Goodies and Daddies

Goodies and Daddies

An A–Z Guide to Fatherhood

Michael Rosen

Illustrations by Caroline Holden

John Murray

© Michael Rosen 1991

First published in 1991
by John Murray (Publishers) Ltd
50 Albemarle Street, London W1X 4BD

The right of Michael Rosen to be
identified as the author of this work has
been asserted by him in accordance with
the Copyright, Designs and Patents Act,
1988.

British Library Cataloguing-in-Publication Data

Rosen, Michael
   Goodies and Daddies: An A–Z guide to fatherhood.
   I. Title
   649

   ISBN 0–7195–4924–8

Typeset in 11 on 13pt Palatino by
Wearside Tradespools, Fulwell, Sunderland.
Printed in Great Britain by Cambridge University Press,
Cambridge.

For Geraldine, Joe, Naomi, Eddie, Laura and Isaac

Contents

viii   *Contents*

Contents   ix

Dad winking by Isaac (aged 3).

Introduction

A quick trip along the shelves marked Health in a bookshop, will bring you up sharp against a large number of books to do with having babies, looking after babies, wishing you had babies; coping with madly clever babies, cleverly mad babies, bad babies, sad babies; food for babies that will make them clever, food for babies that will make them mad; outings for babies, illnesses for babies . . . and nearly all of them are written for women.

There is a rumour going round that men sometimes get involved in some of this, and even that it's become a habit in some homes. On the other hand, there are also rumours that nothing's really changed, it's just that a lot of people, especially women, wish that it had.

With this state of affairs in mind, I've written a book that is about looking after babies and young children. It's for men and it's written by a man, but of course it can easily be bought by a woman with all kinds of hopes in her mind.

I am not a doctor, therapist, counsellor, or guru. I am a writer of children's books and a father and step-father to five children who as I write are aged 14, 12, 10, 7 and 3. I've been married twice, the first time producing two boys (14 and 10), the second time introducing me first to two step-daughters (12 and 7) and then producing a boy of our own (3). This has been described to me as a 'blended family', but maybe that's because when we met we each had a blender . . . It also gives rise to the complaint by one of us: 'Your children are fighting my children and our child started it.'

What follows is a collection of thoughts, memories and tips

based on the past fourteen years. It's in alphabetical order, which seems a suitably random form to express the haphazard way in which delights and problems confront a parent. If I had tried to write the book as a continuous narrative, I don't think anyone would have stayed the course; but assembled like this, I hope a reader will dip-read it on the loo, waiting for a bus, cooking, while the ads come on in the middle of a film, or with the baby on one arm.

The fathering I'm talking about here is not the whole course from soup to nuts. I'm restricting myself to 0 to 5, though as you'll see, children as old as my fourteen-year-old make occasional appearances.

I don't promise any easy solutions; it's not a Dad Construction Kit, where all you have to do is follow the instructions and stick together the relevant parts with a non-toxic glue. In a world where men had had as long a tradition of looking after babies and young children as women, such a book would hardly be necessary – we would just talk to each other. In a world where men who do get involved in such things are often separated by miles and by deep-seated inhibitions, I hope this book will give you confidence, strength and the occasional laugh.

I've tried not to sound bossy – it's a common disease in the battle-worn parent looking at the newcomer. Just grit your teeth when I come on a bit strong and tell yourself that I mean well. I would love to have been able to thank some men for having shown me ways in which to look after young children, but the person who taught me the most was an elderly working-class Irish woman, my first wife's mother, whom my boys knew as Nanna.

Babies' Blotches

Babies in ads are smooth and shiny and glowing – beware! Real babies are often blotchy and flaky. Rashes and blobs appear all over them for no apparent reason. You worry that if you go out with your baby covered in spots people will think it's scurvy or – even worse – it's caused by dirty sheets and male incompetence. ('Tut, tut, if that child had its mother looking after it then it wouldn't have scurvy.') At times I've found myself behaving like some mad explorer, spending whole evenings poring over the islands and seas on a baby's skin.

Other people's babies' blotches always look worse than your baby's. In fact, given that they look so beastly, you can never quite figure out how other parents can possibly love their children. However, just in case you get concerned about your one's spots, here's my journal of discovery.

Sometimes the blotches were pin-points, sometimes splodges, sometimes little white bumps on the face, and sometimes scabby things on his head. (All this as well as NAPPY RASH!) I soon discovered that none of these was leprosy, ringworm, measles or even German measles.

The pin-points were heat rashes. In hot weather, two or three of my children have come up in heat rashes. They differ from the two measles in that they don't spread evenly round behind the ears and across the chest, but erupt in little groups of pin-points anywhere they're hot, like in the crease of the neck, where the clothes are tight, or randomly across the chest. Sponging with cool water is the quickest way to deal with them, but it's more important that they're drinking loads.

Splodges have always been a mystery. At various times I've thought it was soap, the dressing in a new vest, something they'd eaten, a reaction to traffic pollution, a detergent, and so on. They seemed to come and go over a day or so. If it is an allergy, you can try to eliminate the possibilities by going through all the different foods and possible irritants. One Sunday afternoon my second child pigged out on satsumas and the next day he came out in red blotches, round his ribs. That was how we discovered he was allergic to citrus.

White bumps on the face, I was told by various old ladies, were 'milk buds'. They don't matter at all. Scabby things on the head *do* matter, because if they get too widespread, the skin can crack and make the scalp bleed. It's called 'cradle cap'. It's a bit of a drag but the best way to deal with it is very gently to massage an oil into the scalp, leave it for as long as is convenient, shampoo it out, and then brush very gently. You may have to do this once a week for a bit, if it's got bad.

Ringworm does still exist; my citrus-allergic child seems prone to getting it (he seems to be up for any fungus going, actually) and babies can catch it from older children who've picked it up in school. Look out for a single ring-shaped weal, with a different colour in the middle, or a patch of white flakey stuff on the head with hair loss in the middle of it (unlike cradle cap, which tends to go brown). This is one for the doctor. I've found that doctors are really keen on spotty children, who give them loads of things to look up, and lots of interesting questions to ask.

All this is very different from eczema, and should not be taken as minimizing the worry and trouble children and parents go through with this. None of my children has had it, so I won't pretend to be an expert.

Babysitters

I've found that the worst thing about babysitters is that you book them several days before you want to go out, but by the time the day comes round for them to babysit, you're too shattered to want to go out. Too late: they're booked, they come, you go out and sit down in the restaurant, and fall asleep.

I always used to think that records-and-clothes-hungry teenagers would be the most ideal babysitters. Surely they would queue up to come over to watch your telly, eat your cake, and go home with a few quid in their pockets? Not so. All the ones we've had are OK for a few times but then suddenly reveal in some subtle way ('Going out tonight, aren't I?') that they've got their own lives to lead. The other problem with teenagers is that they can lose their grip. One nice lad spent all evening trying to get our three-year-old to bed. She just sat on the sofa staring at him. In the end the poor lad rang his mum, who told him to keep calm. When we got in at well past eleven our little treasure was still there, bright and smiley. The boys, when they were little, all went in for outrageous flirting with the teenage girls and young women – lots of blushing and running around giggling and dropping of pyjama bottoms. Small wonder some of those sitters never came back.

I reckon the worst arrangement is the old ticket system where you have a babysitters' circle. It leads to partners arguing over who's going to do it, or somebody builds up a backlog of tickets and you get to feeling like you want to go round and punch them on the nose. In fact, arguing over whose turn it is, and whether a Sunday morning counts as much as a Saturday night, is one of the quickest ways to lose friends.

By far the best set-up we've had so far is an agency. Everyone needs everyone else in the arrangement; the boss of the agency needs people who are reliable or they get the hoof, the babysitters have made a conscious decision that they need the money and they aren't doing anyone a favour, and you get someone who turns up on time and does the business. If not, you complain. The young woman who comes at the moment is a vegan, and as a result our children have taken to saying things like 'Hamburgers are dead cows, aren't they, Dad?'

Bathtime

I have a photo of myself surrounded by a group of schoolgirls in a child development class watching me bath my first child. The girls are looking on in amazement and horror. This is partly because they're thinking I'm a clumsy old twit who's likely to drop the baby any minute. The other reason is that they are all black, and this is the first time they have ever seen a naked white baby. They were horrified that you could see his veins.

Bathing babies is a tricky business. They are very small and very slippery. This may well sound like an evil heresy to your women mentors, but you don't actually have to *bath* babies. You can lay them on your lap, on a towel, and sponge them down with warm water and hug them dry. Then you don't have to go in for that game of feeling the water with your elbow, supporting the baby with one hand while you try and wash it with the other, all the time putting your fingers in your ears so you can't hear the screaming.

As for bathing: if, like me, you've got big hands, it's a great help. It's really nice getting the baby to play with the water. Do everything slowly and gently; a non-skid mat in the bath is a great help. If you're going to talc them afterwards, don't puff the powder all over them – it only gets into their lungs. Try and avoid extremes of temperature getting in and out of the bath and bathroom (another reason for avoiding it altogether).

When they get older, then it's time to stock up on bath toys. I've found this is a great time to re-live all the nutty things I used to do in the bath when I was a kid. I've taught my kids about drip races, tidal waves, and how to make bubble submarines with the flannel . . . bliss! There's a huge range of toys in the shops involving little blokes diving in, wheels going round, hippopotamuses zooming round in circles, and so on. All jolly good fun, and great solutions to the birthday and Christmas presents problem. Yoghurt pots, plastic bottles, ice cream boxes, bits of wood, lufas, pumice, and the like all have great potential too, and they are all a great distraction from the hell that is called HAIRWASHING.

Bedtime

'But I'm not tired ... can I stay up and watch the football? ...
Tell that story about the time you got lost, Dad ... one more
game of draughts ...'

It's one of the great family battlefields. Just as everyone is
getting tired and ratty there's a whole heap of fiddly, even
more tiring things to be done. Kids see the jugular and go for it.
They are geniuses at devising new ways of delaying bedtime. If
you could do an A-level in bedtime-delaying routines, all kids

under five would pass. I reckon this is a time when democracy has to go out the window. Let's say, that, like us, you do a two-biscuits-before-bed routine. Any child over the age of eighteen months knows how choosing biscuits can take up to ten minutes. You'll end up swearing that you'll never buy a Figgy Roll again. As with any other stage on the journey to bed, you can try one of two things: 1.   offer no choices and, in this case, slam two biscuits down and close the tin quick; 2.   say, 'Time for biscuits. You have five seconds to choose or there *are* no biscuits! One, two, threeeeeee, foooooooour, fiiiiiiiiiiiiiiiive', and again, slam the tin shut quick. It's brutal, but it works.

I've applied this system to bath bubbles, choosing a story book, finding teddies, kissing brothers and sisters goodnight. If I don't, I end up a shattered wreck with no evening left.

Bedtime routines are generally reckoned to be a good idea. It's obviously nice for children to know that there is a set of comforting stages to go through on the way to that strange and lonely place called bed. Going to bed means going to sleep, which means saying goodbye, and no one likes saying goodbye to loved ones, no matter how old you are.

If you're the kind of father who gets home at around bedtime then you may well think that the last thing you can face is playing flannel-submarines and reading *Mrs Tiggywinkle*. The problem is that your partner thinks exactly the same thing. She may have spent the last few hours coping with tantrums, baked beans on the floor, and three pooey nappies. Or she may have spent the last few hours coping with tantrums and the rest at work. So even though your feet feel like someone very large has spent all day jumping on them, now is your chance to get into childcare. If women ever *have* dreamed of men arriving at the door and whisking them away on dashing white chargers, then you turning up and offering to squeeze a kid or two into pyjamas is a very close second best.

I mentioned reading a book as part of the bedtime routine. Perhaps I don't need to wax lyrical about this, but I will anyway. You snuggle up on the sofa with a newly bathed infant, all hot and sweet-smelling, you choose a book between you, and right there you witness the discovery that words and pictures can tickle you pink, terrify you, sadden you, intrigue

you, and so on. And remember, learning to read is not simply the business of deciphering a code ('that letter is "b" and that makes a "b"-sound'). We have to show children that reading is something interesting and pleasurable. With very young children, when we read to them at bedtime we are, among other things, introducing them to the conventions of the book: how books work from left to right, how stories unfold, how pictures and words tell two complementary stories, how the title is on the cover, the fact that it's people called writers and illustrators who make books, and how they have their own styles and so on. All these things we take for granted, but as you're cuddling up on the sofa, it's all going on in the child's mind.

As the late arriver in the house of an evening, this might be the only time you get to see your children before bedtime. So you've got to squeeze all that love and care into one reading of *Where the Wild Things Are* or *Peter Rabbit*.

Go for it! Remember how they didn't want you in the school play? Remember how your dad told you to shut up singing in the bath? Not any more. Now you have a captive audience. You can dish up every mad voice, crazy face and loony noise

that you've ever invented. Children's books are full of grotes-
ques, talking animals, fools, villains, goody-goodies, wind,
police sirens, raspberries . . . it's fantastic. Give it all you've got
and even if it's pathetic, they'll still love you for it.

Sometimes the words in the stories are too hard. No problem, change them or explain them. Keep the flow of the story
going, but don't shout down the questions that your child asks
you. It's all vital pre-reading stuff. Be prepared to talk about
pictures, pointing out interesting bits. Watch out for scarey
things; there's nothing wrong with a bit of a scare, but the child
needs a safety net to fall into. You may have to do a lot of
reassuring, but that's no bad thing. Stories are often about
being reassured that if you oppose badness and danger you can
survive. Children want to know whether they can survive as
well. And a good time to find out, is just before you go to sleep.

See also READING BOOKS

Bedwetting

Beware of bedwetting bores! You only have to breathe a word that one of your children has wet the bed and they come at you like a hurricane. You soon discover that what they're really on about is *shame*. They remember wetting the bed when they were children, they remember their mums or dads getting all screwed up about it and moaning about soggy, smelly sheets. They had children and whaddayaknow? – they got all screwed up about it, too. Then you come along and happen to mention that one of your kids wet the bed last night and – whoosh! they hit you with a great heap of shame dressed up as advice.

If you are armed with a plastic undersheet, a washing machine and big child-sized nappies, bedwetting doesn't have to be a problem as far as mess is concerned. Remember, some people call it a bedwetting problem when it is really that they're not prepared to let their child wear night-nappies for as long as they want or need. The point is that, if a child is over about three and still not dry at nights, the child itself can increasingly take on more and more responsibility about wearing the nappies: buying them, putting them on, taking them off, throwing them away and so on. In fact, the very business of taking charge of the process might help, in the long run, to get the child dry.

We let one of our children wear a night nappy till she was over six because that's what she needed to do. She then very much wanted to get out of wearing them and said several times, unsuccessfully, 'No nappy tonight.' Eventually, I think it was the fact that she discovered she could get up in the night, go to the toilet on her own and put herself back to bed that helped to get her dry.

It doesn't need me to say that some children who have been dry at night but then begin to bed-wet do it as part of some kind of crisis. In situations like this, suggesting the wearing of nappies at night would be, in effect, punishing them, and that's the last thing you want to do. However, if the choice is between being a cold, wet, smelly person and wearing nappies, then it might help. The most important thing, though, is to try to find out where the anxieties are, and relieve them. The hardest thing to cope with is thinking or knowing that you might be the cause of the anxieties: have I been making too heavy demands on her? Expecting her to succeed too much? Are the rows between me and my partner causing it? Is something going on at school that I don't know about? Or it may just be that the child is saying she wants you to spend more time with her. Hmmmmm.

As a footnote: the worst aspect of women being restricted to a domestic role is that this seems to have induced areas of pride where they are least appropriate. So, it becomes a matter of pride that a child doesn't wet the bed. A bedwetting child is a slur on motherhood. Ideally, the great thing about being a bloke and getting involved with things like this means that you don't have to carry this burden. Your kid wets the bed? So he wets the bed. If you're into male competitiveness, then stick to golf and Volvos. Don't turn Monday morning at work into driest bed competitions; it'll be the child that suffers.

Being Around

If I had to say what I thought was one of the most important things about being a dad, it is 'being around'. The worst thing about being a father is that too often, for real or imagined reasons, you have to be out working. Being around means that you are somewhere in the house being available for rows, cuddles, crises, laughs, food, mess and the rest. I've found it very easy to categorize all kinds of little tasks, like fetching children from school, doing shopping with them, feeding them when they're young, as 'not needing my presence'. If they don't need my presence, then I can be elsewhere in the house. If I can be elsewhere in the house, I don't really have to be home at all, and because I don't have my partner's undivided attention I might as well be out having a good time or working somewhere else.

What follows from this is that sometimes the only way you can programme yourself to be around is to take on trivial little tasks like wiping the table or tidying the mantelpiece (or try the trivial big tasks like doing the washing and cleaning the loo), and I've found that it's during these times that you actually make a relationship with your children. It's then that they ask you the really important things, like 'Why do you pee standing up?' or 'Do buffaloes eat spaghetti?' and other vital questions.

Even if you don't do the trivial tasks but you're just *there*, reading the paper, your presence is a great big affirmation that you like the company you're keeping, just as your absence creates the tiny anxiety that home isn't where you want to be and the children aren't who you want to be with. If you are just around, then children will claim you, even if you don't get into

the business of claiming them. I have two step-daughters whom I didn't make enormous efforts to befriend and love, partly because I was so worried that the separation from my first wife was affecting my own 'natural' children. The step-daughters have always had other ideas, and once it became clear I wasn't the enemy, they started making claims on me as a dad. They can only do that if I'm there to be climbed on and argued with.

See also CRAZES, GETTING AWAY

Birth

I'm not going to pretend to be an expert on birth: I'll just tell the stories of the three births I've been at. The first and second were hospital births and the third was at home.

For the first, I went along to ante-natal classes at the hospital where a kind but rather inhibited fifty-year-old woman told us about how the baby grows and gave my partner some exercises to do which I had to do with her. This mostly seemed to involve crawling round the floor on all fours arching our backs, and squeezing each other's arms till it hurt.

Plenty of men find these classes excruciating. In the normal run of pregnancy you may feel irrelevant and pretty useless and then, just to rub it in, you have to turn up in public as the labelled sidekick. 'Ah-hah,' say some women, 'now you know what it feels like to have to go to your work-place parties, and your friends' dos...'. How much value you get out of these classes is closely related to what kind of birth you and your partner have in mind. If you're planning on having a hi-tech, conveyor belt, production-line job, then the birth will mostly turn on the machines and minds of the medics. Your role will be smiling, forehead-mopping and phoning the relatives. The more active a birth the pair of you envisage, the greater your role will be. Instead of just nodding keenly, you may find yourself learning bum-massage, belly-oiling, controlled breathing and something called 'supported squats'. Some of this is part of making the pregnancy-time more enjoyable (if that's the right word), and some of it is to do with rehearsing for the birth itself. In this first birth I was involved with, we either didn't know, or didn't try to know, how we could have done more

about making the pregnancy something *we* were going through
– rather than something that doctors were administering for us.

The last two weeks of this first pregnancy were hell for her
and she lay about in the corner of the room moaning and
waiting. I had no idea what to do about this, and just kept
bobbing up and down hopelessly making encouraging noises
and feeling guilty that it was somehow my fault. It was at times
like these that knowing about massage and the like would have
made us feel less helpless. (Nowadays, there's a clutch of books
on the market including sections on massage in pregnancy.)

We knew when the baby was due because we timed the
length of time between contractions (when they're regular, and
frequent), and an ambulance came to pick us up. Two weeks
before I had done the suitcase bit: packing all the things she
would need in hospital. She couldn't face that because it
seemed too committed. I had a role at last: suitcase-packer-in-
chief.

When it came to the actual thing, she was stretched out on
her back, in what seemed like an operating theatre, on the
hottest day for half a century. The baby seemed to get stuck,
the doctor kept shouting 'push in the bottom! push in the
bottom!', while my partner had me in a kind of neck lock which
meant that for most of the labour my nose was in her armpit.
The number of people in the room went up and up until there
seemed to be a whole crowd of people peering and waiting. A
woman in a short white coat appeared and said: 'Go on, you
can do it', there was some shouting about the cord, and the
baby came out. There were more mutterings about the cord,
which I discovered some hours later meant that it had been
round the baby's neck, but the doctor didn't have time to
explain because he had rushed out of the room to see if the
eggs in the pigeon's nest on the balcony had hatched. They
had, and he was very very excited.

All in all, it had been confusing and worrying. Why did more
and more people start coming into the room? They weren't
students, one of them was an oldish bloke in a blazer. Why did
the baby seem to get stuck? All that shouting about push
harder seemed to be saying that somehow my partner wasn't
doing enough. I think, to be absolutely honest, I thought that

too. Note here: it is terribly easy, as a man, to side with all the men in the room. 'We chaps know how this is done . . . just get on with it, woman, don't be so damned feeble . . .' etc., etc. In actual fact, there was a mini-crisis here: the cord being round the baby's neck is a problem, which in this case was solved by the doctor putting his hand inside and doing a nifty bit of girl-guide knot-work to free the baby. Why wasn't this explained to us? If not during, then after? Perhaps I wasn't bold enough at the time to ask questions. If you don't want the event to be remembered as mysterious and irritating – ask questions. Part of being pleased about having a baby is knowing how it survived the first trial of life.

The next birth started when 'the waters broke', which I discovered sounded like someone tipping out a bucket. The hospital ordered us in straight away and soon we were on the conveyor belt where doctors, midwives and nurses tell you of one inevitable consequence after another – none of which, are you allowed to think at the time, presents any alternative course of action. Because the waters had broken they said the birth was due, even though labour pains hadn't begun. When the labour didn't start, they said to delay any longer would cause infection so they would have to induce. To induce, they put her on a drip. When this didn't work, because they used the wrong dose of drip, they had to hurry the whole thing up with a double dose of drip. Needless to say, the birth itself I can scarcely remember.

In situations like this you are in the worst of all worlds. Without any other source of advice you find yourself nodding and agreeing to everything, even though each one of these steps is debatable and other courses of action are possible. In our case we also experienced the medical cock-up of the induction dose being too low, and so there were several hours of pointless (dangerous?) stress. No one felt it necessary to apologize to us about this; there were just a few hurried mutterings between doctors and nurses, and rapid readjustments. None of this matters if you and your partner are people who want this period in your lives to be done *to* you rather than *by* you. I've felt like this at times. But if you want this time to be something you have some control over, then it is precisely at the moment when doctors are talking injections and inductions that *you* have a role. The key issue is: are the medics taking decisions for their convenience, or for your partner's and yours? If you think it is mostly for their convenience, then basically it's down to you to intervene because your partner will probably be too far gone, too woozy and too preoccupied with herself to be able to take on the medics, too. This is . . . Responsibility. Something I know I didn't take on during this second birth.

The third birth I was at was with my second wife, who wanted to have this her third baby at home – just as she had had her second. The plan was to have an independent midwife and doctor to attend the birth. I think we assumed that the birth would happen in the bedroom. As the contractions started coming naturally we did the un-hippy thing of ushering the children off next door, rang the midwife, and waited. My wife then started walking around the bedroom and I massaged the base of her back. I remember feeling very calm, even madly so, when it slowly crossed my mind that we might be the only ones around when the baby came into the world. I found myself imagining catching babies, footballs, and a Christmas pudding I had once dropped. Every now and then we took a quick peek out of the window to see if there was any sign of the midwife, and then the groaning and swearing started up. (Not from me. I've since been told this is definitely normal!) Just then, the midwife did arrive and my partner rushed off to the loo. The midwife signed me to keep an eye on what was going on, and next thing my partner shouted 'I can feel it at the front!' She knelt forward while I sat on the edge of the bath, the midwife came in and spread a few old terry towels on the floor, and out came the baby.

This was the pregnancy and birth that was the most planned of the three. My wife knew what she wanted to do in the birth, to have it at home and have it in whatever position she would feel most comfortable at the time: squatting, crawling, half-squatting or however. She was also clear about what she wanted from me, in terms of helping her get into those positions, and massaging her. (She didn't ask for ice-packs on her sacrum, but some women find that a great relief.) Having an independent midwife was a great luxury, and she and her doctor colleague were wonderful in supporting the idea that the birth was something *we* did that they supervised, rather than administered. They were also great with our children, spending a lot of time checking dollies' blood pressure and heart beats.

This pregnancy was the first where I felt I got really involved with helping with food. I'm told many women find preparing food either nauseating or an emotional burden (having to think about other people when they would quite like to think about themselves). On top of that, women are bombarded with advice: no booze, no fags, plenty of calcium foods – milk and chick peas (houmous, falafel) – heaps of fresh food, iron-rich foods like beetroot and grapes, plenty of fish. If any or all of this means a break from what she was eating before, then it's a great help if you share it too.

All three of my children are boys (what's the matter with me? have I only got XY chromosomes?), and one feeling I had in relation to all three is how amazed I was that such a large and complete human being comes out. One moment there's no one, and the next something alive and whole appears in the world. At the very moment of birth I don't think I felt that the baby was much to do with me. In each case it took a few days of cuddling, looking, and thinking before I felt it was.

A frequent worry is that the birth itself will be something very violent and bloody. Some people are very worried about pain, sometimes more worried about other people's pain than their own. There's no point in pretending that birth is like going down a slide. Of course there's blood – and sometimes shit and piss, too, but basically that's the human condition. It always strikes me that accepting and even enjoying this side of life is much less undignified than trying to sanitize it and ignore it. Of course, it may be that you have just the same feelings, but when it actually comes to it, you can't help yourself passing out, like many others before you. Remember, there is sometimes quite a good physical reason for this – such as that you haven't eaten or drunk anything for about seven hours, and you've been sitting in some funny position for a lot of the time.

A well-kept secret of mine is that I spent a short time in my life wondering if I would be a doctor. This meant that I did a year of a degree in physiology. I let you in on this exciting fact to explain why I find it very easy to overlook other people's ignorance about how bodies, and in this case ovaries, wombs and vaginas, actually work. I'm not going to sit here and say that every expectant father should read a text book on birth, but you could make a bit of an effort to find out how it all works, if only for the reason that your partner will take this to mean you're interested in what she's going through. It also means you can offer views on what doctors and midwives are saying, when your partner comes back from check-ups. If you think you know it all anyway, here's a quick test: what are the following – the cervix, the second stage, amniotic fluid, and the placenta?

Looking back on all three events, I find I am irritated by how calm I was at the time of the birth itself. Perhaps the calmness was a defence. The actual arrival of a new and very small human being sometimes seems too quick for something that affects your life for so long afterwards. To be honest, I didn't feel very useful at any of the births; I never felt I was doing something special or particular that no other person could have done. None of this is intended to deny that other men have felt exhilarated, excited, and needed or, alternatively, frightened, angry, or shocked. Sitting in the calm of remembering, I feel proud I was there, and warm that I know what my children looked like when they were one second old. As far as relationships with partners are concerned, I don't feel anything mystical or extra-close happened but, of course, if I hadn't been there it would probably have been very nastily disruptive and negative. In one sense I feel more kind of old-soldierish about it: I was there, doing my stuff, and I'm here now to talk about it. I suppose it's a feeling that says: I was reliable, wasn't I? Which feels nice, but a bit boring!

Birthdays

Birthdays are brilliant. Go mad, have cakes, ice cream, choco-late fingers, flash photos, in-laws, balloons, crisps – but don't, *don't* invite hundreds of children. Either you or your partner will ignore this advice, dismissing me as a miserable Scrooge, and you will tell me that making four hundred cucumber sandwiches and playing Pass-the-Parcel was fun. You will have turned a blind eye to the fight over the party-poppers between your little one-year-old and the huge brutal two-year-old next door. You will have ignored the meringue ground into the 100 per cent wool job on the sitting-room floor.

We've institutionalized birthdays to a Sunday tea-time with a visit to the local posh 24-hour deli where they sell things like damson ice cream, tortilla chips and Black Forest cheesecake. In-laws and neighbours can come if they want to, and the odd friend here and there. Anything more than that and we'd go mad.

A father's role at parties is to eat lots of ice cream.

See CHILDREN'S PARTIES

Car Journeys

'Now listen, I can't drive properly with that noise. If there's one more squeak out of them I'm going to stop the car. I can't stand the noise. Why don't they just look out of the window? Give her a drink if she wants one. Who's been sick? Where? Of course I can't stop here. Open the windows. Yes, I do want the radio on, I'm waiting for the cricket score. Well, we would be making good time if we didn't have to keep stopping. Didn't you bring a book she could look at? Yes, I know it makes her sick, but everything makes her sick. I'm not shouting. Isn't she old enough to listen to a tape or something? ... She'll be wearing silk pyjamas when she comes, singin' ay ay yippee, singin' ay ay yippee yippee ay ... there's another blue car, there's another one – see, that makes three blue cars. Now why's she crying? Of course we're nearly there, if she asks are we nearly there once more, I'm going to stop the car, jump out and go for a run in that field ... she hasn't sat on that marker pen, has she? I know it's the waterproof one ... any of those cakes for me? Oh, I missed out on those, did I? Don't let her go to sleep now, she'll never go to bed when we get there ... uh-huh there's a hold-up.'

See also CAR SEATS

Children in your Bed

One of my children managed every night, one way or another, to end up in our bed. This would have been bad enough, but he also managed to end up sleeping with his feet in my ear. And they twitched. Like a lot of other parents, I've had children who've been desperate to be in the bed and never want to leave and others who never really discovered the pleasure and aren't that bothered about it. There are no rules, here.

Starting with the baby . . . do you have the baby in the bed? Factors affecting this decision are: do you have a huge bed? Do you believe that babies need body contact for at least the whole of the first year (the so-called continuum effect)? Do you mind having it off while a baby's in the bed? Babies certainly like being in your bed, but then some people find it difficult ever to get them out. If you object but your partner thinks it's a good idea, ask yourself whether you are against it only because you're jealous of someone else being in her arms (see JEALOUSY). If your partner objects but you think it would be a good idea because you've read a book about it, then tough! It's her milk the baby's after, and if your partner would rather not have the baby nuzzling for it all night, there's not much you can do about it.

As the children get older, many (perhaps most?) parents seem to let them into bed in the mornings, if only at the weekend. There's plenty of stroppy fourteen-year-olds that secretly yearn for this and would jump at the chance if they knew you would say yes and not laugh at them for it. My ten-year-old boy loves it.

Children's Parties

Don't.

See BIRTHDAYS

Cot Moving

A traditional pattern of sleeping arrangements goes like this: newborn baby in carry cot beside your bed so that she can be lifted quickly to be fed in the night. After a while she moves on to having her own cot, on the other side of the room. After a further while, the cot gets moved into a separate room. And last step, after yet further time, is to move the child into a bed.

There are no rules about this sequence – whether you follow it, or not – nor on how long each stage is. Some people have the baby in with them, some people put the newborn baby straight away in a cot on its own in another room. Some people believe that a baby needs almost permanent body contact with another human for around a whole year. Others say that if you teach a baby right from the start to sleep in its own cot in another room, you'll have tranquil nights and a long and happy life. It's an emotional matter, and men tend towards the put-her-in-the-other-room approach while women tend to be more tolerant of the near-at-hand method.

You may hear all kinds of advice on this matter from other parents, your own parents, from books – but in the end, the solution you come up with has to suit your way of life and your emotional outlook. If you try to do something you don't agree with but someone has told you works wonders, then it won't work for you. This is A Thought.

Crazes

My mother had a devastating line: when one of us mentioned a man we knew, she would say, 'Ten!', or 'Eight!' She wasn't giving them marks out of ten – she was describing their mental age. It was only a variation on the old gag about men being little boys. It would crop up mostly because she had heard about some man or another pursuing a craze.

The crunch for us here is when it's Craze versus Childcare. When deep down you know it's your turn to take them to Woolworths, is it really necessary to lock yourself in the darkroom, inspect the fishing flies, or mend the model railway lines? I've noticed how apparently useful tasks like decorating, car maintenance, gardening and the like can be used as a smokescreen for avoiding childcare. DIY can be prolonged for the whole of the time the children are growing up: there's the Sunday morning skip inspection where you really *do* have to poke around in the area's skips to see if tiles, sinks, and wood (always wood) can be salvaged. There's the Saturday afternoon trek to the DIY shops, where long chats about Philips screwdrivers must, but must, be had with those blokes in overalls. And there's the disasters: the wallpaper that doesn't stick, the paint that doesn't match, the cupboards that collapse. It all takes hours and hours and hours, it's all much too dangerous for the kids to help with, and it's all supposedly desperately necessary – 'I'm keeping the home together here, love.'

Dad's Back

If you're in a traditional set-up, out working while your wife looks after the children, then 'Dad's back!' is a moment full of emotion: 'Yippee, he's back, now we'll have some fun', 'Oh what a pity he isn't here more', 'It's all very well for him to come home and have fun with the kids, I have to do all the hard slog all day and he gets the fun stuff', 'I'm completely shattered from all that boring stuff at work and now I'm supposed to be all cheery and hearty the moment I walk through the door', 'I can't stand the noise', 'Look out when your father gets in, he's often tired, hungry and grumpy', 'Have you brought us any presents?'

Then there's stories to be caught up on, and the problem with the minder, the washing machine, the next-door-neighbour's cat, the little one's earache and the lack of buses into town. It's an awful lot of stuff, all jammed into one moment. Ideal for sparking off a row because someone, including you, thinks that someone else is not listening, not caring enough, not being nice enough. Someone might well have a shout and stomp off.

For one man I knew, who lived next door to my parents, coming home was the opposite of all this. It was the only moment in the day he felt truly happy. The moment he was through the door, he was on the floor with the toys. He thought it was the only thing he did in life that was worth anything. I'll never forget the expression on his face when I once said something about the kids growing up quickly. He looked devastated.

Dad's Bum and Dad's Trousers

Women know only too well that it's hard to think about why you should look OK when you're concentrating on someone else. You see, you might take all this fathering business to heart and take it on really seriously, only to discover that you've been attacked by the twin diseases of 'Dad's Bum' and 'Dad's Trousers'. The first indications of the illness might come from your kids. You're bending down or squatting to pick up toys scattered all over the floor when one of your kids says, 'Dad, your bum's all squodgy!' Perhaps they glimpsed it through split pockets, or bulging out of trouser tops as in Plumbers' Cheeks. Everyone gets a good laugh out of it. Don't get ratty with them – they know not what pain they're causing. And it's no use pretending it's because the jumper's too short. Long jumpers hide Dad's Bum but don't remove it, and there's a possibility that its appearance at the bedside has a distinctly dampening effect on the partner's hormones. Beware!

The tatty trousers that should have been changed yesterday go with Dad's Bum – the symptoms here are the saggy crotch and the split pocket. I must admit, I have been suffering from both Dad's Bum and Dad's Trousers for something like fifteen years: I gather that there are remedies to be found in jogging, swimming, and trips to flash jeans shops.

Drawing on Walls

I have yet to meet a child who hasn't at one time or another scribbled on the wall. I remember once when my dad came up to kiss me goodnight, just as I was getting going on the wall next to my bed. In a panic I sat up and tried to cover it. My dad stopped for a little chat while I sat there twisted up against the wall, trying to look natural. After a bit my dad noticed that I hadn't moved from this strange position, and interrupted himself in the middle of the chat to say, 'Hey, what are you hiding there?' 'Nothing, it's OK.' 'No, come on, I can see you're hiding something,' he says, still cheery. I couldn't hide it any longer, and leaned forward. He went bananas. I was about ten at the time.

With little tiny ones, there isn't much point in getting mad at them. You've spent all that time sticking pens and crayons and pencils in front of them. You've applauded every little scribble, you've pinned up the masterpieces ON THE WALL. They put two and two together: great scribbles go on the wall. Why don't I do a short-cut, and get scribbling straight onto it?

One solution to the problem I saw was pinning up lining paper horizontally along the child's bedroom wall. It was a great idea, but it was just loose enough to allow for felt tips to go straight through onto the wall behind.

Lots of 'the only place we draw is on this kind of paper' is in order here, and lightning reactions. More child-centred people assume the worst and suspend all ideas of home beaut. (as the Australians call it) until children leave home.

Dressing

Trying to dress a baby for the first time can be a frightening experience. You think you've pulled an arm off, a finger's got left behind in a babygrow, or a suffocation has taken place under a vest. Dressing a baby is like dressing a screaming rubber doll. First rule: don't do it with anyone watching. It'll take you twice as long and you'll probably end up putting a vest on its legs. Second rule: watch the experts at work and see how they do it. Notice how they hold the arms to get them into the sleeves, which way round the baby is facing at each point in the operation, which way onto the head the vest goes, and listen to the reassuring noises that are being made as the whole thing gets under way.

For those who have no experts to watch, here are some tips:

- When babies are very young you have to dress them as they are lying down, but the moment they begin to sit up you can sit them on your lap, back firmly against your belly, and dress them like that.

- Putting on clothes that go over the heads (vests, jumpers, etc.) must be done by approaching the baby's head from behind. Make the neck-hole of the vest fit over the bump that sticks out of the back of the head, and pull from there. Taking the same garment off, you lift from the front, up over the chin, face, forehead, and off. I'm not one for rules and laws, but this certainly is one. Doing it the wrong way can be painful.

- Putting hands into sleeves is done by you holding the hand

and going down the sleeve with the baby's hand as far as you can go; same with feet and legs.

- In cold weather, woollen vests next to the skin are worth two jumpers on top. Hats, gloves and booties are vital for at least nine months of the year in England.

- Children find dressing very boring except when they can annoy you. So they try running away, hiding their hands and making their feet stick out at a funny angle. Sometimes they grow extra arms. Hit back with tricks and jokes. Try the 'Bye-bye hand' routine: as the hand disappears into the sleeve, pull it out quickly, half a millimetre from your nose, feigning huge surprise. Try the same with the feet. Snags with this: you may have to repeat it every day for four years. Other routines: putting knickers on child's head – or yours (never fails, this one) – and producing lost socks from behind child's ear.

I'm hopelessly sexist about buying clothes, leaving it all to my partner, but have at times made efforts. I have to admit that, when I was more conscientious about it, it was very pleasing buying clothes that looked nice on a young child or, even better, that they said they liked. I was more confident in areas like pyjamas and tee shirts, but I have occasionally graduated to track suit bottoms and shoes. Skirts and dresses – can't manage at all. One thing that intimidated me was that every time I bought something for my second son, it was OK in the shop but by the time he got home, he had grown out of it. The moral of this story is never to take any notice of the signs or labels that say '2–3 years' and the like. Buy big – in a week the garment's shrunk and the baby's grown. If it's really madly too big, it'll fit next year.

Women are brilliant at passing babygear around on a network. Never be too proud to accept anything; it saves you an amazing amount of money.

Earache

Two of my children have suffered very badly from earache. One of them screamed all night and we had no idea what was the matter with him. At about four in the morning I figured it out by going all over him with my hand, pressing gently to see if doing it in any one place made him scream even louder. He did when I got to his ear. So, if a baby screams persistently even though it's dry, fed, winded, wee'd and poo'd and hasn't got a temperature, it may well have earache. If you press very gently with the flat of your hand over the whole ear and it screams even louder, you know it's got earache.

Older children will hold their ear obviously, so you can tell. At various times, depending on the seriousness of the pain, I've been successful with sitting the child upright with a hot water bottle over the ear, plus an infant painkiller – follow instructions exactly. If this doesn't work after a few hours then the doctor has to have a look, because the ear drum can burst and/or something ghastly called a mastoid infection can happen. The point is, if you can disperse the gunk in the ear without going to the doctor, you can avoid having to pump the child with antibiotics, or putting it through various kinds of mini-operation.

The reason why little children are afflicted with earaches is because children under seven have very narrow Eustachian tubes that can't always drain easily. Something went wrong in the design, apparently. If you've never tried homeopathy, then this is where you could start. Various homeopathic remedies will disperse mucus.

Eating Out

Unless you go to Macdonald's, the Happy Eater, and fish and chip shops, eating out with kids in England is often a nightmare. If you have fond memories of you and your partner enjoying nice leisurely meals in super little restaurants, then whatever you do, don't confuse those memories with what you will experience with one or more little ones in tow. Certain strategies are in order. I found that rather than try to coax my children to sit on a chair, it's easier to have any child under two on my knee. Waiting for food to come is always agony, and a few handy games like variations on I-spy, knock-knock and so on are useful.

All my children have always loved to go on sight-seeing tours to the toilets. 'I wanna go to the toilet, Dad', means 'I wanna check out the loo seats.'

Choose simple food, like baked potatoes, and be prepared to eat vast amounts of leftovers, especially of Knickerbocker Glories. Ignore snotty waiters and ask for extra bowls, plates, tea spoons and paper napkins so that all the necessary decanting, dividing up of quarter portions and wiping can take place. Get out before they go on further sight-seeing tours round all the other tables.

Stand by for the loud embarrassing comment announced to the whole restaurant: 'Dad, what's a foreskin?' Or loud singing of 'Happy birthday to you, I want to go to the loo, I want to do a poo', followed by hysterical giggling. Get a babysitter as soon as possible afterwards and go to your favourite restaurant to remind yourselves what it used to be like when you were young and carefree.

Eating out abroad can be tricky, especially in France where the gaps between the courses are longer than the courses themselves. As far as children are concerned this is pure hell. Why does it take half an hour from the time you've had cheese till the orange arrives? I remember on one occasion sitting next to a French family, and little Danielle was about two and wasn't allowed to leave her seat for the full two-hour stint. Every time she looked like she might slide off the edge of her chair, Dad stared at her and shouted, 'Danielle – je te parle!' Presumably this treatment, carried out regularly over several years, trains les petits français. When I tried saying 'Eddie, I'm speaking to you!' he said, 'Yeah, I know, I can hear you, Dad.'

Equality

There's one school of thought that says equality is a nasty idea invented by communists, impossible to achieve and disastrous however you attempt to put it into practice. This school proves its case by saying women can't be boxers because their breasts get in the way and plumbers can't be judges because they don't speak proper.

I'm not ashamed of it. This book is to do with trying to bring about a certain kind of equality. It's based on two ideas: one, that women are human beings; and two, that men are too.

If women are human beings then they're entitled to go out and do whatever men enjoy doing. If women go out and enjoy whatever men enjoy doing, *and* have babies, then someone has to share in the childcare. People with enough money hire nannies, though this still leaves the evenings and weekends. People without have to work it out somehow.

If fathers are human beings too, then one of the ways of proving it is by having something to do with those *other* human beings called children. Fathers who totally avoid childcare always seem to me to be trying to avoid paying their dues as members of the human race.

I'm under no illusion, as they say, that if every father took equal shares in childcare then 'equality' would have arrived. But certain possibilities would crop up: doing different kinds of work changes us. A woman not 100 per cent devoted to the needs of others becomes different. A man becoming in part devoted to the needs of others does too.

Feeding Babies

If you haven't already found out, you will very soon discover that your nipples don't seem to give a baby much of a treat. This means that your role in the first stages when your partner is breastfeeding is limited to such things as finding cushions to jam under partner's elbow, supplying gallons of liquids, not arguing when she says 'Breastfeeding is work, too, you know', answering the telephone, and generally keeping marauders away from the cave.

When or if the dreaded bottle arrives, then let's face it, there is no real reason why bottle filling, cleaning and giving should be a female task. After all, blokes don't seem to have much trouble topping up the oil, water and battery.

Obvious points:

1. Follow the instructions on the side of the tin, EXACTLY.
2. Be neurotically careful about keeping bottles and teats sterilized.

When you're feeding, head off to a room on your own without your partner, mother or mother-in-law – the first few times, the baby will be easily distracted by the smell and sound of mother; and anyway, you don't want to *feel* an incompetent nerd, even if you are one.

Hold the baby firmly in the crook of your stronger arm and focus your eyes on the baby's eyes. Making chooky-chooky noises is not some nutty thing that besets women in their dotage; it keeps the baby focusing, and gives it a sound cue to link with the food. So pluck up courage and make some reassuring noise, such as tongue clicking or a low burbling of the times-tables, accompanied by smiling and much eyebrow work.

Don't jam the bottle in like you're gardening or something; ease it in, and be prepared for the baby to be bored. If it is, wiggle the teat about a bit – remember, a very young baby is basically a mouth with a brain and body attached. Getting through a successful feed is a really nice feeling for the baby, and even better for you. You feel ultra-competent.

The baby will be sick. This may come just at the end of the feed, after an hour's hard work. Bloop! straight over the trousers. And the funny thing is, it always looks like more came out than went in. Now you have to decide whether to try again or leave it for a bit. Mostly, leave it for a bit, because even though it looks like more, it's actually less. Technically, this kind of bloop is really just a high velocity burp. Anyway, who cares *what* it is when your trousers are soaking with warm sicked-up milk? Therefore, come prepared with towel. Forget the PVC apron touch – bloop just pours off it, down your socks.

Panic for first-timers: the baby bloops several times. This happened to me with my first-born so I dashed for help to old Dr Spock and he talked about something where the stomach or gut grows together. PANIC! But then he pointed out that the baby would have to bloop *every* feed and be losing weight for this to be the problem.

See WINDING, WEANING AND GETTING ON TO SOLIDS

Feeding Toddlers

When you're about two or three, then there are loads more interesting things to do than sit around a table chewing: you could be under the table, on the table, sticking lego into the food, putting your finger up your nose, and so on. Remember, so long as a parent isn't stoking a child up with biscuits, sweets and ice-creams in between meals, then at some point or other hunger will get to it and it'll eat. No child will starve itself. The point about the biscuits etc. is serious: a child will quickly learn it can get away with dodging mealtimes *and* get a pound of biscuits at three o'clock. All my kids have tried this on, in their time. What's needed here is *firmness*.

Firmness in this case does not mean forcing a child to eat everything you've dished up and making every meal a battle-ground. It's tough to admit it, but you don't always know best about things like, say, whether a child is hungry or not. But it does mean being consistent: if you say there's nothing else to eat until tea-time . . . then stick to it. Let them know that what you cook is what there is. Don't get up and start cooking something else or they'll soon learn that one, too.

Be prepared to go in for jollying-up exercises. I do: 'here comes the helicopter [spoon heads for mouth] landing now [into mouth]'. And one of my children liked the fork-lift truck routine, with the little bird for variation. Do remember that their arms actually get tired reaching up to the table. If a bit of lap-sitting looks like it'll do the trick, then take it in turns with your partner from meal to meal so you're not having a barney about it.

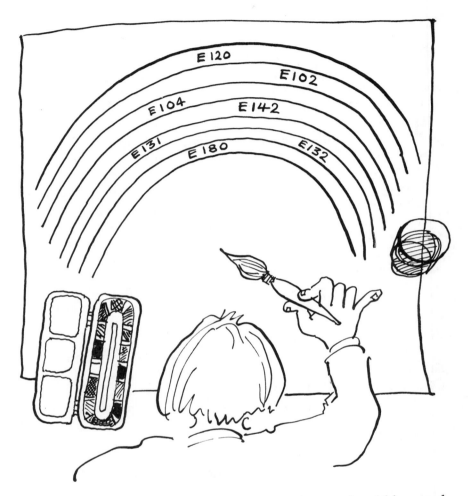

For children to enjoy eating, then mealtimes should be good times in a general sense. Three-year-olds go in for spontaneous singing and hours of knock-knock jokes that don't make sense: Knock-knock – who's there? – Potato – Potato who? – Carrots [hysterical laughter]. Four-year-olds turn their plates of food into film-sets and act out war movies, fairy stories and Japanese cartoons with the peas and gravy. Notice I've left two-year-olds out of this sequence. Two-year-olds are dangerous anarchists and would rather eat under the table or hanging from the lampshade – and often do. One reason for this *may* – and I mean only 'may' – be that you're unwittingly dosing them up with stimulants. Take time out to read the sides of packets of fish fingers, soft drinks and the like and figure out just how many additives you're pumping into your little loved one.

Back to serious things: anything with sugar in is, in its own way, addictive. In other words, once they've discovered the joys of the chocolate biscuit, or whatever, then they'll prefer that to a bit of fish, a tomato, or a carrot. If you are one of the two people in the world who enact a strict 'no sweets, biscuits, jelly, buns ever, ever, ever' routine, then you won't have a problem here and your children will happily munch raw carrots any time of day or night. If, like me and most people, you're a compromise person, and try to dish up fresh veg, salads, fresh fruit, and not too much tinned and frozen food and sweets, then you'll find yourself in the position of saying 'Just one bit of cabbage' or 'One leaf of lettuce, or there's no afters'. Once again, so long as you stick to what you've said on the day, and you stick to more or less the same line from day to day, then it'll work out.

One last do-or-die method I've used goes like this: 'Come on, eat up, it's really nice . . . you don't want it? . . . None of it? . . . OK, I'll eat it . . .' [I open mouth very wide and bring it near the plate, making growling noise]. Sometimes this works and they shout 'No, don't eat it, don't eat it, I'll eat it'. Sometimes they think it'll look really funny and they want to watch you gobble up the mashed-up gunk on their plate. Tough! You have to go through with it so that they know next time you really do mean that you'll eat it. That's what's hard about sticking to your line.

Be prepared to leave their food on the table for a bit, after everyone's finished. I can't think of the number of times my youngest has left a full plate, saying 'I don't want none of it!' and then come back to the table about twenty minutes later and wolfed down the lot.

First Night with Baby at Home

This is a strange and unnerving experience. I spent the whole night listening to him breathing. What would happen if he stopped? How would I know? Do newborn babies dream? Every little snuffle and squeak, I was wide-eyed and staring. I got up at least ten times just to go and look at him to check he was real. What if he's cold? What if he's too hot? Who is he, anyway?

The birth kept going round and round in my head. The very first sight of him. Is a baby a person? What if I'm a complete dead loss as a dad? How would I cope if there was something awful? Is he OK? What if he was Down's Syndrome and they hadn't spotted it? How would we know? What would I do if he was disabled? Would we cope? Will I earn enough money to keep him? Should we move out of the flat, since my flat-mate didn't reckon on this when he sub-let the place to me. Where shall we go? I hope his belly button heals up soon. Ah, he wants a feed. How long's that? Three hours. Must sleep, must sleep.

And all the while, you really can't believe that where before there were just two of you, now there are three. And that is an incredible feeling.

Food and Cooking

How will you be remembered by your children? As the one who, when Mum wasn't there, dished up revolting food? I love my Dad for many things, but when Mum went to evening classes on Monday nights, he would smack his lips and say 'Lovely, cold meat for us tonight, boys.' And we hated it. Chunks of cold, damp meat made Monday nights dreadnights. Yet there was one dish he could make that we absolutely adored. And just to make it taste even better, Mum said it was bad for us. It was a Jewish dish called Matzo Brah (spelling guessed) which involved soaking broken matzos (those large water-biscuit-like things) in water, dunking them in beaten egg and frying the bits in chicken fat. And when we had it he would always say, 'Don't tell Connie I've given you Matzo Brah.' The moral of this story I take to be, that it's not a bad idea to have a few Dad's Specials up your sleeve. Learn what it is to be loved for the food you cook, but get ready to duck if the woman in your life feels undermined. Your line here is: 'But darling, every meal I cook frees your mind.' Well, something like that . . .

One of the most important techniques to get hold of is how to rustle together nice nosh very quickly. And this means nice nosh for everyone: the baby you're in charge of, your partner, friends, anyone drifting in. I've found that the best thing to do is have a repertoire of basics that you can play around with.

Starting with the youngest (see WEANING for first foods, and FEEDING TODDLERS), you want to have a range from emergency rations to extra specials. Emergency rations are things like peanut butter sandwiches, baked beans, fish fingers, bananas, yoghurt, toast fingers, cheddar cubes, tomato segments and cucumber slices. A screaming one-year-old can be silenced in minutes with this stuff, so always make sure you've got supplies handy. Don't use the gooey egg, it's not worth the salmonella risk.

Not so quick and easy are a range of things using cheese, tuna fish, beans, sweet corn, peas, green beans and chick peas, yesterday's boiled or baked potato. Any combination of these, grilled, usually goes down well. The problem with meat is that in convenience form – i.e. sausages, hamburgers and the like – a glance down the list of ingredients gives you much cause for thought, while fresh meat takes time to fetch, prepare and cook.

When it comes to preparing more elaborate things, spurn not the noble casserole and stew. Here you can junk together all your favourite foods and flavours, dish it up to everyone and have some left over for tomorrow to save you time then. I've found that sloppy rather than dry goes down best with younger ones. The cheap and quick way is to literally grab anything you like the taste of, chop it up into half-inch chunks, fling it in a big saucepan, top it up with water and simmer for two hours. Use some or any of the following: potatoes, tinned tomatoes, chick peas, kidney beans, onion, brown lentils, red lentils, carrots, barley, rice, cabbage, parsnip, broccoli, cauliflower, beef, lamb and chicken. For flavouring experiment with parsley, marjoram, garlic, stock cubes, bouillon cubes, mustard, lemon, tomato purée.

If you're looking for quick, tasty and good food, then you really can't beat Italian sauce and pasta. In fact, an Italian sauce is a great basis for loads of dishes. Quick simmer method: mash up tinned tomatoes with a potato masher, add tomato purée, garlic, basil, oregano, tarragon, thyme and lemon rind. Experiment with quantities of it. The minimum cooking time is about twenty-five minutes for the flavours to meld. This sauce you can use with pasta and grated cheese, or you can pour it on any kind of veg, or meat. Optional extras are green and red peppers, capers, mushrooms (see recipe book for the full olive oil number).

As for the pasta, go mad. Get every and any variety you can get. Here is a wonderful chance to give your children choice, food games and fun, and with really good food. My three-year-old and seven-year-old are both addicts. Whenever I say what do you want, they always say 'Pasta' and we go through the coils and bows and tubes and green ones and orange ones. I slop on the sauce with grated cheese, can't fail. Tinned pesto is another winner; dilute it with water rather than olive oil so it isn't too rich, stir it into the hot pasta and add grated cheese.

Rice is another winner especially if you experiment with different kinds of rice: round grain, long grain, white, brown, patna.

Any leftover veg or frozen packets or rice can all be stir-fried. Note: olive oil tastes best: buy the most expensive, extra virgin; use tiny quantities; and get it hot before you add the veg or rice.

Dishing up food can be a wonderful and satisfying business that makes you feel very wanted and loved, but it can also be a heartless and thankless task. Stand by for abuse, sulking, and fussiness. The line 'this is what I've cooked, I haven't cooked anything else' is a vital weapon in your armoury, to which you add 'and you're not pigging out on biscuits instead'. Compromises can be reached over a little bit of picking out of 'bits I don't like, dad'. Not too much, or you'll go crazy. Your general aim is to go for enjoyable but healthy. Try to avoid the usual dad's easy option technique, which is mum cooks but I dish up convenience food. If you do this, you undermine partner's life and child's stomach.

Getting Away

You're each entitled to equal time away from the struggle. If you want to go to an evening class on electric guitar, then your partner is entitled to go swimming the following night. If you think you want to spend a week walking in the Peak District, then your partner is entitled to a week somewhere too. It may never be exactly fair swops, but it should be roughly so, otherwise resentment rears its ugly head. Let's say you both work, and one thing you say you need to do after work is go round to the pub for a packet of crisps and a drink. This is Getting Away. If you participate in or follow a sport, this too is Getting Away. And if it is classifiable as Getting Away, your partner is entitled to equal quantities of it. My going to watch Arsenal on Saturdays equals my wife's swimming lessons.

So far, so simple. Here come the complications: what one person says is Work, the other person might say is Getting Away. Or even worse, what one person says is Work, the other person might say is Not-work. So, if you are both agreed you want children, then getting in money to pay for the household is Work. But then, maintaining the household and childcare are also Work. To illustrate these complications: 'Sorry, love, I had to go off for a drink after work, there was quite a lot of stuff to tie up for tomorrow.' (This could be fibs.) 'While you've been in the pub, I've been getting the tea. I'm going out now, see you!'

By and large, so far in the history of the world, blokes seem to have learnt the tricks of this game much better than women. Sorting out a bit of EQUALITY in these matters may do wonders for your love-life. Women report that sex with a bloke they think is exploiting them is either impossible or unpleasant.

Goodbyes

You can't avoid these. As some children get older, they get more and more unhappy about goodbyes. The problem with knowing more about the world is that you also know more about awful things that could happen to your parents. They could sink with the *Titanic*, drown in a river, turn into a ghost, or whatever. They know it's possible, they've seen it in books, on telly and maybe heard about friends or relations. So goodbyes can get more difficult not less, especially round the age of three or four.

I once saw Sheila Kitzinger handing out a bit of advice on this. She said, why don't you give the child you're saying goodbye to something 'very important' to look after: like a special key ring, or an old bank card. Tell them they've got to look after it until you get back.

I've tried this and it is a great help, especially if you make a fuss about it when you get back, or in the morning if it's when a babysitter comes. In fact, shortly before I wrote this I had The Cling treatment from my three-year-old when I dropped him off at nursery school. Some of the children were painting daffodils, so with him clinging on to my leg I painted a daffodil, one of the nursery teachers hung it up to dry and I said to him: 'Look after my daffodil, won't you? Make sure no one spoils it, so when I come to pick you up I can take it home.' He seemed appeased.

Smaller children can be convinced by cheque books, diaries, watches and the like, but you have to play it for real from start to finish.

Hairwashing

This is one of the great childhood terrors. And they're often afraid of it even before they've experienced shampoo in the eye and water up the nose. Having experienced it, they turn wild. For this I've needed soundproof ears, gritty determination, a firm hand and a good line in bad jokes and jollification. Knock knock – Who's there? Boo – Boo who? – No need to cry about it . . . Mmm, well, it's the way you tell it.

Try any or all of the following techniques. I cannot guarantee success; they have at times nearly worked for me, but you will not get your money back if they fail. Never use adult shampoo; give the child a flannel to put over its eyes; buy one of those brims without a crown; let them feel the water in the jug before you tip it on; hold their head back so the water can't go in their eyes, telling them to hold on to the side of the bath.

I've figured out that the screaming is actually therapeutic. It gives them something to focus on while you do the dirty deed. It's worth explaining to your neighbours what the cause of the noise is: invite them in if they don't look like they believe you. They will never come again.

Health Visitor

In the first days and then at various times in the first year, a health visitor will call. It's a slightly ambiguous moment because they come both to help you and to see if you are treating the baby properly. This means that you may feel you're being snooped on. No matter how nice they are, no matter how they appear to be looking at the baby, they are also making judgements about you.

On one occasion I found myself feeling guilty about the dirty washing-up and then getting irritated by the fact that really the health visitor wanted to see my wife and not me. The point is, they don't really expect to see a man on his own looking after a baby, so if you're in this situation, stand by for one or two little awkwardnesses. One reason may be that the visitor is on the lookout for POST-NATAL DEPRESSION and is suspicious about why the mother isn't there.

If you're an evenings and weekends dad, then the health visitor will be no more than a name.

Helplessness

This is a skill learned at an early age by most men when faced with dirty washing, an empty fridge, a splinter in a thumb, or a screaming younger brother. This develops very neatly into helplessness in parenthood when faced with a pooey nappy, a wet babygrow, an empty fridge, a splinter in a child's thumb, or a screaming nipper.

If this book has any purpose at all, it is to undermine this sense of helplessness. Yet, even as I say that, I can't help admitting that helplessness isn't all bad. Even when we are capable, we still get bouts of helplessness. I've been defeated by buggies that won't fold, lost keys, sleepless babies, car break-downs, diarrhoea (child's, not mine), a bad back (mine, not child's), and rain. In fact, one of the tricks of the fatherhood game is to forego the need to achieve and be a winner. You can admit that some days you feel helpless. Some days you only managed to do one thing: buy some orange juice. Some days all you did was potter about doing nothing and so nothing was achieved . . . and that's OK.

A shady side of helplessness is that you may notice some women are sometimes glad that you feel helpless. It works like this: women were told to do the domestic stuff and childcare. They got good at it. They were proud they were good at it. Then along comes a man and has a go at it and he's not as good at it as they are – or at least, they hope he isn't. Men then think, oh well, they're right, I'm not really much good at it, I'll go down the pub. And we're right back to square one.

Holidays

I was once in the middle of shooting a TV film and the lighting man was showing his family album. Some of the pictures were of him and his children on the beach about fifteen years earlier, when they were toddlers. He looked at them and said, 'You know, when I look at these, there's one thing that bothers me. When I remember that holiday, all I can remember is shouting at the kids for being naughty, but look at them. Look how small they are.'

It doesn't matter how often I think of that conversation, I still know that on holiday there's even more chance of my getting ratty and shouting than at any other time. Why is this? I think one of the reasons must be that, no matter how hard I try, on holiday I always end up thinking about holidays I had when I didn't have children, and I climbed mountains or hitched across France. It's good old boring male egotism. And yes, holidays are potential disaster areas.

The first rule of holidays is that the nicer the place, the more horrible the journey (see CAR JOURNEYS). It's always your flight that sits on the runway for an hour with the air-con switched off. It's only your children that are screaming in the departure lounge. It's only your children that people are praying they won't have to sit next to.

Once there, you face the hard, cruel reality of what shared childcare means when you've got no excuse to nip off to work, phone your friend or see that crucial football match. Will you have the stamina to play dot to dots, build sand castles, and go and see the donkey for the hundredth time?

The problem is that holidays with children have to be family-shaped. It's no use trying to squeeze a baby and a two-year-old into a wild outdoor adventure, or a chic rave. The problem with family-shaped holidays is that they can be boring. In the circumstances, as my wife has to remind me every single holiday, it is grossly unfair on the children to complain to them about it.

I fear I have made holidays sound terrible. They're not. Amazing and wonderful moments can happen. And the best way for them to happen is through not trying. Little children like holidays to be in safe places where they can play about near you and they're not constantly being carted off to see the next fascinating tree, wall, holy fountain, or Olde Inne. Some of the most exciting cave paintings in Europe are in the Pyrenees. My two-year-old's response to these was to fall asleep in my arms, and so for one hour's worth of stooping and bending in the dark I carried him fast asleep past the bison, the deer, the stags and the rest.

The best holidays my children have had have been where there's been a swimming pool, young ones included. I find it difficult to stay in the water longer than four hours at a time, but they don't understand how I can give up so soon. Other highlights: castles, beaches, donkeys, sheep, old-fashioned sweet shops, blackberry picking and ice-cream parlours. Turn-offs: bookshops, churches, Indian restaurants, heat, flies and guides with loud voices.

See EATING OUT

Hugging and Kissing

I'm told some men feel a bit funny about this, especially with boy children. I have to say I find babies very huggable and squeezable. If you don't there isn't anything worse than seeing other people going goo goo, squeeze squeeze all over the place. It seems so phoney. I think the more of the muck and crap you get involved with, the easier it is to feel huggish towards babies. Once you've got into hugging your babies, then there never seems to be any reason why you should stop. As I say elsewhere, my fourteen-year-old hulk still wants cuddles.

Mind you, if you really aren't a hugger then kids are pretty good at spotting the phoney hug. On the other hand, even if you haven't been one, you might find you can grow to like it. Intriguingly, some children are more into it than others. Some like to flop out on your lap and tuck their head into your neck, and give you squeezes, while others keep their distance. You have to respect that.

Mine go in for a mock-up of a demanding-brat routine to disguise the fact that they are – well – demanding brats. It all started with my ten-year-old. At any time between the age of two and eight he would go in for a kind of droopy wail: 'Da-a-a-d, ca-a-a-an I sit on yoooou? D-a-a-a-d, sta-a-a-a-y with meeeee. Da-a-a-a-ad, uppy, uppy', and so on. The only way I could cope was to give him the cuddle but to repeat the 'D-a-a-a-a-d' wail at the same time. This caught on, and now whenever anyone wants a cuddle in our house, they give it the intro of 'D-a-a-a-a-a-d'.

Indoor-itis

This can strike any child under ten after spending too long indoors. The over-tens just get sulky and eat biscuits. Under-tens' symptoms of indoor-itis to look out for are repeated banging of head up and down on sofa, getting into small dark corner of the house and jumping up and down on brother, sister, cousin or friend, heaving on your neck, kicking the skirting board.

Eddie is the main indoor-itis sufferer in our house, so we bought him a 'PT bouncer'. This is a very small trampoline. Every time Eddie starts showing any of the symptoms (normally with him it's all of them at the same time), we shout: 'Eddie – bouncer!' and he heads off and bangs out about a thousand or so leaps.

Other cures for indoor-itis: house-dwellers – open back door, apply short but firm pressure on child's shoulders in direction of open door, count three, close door; flat-owners – hard luck, it's the park, or yet another trip counting paving stones and red cars. I notice that, traditionally, these trips seem to have been designated as Dads' Jobs. Standing in a park on a Sunday afternoon you would think the nation was jammed full of single fathers. I always imagine that this is a consequence of the same little scene played out in millions of houses all over the country just after lunch:

HER: Ooh, it's nice to put your feet up after lunch.
HIM: Yeah, really nice.
KID 1: Park park park park park.

HIM: Hear that, love? She's pretending to be the dog. What's on the telly?

HER: She's saying 'park' with a 'p'.

HIM: Uh-huh.

KID 2: Park park park park.

HER: Ooh, it's nice to put your feet up after lunch.

HIM: I agree.

HER: Shame you can't fit it in this afternoon.

KID 1 AND KID 2: Park park park park park park ... (*until dad grabs football, kite and Sunday newspaper and stumps off with kids*)

HER: Oooh, it's nice to put your ...

HIM: (*leaving*) All right, I heard, I heard.

Jealousy

It's something I've always been reluctant to admit, but there's a very good chance that you will feel jealous of babies and children. I tell myself that it's OK to be jealous but it's not OK if I pretend I'm not, because otherwise it'll come out in some other mean and nasty way. Basically, right from the start, if your partner is breastfeeding this can, deep down, be a big disappointment. Here was this part of my partner that both of us seemed to think me fondling was a good idea. Possibly I told myself that in some way or another it belonged to me. Not in reality, of course, but I had noticed that whereas my partner was quite happy to offer her hand to friends and strangers, she didn't do the same thing with her chest. It seemed like I was in some sort of privileged situation, here. And then along comes the baby, and the little creature has total and unlimited access. And it's not just any old access – it adores it, it gurgles at it, it falls asleep on it, it squeezes it, it devours it. I've been elbowed out.

It's worth putting in a bit of time thinking about this. Find out if deep down you do actually feel fed up about it. If you do, let it out. I've made jokes about it to help me admit what was going on: 'Hey, what are you doing, little one? I thought that was mine!' Meanwhile I've had to face up to some hard truths: my partner's body isn't mine – any of it. If I want my child to be confident and happy then lots of breastfeeding willingly given is a great boost. And there's something else: when finally the weaning takes place, my loved one's nipples may be about as sensitive as boiled cabbage. This may disappoint her but the great feminist guru, Sheila Kitzinger herself, recommends frequent friendly stroking and squeezing. Yippee!

In a rather Freudian way, I've reduced jealousy merely to your partner's breasts (the psychological justification being that it reminds you unconsciously of the time your own mother put away her breasts and seemed to be spending too much time with your father). Obviously, jealousy can hang around in all sorts of places. I am not saying anything dangerously new in noting that some women, especially in relationships where the loving element has gone into decline (or is it *because* it's gone into decline?) put all their affections onto the children, especially a boy. The standard line in situations like this is to blame the woman. Before you leap to curse your partner for giving all her love to the little brat, consider that you might just possibly be partly responsible for the situation. You letting childcare be carried out solely by your partner is her reason for devoting herself to the children, which is in turn your reason for having your nose out of joint. In other words, this whole business of taking over chores traditionally done by women has repercussions that go quite deep. There is the possibility that some traditional resentments can be relieved.

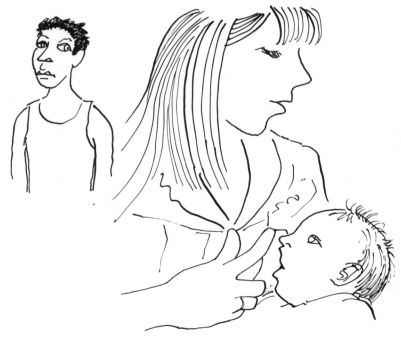

Kids' Cooking

I'm not talking here of older children flinging hamburgers about and begging to make chocolate cookies and honeycomb toffee all Sunday. No, this is the story of the little fingers in the pizza dough and the jam tart. There's no question, small children feel wonderful being part of making food. It may drive you crazy, because you thought you were going to bash out those pizzas in half an hour because you wanted to watch the football. No chance. 'Can I help?' says your two-and-a-half-year-old.

One trick here if you really don't want to take five hours to make those damn pizzas is to privatize your pizzas and give him his own little pizza to make. And remember: his will be the one that tastes the best, and everyone has to clap his pizza.

If you're a dab hand at cakes and so on, then the real interest will be the opportunity to lick the bowl. This is all very well, but maybe you want to lick it yourself. Children are also very good at greasing pans and mashing tinned tomatoes. Wear goggles.

Little Chauvy Pigs

Little boys sometimes go in for being horrible to mum. Freud claimed to know why, but the question for men is what do we do about it? If we dive in as the heavy dad: 'How dare you throw toast at your mother?', all it does is reinforce the idea that men are tough and women feeble. If we do nothing it gives the message you agree that being beastly to mum is a good idea. I suggest the following:

1. When mum's not around you give the little lad an earful about why you don't like these goings on. This avoids upstaging mum.
2. You have an interesting conversation with your partner (!) where in an instantaneous flash of understanding you both come to the conclusion that at the actual moment of the boy's beastliness it's down to her to say 'No, I don't want you to blow raspberries in my face', 'No, I won't get your cornflakes if you yell at me', but *you* will do the support business when you've got the blighter on his own.

P.S. If Freud was right, remember the reason for the beastliness is because he's fed up that mum sleeps with you and/or has had another child.

Middle-Class Curriculum

Whatever the pros and cons of the National Curriculum, it seems to me it has sharpened up the whole question of how parents supplement their children's education. Perhaps all that schools do is confirm children's parents' status, education and ambition. A friend of mine was rather wearily lugging his daughter from a piano class to a computer workshop one Sunday when he looked out of his car window and said: 'I'm just doing the middle-class curriculum.'

I'm sure most people reading this book will know of children who are rushed from piano lessons to swimming lessons then on to theatre club on Fridays, art class on Saturday mornings, dance on Sunday mornings and so on . . . The process used to be restricted to the seven and overs but I notice it's got a hold on the five and unders and now there are singing classes for one-year-olds and poetry classes for two-year-olds and gymnastics for three-year-olds, and the whole thing is matched by hundreds of books guiding you in how to make your child a neurotic – sorry, I mean a high achieving – credit to your skills as a parent.

I can't think of anything more dreary than seeing and hearing tired little children screeching away hatefully on violins, and cursing cold swimming pool water. Somehow you have to juggle with following children's real enthusiasms, putting opportunities in front of them they would otherwise not have, being prepared to drop things when the child is uninterested, helping them achieve things for their own satisfaction rather than yours and the neighbours'. My present fourteen-year-old has never really bitten on any of the things

I've put his way: photography, computers, foreign travel, swimming, football, poetry. On the other hand, he's really taken off on something that I know nothing about, couldn't help him with if I tried, and never see him do: skateboarding. With skateboarding, I guess he feels under no pressure from me, his mother or school. It's totally self-led.

If I were to be balanced about this, then I should be pointing out here the difference between the kind of pressure-cooking I've described and the matter of 'giving opportunities' and 'introducing experiences'. Somehow or another we have to do this without it being a burden to our children, as in 'let's go and look at this old church, it's got a fifteenth-century nave and fourteenth-century font, you know . . .' With very young children, the most important opportunities we give them are space, time, and attention. Rushing them hither and thither dumping them into stimulating classes seems to make them panicky or blasé. This I know from comparing the children I do performances for (it's a kind of one-man show): the most difficult ones to handle are the Sunday morning Arts Centre ones where the super little darlings appear to know it all. In fact, the only time I've ever had my face spat in was by a super little darling.

At home, young children need corners or rooms where they are safe, little chairs and tables, plenty of paints, paper, things to model with (clay, plasticine, play-dough), cardboard boxes, glue, scissors, plenty of books, story-tapes, music-tapes, things to bang and blow, dressing-up boxes and cast-off home items like old telephones, saucepans and the like. With all these things, in conjunction with time, space and attention, they will make more opportunities happen for themselves than you or I can imagine.

Minders

This can be nightmare or bliss. A brief talk with friends will reveal the full range, from over-worked ratty old biddies who plonk the children down in a roomful of potties, toys, televisions and sweets and leave them all day, to brilliant intuitive infant teachers who take them for walks and visits, and find new and interesting things for them to do.

Remember, you are only paying for a minder, not a Suzuki teacher. The abysmal under-5s childcare situation in this country means that nearly everybody suffers: parents, children and minders. Nearly all parties can come out of the situation feeling aggrieved.

So, how to choose a minder? If it's you that's doing some of the ferrying to and fro, then make sure the minder is someone who can cope with a man and isn't overcome with embarrassment every time she sees you. When you're checking out the situation, you need to look at the state of toys, safety of heaters and windows, what kind of food she dishes up, how many children, whether she takes them out, if so, where and why and how does she look after all the children on the roads, is she in a reasonably contented state of mind and not in some lousy relationship where she's being hit or is hitting the bottle.

Of course all this involves scrutiny, and scrutiny can be resented. It's part of the vicious circle of everyone checking out everyone else. You might find, as a man, that this feels like female biz and you retreat in the face of it. Understandable, but if you do, then you have to accept that this gives off very specific messages to your child: 'Dad isn't interested in my life at the minder's . . .'

My partner hatched out a plan with some friends that was something of an improvement. Three households employed two women to look after our children for varying lengths of time in our houses. We advertised for the women, paid them over the rate and during holidays, and we also provided food for the children. About once every six months there was a meeting between people from the three households to discuss things like people dropping out, pay increases, illnesses and so forth. It seemed like one of the best arrangements that I've heard of.

Movement

Most of the baby manuals have nice little charts explaining the stages a baby goes through, hands waving, head lifting, back arching and so on. It can be really nice watching all this. I mean, before I had a baby, I thought babies were little immobile blobs that smelled. I had no idea that right from the start you can see expressions, movements and personality. More than that, there are times early on when you can see changes every day in these movements. This is wonderful.

Several things made an impact on me. If you get to sit with your baby right from the start, watch how it will scan your face. It may feel prattish, but use your face, and your eyes especially, and talk and sing to the baby. Don't worry about what nutty and gooey things come out of your mouth. You'll be amazed how soon the baby starts recognizing you. I nod and stroke the baby's cheek with the back of my finger. Watch out here for the milk reflex, when the baby turns to face the thing tickling her cheek because she thinks it's a nipple.

One of the first things my first wife's mother made us do, after we had bathed our first boy, was to lie him down on his back in front of the fire with just his top on, to let him kick. Then for about five minutes or so, he kicked his little legs. He seemed to love it and my mother-in-law said it would strengthen his legs and back. It was a nice social time, too, when we could all sit round and enjoy the baby.

I once saw a film on TV of a three-month-old baby which aimed to show how babies communicate. They showed how it kept repeating certain gestures. These gestures seemed to be the same for one kind of situation, like wanting something to eat, or wanting to be picked up. The film repeated these situations in rapid sequence, whereupon you saw twenty repetitions of exactly the same gesture by the baby. In other words, what seemed like the slightly chaotic waving we think babies do, in fact had a clear pattern. It was yet more evidence that babies are not blobs. I then went away full of this to watch my little ones and any others I came into contact with and – yes – it worked. Only the other day, I looked into the pram at a friend's baby, and first I saw it read my face and then it made a repeated little move with one arm, then with the other, and a little turn of the head. It was instantly recognizable as a kind of 'hallo'.

For me, the biggest buzz in this area is getting the first smiles. All sorts of things make a baby smile. By the way, some very early smiling, first week or so, isn't actually smiling, it's a bit of grunting to go with nappy-filling. But after a couple of months or so, all sorts of things can make a baby smile, or even better, laugh: making popping noises, little raspberries, nodding and singing, swinging the baby up and down, jigging and singing, squeezing, blowing down her neck, burying your nose in his chest, twiddling your fingers, doing ventriloquist acts with a teddy or dolly. I really got into this, and have spent hours at it. It may sound weird, but being able to make a baby smile and giggle is one of the major achievements I've chalked up in my life.

Nappies

There are probably quite deep reasons why, for some men, nappies represent the last threshold, the one you just cannot bear to cross. Yes, I'll do the shopping, the washing, the cooking, but nappies – no. What is being said here? That handling poo is one of those things with a female label on it? That those same human beings we think look great in those new clothes and smell wonderful in that perfume are also the best at nappies? Perhaps you feel a sense of panic even as you read this. If so, let me say this: first and foremost, getting a baby clean and fresh and dry is a nice thing to do. And if you move in quickly before the mess has had time to oxidize in the air, it doesn't actually smell too bad.

I had a rude awakening to the business long before I had children. My girlfriend at the time was in with a group of women who had decided to play a practical joke on their men. We went over to see a couple and their baby. When we got there, there were two other couples visiting. There was a bit of talking and suddenly I noticed that all the women had gone: there were four men and a baby – as in the film, plus one. We chatted on about football and other manly things for five minutes, ten, twenty, thirty and of course soon the baby started crying. There should have been a camera. We didn't know what to do, who was going to pick it up, who was going to jig it up and down, who was going to see if its nappy needed changing, who was going to do the nappy. In the end all four of us did it. There were eight hands on that baby, pushing and prodding and squeezing, trying to get it right. The whole thing had been a wicked conspiracy on the part of the mother to try and get her bloke to wise up. And this was in the days of . . . the Terry Towelling Nappy.

I guess that nearly everyone reading this will be spared the delights of shaking turds off terry nappies, and seeing stinking buckets of pissy ones standing in the bath. Such pleasures are gone. There really is no mystery about paper nappies, no magic folding tricks, no cunning deals with safety pins. I almost regret that my terry-nappy knowledge is redundant.

If you don't get in on nappies at the beginning, you never will. If you never do nappies, then your child will never see you as someone who deals with the real, basic stuff. Probably most men today are people who were brought up sharing constipation, sore foreskins, funny-coloured wee, itchy bums and the like only with their mothers. This may sound nutty, but I feel really good when I think that my kids have thought that dad as well as mum was a right person to help solve such problems. I was there with the salt water when the sore willy had to be dangled in. I was there teaching them how to wipe bums, and even as I'm writing this, I'm popping out of the room every so often to help my step-daughter massage her belly to help with constipation. All this kind of contact starts with nappies.

What is there to be said about paper nappies? My big mistake is always to yank the tabs too hard, so destroying the nappy in half a second. Over a year this can be an expensive mistake. If you put them on too tight it leads to rashes round the waist, and if they're too loose they leak. If you're confused by the mysticism of the ads, what they are basically saying is that 1. wee next to a baby's skin causes nappy rash; 2. our nappies hold loads of wee; 3. but don't panic because the brilliant way in which we make our nappies keeps the wee away from the skin. If you believe all they say about running shoes, you'll believe this too.

In other words, beware nappy rash. Everybody's life becomes hell when nappy rash is around. Small wonder; I don't suppose *I'd* keep very quiet if the whole of my bum was stinging all day. You only had to show a paper nappy to my second child and his bum would look like a tomato. What to do? The best and most impractical cure for nappy rash is the no-nappy treatment. If you expose most nappy rashes to the air, they go. But of course this also exposes your carpets to wee. This is where you rediscover the prehistoric virtues of the terry nappy. You can lie a baby on them, you can pin them loosely on the child, you can mop up pools with them.

You can buy various ointments that claim to cure nappy rash. The problem here is that they may or may not work, assuming that the newly ointmented surface is not going to get drenched with urine every hour on the hour. In other words, you may need both ointment and the fresh air treatment.

Once cured, you may have to go for the barrier method. Basically this is like fitting a damp course to your house. The old method here is reliable but slow and messy: vaseline. Vaseline makes a great wee-proof layer but when it's at room temperature it can be very stiff and hell to get off your hands. If you leave it on a radiator it'll soften, but then of course you may not be changing the baby near the radiator . . . Less efficient but easier to use and easier to clean off your hands are various zinc oxide creams. Take your choice.

Finally, where to do nappy changing? Much favoured is the changing-mat. It seems at first glance to solve all problems: the offending articles – the pissy pooey child and the pissy pooey nappy – are at arm's length, and any sudden explosions or fountains mostly land on the changing-mat's cleanable surface. So far, so good. But you will soon learn that fountains landing on the changing-mat are not absorbed, but run in rivulets towards the carpet, or much more likely, straight onto the clean vest and jumper. In other words, you need a changing-mat AND a terry nappy to put under the baby.

The other problem with the changing-mat method is the wriggle. As the baby gets older, the more it wriggles. My second child was not just a wriggler, he was a wrestler. It's at times like these you realize you don't have three arms and your head isn't much good at sticking down nappy tabs. Nappy-changing time becomes a time for much shouting, and skilful use of judo holds.

My solution to these changing-mat problems is to put the child over my knees. This way you can hold him down with the same arm that has the hand doing the nappy changing. With a terry nappy over your knees you can catch some of the fountain before it reaches your trousers, and you soon learn a quick upward hoist of the child to make sure you don't get soaked. Women seem generally to disapprove of changing nappies on knees, but it's nice to have individual and freaky ways of doing things. It makes you feel less slavish. With this over-the-knee technique, look out for the flailing feet. The child will learn very soon that as you sit there concentrating hard on wiping and tab-sticking, your chin is getting invitingly near. One kick of that lovely little pink foot and you're reeling. And they love it – cue for giggles and cackles and woman experts sitting around nodding, 'I told you so, I told you so.'

Changing nappies brings you into close contact with every digestive quirk. Even though you may never learn to spell it, diarrhoea becomes immensely important in your life. You discover such interesting facts as that babies on breast-milk only produce a not unpleasant mustard-coloured putty. You will be shocked to find that sometimes this isn't mustard-coloured, but bright green. Do not be alarmed: that's what it does when it hits oxygen. You will discover what babies can digest and what they can't. Sweet corn and raisins will never seem the same again, and the seed distribution systems of tomatoes and the like will become instantly clear to you. To revert to nappy rash – it's not always wee that causes the problem; in my experience, the thing is often triggered off by you being lazy about changing a pooey nappy. You think, OK, leave it just while I finish this cup of tea . . . three minutes . . . five minutes . . . and the damage has been done. It looks OK when you get round to changing it (after seven minutes), but by the time you get to the next nappy, there's the great red raw mess and the uncomprehending, pained eyes looking at you accusingly through the tears: why is my bum burning?

Now for a problem: changing nappies when you're out and about. Notice that motorway service stations have changing facilities in the ladies' loo only. Hard luck if you're on your own, it's the awkward sitting-on-the-loo job. If you're out on your own in other places, watch out for sympathetic old people who are probably thinking that your wife's just died; notice how all your men friends run like crazy at the sight of a baby's bum; observe parents and in-laws tut-tutting and unsure whether you should be doing this at all. Be brave, be bold, do it!

Nursery and Reception Class

This is about as far as this book takes you, up to the door of the first day of real school. It's at this moment you will remember The Cling (see SHAMING UP). What strategy will you use to ensure that your child doesn't hang on to you like a limpet, wailing pitifully? How will you ensure that this day is not indelibly marked in your child's brain as the day you deserted her and left her helpless in the control of totalitarian torturers?

Everyone is wondering this, and everyone is eyeballing everyone else, wondering which kid is going to crack first. Here's my solution: make for the sand-tray and get digging. Don't wait for your kid to go there. Just get over there and stuck in like it's the best thing that's happened since the ice cap retreated. Soon you will have a little cluster of kids around you. 'Hey, this looks good.' 'Yeah, I'm going to bury my Dad in here', says one cheery little girl.

Out of the corner of your eye, you notice that your own little dear is coming over too. Keep digging, muttering about how there's a lot of work to be done here. Other parents may now have run away and left their children in the capable hands of the totalitarian torturer and you. A few other parents are enwrapped in The Cling but trying to find an interesting book. The torturer will probably want to throw you out after a certain time. Pretend that your work in the sand-tray is nearing completion, but it's OK for the others to finish it off. Then quickly mutter to your own child, 'See you in a minute', and get out fast.

If you win this round, the rest is plain sailing till your child enters college, where you have to repeat the routine with the gas-ring in the student Hall of Residence.

Older Kids Attacking Baby

It's true, they do. You turn your back and POKE! In goes a finger and the little tiny thing is screaming. Sometimes they go in for leaving dangerous things in the cot, like a fully-armed Action Man. I shouldn't jest: my older one left a polythene bag in his baby brother's cot with malice aforethought. Beware of the over-keen hugger. 'Dad, let me hold the baby', and a little cuddle turns into a big juicy hug which turns into a half-nelson.

It's all understandable, if alarming. The older child has had you all for himself for the first months and years of his life and then along comes this screaming, sucking monster that every-one comes round to see and pat and hold and go goo-goo-goo at. If friends do come round, insist that they bring something for the older child. If it's couples coming, make them take it in turns to play with the older child. Tell them to avoid bright breezy gaffes like: 'Well, your baby sister looks terrific, I bet you're pleased, aren't you?' and 'Aren't you a lucky little chap to have such a beautiful little girl?' or 'Mum's busy, isn't she?'

The conventional role of the caring, considerate father in this circumstance has often been to take the older child on long loving outings to the zoo. This is probably a mistake. From his point of view, such outings mean: 'Ah, so Mum doesn't love me any more, she only loves the monster. And to prove it, you've wheeled me out of the house so she can get on with all that hugging and kissing with the monster. You're ganging up on me.'

The alternative is that you get stuck in with the new one and let the older one have some good times with mum, when she can reassure him he's a fantastic fellow and she still loves him.

On the Move

Some of the most hairy outings I've gone in for with children have been taking a child with me when I've been doing my show in a school. How did I manage the train journeys to places like Nottingham, taking my books, preparing for a performance, talking to the children and teachers afterwards and then travelling back on the train? All with a one-year-old in tow. In one school, when Eddie was about two, he refused to go into the nursery and so he sat at the side of the stage while I did the show. After about twenty minutes he got up and slowly started to crawl across the stage behind me. I just let him carry on, but then, just as slowly, the head of English in the school got up on the stage and started crawling after him. So there I was in the middle of trying to put something across to two hundred or so children, being upstaged by a baby and the head of English creeping about behind me.

Presumably you won't be quite as daft as I was, but there'll still be times when it's just you, the baby and the outside world. The most important item here is The Bag. If you're lazy and only in on this business as an auxiliary, you will let your partner do The Bag. She will say: 'She needs a drink, here's a change of track suit bottoms, I've put a knife in to peel the apple', and so on. This is all very comforting, but kind of debilitating. I've been like that with my third (our fifth) and it always seems like a reflection on my competence. You may not be so bothered.

What feels best is having your own Bag. You have your own supplies of stuff: terry nappies, baby lotion, vaseline, baby wipes, disposable nappies and so on, just as you have your

own toilet bag if you go away. You then also stuff in changes of clothes, two books (for the child, not you) that can be spun out in case of rained-off outings, long bus trips and the like, and always always always supplies of food and drink. Make sure the drink is really thirst-quenching and not just some sweet sticky thing, and the food is immediately consumable: sealed tubs of baby gunk or yoghurt with spoon, peanut butter sandwiches or whatever. Don't forget three polythene bags for putting nappies in in case you have to bring them home with you, and also for catching sick on board a bus. If there's room, maybe you can squeeze in a comfort toy and an engrossing toy. Lightweight rain gear goes in there too, because it's always too windy and it always rains. Changing-mat users will need a changing-mat.

The Bag itself should either be a rucksack or a shoulder bag, so that you can use two hands to carry the toddler and push the buggy. I used to use a bag that I slung across me so that I could carry him on one hip, the bag on the other. This allowed me to grope in the bag while still carrying the little fellow. The bag itself will need to be washable as it soon gets to smell of old food that you didn't empty out, wee, sick, sour milk and baby lotion. Lovely.

There are two very real dangers about the weather. Babies dehydrate in the hot weather and suffer from hypothermia in the cold, very, very easily. The explanation for this is down to the ratio of a baby's surface area to its overall body weight. Basically, it's as if they've got loads more skin than we have, and so they lose heat and/or water through their skin very much more quickly than an adult. In cold weather, a baby with an exposed head, neck, hands and feet is at risk. In very hot weather, you have to keep pumping in the fluids. The problem with both situations is that babies don't always shout about it to let you know they're suffering. If a baby isn't kept dry when it rains, it loses body heat very quickly straight through the clothes, and gets to a point where it is just as if it were naked. In an emergency, caught out in the rain, shove the baby under your coat, or better still, next to your skin.

Other Guys

It's no use pretending otherwise, being a share-care father can be a bit lonely. There aren't many other men doing it, and whereas women seem prepared to mix with other women on the sole basis that they are mothers, I for one have found it difficult to become friends with a man simply because he's a father. That probably says quite a lot either about me or about men in general. There's no question: in an ideal world, we would be able to behave towards each other in the way that mothers manage, giving each other advice and help on how to cope with teething, nappy rash and sleepless nights. Instead, these kinds of conversation we have with women. I can remember times when it's been me, my young child, a friend and his child, and we've sat and talked about everything *except* the children. It's almost as if we'd been saying to each other: 'Hey, look, we cope with this upbringing game without going in for long boring conversations about the best kind of shampoo, don't we?' Perhaps there's a sheepishness factor to overcome. Or perhaps men aren't very good at doing baby-talk: 'that's a nice babygrow your little girl's got . . .'

So, rather than set up fathers' outings, picnics, play-ins, etc. I've tended just to muck along with the playgroups and outings that local mothers have organized, or just go solo. You may not have much of a choice, but I think I would have learnt all kinds of things if I had done a bit of the socialized childcare with some men around. You see, one of the hardest things is to find your own ways of doing things. I only got to feeling OK about looking after young children when I began to think I was doing it in my own way and not just imitating what women do.

Other Parents (child's point of view)

Some of my fondest memories are of staying round at other people's houses. I was sure for years that a lot of my friends' parents were nicer than mine. I would lie awake comparing all the different kinds of things my friends were allowed to do, what kinds of holidays they had, what they were allowed to eat, what happened when they went to bed. In the long term it was a very empowering thing of my parents to have let me do. They were setting themselves up for comparison. Of course now, as a parent, to think of my own children going to stay with other people feels just a teeny bit threatening! What if my children think that someone else's dad is nicer than me?

Going to stay with friends was something that happened to me after the age covered by this book, but there are plenty of ways you can widen your children's awareness that there are other styles of living. I've found that, right from a very young age, children seem to want to adopt another family or another person. At present my two youngest seem to have adopted Caroline, the illustrator of this book, and want to get over and see her whenever they can. Other times my children have homed in on other parents. Perhaps it's a way of getting looked after without the emotional hassle of your mum or dad breathing down your neck. Where the home your child is attracted to follows the traditional pattern you can, as an active father, come up against some funny situations: you're doing baby talk with the woman of the house and your old friend is sitting there feeling cheesed off and guilty.

See OTHER PARENTS (parents' point of view)

Other Parents (parents' point of view)

I often think of the early days with our first child, going to see some friends who had a child of more or less the same age. It defused all the little petty worries and anxieties and set up a whole new range of the gags and stories that help you cope – like calling newborn babies' poo 'mustard gas', and giving your child's moods nicknames: 'oh, no, he's doing the Screaming Iron Girder Act', a reference to when children go rigid and scream. Their baby was a bit premature, and I also remember going up to the hospital to see him. Barry went behind a glass screen, dressed up in surgeon-type gear, while we looked on. We found that if we shouted, Barry could just hear us. He made a face to show that the baby seemed to look a bit down, so I shouted through the screen: 'Tell him a joke.' Barry mouthed 'What?' 'TELL HIM A JOKE.' Barry looked puzzled. 'ASK HIM, WHERE DO FROGS CHANGE THEIR SKINS?' Barry leant over the incubator and I saw him say, 'Where do frogs change their skins?' He looked back at me. 'IN THE CROAKROOM,' I shouted. Barry went back to the incubator. 'In the croakroom,' he said to the baby.

The baby flourished: now he's fifteen and over six feet tall. It was that first joke that did it.

Pets

Young children love pets. Pets don't always love children. Great big dogs seem to think they're very important, and protect them from strangers. One Great Dane I knew (!) would never let a stranger stand between the mother and the baby in its pram. It wasn't aggressive, it just nudged in and made sure you couldn't get near. Just as well it wasn't aggressive – it was about as big as a donkey.

Cats don't seem to be useful. Young children like poking cats, and cats seem to think that a poke is worth at least a spit and at worst a scratch. Small children and cats clearly weren't designed to be good friends.

Gerbils are a winner if you feel you can look after them as well as a baby, but all young children are animal liberationists in so far as they are very keen on opening cage doors.

Beware of dog do. It is lethal, terrible stuff. Young teething children will quite happily chew a shoe or suck their fingers after they've fallen over in the park. Dog do can carry eggs of a parasite that can make children blind. It's a terrifying thought. You have to be vigilant about it.

Look out for jealous pets. They get all down-at-the-mouth and whiny. If you're holding the baby, a dog will sometimes come up and put its nose on your lap to say, 'me, too'. Pets *must* be kept out of the room where the baby is sleeping. Cats will sleep on babies and possibly suffocate them, dogs might bite, and gerbils . . . well, who knows? Jealous gerbils . . . what an idea.

Play

I must have spent hours, days, even weeks down on the floor building towers, playing dollies' dinners, car races, lego houses or whatever. Play is vital. It's the starting point of all learning. Sadly, its status is low in our culture, where talk is of pushing children from level to level and measuring them in terms of skills acquired.

A lot of adults treat children as if they are really incomplete human beings, waiting to grow up. Evidence for this, they seem to think, is that they don't do real grown-up things, like driving cars, but spend a lot of their time playing. Playing, then, is seen as something childish, unimportant and silly. If you recognize any of this as something you've thought, then now is the time to banish it.

My position is this: we learn through play. Play is where we try out different ways of doing things, in as enjoyable a way as possible. Through play we find out what we can do. Good play breeds more play, more confidence, more ability. Children are brilliant at this and we should help them play in as many areas as possible: with toys, with paper, pens, pencils, crayons and paints, with words, with movement, with climbing apparatus, with voice, with drama, with machines, cooking, and any safe process around. All art, construction, scientific discovery and invention has its origins in play, and in people who are prepared to play.

If you have only one child and this child does not have plenty of other children to play with, then it's you that's got to do the playing. Get down on the floor with those bricks, with the crayons, with the cars and push them around a bit. Think like a child, don't pressurize, don't organize – just play along-

side, adopting suggestions that the child makes: 'Let's feed dolly with a straw.' 'Yeah, let's.'

If you want to occupy your mind with what's going on here, you can see all kinds of concepts being put into place by the child: relationships in space and time, force, momentum, structure, stress, strain. If you get into dramatic play, once again you will see concepts – to do with power, punishment, anger, care, cruelty, fear, kindness – all being worked through in the games. It can get you wondering about stories, films and plays and why we listen to and watch them, or why we don't, as adults, act out power, punishment, anger and the rest.

If you don't want to get into the theory, then just let yourself be a child and enjoy it and see what comes up. Don't take my word for it that it's 'important': play with playing and find out what it means.

Some fun things to do:

- Use dolls, or socks as glove puppets, to do little plays. Remember, you're not into making complete dramas, just little open-ended dramatic contexts. If you listen to children in dramatic play, it keeps going one step forward, two steps backward: they set up a situation, start to act it out and before it finishes, they revise and start up again.

- Buy an easel, loads of sugar paper, a big polythene sheet, plastic aprons, loads of brushes, paint and pots.

- Get toys that offer up possibilities of role playing around them: post offices, houses, people, schools, doctor's sets and the like.

- Get toys that offer up multiple possibilities of construction and shape: play-dough, clay, plasticine, sand and water, blocks, bricks, lego, meccano, construx, quadro.

- Get children into contact with climbing, swinging, pulling and pushing, bouncing, trampolining, dancing.

- Play word-games, do silly talk, make funny noises with your lips, fingers and tongue, go for rhyming, magic words, pretend-words, back-slang, turning words round, spooner-isms, rude words in wrong places.

- Tell stories about the child, listen to stories they tell, write or type them as they are telling them so that you can read them back.

- Have various banging, blowing, plucking and key-pressing instruments that make all kinds of different sounds. Have band sessions to make music.

- Don't get too pedantic about rule-bound games with little ones. Just have matching and finding games.

With very young children, be absolutely fanatical about safety. Examine each toy for its potential to break or fall apart and for bits to get stuck in throats, gouge eyes out, or disappear up noses, in ears or elsewhere. If friends or grandparents give toys that look dangerous, or for too old a child, then simply put them on the shelf for later. As I am writing this, my seven-year-old girl has just fired a sponge gun (that the fourteen-year-old bought for the ten-year-old) into the face of the three-year-old . . . (see PUNISHMENT)!

As a postscript, men are at a possible advantage here. If we really are the immature twits who like kicking bits of leather round fields and hurling darts at the wall that women some-times claim we are, then now is the time to cultivate this spirit. If it exists, play with it. I play, therefore I am.

Playgroups

At the first playgroup I turned up at, a woman called Sue told a story about how she got so fed up with her bloke arriving home late Saturday night and pissed, she tied a knot in his pyjama trousers. Then when he came back she had the delight of listening to him hobbling about at the end of the bed swearing and cursing, struggling to get his legs into the pyjamas. Rather curiously, at the same time another woman there was talking in great detail about the imprisonment of Rudolf Hess.

Playgroups are, quite rightly, story-swapping time for mothers. Then suddenly, out of the blue, comes an alien: a father. Out of the window go all those chats about stitches, pissed husbands, and exercise videos. You are an inhibiting factor. This means that playgroups can be lonely places. Should I be here? Why am I here? How long will it go on? Why doesn't anyone talk to me? Try them if you're prepared to be any of the following: an outsider, or an expert on cars, men's birthday presents, what makes men want to have it off with women other than their wives, how to get boys to pee standing up, and the effects of beer. The other side-effect I noticed was that I was being held up to other husbands as the street goody-goody.

In spite of all this, the little ones usually have a good time and it gives you a chance to see how other people handle their kids, or find out what little tips they've got on where to buy a raincoat. You also see how your child gets on with other children. So if you can cope with embarrassment, it's worth it. It also tests your nerve. Can you stay cool when another kid is poking yours in the eye? Do you stop your kid hoarding tractors and trikes and fighting off nice little children with his

King Arthur's sword? Do you single out one kid, spot the way he rides his trike over other children's feet and dub him a pathological maniac on the verge of a nervous breakdown, drug abuse and murder? Do you hate his mother because of it? Do you want to yell 'SHUTTUUUUUP!!!' at the kid who keeps coming up to you and banging a drum in your face? Do you get in there, start building a lego fairy house and then get upset when none of the children want to play with you? These are some of the pleasant emotions you experience at a playgroup.

Post-Natal Depression

Because this is something that women are seen to suffer, it is inevitably treated as a woman's complaint. However, it doesn't take much imagination to see that being pregnant involves at least two other people: the father and the baby. It may also involve, historically, the mother's parents, the kind of pre-natal care received from midwives or doctors, the kind of labour, the kind of people who were at the labour.

Clearly, for two people to care for a baby together, they also have to care for each other. In the nine months on either side of a birth, most women find desertion, lack of support, indifference, contempt, bossiness, coldness, and so on, almost unbearable. The problem may sometimes be that we never intended to express such feelings, but that's how they came over, and that's how they were taken. Maybe you didn't turn up at a pre-natal class, maybe you came home later than you said, maybe you sit staring at the wall because you're worried about the birth or the baby or money. Everything's very raw and sensitive and feelings of isolation, helplessness, loneliness or an overwhelming sense of weakness and lack of control can lead to a full depression.

What this is all getting at is that, one way or another, we are part of the problem, and part of the solution. This is not to say anyone's at fault, but that to blame the victim, the mother, is precisely what is wrong with, say for example, telling a depressed mother: '*You* ought to see the doctor about it'. Maybe 'we' would be more helpful.

However, if things were as simple as that, there would be no problem. Just to make it really foggy: perhaps you think that what's being asked of you is too much caring, too much support, too much sensitivity. 'Why,' you might ask, 'do you need to rely on me so much? Perhaps the reason why you're getting depressed is because you expect too much from a man. If you didn't expect so much, you wouldn't feel so let down.'

So we are back to that old conundrum of what people feel they are entitled to ask of each other. It's my experience in situations like this, that one partner (or both) appeals to the outside world, citing other couples or experts as evidence that what they are asking from the other is normal and OK; meanwhile, the opposing partner appeals to the outside world as evidence that what the person is asking for is abnormal and unreasonable. It's at moments like this that you realize the word 'love' may simply mean 'equilibrium': two people agreeing on what they think each is entitled to ask of the other. Then a baby comes along and you're trying to work out equilibrium between *three* people. Hard.

Potty Training

This is not a competition. But stand by for the great potty-training races. Conversations with friends soon get down to, 'Oh, isn't he dry YET?' You are soon left thinking that really it's you that's still walking around in nappies. Tough it out. If we make children feel under pressure about their pees and poos, they'll feel under pressure about a lot of other things as well. Peeing and pooing shouldn't be a burden to children, or a performance done to please others. Ideally, the child should get a sense of satisfaction from a job being well done. If you leave potty training to a time when a child *can* appreciate how well it has done, then that is a tremendous confidence-booster, and a cause for self-congratulation to the child.

This said, you may have very little to do with it. You may find, if your child goes to a minder, that the minder is pretty desperate to get her charges out of nappies and 'get them dry' in about two days flat. This didn't stop one of ours needing a nappy at night till she was six, and she would quite often wet herself during the day till she was four. Another one just decided that he wanted to have a go at doing it in the toilet like his older brother, and nothing would stop him. He genuinely did it all himself. My youngest thought that he would keep nappies on till he was three. I suspected he was using it as an excuse to say 'I'm still a baby', so to start off I reasoned with him: 'Don't you think it would be a good idea if you didn't have a nappy? Mummy doesn't wear a nappy, Daddy doesn't wear a nappy, Postman Pat doesn't wear a nappy, the Teenage Mutant Hero Turtles don't wear nappies . . .' and so on through everyone else he knew. This had absolutely zero effect. He clearly thought, 'Yes, I know that Leonardo and Postman Pat don't wear nappies, but I do.'

So I did something that may seem to contradict the self-confidence bit (but remember, he was three). After leaving potties about for a few weeks, and getting him to watch the rest of us on the loo, one morning when I got him up, I took off his night nappy and he walked about with nothing on. I said, 'Tell me when you want to do a wee or a poo.' I figured that he had never really had to think about the actual business of doing it: what it felt like, and so on. Sure enough, first time he wee'd on the floor or, more accurately, on his feet. I don't think he knew what it was at first. I got there with the potty about half way through, to show him that it is possible to catch it. Next time, he called out just as it was beginning so I got there earlier. The third time, he called out just before. Each time, whoever was there made a big fuss of him and said how well he had done. By the fifth or sixth time, he was going to the potty and doing it in there, and he came and showed us the wee or poo he had produced. Huge applause.

Of course, they are never completely dry. Accidents happen when they are so engrossed in a game they leave it too late, so you have to keep an eye open for boys hanging on to their willies and girls crossing their legs. The first few days at nursery or school sometimes need taking gently, with plenty of showing them the toilets and practising sitting on it. Try very hard not to get ratty about accidents; the more ratty you get, the more likely they are to do it again. Whatever you do, don't go in for leaving them in their wet knickers to punish them. On several occasions I've told mine the story of how I was woken up one morning by a phone call from a publisher telling me that my first-ever book was accepted, and as I was standing taking the call with no clothes on, I found it impossible to hang on any longer . . .

If your child is repeatedly wetting itself during the day, then he or she is trying to say something to you about something they're worrying about, such as being bullied at school. Whatever it is, it's unlikely to be anything to do with weeing itself.

Preparing for Fatherhood

One of the first things I found when fatherhood hit me was that, yes, there were things I ought to do, but I couldn't. These consisted of being able to drive a car, earn money, mend toilet cisterns and carry heavy weights. On the other hand, I was good at winding, changing nappies, and putting the baby to sleep. I understand full well that the reverse is probably the case for you. You *can* drive, earn money, mend toilets and carry coal-sacks – all very useful fatherhood qualities, as I've since found out.

So, assuming you've got those before you start and won't be picking them up as you go along like I have, then how do you get your mind round the stuff I *could* do? May I suggest you take up spying? I'm assuming, here, that your partner is pregnant and you're beginning to wonder what the hell is going to hit you. Is the whole thing a dreadful mistake or is it going to be fantastically excitingly brilliantly wonderful? Or something halfway between, like boring? Are you going to be able to carry on marathon running, mountain climbing, ballroom dancing, crossword solving, hang-gliding and part-time brain surgery?

Back to the spying. Very furtively, start father-spotting. When you're out, see if you ever see any men pushing a buggy. Study their faces. Do they look like they've been conscripted by a woman who knows what she wants, or do they look like volunteers? When you go to a party with old friends who have had a child, listen closely to the way they talk. Have they gone completely crazy over what looks to you like a slow-moving piece of pastry? As the baby screams, needs changing, feeding, cuddling or whatever, watch closely who moves first, mum or dad. Does he know where the clean babygrows are?

All questions concerning men and childcare can be reduced to this vital one. In the moments of self-doubt in the middle of the night, in the midst of being asked when it's due, let your mind ask yourself that key question, 'will I know where the babygrows* are?' After you've cleared up that problem, everything's a pushover.

* My editor says: 'Will they know what a babygrow is?' They are stretchy boiler-suits for tiny humans, coming in various colours and patterns including a very fetching convict suit.

Punishment

The old slogan 'You wait till your father comes home' is alive and well. I heard a little boy on the train silenced with it, the day before I wrote this. It's a short-cut to disaster. It signifies dad is the real tough guy in town, while mum is a tender wimp. Mind you, thinking about it, *I* have actually used 'you wait till your mother comes home' to great effect!

Still – no one is perfect, and we are all at our least perfect when it comes to punishment. Everyone gets some of it wrong some of the time, and some of us get it wrong a lot of the time, but most of us think we are doing a better job than most other people.

Wrong things I've done: hit children, mocked them, made them feel small, made other children laugh at the one 'in the wrong', shouted too loud, persisted in being angry long after it was right to do so . . . and I'm sure many other things, too.

Wrong things I think other people do: bribe and blackmail children to be good, lose the power of their punishments by going for the highest stakes too soon, pass on the heavy-duty punishment to another person – nearly always the man.

The great debate between adults, in my experience, is in and around what is permitted. My first memory of my fourteen-year-old's best friend is of him at about eighteen months old, standing in the middle of the dinner table splodging gravy and carrots all over the place. At the time I thought that this was right out of order, way over the top, permissiveness gone mad. I guess the boy's mother thought he was learning through PLAY about serving people.

One of the first bits of shouting and punishing I went in for arose out of panic. My first child was about eighteen months old and I was in the garden of my parents' home. One moment he was in the garden too, and the next he had disappeared. I rushed round to the front of the house and he'd opened the garden gate and was running up the middle of the road, laughing and giggling with excitement. I reached him just before he got to a junction with a fast-running main road. Yes, I shouted and raved, which may or may not have discouraged him from doing it again. Yet, quite clearly, it was my fault he was out there in the first place.

A similar thing happened just recently. I was proud of myself for having picked up a computer very cheaply, and I put it in the room where the children mostly play, saying: 'It's all yours.' Within 24 hours it was smashed. The three-year-old had stuffed a balloon and a toy car tyre down the disk drive. My wife steered me away to a far corner of the house to meditate on computers, three-year-olds, and stupid parents who leave expensive gear too near to them. The most he experienced by way of punishment was a long, boring trip to a computer repairer's. The guy there sorted him out with a bit of eye-balling.

Some fathers reading this may wish to avoid some of the punitive rubbish they experienced when they were young. Surely there must be a better way of going on, and not making children's lives miseries? All this is very much to do with What is punishment for? Why are we punishing children?

Here are some possible reasons:

- to try to make the child behave more like me
- to stop the child hurting itself or other people
- to make the child feel small
- to defend adult space into which children shouldn't trespass
- to make the parent not look bad in public
- to satisfy the norms of institutions outside the home: school, church, granny's house, shopkeepers, etc.
- to make the child learn and concentrate
- to stop the child lying
- to stop the child stealing
- to stop the child from being lazy
- to get the child to eat some particular kind of food

The question now arises as to whether punishments will actually achieve any of these objectives. What punishments do you have?

- shouting no
- hitting in all the various places, with all the various forces
- giving lectures
- withdrawing affection
- ordering TIME OUT
- withdrawing favours
- demanding forfeits in terms of money, work, apologies, explanations
- bans
- restrictions
- swearing

Some people think that rather than treat every crime as if it must be confronted then and there, you should use diversion tactics: your child hits another – don't hit your child as a punishment, since all that does is confirm that you think hitting is a good and potent way of solving problems. What is better, say the diversionists, is to direct your child to something more constructive, like having a cuddle, building a bridge, or jumping up and down on the trampoline.

What it comes down to is that you don't want your child to be horrible and you're trying to figure out ways to bring this about. The problem lies a lot of the time in the fact that children *want* to be horrible. This is in order to express their anxieties, hates and guilts, and in order to find out whether you're capable of really looking after them. If, for a moment, you can stand back and look at a child being horrible, it's worth trying to think *why*.

Here are some of the reasons why my children have been horrible. They've been:

- angry that an older sister can make something that looks better than what he's done
- angry with a younger sister for getting affection that she thinks she didn't get
- repeatedly doing what she's been asked not to do in order to see if mother is strong enough to keep saying no

- angry that you've been away
- lying out of fear that the punishment will be too severe
- being madly rude when visitors come so as to challenge parents in public
- telling tales in order to jockey for favours
- not wanting to stick to agreed limits in order to test parental strength

The 'crimes' I think worth dealing with are ones where the child is trying to hurt someone (including me) physically or emotionally; where the child is trying to deceive people in a malicious way; stealing; not abiding by agreements.

The sanctions I favour, but by no means have the strength or wisdom always to stick to, are:

- TIME OUT
- Withdrawal of favours

Here's a bit of standard two-year-old's carry-on. He's sitting on my lap and suddenly he attacks my face: a quick poke in the eye, heave on the ear, blowing a raspberry up my nose. No point in yelling, no point in hitting back – best thing is withdraw the favour: 'No, you're not staying on my lap, you've just hit me in the face.'

Another one that crops up is a bit of mucking around just as you're about to leave for somewhere. Say you've agreed to go out together and she starts flinging things around. Sit down and, 'No, we're not going to the park, you've just thrown orange juice all over the floor.' One of ours used to go in for a great wailing and moaning and running away just as we were about to leave for a friend's house or the zoo or somewhere. I think it only needed one cancelled outing to avoid becoming prisoner to such tyranny.

- Demanding a spoken admission of what has actually been done – 'I shot the sponge gun in his face' – because young children especially find it very hard actually to admit exactly what they have done wrong, and a quick 'sorry' is sometimes a get-out.
- Making warnings and ultimatums and being consistent and firm about them: 'If you do that once more, then I'm not reading you a story.' *If he does it once more, then you must, must, must stick to your threat. If you can't stick to a threat, don't make it.*
- Not giving in to children's blackmail: roaring, yelling, spitting, tearing, and punching when the child can't get its own way (see TERRIBLE TWOS). Not giving in is of course a kind of punishment, and it's important to insist on agreed ways of asking for and getting things.

Sanctions I resort to but don't think are in the long run effective or right, and probably create as much long-term horribleness as they avoid:

- Shouting your head off: this at least sometimes has the advantage of making you feel better, and there is something to be said for not having to pretend you're not angry.
- Hitting: sometimes I've rationalized this by making the hit not hurt, as in the tap with a finger on the back of the hand to indicate disapproval rather than causing pain.

- Teasing and mocking: this I've done too often, and for different reasons; sometimes so that I don't have the unpleasantness of getting and feeling angry, sometimes to wage parental power games ('I'm more powerful than you because I can make you feel rotten but you can't make me feel rotten'), sometimes in order to get one of them to admit the crassness of, for example, lying – saying that the cat wrecked my ring-backed diary/address book.
- Making unreal demands: asking five-year-olds to tidy a room, and when they don't, bundling all their toys into a bag and saying I was going to throw them all away.
- Reproducing my own parents' way of going on even if I know I hated it and it didn't work! Hearing your own parent's voice as you wade into action against your own children must be one of the most common and the most unnerving experiences of being a parent. It makes you wonder how many generations back a particular tone of voice, gesture, or expression goes. It could be hundreds of years, couldn't it?

One of the most pleasant experiences you can have as a parent is to go places with your children and have people say to you that they're nice, or that they want their children to come and play with yours. When they're older and they go places without you, friends' houses, school or wherever, and people say that they liked your children, that too is a very nice feeling. There are no rewards, no medals in this business, but when people say things like that, it feels good – even if it enrages you, because the child concerned behaves like a little sod at home!

Putting Baby to Sleep

You may not know this, but you are going to become an expert at putting a baby to sleep. There are several reasons for this:

1. Your wife is so shattered she can hardly move, and though she is the mother of the child, necessity is the mother of invention.

2. You are easily able to adopt a scientific approach to the matter: for example, how many jiggings of a pram does it take before the baby nods off? If the jiggings are more frequent, does that make it easier? If the jiggings are gentler, does *that* make it easier? If you rock the baby in your arms, does it help if you sing? If you sing without rocking, does that make things worse?

3. You don't smell of fresh milk.

Hang on. Don't babies just fall asleep? I hear you ask. Some do, yours doesn't. For some mysterious and infuriating reason, babies don't go to sleep when you tell them to. This calls for much of the above rocking, jigging, singing and the like. Maybe, as you reeled out of a late night movie sometime in the past, you may recall having seen a fairly ordinary-looking bloke rushing past you wheeling a pram. He wasn't a madman, he was a father. He had discovered not long before that wheeling the baby round during the day sent it to sleep. He has therefore made a scientific leap into the unknown by imagining that if he does the same thing at night, the little thing will nod off just the same.

Sod's Law says here that when the baby nods off during the day, it's always just before you need to get it out of the pram. At night, when lucky people are asleep or enjoying each other's love, your little one is wide awake looking at the stars and screaming. A mile or so in the pram will usually do the trick, and if you do it fast enough you will up your aerobic breathing to a fitness-improving level.

Lullabies are helpful; I've heard them described as work-songs, and after an hour of rocking a baby, you'll know why.

A further Sod's Law on this subject is that the first three times you try to leave the child after your bout of rocking, jigging and singing, the baby will wake up again and yell. This is why you will perfect the crazy Nifty Norman technique of creeping away from where you have just laid the baby down. You look like Groucho Marx, without the rolling eyeballs.

Reading Books

Someone with my background is obviously going to say something about this being the most important thing in the universe. The argument is this: the written word remains the main source of formal and theoretical knowledge in our culture in spite of film, TV and video. You want your child to have a chance to get hold of this kind of knowledge because it means access to better jobs, explanations of the physical, biological and human worlds around us, information concerning any operation you might want to carry out at home or at work. The problem is that children, in their normal daily life, don't actually *need* to read: they can play, ask questions, watch TV, and guess.

In the nice little cocoon of the children's book world, it's very easy to imagine that everyone *knows* that children's books are some of the most inventive, artistic and creative around. Bold claim! Just take a look at the art work and design of picture books. Give yourself a chance to see the wit and humour. I promise you, reading children's books can, if nothing else, be a relief from adult work.

One of the reasons I say all this is that there is a very easy trap to fall into, as a parent – just simply buying the books you had as a child. Believe me, children's books have got better and better.

So, if you think reading matters, can I suggest you need to do most of these things:

- Be seen reading and using and enjoying the printed word yourself.

- Right from the time your child is three months old, be sure to have books or book-like things for children to possess for themselves. There are plenty of cloth and plastic bath books around on the market.

- Right from the time the child is very young, six months or younger, find a time, every day, to put her on your lap and open the pages of a book or magazine with pictures in it, talking about the pictures.

- Using a library, the child's school or your wallet, bring at least three books a week into the house. Ideally the child should choose some or most of these.

- Never be a snob and refuse books on the grounds that they're not good enough literature. If you think you know a better or more right-on book, get it as well, not instead.

- Look for books with plenty to talk about in the pictures.

- Remember children need, in very broad terms, two kinds of book: ones that offer images and explanations for the material world around them, and ones that deal in some way with the child's emotional landscape – fears, delights, desires, hopes, and the like.

- Don't be fanatical about keeping books tidy, or the child will be discouraged from browsing and playing with books.

- When you read to your children, don't worry about sticking to every word. It's much more important that it's lively and interesting. Have fun yourself, do mad voices, sound effects and musical backing.

- The cuddle is as important as the reading.

- At Christmases and birthdays, don't lumber them with worthy books; find all sorts of fun things like books linked to TV programmes and films, cartoon books and so on.

- Don't force them to read. Just follow their curiosities about books: they ask questions like, what does that say? Why's that in big letters? Is that a 'B'? Remember that reading is not just deciphering letters, it is about discovering that books are enjoyable and friendly, it's discovering that they tell stories that go from page to page, it's discovering that words and pictures sometimes tell two different parts of the same story.

- It may drive you completely spare but you will probably have to read the same dull book over and over and over again. It's happened to all of us. I think there must be something very important going on here: reassurance? continuity? certainty? some emotional key-point in the text that tallies with something they're thinking about? Anyway, stick with it for as long as you can bear, while looking for alternative thrilling books at the same time.

- When and if you go to a bookshop, of course choose books that you think they'll like, but always give them a chance to choose a book for themselves, too. Put a price limit on it, so you're not bankrupted.

All this may convince you, but of course I haven't offered any guidance here on 'what books?' Some authors and illustrators

to look for with the youngest children: Pat Hutchins, Anthony Browne, Tony Bradman, Shirley Hughes, Errol Lloyd, Raymond Briggs, Quentin Blake, Bob Graham, Beatrix Potter, Rod Campbell, Sally Grindley, Martin Waddell.

Various agencies try to help parents choose books: The Book Trust in London produces an annual booklet called *Children's Books of the Year*, there is an organization run by parents, librarians and teachers called The Federation of Children's Book Groups, an outfit called The Good Book Guide has a children's supplement to its publications, there's a BBC Radio 4 programme, for adults, but devoted to children's books, called 'Treasure Islands', there is a magazine called *Books for Keeps* that is totally concerned with children's literature, and there are several books about reading with children. Look out for the ones by Margaret Meek, Dorothy Butler and Jim Trelease. A historical reference book for the real enthusiast is the *Oxford Guide to Children's Literature* by Humphrey Carpenter.

There are several book clubs that help you choose, and take the edge off hardback book prices. The one that advertises the most is the least satisfactory – it's run by Book Club Associates (BCA) and tends to go for safe and classic stuff. Much better is The Red House Book Club in Witney, Oxfordshire, and for books that reflect a non-sexist, multi-cultural outlook there is the really good Letterbox Library. Addresses for all these organizations and contacts are available from any children's librarian. There! If all that doesn't convince you, then nothing will.

Separation and Divorce

As this is a book about parenting and not about how men and women are supposed to get on together, most of what I have to say about this is under STEPCHILDREN. This leaves out the matter of babies and separation which occurs plenty, too.

First days and months after separation: try to keep up as much contact with your child as possible. If you've got your own place, take your child there, no matter how crummy the conditions. It's the contact with *you* that's important. If you're sharing with friends or a new partner, try to come to an agreement that means you see your child at least once a week.

My situation was that I was living with a new partner, and my children came to stay for half a week. They were 4 and 8. I would spend hours every night reading to them and playing games. Even if it didn't reassure them, it certainly reassured me!

What can happen is that one partner, usually the man, asks for access; the couple weren't married, the woman says no. The point here is that unmarried men have no rights. If it were just a matter of 'yes, if he's seriously interested in childcare, no if he's not', life would be simple. A woman who has a baby on her own may well think she doesn't want to share the child with the disappearing or casual lover, and would rather share it with no one, or with a newly-arriving Mr Reliable.

This said, in the cases I know, the bloke's obvious dogged insistence that he did want to do childcare, that he actually did it and the child was happy about it, won the day. Where blokes have blown hot and cold on the child, not turned up for birthdays, or cancelled things at the last minute, they've not succeeded. No matter how reluctant your ex is to hand over her little darlings to the bloke who ratted, cheated, fell apart or whatever, the obvious luxury for her of having no childcare for up to half a week can prove to be an irresistible temptation. Be unreliable about it, and you'll drive her spare and lose the game.

Nastiness is very popular. One or other of you has got lots of really juicy, horrible things to say. Grown-up children of separated parents nearly all say that this is the most unpleasant aspect of the whole thing. Children want to love both mum *and* dad, and don't want to be recruited for let's-slag-off-ex games.

Perhaps some people reading this will be newly-divorced fathers worrying over whether they can cope with young children on their own, or with a new, childless partner. I've found it really useful to keep reminding myself that parenting isn't something we are born knowing how to do. Women have to learn how to do it, too, though of course many women are conditioned into it early (while we were playing guitars, football, cards and so forth). Most of the other entries in this book are my attempts to say: you can do it. You can bath a baby, handle a raving two-year-old, go round a supermarket with a child, and the rest. In your role as a single parent for half the week, at weekends, or whatever, never be afraid or too proud to pick other people's brains, never be ashamed. If you're looking after a child, there are plenty of people around who will be impressed, even amazed, that you're doing it.

This means that you are entitled to enlist help and support from friends – even ones who haven't got children. A friend of mine who has his child at various times during the week just invites himself over with his little girl. There's no reason why he should sit in his flat all alone with her all day Saturday, when he could come over and see me. He knows that like a lot of other men I forget to make a point of remembering his situation, so he has to do it himself.

Sex

Just to remind you, if you're reading this several months after having a baby: this is what you once did to make the thing that is now stopping you from doing it. I'll take this stage by stage.

Pregnancy – my first thoughts were, no contraception, yippee. Sometimes the foetus joined in and jived about a bit, so it was like doing it with someone else in the room. You may find that your partner becomes more interested in sex than ever before, or you may find she is completely turned off it and what she really wants is lots of stroking and massage. Late on in the pregnancy it's still possible, with interesting experiments in angle. Giggling over this can cause the droop! If your partner is past her due date and getting fed up about it, there's some evidence that doing it brings on labour.

After the birth, stand by to be at your most adaptable and most understanding. Firstly, your partner's fanny may well be heavily bruised, cut, torn, stitched and generally mucked about with. You wouldn't be too keen on eating meat and two veg after having all your teeth out. However, do not fear, the self-curing ability of the fanny is a wonderful thing, greatly helped by rest, good food and kindness. Your partner may not only *not* want to have your willy inside her, she may well not want to play games with it either. Her breasts may be leaky and full, she may be desperately tired and emotionally preoccupied with the new creature, and monkeying about in bed may be right off the agenda. This will be tough on your hormones. Try hard not to get whingey about it, or you'll seem very unlovable.

If and when you get down to it again, stand by for interruptions. Sod's Law here says that the moment you're on the job, the baby will cry. Sod's Law also says that, in this situation, the more caring a father you are, the more likely your willy will shrivel. Your first thought will be 'Is it my turn to get up tonight?', which is not the greatest aphrodisiac in the world – and of course, neither is it for the woman in your life.

There is much speculation on the part of men and women at this time about the nature of the fanny itself. If it stretched to let out seven or eight pounds of baby, how can it possibly resume its glove-like form? OK – the fanny is not a tube, it is a set of muscles. Prior to reading this book, either your partner or both of you may have discovered the mysterious and wonderful pelvic floor muscles. To avoid both leaking wee and the rare complaint of a prolapsed womb, your partner would do well to discover pelvic floor muscle exercises. Both the doing of these and the rather nice consequences may provide both of you with hours of endless fun ... well, not hours, but certainly moments.

As you get stuck-in to toddler-hood and second and third children??? – then other factors come into play. Children and childcare take up an enormous emotional space. If either of you separately or both of you together let it take up all the space, then your sex life will sure as hell go down the pan. As is well documented, this means there's a very good chance one of you will go somewhere else for this pleasure. This means that you have to find time for each other. Always and only meeting each other when children are around seems to be quite a dampener on the libido of at least one partner (see TIME FOR YOURSELVES).

The only thing to say about sex when your children get older is that it's worth remembering that they wonder if you're still doing it, and if so, when do you do it. You may regard this as the ultimate taboo and nothing to do with them, but of course this is by no means a 'natural' response. It doesn't take much imagination to realize that more people than not in the history of the world have experienced jigging away on rush mats, hammocks, bunks, and dormitory beds with other people around, often children.

Sex Ed

The more embarrassed you are about talking about sex, the more likely it is that your kids will pick some awful moment to say things like 'Dad, what's oral sex?'

Decide what words you are going to use. Are you going for the Latin ones or the ones they use? My objections to using the Latin ones are that children don't use them themselves, and you probably don't either – the result being that as you start off on the old penis and vagina routine it all sounds kind of holy. So I'm all for willies and fannies, myself.

No question should ever be avoided. Children from two onwards hear about nearly everything from the news, from older friends and relations and eavesdropping adult talk. 'What's sodomy, Dad?' 'Men putting their willies into people's bums', I said. Then you can get onto what the world and you think about it.

I've found that for all ages of child, books are great. There are books suitable for one-year-olds and up. Children can take them away and pore over them and come back and ask questions. Don't worry desperately if you disapprove of some-thing in a book; you can always buy the book and explain why you disagree with it. Buy several.

I gather that some men think that all this is a woman's job. Strange! There's blokes, traditionally the tellers of dirty jokes, leaving women to tell it how it really is. This has to be wrong. If you have a memory of a dad fudging it and saying, 'Ask your mother' or 'Don't they tell you about this sort of thing at school?' Now's your chance to do better.

Shaming You Up in Public

(See SHOPPING and SEX ED)

If you are the kind of person who can be shamed up (as my children put it), then you can be sure that at some point one of your children will do it. If you've got anything that you don't want known outside the walls of your house, if there's any last remnant of dignity that you cling to, if there's some aspect of your children's psychology that you would rather not everyone in the world knew about – forget it. It'll all come out, and always at the worst possible moment.

My first child rather mysteriously spent the first three years of his life never swearing. There he was in the company of a foul-mouthed, blaspheming curser like me, and the little chap blissfully ignored the lot. UNTIL . . . Nanna came to stay. There we were, round the tea-table, no one talking, no sound apart from the dull clink of cups and the soft splat of jam on scone, and the little chap looks up at solid, respectable, Northern Irish Protestant Nanna and says, loud and clear: 'Fuck'. True to form the good lady ignored it completely, didn't bat an eyelid.

If ever you're trying to do anything furtive, sub-legal, covert, underhand, then you can be sure that one of your children will blow it. I'll admit it: I once nicked a supermarket basket. I hadn't brought enough bags to load into the car, and so I tried to slip away with a loaded supermarket basket. Oh, no. No chance. There he is, the little chap: 'Dad, why are you putting the basket in the car?' 'Shush!' 'But Dad, you're not supposed to take those baskets home.' 'Shuttup!' 'Dad, Dad, you'll get into trouble.' 'Yes, I know I will, if you keep shouting about it.'

'But, Dad . . .' Oh, for a gag.

If you're the kind of dad who's going to pride himself on such things as 'my child doesn't wet herself', then you can be sure she will do just that. Our younger girl wasn't too hot at the old urethra control, and chose great moments to let it all flow. We were in a very nice but slightly chi-chi South American carpet shop in the posh part of Melbourne, Australia. There we were, getting engrossed in llama wool and bilberry dye, and whoosh! She let go of a jerry-can-full. And somehow they always manage to get it in their shoes, so they have to squelch all the way home.

The other one is The Cling. You've been rather proud of the way your child is becoming bold and independent. She's only three, but she toddles off to play in the sandpit all on her own. When you walk through the park, she loves to run on ahead. It's looking good for self-esteem – both yours and hers. In fact, you've been raving on about it, in a rather boring and besotted way, to your friends. Then your friends come over. And for five hours, she never moves more than six centimetres away from your face. She sits on you, climbs on you, hangs from you, heaves on you, jumps on you, and constantly refuses to go off and play with the little son of your friends, even though she spent the whole of the previous month pleading with you to bring him over. You will not boast about independence and boldness again for a long time.

The Cling may go on for years. In its later stages it turns into The Lonely Leg. You're sitting on the sofa, reading the paper, and out of the corner of your eye you notice that your fourteen-year-old son, who thinks eating glass is sissy, has sat down too. A few minutes later you find he's got a bit nearer, and then suddenly his leg flops over and lands in your lap. It's the Lonely Leg.

Shopping

One of the great humbling experiences of my life has been taking a toddler and a baby to do the supermarket shopping, feeling that mixture of pride and clumsiness that seems to go with a lot of this fathering business and watching some super-competent mother whizzing round the place with about four kids in tow. The two-year-old always thought of the supermarket as a place where the acoustics were best for screaming. By the time he got out of the trolley, he'd decided that a supermarket was really a gym. 'Yippppeeeee, look at meeee, Dad!' I called it going Insanes-bury's. I always imagined that people were staring at me, thinking I was brutalizing infants. Old ladies always seem to be the worst. They have a way of showing that they disapprove of everything you're doing, even the way you take the baked beans off the shelf. If you do nothing to stop your kid hurling cornflakes about, they tut. If you tell your kid off for hurling cornflakes about, they tut. If you hurl everything into your bags at breakneck speed at the check-out, they tut. If you take half an hour carefully classifying the shopping, they tut. You can't win.

I've tried shopping *en famille*, doing it with the older kids, doing it all myself, and, the last and most common, ignoring the fact that my partner was doing it all. By far the most pleasurable way of doing it is with the older kids. They manage to get fun out of it, they have competitions, drive you mad about asking for things, but are very good at packing at the supermarket check-out. The least pleasurable is doing the whole thing on your own. It's lonely out there among the cereal packets.

As far as the practicalities are concerned, don't be too proud to take a list. I used to think lists were sissy, but after several rows about forgetting the potatoes, I matured. A male approach to shopping is to copy marathon runners and go for PBs (Personal Bests): best times for door-to-door, best times for getting through the check-out, how many times can you get 100 per cent of the list, and so on. A more female approach is to make it an outing: park the car, go round the other shops, have a cup of tea and a bun, do the shopping, choose something you're going to eat when you get back, eat it, put the shopping away.

One tip: don't admit to your partner that one or more young ladies helped you pack the bags at the check-out counter. It is a firmly held belief among women shoppers that supermarket assistants only help harassed looking guys, and that the same assistants stand and stare at women under similar pressure, as if to say that it's women's work anyway.

Sleepless Nights

Hi there! Have you just staggered into a bookshop, your eyes blurred over with tiredness, looking for some simple easy solution to your nights of hell? Are you just going to read this entry, try to memorize it, put the book back on the shelf, dash home and tell all to your loved one? If so, pleased to meet you. I've done the same, many times. In fact, I think I hold the world record for standing in bookshops reading the sleepless nights pages in baby books. Stick with this page, it might be useful . . . and try turning over a few other pages, if only for the cartoons.

Everyone has his own idea of hell, but nothing comes much worse than this. I remember nights of wandering around crazed, days spent apologizing to people that I couldn't talk properly.

It may be useful to think of it in stages. To start off with, waking up and wanting to be fed is simply what newborn humans do. So, how to make arrangements for this to happen? With my first, we used to take it in turns to get up and fetch him from the cot on the other side of the room, my partner breast-fed him, and we took it in turns to put him back in his cot. The nice thing about this is that it's these tricky moments that help make the child matter to you. As he was our first, it was in the middle of the night that all sorts of crises cropped up, vomiting, coughing and the like, and so it was good to share the panic. I used to have a little homily I muttered to myself (it sounds rather sickening in retrospect) as I was being woken up for the fifth time. Still half-asleep I used to grit my teeth and say under my breath: 'It's the name of the game.'

The tough line on babies and nights goes like this: keep

putting the baby down in its own cot, with its own noises, smells, dollies and little routines and keep leaving it, *even if it cries*. In other words, make it accept a routine that fits your lives and the baby will feel more secure because it knows it has this routine. It's been my experience that people who carry out this method tell you that it works perfectly. Their children, they say, sleep the whole night through, and as you listen to them talking you feel like an idiot and a worm. This may be because you or your partner think it is wrong to leave a baby to cry, but even though you think you're being nicer to the baby, you still can't get her to sleep. But I'm not going to say here that the 'tough line' is right or good because of The Thought (as expressed in COT MOVING) which says: 'the solution you come up with has to suit your way of life and your emotional outlook. If you try to do something you don't agree with but someone has told you works wonders, then it won't work for you.'

So the child gets older and she doesn't sleep through the night. You are getting desperate. You're supposed to be getting up in the morning to go to work, your partner too, and you're both completely shattered, you're rowing about what should be done about it, you've heard about wonderful potions and cures that will do the job, you look in the mirror and cannot believe that a face could turn so quickly into a scrotum. Are you part of the solution?

What follows only really applies to children who have begun walking and talking, i.e. after 12 months or so (unless you're part of the 'tough line' school).

1. If all three of you want to survive, then something has to be worked out that is a compromise for all three. Anything that only satisfies one or two parties will be dynamite for the one(s) left out. I remember lying in bed with a three-year-old kicking my ear all night, then getting up at six in order to tell jokes to children in a school two hundred miles away. In the end, all I could do was tell them about the three-year-old kicking my ear all night, which they thought was by far the best of the jokes.

2. If you haven't gone in for routines so far, then perhaps now

is the time to give them a try. The snag is that because the main reason for the child waking seems to be to get at mum, especially if she has been the supplier of breast-milk and most night comforts so far, then the best person to wean the child off waking is YOU. Hard luck.

3. Here are some don'ts that are worth trying, but they have to be tried every night for at least six weeks to see whether they work.

When you get up for her because she is crying:

- don't give her things to eat or drink;
- don't turn the light on;

- don't pick her up, or at most pick her up for no longer than a few seconds;
- don't get into reasoning arguments about moons, ghosts, or the nature of time.

Instead:

- pat her, stroke her, lie her down;
- sing her the same song, every time;
- say to her something along the lines: it's night-time, go to sleep, here's your teddy, see you in the morning, night night;
- leave the room.

If she goes on crying, decide on how long you will let her cry before going back and repeating the routine. Ideally this shouldn't be too short or too long. Too short is one minute, too long is one hour.

Other tips:

- avoid giving her stimulating food before bedtime, e.g. anything with additives and/or loads of sugar;
- try not to let her get loads of sleep during the day to make up for the sleepless nights: this may mean waking her up after half an hour of a day-time doze;
- make sure she is really having plenty of outdoor exercise;
- try to stick to regular routines about bedtime.

All these routines have to be dropped when the child is ill; a sick child is, of course, entitled to as much night comfort as it wants. However, this sometimes means going back, afterwards, to square one on the timetable.

If you are successful in all this, you will feel like a hero. No other exploits, sexual or of derring-do, will match the buzz you will get for having helped in bringing about sleepful nights.

If, like me, you are not successful, then you can (perhaps) console yourself that the whole thing really doesn't go on forever.

Slings, Buggies, Car Seats etc.

Get down to a big store and check out the technology. In a matter of moments you can spend hundreds of pounds simply catering for moving a baby around for a few months. As you clean out your account, you might wonder how people do it who don't spend that sort of money. A quick glance at an African woman in the street, and you see she has tied a cotton sheet around herself with the baby tucked inside, either on her back or at the side. The western equivalent is the sling. The question you might be asking is, 'Will I feel a prat if I walk down the road with one on?' Well, keep your eyes peeled: more and more fathers are carrying babies in slings and then, especially on holidays, moving up to one of those rucksack baby-carriers. I was proudly carrying my first around in a sling in 1976 and it seemed right at the time, if only because we couldn't afford a pram. The baby feels very protected and snug in there, and you can jig it and pat it in response to grumblings and irritations.

Buggies are now wonderful contraptions rather like Rubik cubes. To use them to their full potential of collapsibility and adaptability you need to be good at wrestling with crocodiles. They are not fantastically durable because they are so miraculously light. You have to have a sense of humour, otherwise you'll kick it when you are trying to fit the rain-hood. My first buggy was nicked by a lady whom I saw in a café about half an hour later. When I said 'That's my buggy', she said 'No, it isn't', and I couldn't think what else to say.

Car seats are much simpler, until you get into someone else's car. For some reason you can never quite work out, you can

only use your car seat in your own car. However, they are
ESSENTIAL. You must never travel with a baby on someone's
knee, or in a toddler's chair. I know of one child dead and one
seriously injured in the last five years because of this.

Carry cots give you the chance to have a bit of adaptability.
What you wheel them around in during the day, they can sleep
in at night. It's also claimed that a carry cot can be used in the
car. BUT you must have security belts for it, and some people
say there's a problem with this because the baby can still
bounce out of the cot, even though the cot itself is secure.

Prams are a whole world unto themselves. They are masterpieces of coachwork, upholstery and suspension. They are also
wildly inconvenient if you've got loads of steps, a narrow front
entrance, or a cat (the cat will sleep in it).

So what you have to do is look at where and how you're
going to travel with the baby. Ideally, you want to buy all the
gear you need, and no more. It's quite frustrating either having
something you never use or, alternatively, wanting to get
somewhere easily and quickly but finding you can't because
you haven't got the right thing.

Don't be too proud to accept gifts or cast-offs, or too snooty
to use newsagents' windows for news of second-hand gear.

Smelly Shoulder

How can you tell the difference between an ordinary adult male and a new father? Smelly Shoulder. If you are a keen dad, you will long to pick up your newborn, throw her up in the air, and then listen to the telling-off you get for doing it too soon after a feed while holding her so that she looks backwards over your shoulder. It's then you do little patting things on her back, and you feel all warm and pleased. And it's then that she bloops on your shoulder. It might be a mini-bloop, it might be a mega-bloop, it might even be just a smidgeon of a driblet of a bloop – but believe me, she will bloop.

Bloops are made of milk, and though science tells us that milk takes several hours to go sour, baby-bloop goes sour in about four and a half seconds. For months, possibly years, your shoulder will have little white streaks on it, and you will find that at strange and inappropriate moments a faint whiff of sour milk will reach your nostrils. All kinds of things start smelling of it: roses, car exhaust, lipstick – it's amazing.

Is Smelly Shoulder curable? The terry nappy draped gracefully over the shoulder is handy. A quick change of clothes is OK, but it's better to wash Smelly Shoulder clothes in cool or cold water than in hot, because hot water forces the milk (and smell) in.

Sons and Daughters

One of the toughest women I ever knew once explained to me that all the problems in the world were because of 1. the family, and 2. men in the family. She then went to the States and was last seen in a blind panic because her daughter didn't have a pink babygrow.

I have to say that when I see a three-year-old girl in little patent-leather shoes with heels and a tight skirt, or hear a parent saying to a little boy at playgroup, 'You go and sort out that Jason. Punch him, son', I find myself thinking about what part *I* play in making *my* children stereotypes. How is it that I can be party to a daughter not using all of her body when she runs, or a boy solving all his problems by biffing people? In the end, I can't really escape from the fact that there are ways we as parents prevent girls from being courageous and confident and prepared to take on as many strange and challenging situations as boys do, and there are ways we as parents put pressure on boys to be tough and mean and clever and don't-care-ish.

If you feel like getting into all this, watch the different ways people handle their boy babies and their girl babies. Listen to the tone of voice they use to each sex, listen especially to the differences between what parents say when girls or boys fall over and hurt themselves. As far as girls are concerned, I find myself watching to see if the girls get more favours if they play 'little-me', because encouraging *that* won't do them much good. Do the boys get fewer cuddles than the girls? Is there some cut-off point where boys are expected not to want to sit on a dad's lap any more? In case that worries you, my fourteen-year-old, who frequently doesn't feel in any hurry about getting to twenty, will sometimes plonk himself on me.

It's a real nest of vipers, this one, but broadly speaking I think our girls are entitled to a sense of themselves that tells them they can have a go on computers, speak their opinion in public, climb wall-bars, and punch punch-bags, while among other things boys can do it's also OK for them to cuddle teddies and dads, care about babies, dance, and brush their sister's hair. My three-year-old's favourite pyjamas are the Minnie Mouse cast-offs from his sister.

Stepchildren and Half-Children

I don't know the statistics, but we all know people with stepchildren – me, for instance. There's a lot of it about. Meanwhile, articles and books like this one are always being written about 'families', 'parents' and 'children' as if everyone was living in a mummy, daddy, two children set-up. Hundreds and thousands of people are doing the stepchildren stomp.

To the outsider this can seem like the most fiendish complication in the world. You sometimes overhear a conversation that goes like this: 'Mary has to be at Dave's by twelve o'clock on Tuesdays and we have Barry on every other Friday evening, but only if John is in town, and anyway Karen and Tony are terrific with Steven.' I don't go along with trad thinking in this matter. This kind of thing isn't necessarily either better or worse than the trad set-up. As we all know, some trad families are hell-holes of indifference, neglect or abuse, and some step-families and fosterings are loving nests. What counts in all cases is the 'quality of care'.

That said, stepchildren can be hell. Or to put it more equally, some step-parents are horrible. The step-relationship can be fraught. Here are some of the clash-points:

- 'You don't love me as much as your real children', as one of my stepchildren says. They may be right. But then, why *should* you love them as much? To pretend to is worse than admitting you don't. On the other hand, the stepchild is entitled to fairness in all disputes.

  This may also be a cry from the heart about the 'real' dad: 'real' dad doesn't love me (this can be felt even if he died), so because you're the only dad-figure around, I can blame you for the fact that I think my 'real' dad doesn't love me.

- 'Why doesn't his "real" dad pay for that?' I've thought, if not said. This is the basic meat and potatoes of a lot of step-relationships. Various people in the set of relationships around a stepchild are very good at invisibilizing work. While one adult in the business is swanning it at the theatre, the other one might be washing the child's dirty knickers. While one adult is clocking into work to pay for the kid's shoes, the other one might be sitting with his feet up. If only the solution to this kind of problem was simply for everyone to agree that work wasn't invisible. Instead, there are some-times very strong emotional arguments as to why, even though we're all agreed Jim isn't pulling his weight, it's not worth the aggro to make him do so . . . at least, that's what's often said, but maybe this is a cop-out, and on closer examination it *would* be worth the aggro from your point of view.

- An equivalent cry here is 'Isn't it his turn to have him today?' Plenty of people in the step set-ups have pretty complicated arrangements to try to make it fair and right for everybody. There are emotional needs to be catered for, as well as equality in childcare work. If you're going for real equal time share, some people do it by splitting the week on Wednes-day and Saturday night. And elaborate negotiations take place around times when people want to go away for weekends and at other times. Another system, the one we use, goes like this: for one half of the school term, we have them from Monday night to Friday morning, and the second half of the term we have them from Friday night to Monday morning. This means that things equal out over one school term as regards weekends with or without the children, access to weekday school questions, and so on. Holidays can mostly be split equally in half, or swopped. Our principle is: the less negotiation you do, the better it is for everybody, especially as one side of the business may actually quite like the aggro connected with the negotiating.

- 'We don't speak.' Two parties in the business are not on

speaking terms or are at best abrupt, mean, spiteful and revengeful. In this situation it is very easy for the child(ren) to be pawn(s). I'm sure it's been said hundreds of times, but the point is, such a situation causes a split loyalty in the child. No matter how much aggro the parent might feel towards the disappearing partner, the child is entitled to have plenty of (as much as equal) space with that person. Most withholding and refusing rights of access to children who loved both parents are (outside of abuse cases) adult games and nothing whatsoever to do with the child's needs. Excuses like 'we were never married' won't wash.

- A further dimension is added if you have a new baby. Will the half brothers and sisters go mad with jealousy? Will they compete to be nice to it, or will they compete to see who can be the most horrible to it? With my children, it was a very uniting thing. I half expected that perhaps my youngest would feel usurped and would sit around trying to stop me hugging the new baby, or that my wife's older daughter would be even more miffed than when her younger sister turned up. And believe me, that was bad! But no, everyone seemed really pleased. For a start, they spent weeks trying to figure out what their various biological relationships were. Ever since then, they've spoilt him rotten.

Talking

One of the great delights of having children is listening to them learning to talk. If you think about it for a moment, it is almost as amazing as being born itself. We know how difficult it is to learn a different language from our own: there seems to be so much of it – vocabulary, grammar, sentence order, intonation, pronunciation, different ways of saying the same thing, same ways of saying different things, and so on. Somehow or another these little, fairly helpless creatures of one and two manage to pack away this huge rule-system, so that by the age of five they possess the ability to create most of the common structures of the language.

The fun for parents is listening out for the stages in the child's accomplishment of this. It can be great to keep a note of these as they happen. You find yourself wondering, how come the noises we describe as 'goo goo ga ga' can, in about a year, turn into 'want a drink'? Some nice things to look out for are:

1. The first word. Here you can get into furious debates with people about whether a noise that you know means some- thing – like my first child's 'ma', meaning 'I want some of that' – is a word, or whether the first *recognizable* word is the first, such as 'book' with my first, and 'poo' with my third.

2. Mysterious mispronunciations. Here are some of my chil- dren's: 'smeenge' = machine, 'waywees' = raisins, 'diddits' = biscuits, 'prets' = breakfast, 'brummer' = jam. Don't correct these; it only inhibits their experimentation with language.

3. Lovely invented word combinations: my favourite here is my two-year-old's swear word, 'bear-poo', to be shouted at horrid food, horrid brothers and sisters and horrid parents, as in 'YOU BEAR-POO!'

4. Improvised singing and chanting sessions: 'red bus coming, red bus coming, red bus coming.'

5. Incorrect stabs at constructions: 'Don't starfish don't have legs?' This from a three-year-old is a stab at trying to construct a negative way of asking a question, as in: 'Starfish don't have legs, do they?' 'Starfish haven't got legs, have they?' 'Don't starfish have legs?' The nice thing about his 'mistake' is that really what he was doing was putting together two ways of asking questions. He was doing one of the most fascinating things in the whole business: constructing words and phrases 'by analogy'. That's to say, if I can use the word 'don't' as a way of asking a question, why can't I stick it in front of a statement that I'm pretty sure is true, like: 'starfish don't have legs'?

Listen out for 'teached', 'bringed' and the like, which apply the 'ed' rule of making things happen in the past. The old way of looking at that sort of thing was simply to see the child as being ignorant, but really it's the opposite: the child is applying knowledge of a rule.

Along with 'getting him dry' and 'first steps', this is one of those bits of child care that turn into competitions. You may well have to sit through nutty conversations in which people pretend that they're really pleased someone else's child is speaking before their own, or on other occasions they pretend to be sorry that your child isn't talking while theirs is. No doubt you've heard it before, but I'll repeat it: just because your child makes noises that sound like words before other children, doesn't make her a genius. And the opposite: just because your child starts talking long after other children, doesn't mean she's stupid. The first recognizable word may crop up at nine months or at eighteen months. There may be a long time, say from one to three, when you and your partner are the only people who can understand the little fellow. All the consonants seem to be muddled. All this is quite NORMAL. Correcting little ones, making them say things 'properly', making them repeat things just because you say so, are all disastrous. Enjoying their singing, their attempts at doing nursery rhymes and finger rhymes, waiting for them to spit out the beginnings of a story without interrupting, are all much much more important.

Teeth-Cleaning

You don't need to clean a baby's mouth when it has no teeth in it, but as soon as teeth appear, then it's a good idea to clean them. No one ever completely avoids feeding their babies something that will rot their teeth.

Teeth-cleaning comes into the category of chores-that-need-jollying-along. When I'm doing the brushing, before they've learnt how, I go in for various kinds of lunacy: 'Say ah! Say eeee! Say pickled onions! Say ah! Say eee! . . .' and so on. It's also nice to get them to choose their own toothbrushes regularly.

When they're very young it's down to you to do the cleaning, so really go for it: 'upstairs at the back one side', 'upstairs at the back on the other side', 'downstairs at the back one side', 'downstairs at the back the other side', 'upstairs at the front', 'downstairs at the front'. If you say all that, then it gives them a check-list to use when they come to clean their own teeth.

Some kids are prone to mouth ulcers. Weleda make a really good mouthwash you can get from health food shops (leaving me to repeat the pathetic joke, 'Take me to your Weleda').

While getting kids to choose their own toothbrushes is good for awareness, watch out for toothpastes. Rather incredibly, a lot of them actually contain sugar!

Teething

For a reason I haven't figured out yet, we are made without holes in our gums for the teeth to come through. This means that as the teeth grow they have to cut through the gums. Quite clearly, this is hell for the person this is happening to, who can be anything from a few weeks old to up to two years before the whole beastly business is over.

Teething babies and toddlers dribble and sometimes get blotches on their cheeks and neck. They wail and rub their ears and sometimes smell of pear drops. Rubbing their gums with your finger can sometimes relieve them, sometimes make them furious.

It seems that at certain stages of teething rubbing the gums with something hard can be a relief to little ones. The theory behind the rusks you buy from the shop is that they are hard to start off with, and when they get wet they don't break off into little hard bits that could get stuck in the baby's throat, but get soggy instead. But watch out for these rusks: they're mostly jammed full of sugar. So as you relieve teething pains, you rot their teeth. Brilliant. This also applies to the gels and so on you can get from chemists.

Toast is a reasonable substitute for rusks, but you'll notice that the child sometimes takes matters into its own hands and grabs dolls' arms, chair legs, spoons – anything hard to stuff into its mouth. One of my mother's favourite stories was about a friend of hers who was studying medicine when their baby was young. At various times, human arm bones had to be rescued from the child's mouth.

Night times can be difficult when a child is teething. You can sometimes tell if this is the problem because of the way they thrash their head about, as well as from the other signals I've mentioned.

Terrible Twos

It's a generally held view that two-year-olds are horrible. This is partly right. Any parent will tell you that from about two years old till about three and a half, there can very easily be daily tantrums, yellings, rages and wobblies over the most incredibly simple things. I remember breakfasts when the two-year-old said I took the cornflakes off the shelf when he wanted to do it, mornings when I said it was too cold to go out without his coat on, evenings when I put the toothpaste on the toothbrush before he had a chance to put water on it first, tea times when I said no more biscuits, and each time it was worth a tantrum.

First thing: don't panic – it's going on in millions of other people's houses at the same time. In fact, the less you panic the sooner the wobbly will die down today, and wobblies in general will pass away. Wobblies feed off parents panicking.

Secondly, remind yourself that nearly every one of these wobblies is about power. It's as if every wobbly is a set of questions: how grown up am I? Are you strong enough to deal with me? What are the limits to what I can do and can't do?

How grown up am I?
This means that we have to keep telling them: no, you don't decide whether it's warm enough to go out without a coat, I decide because otherwise you get ill. On the other hand: sorry I wet your toothbrush, you *can* wet your own toothbrush, because you *are* big enough to do that on your own, and so what if you do spill water on the floor, it's no big deal.

Are you strong enough to deal with me?
Because if you're not, that means I'm stronger than you. I know

I'm just a very small thing who is afraid of loads of things . . . please be stronger than me so that you can look after me.

This means we have to say things like: it's no use you shouting, it won't get you more biscuits. I have decided. If you go on shouting, then I'm not saying anything else to you until you stop.

What are the limits to what I can and can't do?
Because if you don't tell me, or if you keep changing your mind, I won't know where I fit in in this world.

This means saying what the limits are and sticking to them. People imagine that it's the limit itself that's important, when really it's the fact that you stick to it that is important. In other words, it's much worse to say 'No jumping up and down on the sofa' but only stick to the rule a third of the time than it is to let them jump up and down on the sofa all the time, but have something else that you're consistent about.

Sometimes the Terrible Twos seem to last forever. Yes, you may well find that friends shun you, people stare at you like you're some mad sadist when your little darling throws a wobbly in Sainsbury's because you say 'you're not buying a cake this week'. Yes, I have had rows with my partner about what to do, but actually the children have learnt that one parent does it one way, and the other does it another way. That sort of thing matters much less when you're each doing childcare: 'Buy me a bun. Mum always buys me a bun in this shop.' 'Well, I'm not Mum. I'll buy you a bun when you don't nag for one.' And the two approaches can exist side by side. But remember, the Terrible Twos do pass eventually, and the calmer and more consistent you are, the quicker it will happen.

Time Out

This is not your time out (see TIME TOGETHER and GETTING AWAY). It's one of those funky little American terms for something really important. There's usually a point, when children are relating to each other (and to grown-ups), at which the temperature starts going up, voices start getting screechy and things start falling off tables. This is where you bring in 'Time Out'.

Rather than trying to solve the argument, or getting into elaborate negotiations about who really smashed the lego tower, you simply separate the sparring partners. Where this is two or more children, they just have to go to different rooms, to different activities (see INDOOR-ITIS), or simply in different directions. Where this is you and a child, the same thing applies. Sometimes, rather than have a row it is better simply to excommunicate either yourself or the child. So: at tea time, one of the kids is playing up, pushing at the beans ('Don't want beans'), the other kids are laughing, you're tired and ratty and feeling put-upon for reasons you haven't figured out yet ... what to do? Rather than scream at the offending kid, which will wind all the others up even more ('Hey, Dad, your nose goes red when you get angry'), what you do is simply send the offending one out.

Devise a regular place if you like, preferably boring and unattractive. Don't over use it, but have it as a reference point for all disputes. If the children are fighting while watching TV, warn them they'll get the separation treatment. If you only have one kid then this is a very powerful sanction, because the basis for the argument between you may be about demanding something from you. A lot of rows are really trials of strength, and to pursue the row is a kind of weakness. The way to show that you mean business (in a situation that matters) is to withdraw from the row, take Time Out.

If all this sounds reasonable, and even more – you are actually able to carry it out – there may be one other problem. Your partner may think it's cruel, may think it's unreasonable, may think it's some horrible male way of going on; or, to be fair, may think it's a good idea, but not for her, thank you very much. So you're into negotiations; but remember, you don't have to agree on this. So long as you are doing your stint of childcare, you're entitled to do things your way.

Time Planning: The Caterpillar Principle

This is a metaphor, a symbol for a day in the life of your family. If you're yet to have a child, then I think you may well find that the most valuable commodity in your life will become Time.

Watch a caterpillar. Notice that sometimes one part of it all squashes up and another part stretches. Notice also that it isn't always the same parts that squash and stretch; any part of the caterpillar can do this. And, finally, notice that though the caterpillar appears to lengthen and shorten, in actual fact it is in essence the same size.

Is this useful? Is this helpful? I find it so, though sometimes I call it the concertina principle. The point is, every day is the same length. Therefore:

- The caterpillar needs to be fed. In practical terms this means that there are a set of fixed jobs that have to be done, no matter what happens. Money has to be obtained, food has to be fetched, children have to be attended to, taken to school and so on, and all these jobs are of equal status. This means, if one person doesn't do it, then the other person has to (one person has to stretch more to do more, because the other person has contracted, to do less). Most blokes don't know this, and if they do, they pretend they don't.

- Whatever takes up more time means less time on something else. This means that the longer you stay out, the less time you will see the children, the less time you will see your partner, the more ratty and resentful people will be with you.

- A lot of activities that don't have a fixed length of time will simply expand to fit the available space. This means that if you agree that you both need to do a big clean up of the place, you may *think* it can all be done on Saturday, but it will certainly take the whole weekend.

- Some things that get squeezed out of the timetable today will still be there tomorrow. According to this principle, washing up doesn't go away. Where this principle breaks down is in TIME TOGETHER. Here it is quite possible to squeeze out Time Together today, and the next day, and the next, and it never comes back.

Time Together

So there you are sitting having one of those nice conversations about the world and life, just like you did when you first got together, and every time you try to say something it gets interrupted by a nappy or a fish finger.

Being a caring father and work-sharing round the house may well be a democratic way of running the factory called Home, but it may also be a complete sexual and emotional switch-off. There have been whole periods when me and my partner have only met over a chore, and I have begun to resemble a potato sack. I've started thinking that what I really need is some time for GETTING AWAY. Maybe I was wrong. In order for the whole thing to work, what we actually needed was Time Together.

This is all very complicated. How do you know how to balance what's best for you, best for the relationship, best for the household? Obviously there are no simple answers, but if you never go out together without the children, it might just possibly be the reason why you've stopped being nice to each other (see SEX).

I've always been jealous of people who have relations who love baby-sitting. That's one obvious solution; the only other one is the BABY-SITTER.

TV Watching

Telly gets rationed in our house. This is because if I say to my children 'You can watch as much telly as you want to', they do. They watch all of it, all the time. What does this mean? Mostly, I think it means that in a competition between watching TV and doing homework, talking to me, going for a walk, reading a book, playing with toys, then usually watching TV wins. The point is, TV is very attractive, very clever stuff that very clever, attractive people spend an enormous amount of time, money and brainpower on. When it finally comes down to it, the whole thing looks and feels a good sight more clever, attractive, and expensive than me, or any of us: small wonder they rush off to watch it all the time.

My gut feeling is that in order to operate in the world, children need plenty of practice choosing, making and doing things for themselves. This may be painting, talking, playing with toys, doing little plays, even arguing or fighting or anything else that involves active engagement and participation. The problem with the telly is that the only role it gives us is spectating, which should ideally be only one of many kinds of things a child gets up to. However, if you can pull the spectating of telly into something you talk about with your children, then it is turned into a more active process. The child's view meets someone else's view, and debate and argument challenge the omnipotence of the screen.

All this may seem crazy, thinking of a one-year-old and children's telly. Do you really want to get into a deep discussion with her about *Rainbow* and *Playdays*? Why not?

As an afterthought, I'd say that it's very easy to become anti-telly with children around; they seem obsessed with it, yak on about it at tea time, act out adverts, and burst into tears if they miss their favourite programme. I've found that saying 'but it's only telly' doesn't go down too well. But then, from their point of view it's a shared talking point with all their friends. The more TV they watch, the wider range of talking points they have. As educational experts go about their business, they quite often lament the passing of the time when shared talking points were such things as *Peter Pan*, *Alice in Wonderland*, and Caesar's *Gallic Wars*. What has happened is that children from the age of one and under have built up a *different* set of talking points, and one that parents and teachers have very little control over. Quite often it seems to be this lack of control that is so irritating: 'why do the little blighters take more notice of that berk doing the birthdays on children's TV than of me?' But of course, that is precisely why they take more notice – *because* he isn't me, Dad, the one who tells them off.

It sounds very goody-goody, but if you sit about talking to children, helping them make things, if you take your kids out and do things with them, then at least telly has to compete with life, and isn't left to win hands down.

Weaning and Getting onto Solids

You are in an ideal position to do this, especially if it means coming off breastfeeding. It's actually quite hard for a woman to persuade a little person who has had all the fun and warmth of a juicy nipple in its mouth to enjoy the feel of a spoon and a bit of mashed carrot. Every time she comes for him with a spoon in her hand, he knows that there's a nipple at the other end of the arm – well, nearly, anyway. So, quite often he roars and shouts and tries to get down mum's blouse. (As we know, this kind of behaviour by little boys can carry on into later life – in slightly different circumstances, though the psychologists tell us the cause may be the same.) So you can now move on from being the expert winder to become an expert weaner.

The food: it should be warm and juicy; avoid all additives, salt and sugar (read the sides of jars and tins); preferably use a suitable bit of the food you're having; use a blender if you've got one, though the back of a fork will work perfectly OK on a bit of potato; don't give them egg till they're a year old; in early days, avoid strong herbs and spices – think bland; only introduce one food at a time.

Feeding: the first time I tried this, I'd sit my oldest in the chair and very carefully dangle the spoon in front of his mouth, hoping he'd make a dive for it. Funny thing, he didn't. Then we went to Ireland to meet his Nanna. She was appalled at such pussy-footing. 'You'll never stop nursing him [breastfeeding] like that,' she said. 'He'll be taking you to school with him.' At that she grabbed him, tucked him into the crook of her right arm, held the bowl with her right hand, and started diving in and out of the bowl with the spoon in her left. 'Keep it flowing,' she said. 'Don't give them time to think about it.' It all looked a bit brutal to me, but it certainly worked. It makes sense, because why should the baby have to lose both the nipple (or bottle) as well as the hug and the eye contact?

Drinking is an interesting game. The conventional route is nipple to bottle to sucky cup to real cup. Do you know what a sucky cup is? This is one of those pieces of apparatus which becomes totally indispensable to your child's life, and yet in an odd moment of contemplation you find yourself wondering, did cave people have sucky cups? Probably not. Anyway, they are plastic cups with lids that funnel into a kind of flattened nipple. In the 'nipple' is a set of tiny holes specially designed to get blocked up with the fibres in orange juice, harbour filth and germs on the inside, and be chewed by your child. This sounds very defeatist and cynical, but such a feeling is mild compared to the fervour with which the little ones scream: 'CUPPY-CUPPY! DINK! DOOCE!' with hands outstretched. You will learn to love the sucky cup, the glazed eyes of the child locked on to it, the mad gulping noise from the throat and the soft hissing of air rushing in. Music!

To return to force feeding – this phase doesn't have to go on long, and soon they're sitting in a high chair lobbing food all round the room, playing games by turning their head away just as the spoon is supposed to go in the mouth, so – doink! straight in the ear; keeping their mouth open after the food has gone in, so – gggeee, down the chin; keeping their mouth shut so you can't get the spoon in, and so on. I've had all this and more, and this was when I dug down into the much needed repertoire of funny faces, funny noises, impressions of aeroplanes, birds, octopuses, and songs beginning with: 'here comes the . . .'

Also good fun is when you get onto 'finger food'. Chop up cheese, apple, fish fingers, toast into little cubes and let them feed themselves. This gives them independence and the joy of feeling their nosh. It might mean that they *also* want to get their fingers in the mash and gunk that you want to feed them. Either way, be prepared for gunk, cheese cubes, toast fingers, flying round the room. Whatever you do, never try to pick up this stuff while they're eating, because they'll only lob more just to watch you picking it up – and anyway, while you're bending over they always aim it down your neck. At some point you should let them have their own spoon while you're trying to feed them with yours. This means that sometimes you end up fencing. On the other hand, while they're busy concentrating on lifting the spoon, you can get three mouthfuls in. I remember a woman saying to me: 'If there's one thing I really love, it's seeing her putting away a plate of food.' I know what she meant. Seeing a little child attacking some food with enthusiasm is a really nice thing to watch.

Winding

Two schools of thought here:

1. Winding is totally unnecessary; if they want to burp, they'll burp, so why go through all that flap and palaver? There's no evidence that all that banging and squeezing makes them burp. Anyway, you try getting really hungry, going out to a nice Italian restaurant and being dragged away from a juicy spaghetti bolognaise every few minutes to have your back walloped. Anyway, no one winds piglets, and they seem to manage.

2. Winding helps them feed because their little bellies get full up with air, which stops the milk getting down. Also, if you burp them it prevents the high velocity burp that means total bloop at the end of their feed. Air in their bellies gives them cramps and pain while they're feeding and puts them off their sucking.

Choose whichever line suits you: the little darling will survive either way. However, if you plump for 1. you will find that winding is one of those folk-truths you may find it impossible to argue about with People-who-Know. They may brand you a dangerous hippie revolutionary.

One advantage with winding, it's something you can do (or pretend to do) so that you're not just left gawping at breast-feeding time. However, don't feel that winding equals thumping the poor little thing. I have big hands (you may not), and I found it quite easy to sit the baby sideways on my right knee, supporting it with my left hand round its chest, my right hand pushing up the spine, gently but firmly straightening the back and lifting the rib cage. I suppose what this does is alternately squeeze and release the bag-like stomach. This means success – whether there was a burp in there from the feed or not, the baby'll burp all the same. You may even become known as an expert winder. Gold medals are hard to get in this game, and you'll need whatever's going. Anyway, whatever you do, avoid all that banging and thumping. It must be horrible for the little things.

THE ONE THING

to win at the game of business

CREEL PRICE

WILEY

John Wiley & Sons Australia, Ltd

First published in 2012 by John Wiley & Sons Australia, Ltd
42 McDougall St, Milton Qld 4064

Office also in Melbourne

Typeset in Bembo 11.5/13.5pt

© Creel Price 2012

The moral rights of the author have been asserted

National Library of Australia Cataloguing-in-Publication data:

Author:	Price, Creel.
Title:	The One Thing to Win at the Game of Business / Creel Price.
ISBN:	9781118305201 (pbk.)
Notes:	Includes index.
Subjects:	Decision making.
Dewey Number:	658.403

Cover design by Michael Freeland

Printed in China by Printplus Limited

10 9 8 7 6 5 4 3 2 1

Disclaimer

The material in this publication is of the nature of general comment only, and does not represent professional advice. It is not intended to provide specific guidance for particular circumstances and it should not be relied on as the basis for any decision to take action or not take action on any matter which it covers. Readers should obtain professional advice where appropriate, before making any such decision. To the maximum extent permitted by law, the author and publisher disclaim all responsibility and liability to any person, arising directly or indirectly from any person taking or not taking action based on the information in this publication.

Contents

About the author

Creel Price is one of Australia's most dynamic entrepreneurs and leading business minds. He founded eight businesses before he left school, and went on to co-found Blueprint Management Group at the age of 25. He started with just $5000 in capital, and sold it within a decade for over $100 million.

By the time he retired from Blueprint it employed over 1000 people and had achieved a host of industry awards as one of the fastest growing businesses in Australia, including *BRW*'s third- and sixth-fastest growing company in Australia (FAST 100), *My Business* magazine's Best Medium Business and Best Overall Business, and Deloitte Fast 50 Asian Technology Company.

Creel is a serial entrepreneur, high–octane adventurer and passionate educator, and divides his time between the following three endeavours that he sees as the key to inspiring a 21st century 'Entreprenaissance', and revolutionising business as we know it:

Entrepreneurs

Through his business Accelerate Global, Creel helps business owners of all types and sizes achieve their endgame faster. The Accelerate methodology is used in Sir Richard Branson's Centre for Entrepreneurship in South Africa and Jamaica — a contribution that led to Creel being recognised as the Virgin Unite Global Entrepreneur of the Quarter in 2010.

Socialpreneurs

Creel is a pioneer in the development of a new model of business that combines commerce with social good. Creel works on projects around the world, including in Papua New Guinea and Zimbabwe. He is the outgoing Chairman of Global Ethics Australia, an organisation that launched Love One Water in Australia, where 100 per cent of the profits fund Play Pumps in Africa. This organisation has donated over $5 million to charity worldwide.

Kidpreneurs

Based on his own experience growing up, Creel is helping inspire the next generation of entrepreneurs through his foundation, Club Kidpreneur. The foundation is a social enterprise committed to assisting youths to start and grow their own micro-enterprises, so that one day they may choose entrepreneurship as a career. Creel has co-authored a kids book called *Curtis the Kidpreneur*.

Acknowledgements

This book is testament to both the great team that helped knock it into shape, and the great team that helped knock me into shape so that I was able to succeed at business against the odds in the first place.

Firstly, I would like to acknowledge all of the staff, clients, suppliers, mentors and supporters (too many to name!) that Blueprint was fortunate to engage. Much of the wisdom in these pages is from, or because of, you. To my business partner of 10 years Trevor Folsom, whose friendship, vision and ability to keep a lid on my idiosyncrasies made business both an insightful and memorable ride. And finally, thanks to my family and friends, who kept me grounded and gave me the support to continue when others would have faltered.

Like the publication of any book, this was the usual roller-coaster ride of realising half way through that you have bitten off more than you can chew. It has been full of people who contributed knowledge, direction or steely determination to set deadlines and meet them. To pick from the multitude of knowledge contributors who have framed my thinking more than any others, I couldn't go past acknowledging the sustained input of my executive coach Michelle Duval, my one-time apprentice Emma Weber, and Matt Church of Thought Leaders. And of course thanks to the hundreds of entrepreneurs who have participated in my programs and shared their highs, lows and learnings with me. Being a part of their journey has helped to validate my theory as not merely something that worked for me, but something that works regardless of the business stage, industry type or entrepreneurs' experience.

Thanks to Lucy Raymond and the rest of the team at John Wiley & Sons for having the courage to publish a book less populist than most, but hopefully one that will make a lasting difference to entrepreneurs prepared to take the lessons and implement them. Thanks to my life partner Tania Purcell for being fiercely protective of my brand and design standards in a mission for the project to be more Apple than IBM. And lastly, the rock behind *The One Thing to Win at the Game of Business* was my structural editor, Karen McCreadie, who took on the mammoth task of ordering my disordered thoughts, editing out enough material to fill three books, and considering the detail when I had already moved on.

Introduction

Life is the sum of all your choices.

Albert Camus

Most people start a business venture to achieve some combination of time and financial freedom. They seek to do what they want to do, when they want, where they want and with whom they want. They are dreaming of the High Life. In most cases, however, the entrepreneur soon discovers the High Seas — a point where every day is a struggle just to keep your head above water. Instead of freedom the entrepreneur feels completely overwhelmed as they battle to make ends meet, working ever-increasing hours with no end in sight.

I started my first business when I was 11 years old — a strawberry business that went on to be one of the main income streams for my family. After a string of subsequent kidpreneur businesses, my next foray into the business world was when I cofounded Blueprint with my friend Trevor Folsom — a business that at the time was not in any specific industry or even had a specific type of business. Rather we started a business to find out about business. We chose the name Blueprint to signify that we were searching for the formula of why some businesses succeed and others fail. Defined as a model or prototype, the word *blueprint* seemed to embody what we were searching for as much as what our business did, given we intended to have a group of companies under the Blueprint banner.

We founded businesses in industries as diverse as finance, marketing, call centres, recruitment, e-commerce, insurance and training. During that time some of the ventures were wound up, some stagnated in mediocrity and some were successful beyond our wildest dreams. They all showed promise; they all inspired us enough to turn the idea into a business; they all filled a niche in the marketplace. Yet it has taken me years to decipher what separated the successful businesses from the also-rans.

If you think about individual business success stories it's easy to come up with reasons why that business succeeded. Some would say business success is a result of luck, chance or determination, or that it's not what you know, it's who you know that separates the winners from the rest. Some might put success down to innovation, creativity and sheer hard work. Others might suggest that marketing or raising start-up capital is the key to success. Some would say you have to get the right team together or that it's all about sales. Others might advocate creating systems as the secret to success. There are as many reasons and opinions as there are businesses, and all of those things can be important.

Despite our business success being less publicised than those of many of our entrepreneurial peers, I was often asked to speak to business groups about our rags-to-riches story—how we started out with a $5000 investment each and sold our company within a decade for a nine-figure return. The Blueprint story inspired my fellow entrepreneurs as much for our numerous failures as for our hard-fought successes. Our business wasn't in a sexy industry—our anonymity was largely due to the fact that we mainly worked behind the scenes for corporations, preferring to let our clients take the glory. Nor were we one of those instant IT success stories that seems to raise huge amounts of capital and sell their companies for millions of dollars without ever having turned a profit. Instead it was our ordinariness that struck a chord with entrepreneurs—giving them hope that if we could achieve entrepreneurial success without external funds, lucky breaks and media hype, so could they.

What really captured my imagination was that everyone wanted to know if there was One Thing that underpinned our success—what was the one thing that made Blueprint one of the fastest growing businesses in Australia year after year? What was the one thing that enabled us to build our company to over 1000 employees within a decade? What was the one thing that helped us grow our business without external capital and exit it for over $100 million? The questions were often focused around this notion that there must be one thing that made all the difference.

In a world that is constantly changing, where we are faced with endless choices and have access to vast amounts of information at the touch of a button, the entrepreneurs and business owners I was speaking to were desperate to find a way to cut through the clutter and hone in on an area or insight that could fast track their business success. They simply didn't have time to study all the possible solutions, so the idea that there really could be One Thing was extremely appealing.

Was there really One Thing? Was there really a simple answer amongst the chaos? Was it even possible that in the vast amount of information, knowledge and expertise that is required to create a successful business there was one skill above all others that could transform any business? Was there one definitive skill that crossed knowledge barriers and remained true and relevant regardless of function, business type or industry? Was there one skill that would enable entrepreneurship to be trained regardless of industry or breadth of experience?

What started as a little idea got under my skin and turned into a burning desire to know more so that I could prevent entrepreneurs having to make the same mistakes I made. Plus, perhaps more importantly, if there was One Thing and we could identify it, then entrepreneurship could be taught to anyone.

General wisdom maintains that entrepreneurs are born not bred. This is a limiting and defeatist attitude that declares that entrepreneurship cannot be taught. Some people are born with stronger entrepreneurial attributes, like drive, resilience and pragmatism, but I fundamentally believe that anyone can learn how to be a successful entrepreneur. I once bought into these ideas of born with the skills and learn through hard knocks, and as a result I wasted years making business far harder than it needed to be. And that easier way is not formalised study in isolation. In fact I completed an undergraduate degree in business, but very little of what I learned was useful or ever applied in my own business. Fortunately, these days it has been recognised that theoretical teaching alone is insufficient and it is now often supplemented with real-life experiences.

With business failure rates at astronomical levels this head in the sand approach to entrepreneurial training is clearly not working. It's fine for the 20 per cent of businesses that make it to five years and beyond, but what about the anxiety and carnage created by the other 80 per cent of businesses that don't survive? Business ventures that waste the entrepreneurs' time, money and energy, leaving a legacy of broken dreams and disappointments for the owner, employees and customers involved.

Yet it's little wonder that entrepreneurs don't invest in their own training, given the breadth of study they would need to cover—few professions require such a diverse mix of skills, from sales and marketing to finance to HR to strategy and management. And few professions are as demanding of your time as having your own business. If you didn't learn business before you found yourself in business, you're not alone. Yet it still amazes me how few entrepreneurs invest in training. To be an engineer, doctor or scientist takes years of study—and the role of an entrepreneur is no less exacting or difficult. Business owners need to know a huge amount just to get by, never mind succeed, and that can be incredibly overwhelming.

I think part of the reason there is little light shed on how to become a successful entrepreneur is that it's a complex subject with many moving parts and so many different industries with their own specific quirks. Yet it's my belief that if you can name it you can train it. And if we can identify the One Thing that really makes the difference then we can take the unwieldy world of entrepreneurship and make it genuinely accessible to anyone so that they can massively improve their chances of success.

Following the sale of Blueprint I dedicated my time to uncovering that One Thing. My ambition was to create a formula for being successful at business that you could master over time in your own time—a practical methodology that could be easily applied to your business, regardless of its size, complexity or industry. This book documents that formula and, so far, this One Thing has helped train thousands of entrepreneurs, intrapreneurs and CEOs around Australasia and the UK. This One Thing has also been taught and incorporated into the teaching curriculum at Sir Richard Branson's Centre for Entrepreneurship in South Africa.

In this book you will learn what that much sought after One Thing is, why it's so vital for business success and, perhaps most importantly, find a step-by-step guide on how to implement it in your business. You will discover tools that will help you use the One Thing for fast, effective outcomes.

I hope you share my excitement in discovering something that just may be the missing ingredient for your future business success. Not to mention a tool to help you manage the overwhelmed state so often felt in business, and effectively navigate those treacherous high seas, enjoy the process and arrive safely at the high life you deserve.

Part I

Decisionship in theory

Nothing is more difficult, and therefore more precious, than to be able to decide.

Napoleon Bonaparte, French military leader

Chapter 1

What is decisionship?

I discovered the One Thing every entrepreneur needs for business success in a strange and unexpected situation. Ironically I wasn't even in a business environment. I was sailing off the Australian coast; it was the middle of the night and we were in trouble. The headsail of my ill-equipped yacht had become dangerously entangled and we found ourselves struggling for control of the vessel with a storm front approaching, a big swell, and the nearest port 60 kilometres away.

A real life version of the High Seas came about after I thought I had made it to the High Life and I had proudly purchased my own yacht. What I had naively left out of my dream to cruise the world's oceans was an ability to sail. I thought I would learn on the job (sound familiar?) and then, with a bit of false entrepreneurial courage, I decided to sail 250 kilometres down a notorious stretch of coast at one of the wildest times of year; in fact we were only one day behind the Sydney to Hobart Yacht fleet—a race considered one of the world's toughest.

Our ordeal lasted nearly six hours with the coast guard on stand by for a mid-sea rescue and the whole time my heart was in my throat as I contemplated all sorts of grisly scenarios. To make matters worse, my parents had been woken up and told by police that I was in the midst of a rescue attempt.

Our saving grace was that my friend Stuart was on board and he had a wealth of sailing experience and took over command of the yacht with a steely calm that was genuinely inspiring to witness. He proceeded to take in the developing data of our situation and make informed decisions accordingly, without fuss or hesitation. He encouraged confidence in his crew and refused to abdicate responsibility to the coast guard. A coast guard rescue would have been dangerous and would have come at the expense of the vessel. In essence, from years of experience he recognised his job was to make a series of decisions and live and die by their outcomes.

As we sailed into port safely just as dawn broke, I had an epiphany. I suddenly had complete clarity that, like the captain of a ship, the role of an entrepreneur is as simple as making a series of decisions and living with their outcomes. While the high seas are inevitable, it is the entrepreneur's role to grab the helm and take charge of their ship. It is the entrepreneur's role to encourage confidence in their team and not to abdicate responsibility to anyone else. I realised that the One Thing entrepreneurs require more than anything else is to recognise that their role, in its simplest form, is to make decisions — to train their ability to make faster, better-informed decisions without anxiety, or angst. To master the art of what I have come to call 'decisionship'.

> The One Thing entrepreneurs require more than anything else is to recognise that their role, in its simplest form, is to make decisions.

Back in my business with this new way of looking at the world and my business career, I suddenly knew for sure that entrepreneurship is decisionship. I could now clearly see that the turning point for my successful businesses had been a series of well-made decisions and that, likewise, the turning point to failure for those who didn't realise their potential could be mapped back to a series of poorly thought out decisions or missed opportunities caused by indecision.

Business success and business failure can almost always be traced back to good or bad decision making. There may be a million things that contributed to a certain situation, but ultimately it's not about what happens in business, it's about what you do about it. It's about the decisions you make, the decisions you refuse to make or take too long to make, and the simple little errors of judgment. It's about right decisions that went wrong over time or were not fixed fast enough and about decisions made too early without all the facts.

Just think about it for a moment:

- What is it that made Microsoft a corporate superstar?
- What is it that made Apple rise and fall and rise again?
- What it is that has transformed Facebook into a global phenomenon with over 800 million users?

- What is it that makes Google so popular and profitable?
- What is it that led to the collapse of Bear Sterns?

The answer is always the same: the decisions that were made. After writing a research paper focusing on leadership decision making in business, Dr Hossien Arsham, Distinguished Professor in Business Statistics, Decision Science and Systems Simulation at the Merrick School of Businesss at the University of Baltimore said, 'Decisions are at the heart of leader success, and at times there are critical moments when they can be difficult, perplexing, and nerve-racking. However, the boldest decisions are the safest.' Along the same lines, management guru Peter F. Drucker has said, 'Wherever you see a successful business, someone once made a courageous decision.' Your business started with a decision — you just need to realise that is only the beginning: choosing to be in business is choosing to be a prolific decision maker.

Let's just take one of these companies to illustrate the point. When Apple made a decision to have its own software for its computers it was a masterstroke that will continue to gain them a reputation for stability, simplicity and virus-free computing. In addition this ground-breaking decision would enable them to generate significantly more revenue streams, and the ability to launch products with embedded software faster. Yet despite early success the business made a series of average decisions that saw the shares in the company stumble. And here the decisions started again — it was decided to bring back the founder and former CEO Steve Jobs to give them direction. Since this decision Apple has again become a powerhouse in the IT industry and continues to outpace the competition. Sadly, Steve Jobs has now passed away, but Apple lives on. It is, however, always possible that Apple's run of good decisions may end, or a competitor may make an even better decision and race ahead.

The pages of corporate history are littered with examples of good and bad decision making in action. We may know more about the decisions big business make because they are reported in the media, but the importance of decision-making skills is as valid for the small and medium businesses that make up the backbone of most economies as it is for the global brands.

If you peek behind the rhetoric and opinion about what makes or breaks a company, their success or failure always comes down to a decision or a series of decisions. It's my view that everyone can learn to be a successful businessperson or entrepreneur by understanding the science behind making effective decisions—a specially developed methodology I call decisionship.

The nature of decisionship

Decisionship is simply your ability to make faster, better-informed decisions without the anxiety. And crucially it's about focusing your attention on the decisions that matter. We all make hundreds of decisions a day, ranging from what to put on our toast in the morning to where to book the family holiday or whether to hire that new staff member. From a business success perspective, some decisions are clearly more important than others. And yet all too often I've seen entrepreneurs and business people flounder not only because they can't make decisions fast enough but, perhaps most importantly, because they can't separate the ones that really matter from the trivial white noise of everyday business life.

If I look back at the decisions that made a difference to the success of Blueprint I remember the moment I decided to go into business with Trevor rather than go it alone; I remember stretching our budget to afford a city office rather than one in the suburbs; and I remember choosing a particularly enthusiastic employee over other more proven recruits who would go on to play a big part in our future. I remember the day we decided only to do business with larger organisations and when we sacked one of our biggest clients because it was not aligned with our culture; I remember the numerous decisions turning down tempting but misaligned funding offers; and I remember deciding to retire so that the business could be sold with a full management team in place. I also remember the decision to accept an offer to sell the business the same week that Bear Sterns started to crumble and the global financial crisis ensured companies started to implode around the world. I also remember watching from the sidelines after selling the business in the nick of time as subsequent indecision and poor decisions slowly killed the business over the next two years.

In short, our business journey can be summed up in every decision we made—for better or for worse. Every entrepreneur needs to learn how to accurately assess decisions from all angles and focus on the ones that create the most positive forward momentum. And while our business growth by most comparable standards was considered super fast, I look back and think that, if I had known then what I know now about decision making, we could have achieved twice as much in half the time. And I now see it as my mission to help other entrepreneurs radically fast track their business success though this innovative methodology.

No longer will you have to wrestle with thorny business problems for weeks on end. You won't need to drive your partner and friends nuts going over the same ground because you don't know what your best next step is. You won't need to switch your focus every five minutes depending on external circumstances or who or what crisis shouts loudest! In short, you don't need to go through your business life riddled with anxiety about the inevitable decisions you have to make as a business owner—instead you simply embrace the art and science of decisionship, a decision-making tool that allows you to navigate the hotspots and cut through the difficult business phases as fast as possible.

> Every entrepreneur needs to learn how to accurately assess decisions from all angles and focus on the ones that create the most positive forward momentum.

So let's consider the definition of the One Thing that will make a difference to your business:

Decisionship = making faster, better-informed decisions without the angst.

The components of good and bad decision making

The three components that contribute to both good and bad decision making are:

- speed—how fast or slow you make decisions
- being informed—how much information you have regarding your decisions
- angst—how much anxiety and stress are experienced around the decisions you make.

Everyone makes decisions differently. Within that uniqueness lies some fundamental components that can be either a blessing or a curse. It is the combination of these three decision-making components that creates your decision-making profile and consequently determines how good you are at making fast, effective decisions that accelerate your business without stringing you out!

Speed

Let's first look at decision speed. Being either too fast or too slow in your decision making could hold your business back. We have all had the experience of working with or for someone who is a decision-making speed machine. They make decisions every second breath, only to change their mind the next day! If I'm honest, that used to be me. I would drive people nuts because I'd decide on a certain decision and then change my mind a week later. I was even given a nickname—Wasabi. A somewhat apt label that summed up my ability to make up words (as you will discover) and my tendency to get over-excited and let loose my latest genius strategy only to change it within days or even hours. The look of shock on my exasperated employees' faces apparently mimicked the look you get after eating too much Japanese mustard. When I found out about the nickname I grew to embrace this facet of my personality, but it did make me think about my chaotic decision-making process and its impact on others.

Working for people who are too fast to make decisions, especially if they subsequently change their mind, can be really frustrating for others. It's also incredibly inefficient and erodes your credibility because you don't always do what you say you will do. Equally frustrating is someone who takes too long to make decisions. They hesitate like the proverbial rabbit caught in the headlights, as if the decision needs time to mature—to let you sweat out a result before they can honour you with an answer. The procrastination of these slow decision makers drives their team to distraction. The employees are internally screaming, 'Make a bloody decision already!' You can see this type of decision making on the roads—it's the ultra-cautious person wanting to turn into a road yet by the time they have made a decision an oncoming car prevents them going anywhere. Their hesitation becomes a danger to everyone.

> Effective leaders are decisive—differentiating between when urgency requires ultra-fast decision making and when a more measured approach is necessary.

Being informed

Similarly, there are two ineffective extremes when it comes to be being informed. They can be equally frustrating when an entrepreneur is too pronounced in this area. On the one hand you have leaders who will go to the ends of the earth to gather information, proclaiming that they need more data—so much so that they miss the decision-making window. Entrepreneurs who are too focused on information can lose credibility with their employees because the people waiting for the decision give up. They stop believing that anything will happen. And perhaps worst of all they stop coming up with creative solutions and innovative ideas that could benefit the business, because they are asked to provide indisputable proof, which is often impossible and soul destroying.

The overly informed decision maker also misses opportunities. A certain amount of data is useful, yet we have all been witness to information overload—watching as conflicting information or research makes decision making even more difficult. Drowning in business cases and research is not always the answer to good decision making—it is all about gathering the appropriate information from the most appropriate sources and realising decision making is about both informed guesswork and foresight.

At the other extreme is the ill-informed decision maker: someone who has a disregard for facts and jumps to conclusions left, right and centre, telling you it's down to gut instinct and experience. The problem is that gut instinct and experience are often used as the cover story to justify hasty decisions. Having your head in the sand and refusing to accept the reality of a situation is clearly not the best way to make successful decisions either. Many entrepreneurs fall into this decision-making habit around their financial position—not having enough accurate data about what they can afford keeps them in the dark and often sends them broke in the process as they write cheques they can't afford.

> Effective leaders have decision support structures that give accurate and timely information to help them make informed decisions.

Angst

The final component of decision making is angst, or anxiety. At one extreme you have the entrepreneurs who are cavalier, and at the other those who are overly anxious. Cavalier or flippant decision makers show bravado that is often a mask for denial. In an effort to ignore the negative or simply ignore the facts they tune out their emotions and disengage from the consequences. This will inevitably lead to poor decision making because not enough foresight or thoughtfulness is applied to the decision-making process. They think that they should be one step removed from the decision, when in fact some emotional attachment to the outcome is essential. They wrongly believe that business is all about being hardnosed or detached from feelings of fear and concern. There is a famous although anonymous quote about harnessing the power of nerves that suggests, 'butterflies are necessary, the secret is to have them flying in formation'. Similarly a certain amount of anxiousness for the outcome of your decision is healthy.

At the other extreme, people who are overly worried about the consequences rarely make the best decisions. They might suffer from pre-decision anxiety where they run the decision over in their mind, scared of putting a foot wrong. This can lead to a delayed decision and the choice of an overly safe option, which is often counter to entrepreneurial success. There is also post-decision anxiety, where the decision maker frets over whether they made the best choice rather than accepting that the decision has been made and moving on. It's debilitating for a business, and opportunities are missed, if you're always looking backwards.

> Effective leaders take responsibility for making decisions seriously yet realise their role is to make decisions, so they are prepared to live with the consequences rather than be overly anxious about the outcome.

The need for balance

A really good decision maker is balanced. Just because you are fast at decision making doesn't make you better than someone who is more considered. Getting depth and breadth of data doesn't always lead to making better decisions than the person who gets just enough information. And just because you don't stress out about decisions doesn't mean you make better ones than the person who does. Good decision making is not about any one of these components—it's about creating a balance between the three. Right now, as you read this book I would guess that you are either too fast or too slow in your decision making—a problem that is likely to be connected to the fact that you are either too informed or jump right in without any evidence or insight. And as a result you will be far too anxious or far too flippant.

Decision-making profiles

So what are the personality types that make up your unique decisionship profile? Essentially they combine some of the following extremes:

- *Procrastinator.* Someone who is indecisive and continues to delay decision making until later.
- *Bull at a gate.* Someone who makes overly rash decisions, often only to change their mind.
- *Head in the sand.* Someone who doesn't consider the relevant information before making a decision.
- *Data junkie.* Someone who needs every last bit of information before making a decision.
- *Worrywart.* Someone who worries and stresses about even the smallest decisions.
- *Happy-go-lucky.* Someone who doesn't consider the full impact of their decision making on their business and others.

If you are interested in discovering your decision-making profile then download the diagnostic at my Accelerate Global website here: <www.accelerateglobal.com/decisionmakingprofile>. We developed this diagnostic tool with the help of a psychologist in order to help you determine your decision-making profile. Alternatively you can simply re-read the information above and determine which category rings true for you. Either way it's important that you become more consciously aware of your current decision-making profile so you can correct any shortfall and become a more balanced decision maker.

One of the things that I get entrepreneurs that come through my training program to do is to practice decision making outside their business. Let's say you did the diagnostic and it reported that you're a procrastinator, or you recognise the description of the procrastinator. For the procrastinator, the activity is that, next time you go to a restaurant and open up the menu, you have to make an instant decision. Or if you're going to a book store to choose a book, you should scan the shelves, but recognise that the first book that jumps out at you is probably the right book for you. This will start to re-program your mind and help you to make faster decisions, which can then help in your business life. According to American author and futurist John Naisbitt, the ability to make choices in this way is essential. He adds, 'Intuition becomes

11

increasingly valuable in the new information society precisely because there is so much data. Unless we learn to trust our first response we are in danger of suffering from increasingly bad cases of analysis paralysis.' Follow your initial response for some small decisions first, regardless of the information available, so you get more comfortable with making decisions without mountains of data.

If you already make faster decisions, but those decisions turn out to be wrong, then maybe you could try sleeping on a few of your decisions before finally communicating that decision to the people inside and outside the business. If you make decisions with too little information, maybe you need to get into the habit of seeking more information so that you stop yourself jumping to conclusions. Consider the people you already know or have access to that could help you verify the facts. Work out what additional research you need to conduct and then make an informed choice. If you're naturally anxious, you need to ask yourself, 'What's the worst thing that can happen as a result of this decision?' And you need to remind yourself that it's impossible to be a successful entrepreneur without mastering decisionship. There is no guarantee — that's the scary and exciting part of entrepreneurship. And finally, if you're indifferent or blasé about your decision making, you need to ask yourself, 'What are the consequences of making this decision on the stakeholders and the business?' Or, 'What's the opportunity cost of the decision and maybe I need to start to do some kind of financial cost–benefit analysis or a survey of the stakeholders in order to get more feedback?'

No-one is an absolute procrastinator or absolute bull at a gate — we are all a unique combination of the various types and often our decision-making profile changes depending on the situation; but knowing your profile should give you a better idea of the things that you can start to work on.

Mastering decisionship allows you to make faster decisions — but they won't be rash decisions. You will gather enough information that is commercially viable and you will draw the best conclusion from that information to remove the stress.

But decisionship isn't just about how to make faster, better decisions without the stress: it's about being able to systematically identify and deal with the decisions that will alter the trajectory of your success. Not all decisions are created equal, and it's imperative that you have a framework to assess decisions so you can consistently and quickly identify the ones that are going to accelerate your business.

This book will introduce you to your entrepreneurial eye so you can begin to think like a master entrepreneur—to look at problems and opportunities through the eyes of a Branson, Jobs or Gates. If success or failure comes down to your ability to make fast, appropriate decisions at the right time, then providing a tool to assess all your decisions will allow you to do that—whether you need to make some product development choices, merger decisions, or even if you want to help your child decide on a career path.

Good decision making is not an innate ability—like most things it can be learned and improved with practice. Chapter 2 will help you appreciate the traps and pitfalls that can so easily conspire against good decision making.

Key points

» Business success and business failure can almost always be traced back to good or bad decision making.

» Every entrepreneur needs to learn how to accurately assess decisions from all angles and focus on the ones that create the most positive forward momentum.

» Everyone can learn to be a successful businessperson or entrepreneur by understanding the science behind making effective decisions—a specially developed methodology I call decisionship.

» Decisionship = making faster, better-informed decisions without the angst.

» The three components that contribute to both good and bad decision making are speed, being informed, and angst, or anxiety. A really good decision maker demonstrates balance between all three.

» The combination of the three decision-making components creates your decision-making profile and determines how good you are at making fast, effective decisions that accelerate your business without stringing you out.

» The six decision-making profiles are procrastinator, bull at a gate, head in the sand, data junkie, worrywart and happy-go-lucky. Find out which one you are at my website at <www.accelerateglobal. com/decisionmakingprofile>.

Chapter 2
The anatomy of decisions

Before we get into the formula for how to train your entrepreneurial eye in decisionship, it's important for you to understand just what you are up against.

The one common denominator with all entrepreneurs is that we are human beings. It's an obvious point so it's usually not mentioned in business books. But being human creates its own set of challenges before we even get to specific business-related challenges. These challenges are a result of how we have evolved, how we learn and how the brain functions.

One of the best things I did during my business career was work closely with my executive coach on how to prevent limiting beliefs hindering my ability to be a successful entrepreneur. To be honest, I was somewhat sceptical of new age coaching, but by chance I met Michelle Duval, a leading executive coach, at a training course I was attending. At the time I was drowning in the sheer diversity of tasks I needed to do and challenges I was coming up against. As a result, the chinks in my interpersonal skills were starting to show and I was beginning to see how I was at least part of the problem, but I couldn't see a way to fix it. I began working with Michelle and I was blown away not only by how important self-knowledge is but also how powerful it can be when you put it to good use. Subsequently working with entrepreneurs that come through my programs I have observed that what holds them back is not just a lack of knowledge of business, but a lack of knowledge of themselves and how they react in certain circumstances, particularly around decision making.

> The one common denominator with all entrepreneurs is that we are human beings. It's an obvious point so it's usually not mentioned in business books. But being human creates its own set of challenges before we even get to specific business-related challenges.

Objective and subjective decision making

To delve into why this is the case let's first consider the two different ways to make decisions—subjective and objective. Subjective decision making brings in personal opinion. It is impossible not to bring past experience, strengths and weaknesses to the decision-making table when you are making subjective decisions. Objective decision making on the other hand seeks to minimise the impact of opinion and emotion, and looks at the facts instead.

Much of business theory is focused heavily on objective decision making. The idea that business is an unemotional entity is still very much alive and well in business. The notion that staff should leave their personal problems at the door or remain unemotional at all times if they wish to appear professional is still part of corporate culture.

Only business isn't just an entity—it is a collection of human beings with all their inherent quirks. It is impossible for people to leave their emotions at the door. Our reliance on objective decision-making tools is negating the very thing that often makes great businesses great—their people.

The dilemma is that objectivity and subjectivity are both essential parts of good decision making and yet they are performed by very different parts of the brain, and people usually exhibit a natural inclination toward one over the other.

How the brain processes information

There are many different viewpoints about the detail of how the brain is structured and I am no neuroscientist, so I'm not going to get too technical. We will use neurologist Paul MacLean's model of the triune brain for simplicity's sake. There are those that argue this isn't strictly correct, but for our purposes it's adequate and easy to understand.

As we have evolved, so has the brain and its capacity. The oldest part of the brain is the reptilian brain, which is the domain of instinctual behaviours. As we became more sophisticated the limbic system evolved around the reptilian brain; this is the emotional part of the brain. Finally the neocortex, or rational brain, evolved around the limbic brain, and this is the part of the brain responsible for language, planning, abstraction and perception. I'm not getting into which bits are subconscious and which are conscious because that argument is still in progress, but suffice to say that within the complete brain there are things we are conscious of and things we are not conscious of.

You don't, for example, have to think about breathing. Your liver performs over 500 separate functions in the human body. Do you even know what they are? I certainly don't but thankfully we don't need to as our body knows and will just get on with the job. When a woman gets pregnant she doesn't need to think about how to grow the foetus or what chemicals her body needs to release and when, so the baby develops normally — everything is done without any conscious thought.

Essentially we have a conscious mind and a subconscious mind. What we refer to as the conscious mind is mainly made up of the neocortex and in particular the frontal lobe of the neocortex, which is responsible for such things as creativity, decision making and planning. Most of the higher mental functioning that makes us human is connected to the frontal lobe.

We make sense of the world by filtering the information in the outside world through our five senses into our internal world. In his book *Flow*, psychology professor Mihaly Csikszentmihalyi says:

> At this point in our scientific knowledge we are on the verge of being able to estimate how much information the central nervous system is capable of processing. It seems that we can manage at most seven bits of information — such as differentiated sounds, or visual stimuli, or recognizable nuances of emotion or thought — at any one time, and that the shortest time it takes to discriminate between one set of bits and another is about 1/18 of a second. By using these figures one concludes that it is possible to process at most 126 bits of information per second.

Csikszentmihalyi goes on to calculate that in a lifetime of 70 years, counting 16 hours of waking time a day, that equates to 185 billion bits of information, and it is out of that information that every memory, thought and feeling and action is extracted. He concludes by saying, 'an individual can experience only so much. Therefore, the information we allow into consciousness becomes extremely important; it is, in fact, what determines the content and quality of life.'

The fact is that we are privy to infinitely more bits of information than we will ever be consciously aware of. Even the 185 billion bits over the course of a lifetime equates to a small percentage of what we could be aware of. Needless to say, if we were to become conscious of all that data we would go insane, so our brain operates as a screening system which vastly limits what we are consciously aware of.

This is why having a clear vision or concrete goals is so important, because they instruct your brain what you want to be made conscious of. You will begin to see opportunities and ideas that would have otherwise been missed.

We are literally being bombarded with information all the time through our five senses. It follows therefore that we have to take control of that process in a much more meaningful way if we ever stand a chance of making good, effective decisions. We have to decide what to focus on and how to tailor decision making to our own unique beliefs and aspirations. We have to decide what our goals and preferences are and take steps to move toward those objectives. And we have to be aware that many of the decisions we think we are making objectively or consciously are nothing more than a subconscious, knee-jerk associative response to a past event.

> Many of the decisions we think we are making objectively or consciously are nothing more than a subconscious, knee-jerk associative response to a past event.

The influence of associative conditioning

Another way that the brain deals with the vast amount of data that is coming its way is through a process called associative conditioning. When we are kids we learn by association. Say you are in the kitchen with your mother and she turns her back for a second and you cut your fingers with a knife. In that moment of pain your little brain will scan the environment, and log and categorise everything about the scene so it can be used for future reference. Fast forward 20 years to a time when you don't even consciously remember that incident with the knife when you were three, and you are extremely wary around knives. You prefer to get your partner to chop up vegetables even though you're not sure why and it seems really silly. So you think you are making a decision to ask your partner to chop up the vegetables when in fact it's a knee-jerk associative response to a long-forgotten memory—buried deep in your subconscious mind.

One of the most helpful descriptions I've ever found about what's really going on in your mind comes from Bruce H. Lipton's fantastic book *Biology of Belief*. He says:

> The conscious mind is the creative one, the one that can conjure up 'positive thoughts'. In contrast, the subconscious mind is a repository of stimulus-response tapes derived from instincts and learned experiences. The subconscious mind is strictly habitual; it will play the same behavioural responses to life's signals over and over again, much to our chagrin.

You have probably experienced this yourself—I know I have—where you have been in conversation with someone and they have said something. Next thing you know you're really annoyed and storm off. After the red mist has settled you're actually really confused about your overreaction. It wasn't rational or logical, so why did you react that way? Why did you decide to go on the defensive? You didn't—you didn't decide anything. Your brain scanned your memory banks and associative connections and found a match from a long-forgotten episode that caused your reaction. You didn't 'decide' anything—your subconscious reacted.

And here's the really scary bit, according to Lipton: 'When it comes to sheer neurological processing abilities, the subconscious mind is millions of times more powerful than the conscious mind.'

This means that unless you take charge of the decision-making process and consciously direct the information you assess in a systematic way, you will rarely arrive at the right choice and are instead at the mercy of both your subconscious mind and the colossal amount of information that is available to distract your attention at any given moment.

Harnessing biology for business decisions

The simple fact is that you and I make more decisions before breakfast than our ancestors made in a month. Everything is speeding up. Change is the only consistent element in modern life. If you add business to that life, you have expanded the information base even more.

If you need more convincing, just think back for a moment to when you started your business—you decided what industry to be in, you decided what product or service to offer in that industry and what your selling proposition would be. You decided your business name, the look and feel, and logo; you decided on an office space or to work at home; and you decided how much money to invest and what start-up costs to spend it on. You decided whether to get a business partner or go it alone. And this was all decided even before you opened your doors for business.

Yet possibly the biggest decision of all was getting into business in the first place. The catalyst may have been that you were made redundant and thought, 'It's now or never'. Perhaps you just had one too many annoying bosses and decided there had to be a better way. Perhaps you found yourself in business almost by accident as you did some extra work for someone and your moonlighting took off. Perhaps you spotted a gap in the market and dived in before someone else filled it. Whatever the reason, you went from being a talented specialist in a particular area to having to be a generalist in a host of important business functions that include a dizzying array of skills from sales to operations, marketing and IT, human resources and leadership, to customer service and finance.

If you are like most entrepreneurs it doesn't take long before the wheels fall off and the entrepreneurial dream is nothing but a distant memory. Your aspirations of control and freedom have degenerated into chaos. Your 9 to 5 has turned into 5 to 9 and you actually make less money than you did as an employee! And it's all a bit of a shock.

That shock comes from the day-to-day reality of what's actually involved in starting and running a successful business. Most professionals study for four years to be good at one business function—they dedicate their entire lives to perfecting their knowledge and expertise in that one business function, and yet we go into business for ourselves and we have to become an overnight expert in all the business functions. And we wonder why we're stressed!

By going into business for yourself you massively increase the amount of data that is knocking on your brain to get in. But the biology that you have to process that data is exactly the same.

And that's why decisionship is so vital to your business success. If you can appreciate the biological challenges that contribute to poor decisions in everyone, not just the inexperienced, then you are one step ahead. If you can embrace a methodology that actively overcomes those biological challenges by establishing a platform of certainty and then following a process that quickly and efficiently makes a decision, then you are two steps ahead. And if that methodology also provides you with a way to validate and verify your options in accordance with known business strategies, insights and observations, then you will be able to accelerate your business growth exponentially.

Without intervention, the decisions we make are largely dictated by what has gone before—the way we were raised, our schooling, and the experience we have had to date in business. To overcome this we need to focus on bringing both subjectivity and objectivity to decision making without becoming overwhelmed by all of that white noise.

The decisionship methodology described in the next chapter gives you a model for training your ability to harness the power of both the unconscious and subconscious mind to make better subjective and objective decisions—decisions that take into consideration future dreams and goals, the lessons from the past and your innate ability to be decisive in the present.

Key points

» The one common denominator among all entrepreneurs is that we are human beings, which creates its own set of challenges before we even get to specific business-related challenges.

» There are two different ways to make decisions—subjective and objective. Subjective decision making relies on personal opinion, past experience, strengths and weaknesses. Objective decision making seeks to minimise the impact of opinion and emotion, and concentrates on facts.

» Much of business theory is focused heavily on objective decision making, but businesses are a collection of people, so subjectivity is impossible to avoid.

» Objectivity and subjectivity are both essential parts of good decision making, but they are performed by different parts of the brain, and people usually exhibit a natural inclination toward one over the other.

» To improve decision making, you must be aware that many of the decisions you think you are making objectively or consciously are nothing more than a subconscious, knee-jerk associative response to a past event.

» Unless you take charge of the decision-making process and consciously direct the information you assess in a systematic way, you will rarely arrive at the right choice. Instead you will be at the mercy of both your subconscious mind and the colossal amount of information that is available to distract your attention at any given moment.

» If you embrace a methodology that actively overcomes the biological challenges we all have, then you are two steps ahead. If that methodology also provides you with a way to validate and verify your options in accordance with known business strategies, insights and observations, then you will be able to accelerate your business growth exponentially. I call this methodology decisionship.

Chapter 3

The entrepreneurial eye

So how do we train this crucial entrepreneurial skill of decisionship? Don't good entrepreneurs merely make decisions based on gut feel? The answer is in part yes, in part no. Yet for me the more pressing question is how do good entrepreneurs effectively develop and use their gut feel? It's my belief that you can improve your ability to use gut feel or intuition to make decisions by first becoming aware of the process and then working on the areas that will dramatically improve that process until it becomes instinctive — to be used in real time in real situations.

It is about training your ability to look at problems and opportunities through the eyes of a master entrepreneur, and to develop a third eye, or what you might call your entrepreneurial eye — a special skill that will enable you to start making better decisions until you're a master entrepreneur yourself. As you enter this new world of looking at problems and potential opportunities as merely a group of decisions that need to be made, you will start to view things differently. It will feel a bit weird and clunky initially as you go from clarity to confusion to clarity again. But once you get used to using your entrepreneurial eye you will be amazed at how much clearer you will become on your business and your role in it.

I liken it to a visit to the optometrist. Most people have had the experience of having their eyes tested. I'm actually very short-sighted although I never realised it until I was in my late teens. I just thought my sight was normal — that neon signs were meant to be blurry and that it wasn't just me that had to get out of the car to read street signs. Then during a university lecture when I couldn't read the slides a friend handed me his glasses, and suddenly I knew my eyesight was holding me back.

My first eye test, shortly thereafter, was a revelation. I remember sitting forward in the chair with my chin held firmly in place while I had this weird binocular contraption pushed up to my face. As I sat there in the dark staring up at the alternating geometric shapes and symbols on the wall in front of me the optometrist went through a series of lens combinations for each eye. It was a sequential process of finding out which of two alternatives was better. Depending on my response she would alter the next lens until I could see with absolute clarity. I couldn't believe how crisp everything looked. I couldn't believe how far down the letters I could read without squinting. Everything seemed brighter—more alive.

I was reminded of that experience as I became obsessed with finding the One Thing and developing a way to help fellow entrepreneurs achieve the same sense of clarity in their business. I wanted to find a way to be able to train their entrepreneurial eye to look at problems and opportunities with more clarity and to therefore make faster, better-informed decisions with less stress. Remember, good decision making is not just about the outcome. We have only so much time and we have only so much attention, so good decision making is also about identifying what decisions need to be made and in what context, following a proven process to make them, and then reviewing the results and learning accordingly. The entrepreneurial eye is the theoretical model that demonstrates what decisionship is all about. See figure 3.1 for an introductory look at the eye.

Figure 3.1: an introductory model of the entrepreneurial eye

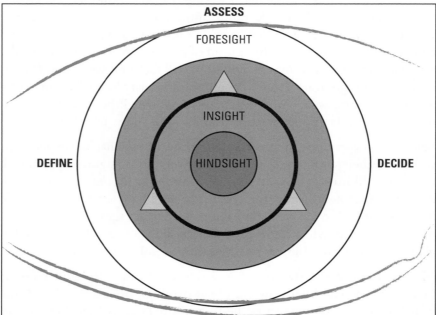

Each sight of the entrepreneurial eye has its own levels of enquiry and depth, which help you to assess the decisions from every possible angle and will be explained in greater detail in parts III, IV and V of the book.

The decisionship process: define, assess and decide

To train your entrepreneurial eye you need to follow the three powerful steps in the decision-making process:

Step 1: define

Step 2: assess

Step 3: decide.

Step 1: define

This step is all about getting really clear about the choices you have to make. You may have heard that the question is more important than the answer. Well, this is especially true for making decisions. Turning the problem or opportunity into a question that can be answered, or into an affirmative statement, is the first step in the decision-making process.

Step 2: assess

This step is about assessing the options for a particular decision. You need to bring three sights to bear when assessing the relative merits of two courses of action—foresight, insight and hindsight. Considering these 'sights' or different perspectives helps to harness both the conscious and subconscious parts of the brain and harnesses the power of subjectivity and objectivity in the decision-making process:

- *Foresight*—the ability to predict what might happen or what you want to happen in the future. This assessment process uses the six lenses of clarity to help the entrepreneur consider the future impact of decisions on themselves and their business. (The six lenses encourage you to answer questions about what you want to achieve personally and what you are striving for in the business—before you make any decisions. Each lens approaches you and your business from a slightly different angle and will be explored in greater detail in chapters 8 and 14). Think of foresight as the prescription for the lenses that make up the new set of glasses that allows you to see more clearly. Foresight is all about *clarity*.

- *Insight* — the ability to use all of the information you have at hand to make decisions in the present. This assessment process uses a decision-making methodology I call the perpetual growth principles (PGP) — four powerful business principles that if harnessed will naturally accelerate the development of your business. The PGP looks at the decision from the perspective of reducing the negative (frictions), fostering the positive (actuators), minimising the things that can slow business growth (mass) and maximising beneficial outcomes for as many stakeholders as possible (balance). The PGP will be explored in detail in chapters 15 to 20. If your decisions meet these principles then your business will thrive — it's as simple as that. The PGP brings objectivity to your decision making. Think of insight as what your new set of glasses allows you to see both up close and in the distance. Insight is all about *focus*.

- *Hindsight* — the ability to reflect on your decision bank, or decisions from the past, to learn and evolve for future decision making. This assessment process uses data generated from past decisions you have made and the learnings of other entrepreneurs and advisers in order to give your decision making both objectivity and subjectivity (see chapters 20 to 21). Think of hindsight as making sense of what you have seen and done before. Hindsight is all about *perspective*.

Step 3: decide

The third step is all about making a decision and getting into action. Too many entrepreneurs make decisions but never follow through. The decide step will help you implement your decisions to fast track your business and move you onto the next decision.

Once you learn how to train your entrepreneurial eye you will look at the world through the eyes of a master entrepreneur. Let's briefly look at how you can develop your foresight, insight and hindsight, and where each of the elements fit into the entrepreneurial eye model.

Using the entrepreneurial eye

Once you become more familiar with the entrepreneurial eye you can use the model as a prompt to ensure you always consider foresight, insight and hindsight when making a decision. You will soon skip quickly through the various elements so that you can make fast, effective decisions without the angst. It will become second nature—yet like any ability it will take practice and repetition to master. In time you will develop your own preferred decision-making style by taking elements of the decisionship methodology and finetuning it to suit your own special needs.

You can use your entrepreneurial eye reactively when you have a decision to make and you need to consider the options. For example, if your competitor lowers their prices and you need to consider whether you will react or keep your prices the same; or if a staff member resigns and you need to consider replacing them or making do with someone already on the payroll.

Alternatively you can use your entrepreneurial eye proactively to make decisions on your business model using the six lenses, or as a way to decide on business strategies that will foster the PGP. For example, you may wish to review your business priorities, choosing the most important things for growth, or you may want to decide on when you plan to exit your business and for how much.

> You can use your entrepreneurial eye reactively when you have a decision to make and you need to consider the options.

The benefits of the entrepreneurial eye

The entrepreneurial eye will help you make faster and better-informed decisions without the angst.

Faster decisions

Being able to quickly turn problems or opportunities into questions that need to be answered will help you make faster decisions, rather than being left swimming around in indecision. For instance, knowing you don't have enough customers doesn't help you make a decision. Rather, defining the question as 'Should we use sales or marketing to increase the number of our customers?' gives you a question that your entrepreneurial eye can quickly act on.

Also, the foresight gained from the pre-work on the six lenses of clarity allows you to immediately rule some decisions out. For instance, once you are clear on your values, you can make employment decisions much more quickly by ruling out candidates that don't fit. If you are clear on your weaknesses then you can make decisions that won't need to rely on these inadequacies and instead will be able to play to your strengths.

Better-informed decisions

One use of the six lenses of clarity is that you can look at a problem or opportunity from six aspects, making your decision more rounded and ensuring you don't forget to think about an area which isn't natural for you to consider. For instance, one of the six lenses of clarity is called the progress lens, which looks at the various business stages from start-up to exit. Each stage requires different skills and different focus so it's essential to appreciate what stage your business is in at any given time. If you aren't normally adventurous, the progress lens will give you assurance that you will need to be a little out of your comfort zone as you go through the various stages of business growth.

Even more powerfully, once you are familiar with the PGP of insight that underpin fast business growth, you will also be able to easily identify no-brainer decisions. If, for example, you are considering purchasing a new computer system that increases complexity and cost, and takes your focus off bringing in revenue and will probably de-motivate your employees, then you will quickly decide not to proceed. You don't have to spend hours wrestling over what to do because the model will help you decide.

Decisions without the angst

Business is not about absolutes. There is rarely a perfect decision, given we are working in a less than perfect world. However, by using a proven decision-making methodology you will gain the confidence to make decisions and live with the consequences. The decision bank that helps you develop hindsight will remind you that sure-bet decisions are fallible and that long-shot decisions can be a runaway success.

Once you begin to see your business through your newly acquired entrepreneurial eye you will view business differently, and everything will become an exciting opportunity or a thrilling challenge. The anxiety and stress don't disappear entirely, but you can manage them in a constructive manner. You put yourself back in control rather than being tossed about at the mercy of one crisis after another.

You will develop clarity; you will learn how to make choices that capitalise on the best opportunities; you will learn the most effective way to overcome problems and obstacles; and you will learn how to proactively direct your business toward your endgame goals. And mastering this One Thing gives you a framework to easily maintain your chosen course.

The rest of the book is dedicated to exploring decisionship and helping you appreciate the various working parts of each lens of the entrepreneurial eye model so you can see their relevance to your daily business life. You don't have to panic and start from scratch for every major or minor decision, weighing up pros and cons until you can't think straight. You won't be overwhelmed by what's ahead—you will simply focus your entrepreneurial eye on the choices to make, assess them consistently and make the best choice. And you will look back at poorly made decisions with interest, not regret, knowing the experience will improve your future decision making.

> Business is not about absolutes. There is rarely a perfect decision, given we are working in a less than perfect world. However, by using a proven decision-making methodology you will gain the confidence to make decisions and live with the consequences.

The remainder of the book is split into parts giving you greater insight into the process and how to bring it all together. I have also included case studies so you can see how decisionship works in the real world, so you may be inspired by the methodology and invest the time to become proficient at the decisionship methodology.

- Part II is an overview of this powerful decision-making process.
- Part III explores how to use foresight effectively.
- Part IV explores how to use insight effectively.
- Part V explores how to use hindsight effectively.
- Part VI brings everything together and looks at decisionship in practice.

I have used the One Thing to grow my business and have since helped thousands of other entrepreneurs implement the methodology in their businesses.

Armed with the methodology explained in this book you will learn:

- how to love the challenges of being in business
- how to set and achieve your goals
- how to start, grow and exit a business faster
- how to develop an effective business model
- how to turn problems and opportunities into accelerating decisions
- how to treat business like a game and start playing to win.

And trust me, if you can do that One Thing then you are well on the way to the outcome that inspired you to start your business in the first place.

Key points

» Decisionship is about training yourself to look at problems and opportunities through the eyes of a master entrepreneur, and to develop a third eye, your entrepreneurial eye. Using your entrepreneurial eye is a special skill that will enable you to start making better decisions until you're a master entrepreneur yourself.

» To train your entrepreneurial eye you need to follow the three powerful steps in the decision-making process: define, assess, decide.

» Define is about being clear about the choices you have to make. Turning the problem or opportunity into a question that can be answered or into an affirmative statement is the first step in the decision-making process.

» Assess is about assessing the options for a particular decision. Bring the three sights—foresight, insight and hindsight— to bear when assessing the relative merits of two courses of action.

» Foresight is the ability to predict what might happen or what you want to happen in the future. Foresight uses the six lenses of clarity, which encourage you to answer questions about what you want to achieve personally and what you are striving for in the business, *before* you make any decisions. Foresight is about *clarity*.

» Insight is the ability to use all of the information you have at hand to make decisions in the present. Insight uses a decision-making methodology called the perpetual growth principles (PGP)—four powerful business principles that if harnessed will naturally accelerate the development of your business. Insight is about *focus*.

» Hindsight is the ability to reflect on your decision bank, or decisions from the past, to learn and evolve for future decision making. Hindsight uses data generated from past decisions you have made and the learnings of other entrepreneurs and advisers to give your decision making both objectivity and subjectivity. Hindsight is about *perspective*.

» Decide is about making a decision to get into action. Too many entrepreneurs make decisions but never follow through. The decide step will help you implement your decisions.

» Once you learn how to train your entrepreneurial eye you will look at the world through the eyes of a master entrepreneur.

Part II

Overview of the decision-making process

We enjoy the process far more than the proceeds.

Warren Buffett, investment guru

Chapter 4

A powerful decision-making process

You probably already have some form of decision-making process—we all have. After all, we have been making decisions all our lives. The problem is that our decision making is often unconscious and ad hoc. It's likely to vary depending on the situation and the gravity of the decision and the results are, at best, mixed.

The three-step process of decisionship—define, assess and decide— merely seeks to formalise the procedure you probably already follow to some extent, while adding the precision that comes with viewing all decisions through the entrepreneurial eye in a consistent way. It is this consistency of treatment that allows for better, faster decisions without the angst.

At first glance the three-step process looks too simple to be useful. But it's amazing how many entrepreneurs I have observed who continually miss one or more of these crucial steps.

There are those entrepreneurs who rush to the assess stage without really defining what the challenge is. The result of inadequate definition is that you can end up solving the wrong problem or being sidetracked before you resolve the real problem. Then there are those who define the challenge and swiftly decide on a solution without ever really assessing the solutions on offer. They don't think back to similar situations and they don't seek advice from others or consider all the angles and possibilities; instead they jump to decide—often with disastrous consequences. And finally there are the business owners who avoid the decide stage like the plague: they are happy to define and assess the challenge, but when it comes to making a decision and taking action against that decision everything grinds to a halt. Too many entrepreneurs make decisions but fail to follow through. Formalising this three-step process and getting into the habit of following all three steps will massively improve your decision-making skills and confidence.

There is an obvious advantage in being able to use a powerful decision-making process that focuses on these three steps, because it ensures that you focus your time and energy on the most important decisions at the appropriate time. Using this process can help you quickly identify what decisions *can* be made, rather than being constantly overwhelmed by all the decisions that *could* be made—including the ones that you have no control over or are too abstract for you to be able to make any headway on. Following a proven process will also ensure you make better decisions more often and you can do so in the quickest possible time, so that they can be implemented and you can move on. And finally, completing the process will ensure that you aren't merely making decisions but that you are actively implementing them so your business can grow and prosper.

This would be the same process you would follow driving your car to an important meeting only to be confronted by a traffic jam. Your mind will automatically define the problem or opportunity into an actionable question such as 'Should I stay on this route or turn off to a longer, less straightforward but possibly quicker route?' You would then mostly subconsciously assess these two options with a thought pattern something like this: foresight—while the alternative route looks free-flowing it is likely to have its own congestion at the bridge/intersection/lights; insight—travelling at this speed on this route I will be 10 minutes late, while I'm unsure whether taking the other route will make me any earlier and could even make me later; hindsight—when I lose patience and change routes it usually ends in disaster. So your assessment might be to stay on your current course. Having decided this you might include in the decide step a decision to call your client and alert them to the likelihood you will be 10 minutes late.

If you drive a car you should be able to relate to this somewhat laborious outline of what your mind manages in a matter of seconds. And to my mind this is the power of decisionship—it allows us to unpack a process that we already use so that we can repack it for better decision making that can still happen very quickly. I remember when I first learnt to drive I was conscious of every working part of the car—the accelerator, brake, clutch and gear stick felt like they each needed my undivided attention, but as I became more competent driving became instinctive and I could enjoy it without thinking how I was doing it. Decisionship will become as simple and natural as driving a car if you persevere with me through each of the steps I outline.

To further demonstrate the power of following a process I will shortly run through a business example. Before I do, I want to share with you a theory that Michelle, my executive coach, shared with me that has helped me tremendously—I call my version of it brick theory. Remember Csikszentmihalyi suggests, 'An individual can experience only so much.' Each person only has so much mental capacity. This isn't about intelligence: it's about how much we can process and attend to at any one time.

Brick theory

Brick theory is my simplification of this idea. Brick theory is essentially trying to get on to paper all of the things that are swimming around in your brain. Each of these items or bricks takes up mind units. Let's assume that everyone is endowed with 100 mind units, and the number of mind units taken up depends on the particular problems, opportunities or tasks on any given day. Sometimes the least important things—like remembering to pick up some milk or buy a birthday card—can take up the most mind units. The pressure to remember little things can eat away at mind units that really would be better paying attention somewhere else. The other ferocious eaters of mind units are the things that we don't or can't control. How much time do you waste regretting past choices or thinking about things you can't change or don't influence? These things are really counterproductive and yet they float around in your mind and you're probably not even aware of how often you think about them. Until you put them down on paper they are simply swimming around in your unconscious brain.

> Brick theory is essentially trying to get on to paper all of the things that are swimming around in your brain. Each of these items or bricks takes up mind units.

Brick theory states that if you can become consciously aware of the things that are taking up your mind units, then you can split them into those things you can do something about and those you can't. Undertaking this simple exercise immediately releases unproductive mind units so you can focus your free mind units on things that do really matter and decisions that do really need to be made.

Taking control when you feel overwhelmed

You have probably heard the expression hitting the wall, when someone becomes so overwhelmed with their job and the things they need to do that they can no longer function properly. The sheer number of tasks and decisions they need to make becomes so overwhelming that they effectively shut down—perhaps you've experienced it yourself. When you have run out of mind units or have no head space to think about anything then you are far more likely to make poor decisions. All your mind units are taken and until you can free some up you will not make effective decisions.

This would occasionally happen to our staff, and then we would have to send them on an impromptu holiday to recover. In fact, it happened to me once when we secured a new client and I recall working 112 hours in a seven-day week. I came away so overwhelmed and tired that I could hardly speak the next week: even responding to the simplest request took forever. I had hit the wall, which happens when you have run out of head space and don't have any free mind units.

> When you have run out of mind units or have no head space to think about anything then you are far more likely to make poor decisions.

The first step, therefore, is to gain some control over the situation, and the best way to do that is to consciously list all the things that are currently using up mind units. Write down the 10 most pressing things on your mind in your personal life and your professional life. If there are more write them down until you have emptied your mind onto a piece of paper. You'll be surprised at how free you become, just simply by writing them down, and you'll be surprised about how many of your personal bricks are actually impacting your business life, and how many of your business bricks are actually impacting your personal life.

Just articulating what those things are can help to crystallise what you need to do to break out of the inertia and get back into action. What I so often find with entrepreneurs is they will agonise over the smallest decisions or put off minor choices that could potentially free up mind units. Conversely they will rush major decisions, which will inevitably make matters worse. Everyone has things in their personal life that take up mind units and everyone has things in their professional life that take up mind units. If too much of your brain capacity is being used or too much of your attention is drawn away by other things, then your ability to make good, effective decisions diminishes. You've probably experienced this yourself where you have so much to do you can't get yourself to do anything.

Which bricks matter?

The next task is to work out which bricks you can and should do something about. Stephen Covey in his book *Seven Habits of Highly Successful People* developed a theory around urgent and important decisions that you may have come across. Essentially, you need to work out which decisions are important and which decisions are urgent, and they're the ones you should focus on as a preference.

While I think this process has a good application, it is not so powerful if your available mind units are getting quite scarce; that is, if you are starting to have difficulty thinking clearly. Rather it is my belief that you should instead focus on what you might call the low-hanging bricks, or petty tasks, first. Essentially, you should identify the bricks that are a major distraction that could be fixed with a minor time investment. By removing these first, you have more time and attention to deal with the urgent and important decisions. These low-hanging bricks might include a dreaded phone call to a client, an emotionally charged staff reprimand, or maybe challenging your business partner around something or even booking a visit to the dentist to get that toothache seen to. Each of these could take less than five minutes to action, yet rather than just do them you let them fester, chewing up mind units as you do and making you less effective in all your other decisions. They're like the proverbial pebble in your shoe.

Whether you consciously follow the decisionship methodology or not, you will be following something close to this process. To give real clarity about the stages of that process, the following three chapters will go into greater detail about the three stages: define, assess and decide.

Key points

» Most of us already have some form of decision-making process, but our decision making is often unconscious and ad hoc. It's likely to vary depending on the situation and the gravity of the decision. The results are, at best, mixed.

» The three-step process of decisionship—define, assess and decide—formalises the decision-making procedure while adding the precision that comes from seeing all decisions through the entrepreneurial eye in a consistent way. Consistency of treatment allows for better, faster decisions without the anxiety.

» The three-step process ensures that you focus your time and energy on the most important decisions at the appropriate time. You can quickly identify what decisions *can* be made rather than being constantly overwhelmed by all the decisions that *could* be made.

» Brick theory recognises that we have only so many mind units to process what needs to be done. If there is too much going on we can easily become overwhelmed and unproductive. Dump everything that's swimming around in your brain down on paper.

» If you make yourself consciously aware of the things taking up your mind units, you can split them into those things you can do something about and those you can't. This immediately releases unproductive mind units so you can focus your free mind units on things that do really matter and decisions that really do need to be made.

» Focus on the low-hanging bricks, or petty tasks, first. Identify the bricks that are a major distraction and could be fixed with a minor time investment. Removing these first gives you more time and attention to deal with the urgent and important decisions.

Chapter 5

Step 1 of decisionship—define

The define step in the decision-making process is all about coming up with the right questions to ask without thinking about the answer. All too often entrepreneurs and business owners launch themselves into solution mode without any consideration of whether they are solving the right problem.

Unexpected decisions

Let me give you an example of a powerful decision definition in our business. It was about three years into business and we were ticking along fairly nicely, we had four businesses and each of them was successful in its own right, turning over a decent amount of revenue—although, to be honest, we probably didn't do our accounting all that well to work out which one was the most profitable.

As we started to consider our next level of growth, Dick Shaw, our chairman at the time, asked us, 'Okay guys, which two of these four businesses are you going to stop focusing on?'

Somewhat stunned by Dick's question, we looked at him aghast, as if he had insulted us, and we were quick to use the company spiel to convince him that each businesses was integral to our product mix and vision. Fortunately Dick persisted and convinced us that we were never going to be able to grow if we didn't start to really focus, and the only way to achieve this was to rationalise two of our four businesses.

This ended up being a very insightful question, something we couldn't have asked ourselves given how close we were to the business. And with the question now defined, Trevor and I could start assessing which of the businesses were the most worthy of our focus to achieve our growth objectives. Surprisingly, within months we decided to close our recruitment and training businesses, which were, at the time, our biggest revenue generators, but we knew this wasn't where we had the biggest growth potential, passion or differentiation. With new, invigorated focus, it didn't take long before our marketing businesses were starting to achieve what we had originally envisaged for them.

Making this somewhat unexpected and courageous decision turned out to be one of the best decisions we ever made, and it proved to me the importance of defining the right question at the start of the decision-making process. That is, however, one of the hardest parts in the process.

The five elements of the define process

The objective of the define step is to reach a point where you are able to identify and focus on the key options to consider. These options must be refined into short, punchy, affirmative questions as you move into the assess step. Your job is to identify the most pressing issues, quantify those problems or opportunities in as much detail as possible and finally narrow the possible outcomes down to the two most plausible options so you can assess them fully in order to make the best possible decision in the shortest possible time.

There are five elements to the define process:

- view — identifying a problem or an opportunity
- illumination — separating facts from feelings
- transparency — identifying the size and type of decision to be made
- screen — deciding whether to defer or delegate
- focal point — identify options and create an affirmative question.

View — identifying a problem or an opportunity

The basic premise of the define part of the decision-making process is to become really clear about the question you need answered and the decisions you need to make. This can only happen once you take stock and articulate all the problems and opportunities that are currently filling your head space.

Go back to the brick theory model (in chapter 4) and write a list of the problems or opportunities that are currently keeping you awake at night. List everything you can think of so that you empty everything from your head and put it on a piece of paper. For example, a problem might be poor cash flow, which is causing major accounting headaches; an opportunity might be a government tender that will offer three years of continuous work.

Problems and opportunities arise reactively or they are sought out proactively. In the beginning most entrepreneurs are firefighters, shifting their energy and focus from one emergency situation to another. They rarely have the luxury of proactively looking ahead so they can pre-empt or avoid problems before they arise, or seize opportunities in a more constructive manner.

There are five elements to the define process: view, illumination, transparency, screen and focal point.

Decisionship gives you the tools to reverse that situation, because it will ensure that most of your decision making will become proactive, and you will be working on the business ahead of time. There will always be reactive situations that arise, but they will no longer be the norm.

I used to run my business like ground zero of a disaster zone. I would be answering phones, sometimes two at a time; there would be a queue of people at my door waiting for my opinion or approval on something; unread emails would keep mounting up; and my in-tray would pile head-high with all the tasks and projects I was looking after. While I enjoyed the adrenaline, it was ineffective for my staff and the business. Also, it often meant that the real problems or opportunities were missed because they didn't seem as urgent or they weren't shouting the loudest for my attention.

It took me a while to realise that not only did I need to empower people to be responsible for making decisions themselves but that I needed to turn my disaster zone into something more resembling the emergency room of a hospital — in short, I needed to get better at performing triage. Triage is the process ER nurses go through to split patients into three groups: those who can wait, those who are too sick to help and those who need immediate attention.

You can only achieve triage in your business if you list the problems and opportunities facing you and then choose the one you are going to work on. This removes the vagueness of so much stuff to do and helps you identify one focus point so you can get to the root of the problem or opportunity. Say the problem is cash flow. With some contemplation you might realise that the shortage of funds is actually being caused by late payments by your debtors. While poor cash flow is the outcome, it is not the core problem. So you might state the problem in a form that makes it something more solvable and less vague or contextual—changing it from, 'How can I fix my cash-flow problems?' into 'How can I reduce my average debtor days?'

Look at the problem or opportunity in a way that can allow you to begin to get really clear about the crux of the situation. The business environment is littered with company failures because entrepreneurs have been trying to solve the wrong problem or capitalise on the wrong opportunities without getting to the root cause. You need to consider how to quickly arrive at the core problem or opportunity as the first step in the decision process.

Illumination—separating facts from feelings

Once you have identified the most pressing problem or opportunity and have expressed it in a way that gets to its core, the next step is to drill down to shed light on the facts and feelings.

Establishing the facts and feelings around each problem or opportunity allows you to separate the emotional from the rational. When you make reactive decisions they are often born of panic or emotional knee-jerk reactions. It's easy to let yourself become overwhelmed by what's ahead of you and lose sight of what's really going on. Add emotion to rumour and it's suddenly fact. Add emotion to possibilities and they can easily spiral into absolutes.

What are the facts?

Your job is to separate facts from feelings and add some specifics to what you think you know so you are in a stronger position to make choices. Adding specifics to the problems and opportunities on the table will allow you to gain control over the situation. Often it is the uncertainty around the problem or opportunity that causes stress, so taking steps to isolate the facts can by default remove a great deal of that uncertainty and allow you to see what you still need to find out. For instance, assuming that a recent increase in interest rates is the reason your customers aren't buying is not a fact. Sales slumping by 25 per cent is a fact. It is a fact if you conduct a survey of a hundred customers and find that 72 per cent of customers nominate interest rates as the major reason for withholding buying decisions.

When sourcing the facts you need to consider the real and known information that is currently available about the problem or opportunity. If you don't know for sure, then you discount the fact. Focus on removing as much of the uncertainty as possible by gathering concrete, verifiable and accurate facts.

What are your feelings?

Decision making is not always a rational or logical process, simply because we are human beings. As I mentioned in chapter 2, our decisions are often not decisions at all but conditioned reflexes made as a result of long-forgotten lessons or associations. This means that, whether we like it or not, we will inevitably bring our feelings and emotions to the decision-making table. Trying to articulate those feelings brings greater clarity to the situation and allows you to move forward. There is no point denying you are feeling anxious or scared or bored by the options. It's far more constructive to acknowledge how you feel so you can assess if those feelings are playing a part in your willingness or unwillingness to address this problem or capitalise on the opportunity.

If, for example, you are experiencing cash-flow problems that are putting a real strain on your business, you might realise that you need to bring in at least $50 000 within two weeks or you are going to be in serious trouble. You may feel upset about this and feel like you are letting people down. You may also realise that you feel embarrassed about chasing a certain client for payment because that client is a friend or a family member. You may be avoiding the discussion to save face, or perhaps you know that the client is also having problems and you don't want to add to their burden. The simple act of acknowledging the truth of how you feel in this situation partially frees you from it and allows you to find a more rational and appropriate response. Once you acknowledge your feelings, you are often liberated from that feeling. If you can say to yourself, 'I am not making the call that will solve this problem because I don't want to bruise my ego', it suddenly seems very trivial and you can take the appropriate action. But until you acknowledge those feelings you will probably come up with 101 reasons why you are not doing what you know you need to do.

Likewise, rational decisions based on facts don't always trump emotional decisions. Consider a decision of whether to hire someone who has a great résumé full of relevant experience or someone without the experience but that you have a good feeling about. This is a case where feelings shouldn't be ignored. You will be much more motivated to train and inspire someone, and be more excited to come to the office yourself, if you are surrounded by people you like and who make you feel good.

Documenting the facts and feelings around a given problem or opportunity allows you to remove the clutter and the noise that can so easily distract you. This illumination of relevant information and feelings will ensure your vision is not clouded by misinformation or misplaced emotion.

Transparency—identifying the size and type of decision to be made

Identifying the size and type of the decision allows you to gain some much needed transparency on how to determine which decisions justify lengthy consideration and which can be dealt with by a quick yes or no. It is dealing with the transparency around decision size and type that will enable you to make much faster decisions and have a lot less anxiety about them.

The size of the decision to be made

The reason it's important to split by size is so that you can gauge how much time you should be spending on the decision. All too often entrepreneurs and business owners spend way too much time on minor decisions and nowhere near enough time on the really mega decisions. There is also the misconception that entrepreneurs have to be right all the time. Not only is this untrue, it's also unrealistic and adds a huge amount of pressure to already difficult decisions. You don't have to be right all the time to create a very successful business.

You just need to be right some of the time. Clearly the bigger the decision the more important it is for you to get it right more often, but there is still a margin for error. I like to break the size of decision down into three categories, each with its own approximate margin of error. This helps me determine how much time to spend on each decision and how much stress and anxiety I'm willing to endure to make it. These are my categories:

- *Minor.* These are day-to-day decisions and you need to be right 25 per cent of the time or more. An example might be the decision to purchase a new printer.

- *Major.* These are larger execution decisions and you need to be right 50 per cent of the time or more. An example might be whether to employ a new receptionist.
- *Mega.* These are large business-critical decisions and you need to be right 75 per cent of the time or more. An example might be whether to bring a business partner or investor into your business.

Starting to include transparency around which decisions are minor, major and mega decisions will help you grow your business faster because you will be making more decisions. Playing with these percentages is the gamble that is entrepreneurship, and the risk is always part of the adventure. It's unreasonable, however, to expect that you can get all decisions right all of the time. Rather, acknowledge that you made the best decisions you could at the time with the information you had available, and don't beat yourself up about past decisions. Learn from the experience in order to make yourself a better decision maker—which is exactly what we will cover in the hindsight section in chapters 21 and 22. Making mistakes is the most important and the most underrated element of success—you simply can't succeed in a major way unless and until you have screwed up a few times.

The type of decision to be made

Another classification that aids transparency is understanding the type of decision you have to make. If you can quickly catalogue a decision into a type, you can then recall the process you like to use to assess decisions of this nature. There are five main types of decision that you will encounter in the course of your business:

- employee decisions
- resource decisions
- financial decisions
- sales decisions
- strategy decisions.

The reason categorising decisions by type is so helpful is that it allows you to quickly move though the definition step and move into assessment. Once you get the hang of decisionship and the process involved, then you will be surprised at how quickly you create your own routines around each decision type. Following is my routine for each type, which you might use as a guide or come up with your own.

Employee decisions

Employee decisions deal with hiring, firing, managing and motivating staff. We developed a formula for dealing with these types of decisions that would save us a huge amount of time and this helped create consistency in our leadership style.

For example, when I consider hiring a new staff member, my mind will immediately run through certain questions:

- How can we reposition someone already in the business rather than employ someone new?

- How can we employ someone on a casual basis so we can try before we buy, rather than committing to permanent employment from the outset?

- How do we make sure that we don't pay the maximum salary by negotiating opportunity or training, or factoring in a success fee?

- What is the real cost to the business once we factor in salary, incentives, management, office, phone, employee taxes and other expenses?

- How will this person increase (or secure) our revenue by three times, or reduce our expenses by two times?

Resource decisions

Generally resource decisions are about purchases for everything other than employee resources. Examples include your choice of office and where you source your raw materials and one-off purchases such as office technology, promotions material, furniture and office fit-out, as well as ongoing purchases, such as communications, accounting, legal, stationery and travel.

When I identify a problem or opportunity as a resource decision — perhaps I need to buy a certain piece of equipment — I would immediately run through a routine of questions:

- For the same amount of money, what else would be a better use of these funds?

- Is this a nice to have or a need to have purchase?

- How can we negotiate the price and terms to defer some of the payment?

- How can we protect ourselves so that we have an unwind provision if the equipment doesn't perform or is delivered late?
- What is the real cost of the purchase? (Include implementation, maintenance and other costs.)

Financial decisions

Financial decisions are to do with the impact of decisions on your cash flow, profit and loss and balance sheet. These might include how you are going to finance your resource purchases, decisions around customer and creditor terms, how to raise funds for the business and decisions around your exit, such as whether to use a trade sale, merger or share market float.

If I were making a decision to consider the appropriate exit offer, for instance, I would ask:

- Am I receiving cash or shares, and what are the tax consequences?
- Do I get all of my funds up front or is there an earn-out, where I get paid on the future success of the business?
- Do I need to continue to 'work out' my time in the business, and if not, what are the restraints of trade around working for someone else in the industry or setting up a similar business?
- Will the incoming investor or purchaser look after my clients and staff, and continue the legacy that I have started?
- How long and drawn out is the sales process and due diligence likely to be?

Depending upon the answers to the above questions, it could mean that a $10 million offer for your business may be more attractive than a $20 million offer.

Sales decisions

These are decisions that help you attract, retain and grow customers and clients. They might be about marketing, your sales team, your offer or your sales process, or they could relate to individual clients, such as pricing, account management and communication decisions.

If the sales decision is about whether to set my price high or low I might consider the following:

- At what end of the scale will my price fit compared with my competitors'?

- How powerful a motivator is price for my customer segment?
- Is there enough margin in each sale including enough margin to pay for sales?
- Based on some estimates of sales numbers at each price, which price maximises my gross profit?
- Which price will help me consistently grow revenue in the medium to long term?
- What are the impacts if there is a fall off in sales due to something out of my control?
- Which price will be the easiest to achieve break-even point?

Strategy decisions

Strategy decisions are decisions that will underpin the future direction of the company—think decisions to expand (geographically, products, revenue); decisions on whether to target specific market segments; decisions on whether to conduct functions in-house or outsource; decisions to change organisational structure through consolidation, decentralisation or re-engineering; decisions to change your brand image or unique selling proposition; decisions to move office; decisions to increase capacity; or decisions to get a business partner.

If I were making a decision about whether to conduct a function in-house or to outsource, I might consider such questions as:

- Does the function need to be part of our core expertise and intellectual property?
- How much will the quality, cost and timeliness of the function impact our reputation with our clients?
- Are there current outsourcers that handle this type of function for a similar industry?
- What are the full costs, including the implementation and management time?
- If we need to increase or reduce capacity or demand, which would react quickest at the least cost to the business?

Once you can identify the decision by type, you can then quickly replicate the process that you have used before for these types of decisions. Considering the type as well as the size of decision will give you more transparency to see inside the decision and how it will have an impact on your business.

Screen—deciding whether to defer or delegate

Once you have identified all your problems and opportunities, you will realise you can't deal with all of them. Some are going to be more important than others. Establishing the facts and feelings surrounding the options and also separating them by size and type can help to determine the order in which you need to deal with the various problems and opportunities.

One of the traps that entrepreneurs fall into is that in the rush to get things done or move through the to-do list, they make decisions before they need to be made, or make them out of sync or without the right information. To rectify this you need to learn how to defer decisions until a later date. That way you still take action, you just defer the decision until a more appropriate time.

Another entrepreneurial trap is being the only decision maker in the company. You might talk about the company being a team and how you want to empower your staff, but when push comes to shove very few decisions are genuinely left to your staff. If you want your business to grow, effective delegation is crucial, otherwise the company will only be as big as your own personal capacity for decision making, and considering there are only 24 hours in every day, that's never going to be that big. You need to learn how to delegate effectively, too.

The screening step in the decision-making process ensures that you focus on making the most important decisions at the most relevant time by ensuring you defer and delegate:

- Defer decisions that are best postponed until a more appropriate time.
- Delegate decisions for which someone else should hold responsibility.

Deferring decisions

When you defer a problem or opportunity you actively decide not to make a decision, and this can be very liberating. Not making a decision is still a decision, but it frees up mind units for you to focus on other things. For every decision you need to make consider:

- Is now the best time to be making this decision?
- Is the effectiveness of this decision dependent on a separate event or different decision?

- Is there more information we need before we can make a decision?

We talked in chapter 4 about brick theory and why it is important to free up mind units so you can become a more effective decision maker. Sometimes even if you have cleared some of the major distractions and split the problems or opportunities into size and type, there can still be problems floating around in your mind. Sometimes it's not possible to solve that problem right now or you don't have the information necessary to make a decision, so it sits in limbo in your mind, taking up space. A great way to handle this is to still look at the problems but actively decide not to decide yet. That way the decision is shelved in your brain and you can use that mental capacity to work on other things. This puts a framework around the decision, which brings clarity and a timeline to the process. You may for example decide to reassess the issue in the new financial year or by a certain date. You can also defer based on a contingency, so you may decide to defer the decision until you hire a general manager or until you get a new client or until some other catalyst occurs, such as your sales volume reaching a certain point. You might defer until you have a certain amount of data or until the results of a particular survey are in, or some financial analysis has been conducted or when the end-of-year results come back from the accountant.

Although this mental shelving may seem odd or unnecessary, if you don't take this step and defer the decision to a later, specific time, the problem continues to interrupt your thoughts and will continue to distract you from other matters that you *can* solve.

Delegating decisions

The art of successful delegation is something that many entrepreneurs and business owners really struggle with. In most situations they started out alone, and so the founder was once the only employee. The business may grow initially but eventually it will level out because the owner believes they have to make every decision themselves. They are secretly quite proud of the fact that every day there is a line of people outside their office waiting for them to make a decision. But ultimately this approach is killing their business. It slows everything up, prevents employees from growing and developing in their roles, and removes any sense of pride or reward in those roles. And it leads to poorer decisions. There is no way that the business owner can stay across every part of the business in the same way that he or she did in the early days. As a result, the people that are in the best place to make those decisions, have ownership of those decisions and action them, are effectively removed from the decision-making process. And that's a major mistake.

Splitting problems and opportunities into categories according to their size facilitates effective delegation because it allows you to delegate some of the smaller decisions to other people. This in turn allows you to gain more confidence in your team members and it also helps their individual development, and increases the level of satisfaction and reward they get from their role. If they screw it up, it's not a disaster and everyone can learn and grow from the experience.

In addition, separating the problems or opportunities by type also allows you to delegate to the right person. If, for example, you decide that you have an employee problem, then it makes sense for your HR person to handle it. Or to at least have them involved in the process. If the problem or opportunity is IT related, then it should be delegated to the person responsible for IT. Identifying the decision type helps to identify to whom the decision should be delegated.

Whoever you delegate to, you need to assign final responsibility to a particular person. Even if there is a committee pulled together to discuss the problems or opportunities, one person must be accountable for the final decision. People need to be empowered to know that they are trusted to make decisions and that you accept that they won't always make the right one. Making mistakes is part and parcel of becoming a better decision maker, and this is as true for your people as it is for you.

One of the best things that ever happened to me and our business was when, about three months in, I accidentally threw away my mobile phone in a McDonalds rubbish bin. At first I was lost without it and realised just how dependent I was on having constant access to everyone. But I didn't buy a new one. Instead it became a fantastic delegation tool. If I left the office or went on holiday the people left behind knew they had to make the decision because I couldn't be contacted. So people were much more empowered to make decisions and it helped to create a culture where people asked for forgiveness rather than permission. In fact it worked so well I didn't have a phone for the remainder of the time I was in business.

Your people will screw up! There will be times that you regret the choices made by others. You will hear, 'Oops, I messed up', but in the long run you will always create a better, bigger and stronger company if your people are liberated to make mistakes. Generate a culture where people ask forgiveness rather permission. Confidence breeds confidence. And, ironically, making a real mess of something and surviving it or working out how to fix it can be the biggest confidence booster of all.

In deciding if you should delegate the decision consider:

- Is this decision mine to make?
- Am I the best person to make this decision? If not, who is the best person?
- Is there someone else, with more information, knowledge or expertise in this area that is better suited to making this decision?

Be honest with yourself about your current decision-making process. Are you avoiding making decisions because of fear or discomfort? Are you making decisions too quickly, before you have all the information? Learning how to effectively defer or delegate a problem or opportunity will free up your time to focus on the things that only you as the leader and owner can focus on, and it will massively speed up your business growth.

Focal point: identify options and create an affirmative question

The fifth and final element that makes up the define step of the decisionship process is to convert the problem or opportunity into an affirmative question, which is essentially a focal point of two options. Creating two options narrows the focus, makes life easier in the assessment stage and helps your brain make fast, better-informed decisions without anxiety or stress.

Identify options

It's essential to sit back and really think about the various options available to you for each problem or opportunity you are reviewing. And that means thinking the unthinkable. You are not interested in just the obvious possibilities: think outside the box to come up with more radical and unusual options. It's also good to ask other people involved in the challenge what they think and discuss the issues with an adviser. Advisers can't make decisions for you but they can help to point you in the right direction to consider alternatives you may not have thought of yourself.

You can also gather options from reading books or visiting online communities. There are hundreds of business communities where people will gladly share their thoughts and ideas about your particular situation.

The objective is to come up with a comprehensive list for the problem or opportunity you are examining and then whittle them down to the one or two options that are the most promising. By consciously considering and disregarding the other options you actively narrow your focus, which makes the decisionship process come alive. I will get to why this is the case shortly — but first let's consider how to reduce the options from the many to the few.

Traditional ways of narrowing down the options include:

- using criteria
- going on gut feel
- using scoring
- using false ranking.

Using criteria

Using criteria effectively involves first developing some conditions or constraints against which you would assess all the options. For example you may decide that you need to find a solution that can happen immediately, will cost less than $50 000 to implement and will reinforce your brand. Any option that does not meet those criteria is then ruled out. If you don't manage to reduce the options to two after this process use one of the other methods to finish the discarding process.

Going on gut feel

Some of the options you gather will just be untenable from the start. You may just have an instinct that certain things may or may not work. Instinct is a highly underrated part of business success, and because we don't understand it or can't explain it, we often discount it.

I'm a great believer in instinct and gut feel, and certainly in the many biographies that I have read over the years it has definitely played a large part in some of the most successful businesses. Ray Kroc, the founder of the McDonald's chain, has said that he followed his funny-bone instinct when deciding in 1960 to borrow $2.7 million, against his lawyer's advice, to buy out the fast-food franchise that he had. Writer Malcolm Gladwell talks about intuition in great detail in his book *Blink*. He refers to this instinctive insight as 'thin-slicing', which is our innate unconscious ability to find patterns in situations and behaviour based on a very narrow slice of experience. Gladwell, too, suggests that instinct is hugely undervalued in the modern world — especially in business.

There is a lot to be said for trusting your initial response. And while we may not fully understand it I think we would be crazy to ignore it. So if any of the options feel right or wrong then trust that knowing, and whittle down your choices still further.

Using scoring

The third way to eliminate options in this pre-assessment stage is to score each option and eliminate the options with the lowest score. Simply list each of the possible options and assign a score out of 10 next to each option. Don't think too much about the score. You don't need to agonise about it. Seeking to assign a score gives you another way to tap into your intuition. If for example I asked you to rate yourself as a leader on a score of 1 to 10, you would instinctively give a response. You may not be able to explain why you gave that score or even be able to justify that score, but it would feel right to you. Scoring the options allows you to actively access that inner knowing, especially when you work in a relatively rapid fashion without second-guessing yourself.

Using false ranking

False ranking is the method we often use in the entrepreneurial training programs that I run. Start by labelling the options down the page from 1 to 10, or however many options you are considering. Next ask yourself if option 1 is better than option 2. Add a tick next to the one that you consider is the better option of 1 and 2. Then ask yourself if option 1 is better than option 3 and assign a tick to the better option between those two. Then ask yourself if option 1 is better than option 4 and assign the tick. Continue until you have compared option 1 to all the other options. Then move on to option 2 and ask is option 2 better than option 3 (not 1) and assign a tick next to the better option. Is option 2 better than option 4, and so on, until you have been through all of the subsequent options — noting that as you proceed down the options each is compared with fewer and fewer alternatives.

Once you have finished the comparisons, count up how many ticks each option received, and select the two options with the highest number of ticks to take into the assessment stage for further investigation.

The objective is to arrive at the best two options. Simply use the above assessment techniques incrementally until you arrive at two options. Although this process may sound long-winded, it may be that you have two options left after using criteria for pre-assessment so you won't get this far. Besides, as you become more and more familiar with the process you will be able to whiz through the define stage in a few minutes. It's just a matter of practice.

Creating an affirmative question

Once you have arrived at the two options that are most worthy of your consideration, it is time to express the problem or opportunity as an affirmative question. This takes a vague problem or opportunity and converts it into action-oriented language.

Our aim is to get to the point where we can create two choices:

- an either/or decision
- a yes/no decision
- a do something/do nothing decision.

If you have a list of 10 things, then it's very difficult to choose. If, on the other hand, you can whittle the choices down to two and express them in one of two ways (either/or, yes/no, proceed/don't proceed), then you give yourself the very best chance of moving quickly through the decision-making process.

You are also less likely to get overwhelmed by two choices because, like a computer, our brains think fastest and engage the subconscious brain much more effectively when we ask it questions in binary, that is, a question with one of two answers. The other advantage of two choices is that there will be less information gathering if there are only two options to consider.

The idea of the define stage is to get really clear on the problem or opportunity you are seeking to address and have it worded so that your brain is ready to use foresight, insight and hindsight to assess the best course of action.

I must confess that this is the part of the decisionship model I initially struggled with the most, even though I wholeheartedly believe in its power. As I mentioned previously, entrepreneurs are traditionally very quick at getting into solution mode without properly identifying the problem, and as a result they often end up solving the wrong problem. Or they become so lustful of every opportunity they can never make a decision or gauge which opportunities are worth pursing and which are wasting their time.

> What you are aiming for is to create an action-oriented affirmative question that clearly states the problem or opportunity.

Defining the problem or opportunity removes that possibility by concisely nailing it through the creation of an affirmative question. And this is a great way to focus your mind on the right question so you get the very best result. What you are aiming for is to create an action-oriented affirmative question that clearly states the problem or opportunity, and the two alternative choices or options. It is also important to be specific when outlining the choices or options. For example the option to hire a general manager might be expressed, 'Hire a general manager on $100000 by July?'

The choice to proceed with something or not to proceed is not always as powerful as a choice between two discrete and different options. This is because you might be unduly influenced by your natural inclination towards purchasing or not, being in action or not, or preference for the status quo. For instance, in the example of whether to hire a general manager, rather than framing the question as 'Hire a general manager for $100000 by July or not?' my recommendation would be to compare it with something of similar value that would solve a similar problem or capitalise on a similar opportunity. For instance you might frame the question as 'Hire a general manager for $100000 by July or spend an extra $150000 a year to incentivise our alliances?' (Note that the real cost of an employee is usually the salary plus an additional 50 per cent for associated costs.) Comparing two similarly attractive and possibly effective decisions makes the process more useful and insightful, even though it does require more thought.

The final step in creating an affirmative question is to include a punchy reflection of the problem or opportunity that we uncovered in the first step. This should be framed as a question at the front of the two options and will generally start with 'Should we' or 'When will we'. So again, looking at the general manager example, the full question might then become 'To help our business grow to the next level should we hire a general manager for $100 000 by July or spend an extra $150 000 a year to incentivise our alliances?'

Improving decisions and the business

Once you have completed the define process you may realise that there is a bigger question that you need to decide on first. So you might go through this process and realise that the bigger problem is how we generate an additional $250 000 before we can even think about hiring a general manager. But wouldn't you rather realise that *before* you have hired a general manager and become stressed about cash flow? Part of the value of the define stage is that it shines the light of clarity into the business and decision-making process so you know what decisions you need to be making and in which order.

At the start of this chapter I shared a story about how our chairman helped us clearly define an affirmative question about which two of our four businesses we should rationalise. This was a pivotal decision in our business and it arose because of a good, albeit unexpected, definition of an affirmative question. In fact, it took me a long time to realise that our board meetings shouldn't merely have an established agenda of topics to cover. To maximise the effectiveness we set aside 30 minutes to cover what had happened in the business, but more importantly to use the remaining time to seek advice on future decisions. Usually we would have time to cover three big decisions that we started to get better and better at defining. The more specific we became, and the more notice we gave our advisers about what decisions we were aiming to make, the more value we got, the better decisions we made and the faster our company grew.

This process was so successful in defining the agenda for our board members that we started to adopt this practice in all of our meetings in the business. Meetings that used to take hours and degenerated into nothing but a talk fest, with little being resolved or actioned, were transformed. They became shorter and much more useful once they were framed around a group of decisions that needed to be made. I believe that if you create all your meeting agendas around well-defined forward-focused decisions that need to be made, you will massively improve the effectiveness of meetings. Here are some example agenda items and what they could be changed to with some better definition around an affirmative question:

- Sales strategy might be converted to something like 'Should we continue to spend effort selling to companies with fewer than 100 staff?'
- Cash-flow issues might be converted to 'How can we get our average debtor days down from 45 to 30 days?'
- Capacity problems might be converted to 'What revenue do we need before we move to a larger office?'

To help you conceptualise how you might use the define process in your business, let me give you an example of a decision that needed to be made by one of the entrepreneurs in my training program.

Case study: Jeremy — to wine bar or not to wine bar?

Jeremy, who had a successful veterinary wholesale business, was losing interest in his current business and was considering opening a wine bar as a side venture, something he was tremendously excited about. In fact, he spent hours every week thinking about how and when he would capitalise on the opportunity, yet it was having an adverse affect on his ability to be an inspiring leader for his business. By fleshing out the problem and opportunity he realised that he wouldn't be able to start a wine bar without first completing a succession plan for his business. So, rather than consider when to invest in the wine bar, the problem to solve first became when and how he could execute a succession plan that would keep the business growing and the clients and staff motivated.

The facts around this situation were that the business was making profit of $450 000 per year. He had nine direct reports but he was the only client account manager, and so he delivered all the sales pitches. And there were very few docu-mented systems in place. His feeling was that there was no-one in the business who was appropriate to take over from him, and that his staff would welcome a change in leader as he was probably not that empowering—Jeremy liked to make the decisions. He was also worried that bringing someone in from the outside would take a long time to find and train, or that they would ruin the business.

Jeremy recognised that the decision was probably categorised as a mega decision, as the future of the company would depend on how successful the outcome was.

The decision was a combination of an employee and a strategy question — so he would have to factor in all of the costs associated with their employment.

Considering the screening stage, Jeremy knew that he was the only person that could make the decision so this couldn't be delegated, and secondly he couldn't afford to defer the decision because he really needed to have a clear path for him to be re-motivated into his business — so he gave himself a week to decide on a course of action.

And lastly, he came up with five alternative strategies or options that might be worth considering in order to execute a succession plan: to hire a general manager now; hire someone temporarily to systemise the business and then recruit a general manager; get a business partner; exit the business now and let the incoming investor manage the succession; or merge the business with a competitor who had the management capability. One of his criteria for choosing appropriate strategies was an ability for him to get at least $5 million as an outcome if he sold his business outright. This helped him rule out the competitor option and the immediate exit. His gut feel was that the business wasn't ready financially for a general manager now. So he was left with a choice between two options. These options were then framed as this affirmative question: 'Would the best succession plan be hiring a temp project manager for six months until the business is system-ised and is ready financially for a GM, or should I find a management-oriented business partner to buy 25 per cent of the business to help pay for themselves?'

After assessing the two options he followed the decisionship process to assess the options using foresight, insight and hindsight, which we will get to soon. The clear winner was to hire the temporary project manager for six months. The best part of this decision was that he could implement it immediately, and he soon found a suitable project manager which created an unexpected ending. Enjoying his work with the senior project manager he had hired helped Jeremy see his business with new eyes, and Jeremy's passion for his business was reinvigorated. This passion turned into a better leadership style and company culture, and within months the business was booming beyond Jeremy's wildest dreams. The additional cash flow has helped him open the wine bar and employ a manger for it, so he can remain CEO of his business until he achieves a financial exit.

Jeremy could see that the work he completed in getting a clearly identified affirmative question helped him make a well thought through decision in the assess process, which is what we are going to discuss next.

Key points

» The define step in the decision-making process helps you come up with the right questions to ask, without thinking about the answer. Entrepreneurs and business owners often launch themselves into solution mode without any consideration of whether they are solving the right problem.

» The define step aims to get you to a point where you can identify and focus on the key options to consider. Refine the options into short, punchy, affirmative questions as you move into the assess step.

» The five elements to the define process are view, illumination, transparency, screen and focal point.

» *View* is about identifying a problem or an opportunity. This can only happen once you take stock and articulate all the problems and opportunities that are currently filling your head space.

» *Illumination* is about separating facts from feelings, so you can separate the emotional from the rational. Reactive decisions are often born of panic or emotional knee-jerk reactions. Separating facts from feelings prevents this from happening so easily.

» *Transparency* is about identifying the size and type of decision to be made so you can determine which decisions justify lengthy consideration and which can be dealt with by a quick yes or no. Considering the type as well as the size of decision allows you to see inside the decision and how it will affect your business. The result is much faster decisions and a lot less anxiety over them.

» *Screen* is about deciding whether to defer or delegate. Once you have established which decisions are more important, and recognised you can't deal with all of them, you will need to defer or delegate.

» *Focal point* is about identifying options and creating an affirmative question. This final perspective converts the problem or opportunity into an affirmative question, which is essentially a focal point of two options to narrow the focus. It makes life easier in the assessment stage and helps your brain make fast, better-informed decisions without anxiety or stress.

» The define stage shines the light of clarity into the business and decision-making process so you know what decisions you need to make and in what order.

Chapter 6

Step 2 of decisionship—assess

Having first defined the problem or opportunity and converted the challenge into a specific affirmative question with two choices, it is now time to assess those options. Never enter the assess stage without adequate and thorough definition of the options. A well-defined affirmative question with two options will make all of the difference in the assess step.

The decision-making personality types

In chapter 1 I briefly introduced you to the various decision-making personality types. During the assess stage these traits can really cause some damage, so it's important you understand them in greater detail and appreciate the common pitfalls of each type so you can recognise the behaviour and take evasive action to move forward.

The procrastinator personality

The procrastinator delays making a decision. There doesn't appear to be a good reason for slowing down the assessment process—it just seems to happen that way! Maybe they think that by delaying or going at a snail's pace the world will conspire to make the decision for them. This is in fact exactly what usually happens—their inability to decide on a course of action turns into a self-fulfilling prophecy. For instance, the delay in formalising a salesperson's commission scheme results in the staff member leaving. The failure to take legal action against an outstanding debtor becomes redundant when they go out of business owing you funds. The delay in deciding when to bring on a business partner results in a talented colleague perfect for the role finding another opportunity. Or maybe the procrastination around how to become a thought leader in your industry results in someone getting there before you.

Procrastinators need an assessment methodology, or a tried and proven process to follow in order to help them make faster decisions with more confidence.

The bull at a gate personality

This is someone who uses their gut feel to make lightning-quick decisions between two courses of action. They seem to go eeny, meeny, miny, mo, let's go with option 1—not because it's been carefully considered as the best course of action, but because they think that making any decision is better than making no decision. They feel that any hint of indecision is an affront to their ability as a legitimate entrepreneur.

Unfortunately the bull at a gate assessment relies on luck and chance, and unless an entrepreneur has decades of experience they are likely to make too many mistakes using this as a methodology. The bull at the gate personality also changes his or her mind too often, which is a source of frustration to everyone involved. I recall with some regret one of our bull at a gate decisions to expand our offices into another two capital cities shortly after we started our business. It was a rushed and poorly considered decision, and within six months we had retracted it. It was a costly and time-consuming error that could have been easily avoided if we had just assessed the options thoroughly.

Speed kills and this can also be the case with decision making when it is taken to the extreme. Following a rigorous process for assessment will help those that have a tendency to be a bull at the gate to slow down, or at least make fast decisions using a better rationale.

The head in the sand personality

This person doesn't gather an appropriate amount of information about the choices available to them before making a decision. Like the bull at a gate decision makers, those who have their head in the sand leave themselves open to making poor decisions. I have seen entrepreneurs make decisions to build software in-house without any understanding or technical knowledge of what's involved and how huge a job that can be. I have had friends become the winning bidders at house auctions without realising they need their loan pre-approved in order to give the deposit, and I have witnessed the huge disappointment when a manager has employed a litigious employee because they don't think to do past-employer reference checks.

Assessing the choices available to you based only on what you know can be ignorant, arrogant and downright dangerous. You need to be appropriately informed before making a decision.

The data junkie personality

At the other extreme is someone who needs every last bit of information for every possible choice before they can make a decision. This decision-making profile can get stuck in the define stage because they won't narrow down their options. And once they finally arrive at the assess stage, they want to conduct every possible bit of research. They want to conduct surveys and gather masses of data, but often just to prove or verify their original opinion anyway. You need to gather appropriate amounts of information in order to make an informed decision. That doesn't mean, however, that you can cherrypick the information that confirms your original theory because that simply pollutes the process.

Excessive or selective data gathering slows the decision-making process down and can result in missing opportunities or problems. It can also result in data overload, where too many opinions or conflicting information makes it extremely difficult to distinguish between options.

You will often read in newspapers where politicians get this wrong. They will conduct comprehensive polling in order to get their constituents' opinions and will then change their policies to ensure they can maximise votes, only to find out on election day that opinions and reality are two different things. Like me, you might have also witnessed decisions made by committee, an outcome that generally gives a safe result but rarely a brilliant one.

We slipped into this habit with one of our choices of logo — we used a democratic process to decide, only to realise we received a middle-of-the-road design rather than something more dynamic which would have been in tune with our corporate image. You need to be appropriately informed without becoming a data junkie when you assess and choose between options.

The worrywart personality

Someone who worries and stresses about even the smallest decisions has even bigger worries when they are confronted by too many choices to assess. Worrywarts freeze at the thought of decision making. They are often unable to sleep as they stew over a choice or regret a previous decision. Too much pressure from an over-anxious boss stresses out employees to the point where they also become nervous and hesitant about decision making, and before you know it you have bred a culture of indecision and worry in your company.

Throughout history the major success stories are often defined by audacious decision making. The super-successful have not worried excessively about guaranteed success or what people will think, rather they spent their time proving it instead of worrying about it. Worrywarts will rarely choose a course of action that is non-conventional and, whether you like it or not, it is these ideas that will make history and entrepreneurial success, not the middle-of-the-road ideas. You need to start to assess decisions without too much angst.

The happy-go-lucky personality

This is the personality of someone who chooses alternatives without much regard for the holistic picture. Where the worrywart stresses about what others think and how to guarantee success—which is of course impossible—the happy-go-lucky personality doesn't give enough consideration to the consequences of their actions. Happy-go-lucky decision makers say to themselves, 'I have no idea how this is going to turn out, but I'm willing to take the risk anyway'.

I have seen entrepreneurs temporarily discount their products to clear stock, only to set in motion a price war with competitors that erodes their profit margins many years later. I have seen threats of legal action ignored until the problem escalates into a disaster that consumes all of the entrepreneur's time. And in my own business, my tendency toward this personality trait resulted in me having to lay off a huge number of staff.

When assessing decisions it is always advisable to consider the impacts on other initiatives, parts of the business and stakeholders. In fact, we will shortly be looking at how to develop foresight when assessing decisions, and this can help overcome a tendency towards the happy-go-lucky personality.

So the key to being good at assessing the relevant options is to be neither too fast nor too slow, neither too informed nor too ignorant, and being mindful but neither anxious nor flippant.

Are you a satisficer or a maximiser?

In his excellent book *Paradox of Choice* (2004) author Barry Schwartz discusses the merits of satisficing instead of maximising—a theory developed by the Nobel Prize–winning economist and psychologist Herbert Simon in 1956. Satisficing explains the tendency to select the first option that meets a given need or select the option that seems to address most needs, rather than the optimal solution for which maximisers are always searching.

To demonstrate this Simon gave two examples. The first is about a task to sew a patch onto a pair of jeans. The best needle to do the stitching is a 10-centimetre-long needle with a 3-millimetre eye. This needle is hidden in a haystack along with 1000 other needles varying in size from 3 centimetres to 15 centimetres. Satisficing claims that the first needle that can sew on the patch is the one that should be used. Spending time searching for that one specific needle in the haystack is a waste of energy and resources.

The second example describes a mouse searching for cheese in a maze. The mouse might begin searching for a piece of gouda but, unable to find any, would eventually be satisfied and could suffice with any piece of cheese, such as cheddar—the mouse would be satisficed.

Schwartz argues convincingly that one of the issues of modern living is the myriad of choices available to us. The paradox is that less choice results not only in better decisions but also in more decisions more often, and happier consumers—whereas an abundance of choice leaves decision makers overwhelmed and some simply don't decide, or decide and live to regret their decision.

On face value, maximising (finding the optimal solution) appears more appealing than satisficing (settling for an okay solution), but I put Schwartz's theory to the test myself and realised quick decision making can in fact make you happier and save you a huge amount of time.

Needing to book a yacht and a French villa for my European adventure, I first decided to use maximising for the three-week yacht charter (my default booking technique for holidays). On the internet I mulled over 200 yachts in every size imaginable and compared costs and benefits. Each had widely different cabin layouts and pick-up locations, and they were different ages, too. I would select a finalist and then spend days considering whether this was the best — invariably then continuing to look for a better option. After weeks of searching I finally settled on a 2005 model 54-foot monohull out of Salerno in Italy. The upside of the yacht was the roomy main cabin and cockpit, and the downside was the hull speed and modest size of the owner's accommodations.

My second task, of booking a villa for a fortnight, I approached with a satisficer attitude — I determined the region, proximity to a major town, number of rooms, price range and general feel (we wanted something that looked and felt provincial). Within an hour of looking I had found something suitable, sent an email to check availability and by the next morning, when I received confirmation from the owner, booked it.

The learning I took out of the experience was twofold. First, being a satisficer saved a huge amount of time — I spent maybe two hours on the villa selection and 10 hours on the yacht selection. But the biggest learning was the buyer's remorse I felt about the yacht selection. And this is why Schwarz believes consumer societies with vast choice aren't as happy as societies with fewer choices. Sailing the yacht around Italy was awesome but I did constantly think about the yachts I nearly hired at various times — on a long day sailing to Capri I kept thinking that if only I had chartered that faster Swedish yacht we would be there by now. And sleeping at night and waking up to bang my head on the cabin roof, I would think, that wouldn't have happened if I had chartered that older yacht that had the bigger owner's cabin.

My experience being a satisficer with the villa booking was entirely different and somehow more enjoyable. Because the villa I chose was the first and best I saw in my brief search I had no regrets; I had nothing equivalent to compare it with, so went home happy, thinking we must have booked the best villa in France. The result was a strong lesson to me — utilise some of the satisficing habits, like pre-thinking your critical assessment criteria, and you will make faster decisions with less opportunity for regret or anxiety.

The decisionship theory capitalises on this by creating a framework for pre-thinking, and a quick and easy assessment methodology to compare choices. There are three elements or sights to consider during the assess step. In its simplest form, assessing is about using *foresight* to get clarity by considering how the proposed decision or course of action will likely pan out in the future; focusing your *insight* on considering the pros and cons of each course of action; and using the perception of your *hindsight* to take learnings from the past and check that you're not repeating bad habits.

As you become better at decisionship, this will happen instinctively in a matter of seconds, but until then you need to develop your skills. In short, you need to train your entrepreneurial eye in foresight, insight and hindsight. These three sights can then work together so you can harness your conscious and unconscious brain.

> Decisionship theory capitalises on [satisficing] by creating a framework for pre-thinking, and a quick and easy assessment methodology to compare choices.

Developing foresight skills

Foresight is the ability to predict what might happen, or what you want to happen, in the future. If you are clear about your future then this clarity will help guide your future decision making. Think of foresight as the prescription for the lenses that make up the new set of glasses that allows you to see more clearly — it's all about clarity. To help train your entrepreneurial eye to have foresight, or provide better clarity on you and your business, you need to work on a series of reference points that will help future decision making. These reference points encourage you to consider your business from a number of different angles so that you are more conscious of what you want to achieve and why. Foresight requires some pre-thinking, so you really understand yourself and your business and can then use that information to bring foresight into your decision making and save time. Having completed the pre-thinking, your decisions will become much quicker because you will be able to quickly assess whether a course of action is taking you closer to your objectives or further away from your objectives.

To develop your foresight you should work on the six lenses of clarity: the passion, philosophy, proficiency, progress, prototype, and plan lenses. These six lenses are located in the outer foresight ring of the entrepreneurial eye model (see figure 6.1, overleaf).

Essentially there are three lenses focused on you as an entrepreneur and three focused on your business. One of the mistakes entrepreneurs make is that they assess decisions about their business in isolation, asking,

'Which option is best for the business?', when in fact they should be assessing choices based on their own skills and needs, as well as what the business needs.

Figure 6.1: the six lenses of clarity in the entrepreneurial eye

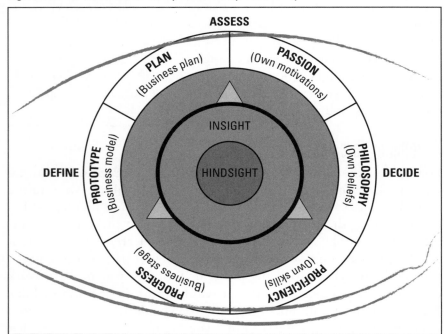

First, they should be considering themselves: 'Which option will keep me motivated, match my beliefs and values and play to my unique skills?' And this is exactly what the first three lenses cover—providing foresight around the following:

- *Your own motivations.* This involves figuring out why you are in business and what you want to get out of it. You need to start assessing choices that help you get to your endgame faster. For example, a decision to bring in an investor would clearly need to include the foresight of when and for how much you want to exit your business. This is the passion lens.

- *Your own beliefs.* Focus on your unique set of personal values and how these can come out through brand and culture in your business. You need to assess choices that are on brand and aligned to your values, and build the type of business that resonates with you. One example could be a decision to use cheap labour in poor conditions, which might not fit with the values you hold. This is the philosophy lens.

- *Your own skills.* Life's too short to be doing what you don't enjoy or aren't good at. You need to start assessing choices that play to your strengths and create a role that you love. As an example, a decision to do a high-profile launch around the country would not be a great idea if you weren't good at presenting. This is the proficiency lens.

Having foresight around these three lenses will help you assess decisions based on whether the options match what will be right for you individually.

Next we need to consider decisions that will be right for the business: 'Which options will get us to the next stage, help build our business model and adhere to our plan?' These are the questions covered in the final three lenses, which provide foresight around the following:

- *Business stage.* Most successful businesses tend to follow a well-trodden path from start-up to exit. You need to start assessing decisions differently depending on what stage your business is at, and there are critical success factors involved in moving to each new level toward the ultimate vision. An example might be choosing to expand internationally before you have proven your formula, which could have disastrous results. This is the progress lens.

- *Business model.* Too many businesses remain in mediocrity because they don't optimise a well-considered and profitable business formula or model. You need to assess decisions that will help you develop and then replicate this formula. As an example, a decision that gives you the opportunity to experiment with two different scenarios may be worth pursuing so you can develop your ideal business model. This is the prototype lens.

- *Business plan.* A shortcoming of many entrepreneurs is their inability to stick to a plan. You need to start assessing decisions based on adhering to your pre-agreed priorities. As an example, a decision to take advantage of a new business avenue that would distract you from your core priorities may not be such a good idea. This is the plan lens.

Having foresight around these three lenses will help you assess decisions based on their likelihood to help your business grow. Combined with the three individual lenses you will be ensuring your business is growing in a direction aligned to what you want as an entrepreneur.

In part III we will discuss how to develop foresight around each of these six lenses in more detail.

Developing insight skills

Insight is the ability to use all of the information you have at hand to make decisions in the present. Think of insight as what your new set of glasses allows you to actually see both up close and in the distance — it's all about focus. Insight will enable you to focus on the most important problems and opportunities and send the crucial data to your brain, which then helps you make sense of what you are seeing and what you plan to do about it. To help train your entrepreneurial eye to have insight the entrepreneur needs to develop a decision-making methodology that they can rely on to help them make faster, better informed decisions without the anxiety.

> Insight is the ability to use all of the information you have at hand to make decisions in the present.

The four business principles for developing insight

My insight methodology is called the perpetual growth principles (PGP), and is made up of four principles:

- reduce frictions
- foster actuators
- minimise mass
- maximise balance.

The PGP are located in the middle insight ring of the entrepreneurial eye model (see figure 6.2).

Reduce frictions

Business success is about having the time, money, knowledge and momentum to grow your business. It is the shortage of these core elements that cause eight business frictions that slow your business down. These business frictions, such as lack of funding and lack of support, will be discussed in more detail in chapter 16. If you can identify the friction then you can make decisions by assessing whether the decision is likely to fix the friction, or at least not make it worse. For instance, if your biggest friction is a lack of funding, a decision to take on a new client who pays in arrears might be disastrous and even send you broke. Overcoming business frictions will ensure that your business can grow unhindered. The frictions form the bulk of the middle insight ring of the entrepreneurial eye model because they give entrepreneurs the biggest insight when assessing the best options.

Figure 6.2: the perpetual growth principles in the entrepreneurial eye

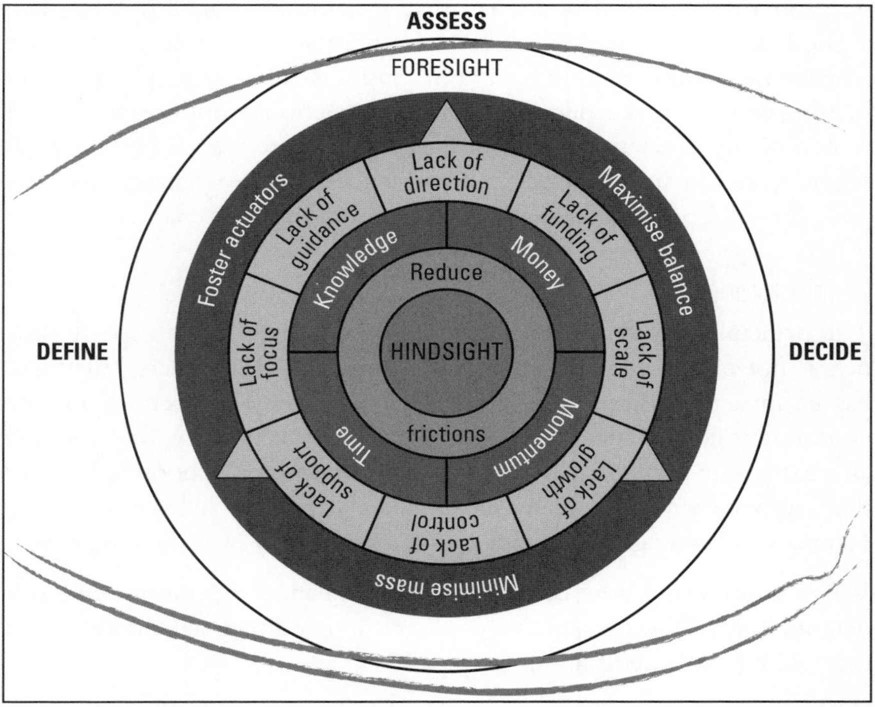

Foster actuators

The opposite of a friction is an actuator. Instead of holding you back, actuators can propel your business forward (they will be discussed in detail in chapter 17). The eight actuators include things like simplicity, empowerment, innovation and replication. Once recognised, these positive forces can be sought out when you are assessing the best decision options. For instance, a decision to sign a five-year office lease won't allow you flexibility, which is one of the powerful actuators needed for you to grow quickly, despite this creating a lack of predictability in your business. If an option has the potential to harness more of the actuators than an alternative course of action, it will have more chance of propelling your business forward.

Minimise mass

Contrary to popular belief, more is not necessarily better. So many entrepreneurs have too many expenses, too many products, too many staff, too many target markets and too many locations. For instance, a decision to develop your own software in-house might not be such a good decision, as it will increase the number of people needed and management time required in your business. This principle is about helping you to make decisions where you choose options that don't unnecessarily overburden your business with more mass. The four areas where you can inadvertently take on excess mass — people, products, purchases and processes — will be discussed in detail in chapter 18.

Maximise balance

This principle is about the recognition that a business is not a silo. A business is not only a network of important internal stakeholders, but it also has an impact on indirect stakeholders, such as family, competitors and the community. For instance, a decision to put up your prices without adding any extra value may harm your client relationships. Choosing options that are win–win for as many stakeholders as possible helps ensure your company not only grows quickly but also sustainably over the long term.

When considering how best to maximise balance you must view your decisions from the perspective of direct and indirect stakeholders, and this will be explained fully in chapter 19.

By considering options using the PGP — four universal business perspectives — you will bring a level of insight to your choices like never before. Part IV discusses in detail how you can develop your insight to quickly and easily make decisions using this proven formula.

Developing hindsight skills

Hindsight is the ability to reflect on your decisions from the past to learn and grow for future decision making. Think of hindsight as making sense of what you have seen and done before — hindsight is all about perspective. To help train your entrepreneurial eye to have hindsight you need to build a decision bank or databank of decisions made, and their consequences. That way you can actively and consciously learn from the past: what went well and what could have been improved with hindsight or perspective.

To train your entrepreneurial eye on hindsight there is a regular process to follow — a process which involves the development and interrogation of a decision bank. As you can see in figure 6.3, the decision bank is located at the centre of the entrepreneurial eye model.

Figure 6.3: the decision bank in the entrepreneurial eye

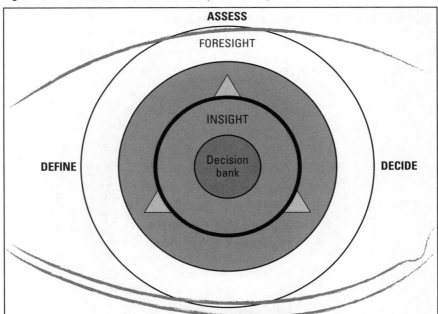

A decision bank is essentially a database (manual or electronic) that stores your past decisions in a way that will help your future decision making. Too many entrepreneurs don't reflect on the decisions they have made to work out whether they were successful or not. As a result they can't then reflect on the lessons of that decision, take them forward and apply the learning to future decision making. For example, one of the decisions we included in our decision bank was around hiring staff: wherever possible, we would hire them on a casual basis before taking them on permanently. When we adhered to this learning we got more motivated, more productive employees who enjoyed and fitted into our culture. Assessing decisions using foresight and insight is useless if you don't also develop and reflect on your hindsight.

In part V we discuss in more detail how you can capitalise on the power of hindsight in your decision making.

Decisionship is a proven process for decision evaluation, and the entrepreneurial eye model provides a visual reminder of all the sights or perspectives you must consider during that process. Figure 6.4 shows the full entrepreneurial eye model, indicating the elements contained within each sight.

Figure 6.4: the complete model of the entrepreneurial eye

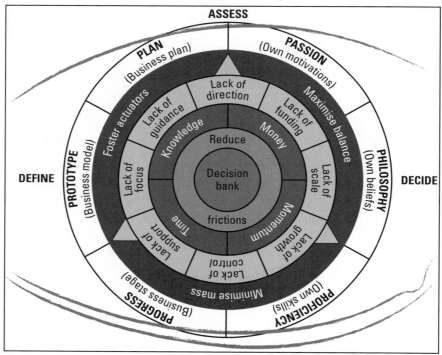

Once you have thoroughly assessed the options you need to make a decision on, you need to follow through. The next chapter will explain how best to do this.

Key points

» Never enter the assess stage without adequate and thorough definition of the options. A well-defined affirmative question with two options will make all the difference in the assess step.

» During the assess stage your decision-making personality type can cause damage. You must be neither too fast nor too slow, neither too informed nor too ignorant, and neither anxious nor flippant.

» Decisionship creates a framework for pre-thinking, and a quick and easy assessment methodology to compare choices.

» The three elements or sights to consider during the assess stage are foresight, insight and hindsight. They work together so you can harness both parts of your conscious and unconscious brains.

» Foresight is the ability to predict what might happen, or what you want to happen, in the future.

» Foresight focuses on the six lenses of clarity: the passion, philosophy, proficiency, progress, prototype and plan lenses, which are located in the outer foresight ring of the entrepreneurial eye model.

» Insight is the ability to use all of the information you have at hand to make decisions in the present.

» The insight methodology is called the perpetual growth principles (PGP), made up of four principles: reduce frictions, foster actuators, minimise mass and maximise balance. They sit in the middle insight ring of the entrepreneurial eye model.

» Hindsight is the ability to reflect on your decisions from the past to learn and grow for future decision making—making sense of what you have seen and done before.

» To train your entrepreneurial eye on hindsight you need to develop and interrogate a decision bank, which is located at the centre of the entrepreneurial eye model.

» Decisionship is a proven process for decision evaluation, and the entrepreneurial eye provides a visual reminder of all the sights or perspectives you must consider during that process.

Chapter 7

Step 3 of decisionship—decide

Entrepreneurs are notoriously good starters. They have loads of great ideas and are excited and energised at the start of a project or venture, only to lose interest as the business idea flourishes past the interesting phase. As a consequence, they are often great starters and lousy finishers.

To counter this tendency, the third and final step of the decisionship process is decide, which includes all the vital components to ensure that your decisions are implemented, and not ignored, delayed or forgotten. Making a decision is one thing. Following through on that decision is quite another.

The word decide comes from the Latin word *decidere*, which means 'to cut off from'. The idea is that when you make a decision you cut off from any other outcome or option. And yet, as we all know, very few people have the natural ability to consistently follow through on all their decisions. Most of us make decisions all the time that we either forget or have no real intention of following through on—either consciously or subconsciously. In reality it is amazing how many entrepreneurs make decisions but never action them or see them through to fruition.

This tendency to procrastinate on decisions has been discussed by many renowned philosophers and psychologists. Back in 1953 Dr Sigmund Freud, neurologist and founder of psychoanalysis, developed a theory of how anxiety creates a mental response in our brains that leads to procrastination—further reinforcement that if you can develop an ability to make faster, better informed decisions without the anxiety you are more likely to succeed in business.

I'm sure there are hundreds of other reasons and theories about why people procrastinate, but for me the reasons are not important. What is important is to understand that making the decision is the beginning, not the end. You need to have a process for taking the decision and bringing it to life, otherwise the chances of it being actioned are radically reduced—regardless of who you are and how committed you are to the decision. Life has a habit of getting in the way of even the most committed individuals.

A decision without action is as useless as procrastinating about the decision in the first place. Any decision will come alive only once it's put into practice. And it is this actioning process that separates the successful entrepreneurs from the rest. There is nothing to be gained from making loads of decisions only to do nothing with those decisions. The decide step is therefore more than just about highlighting the best option and committing to a particular course of action: it's about putting in place a protocol to ensure your decisions are effectively actioned.

The entrepreneur's curse

Before we go through this protocol I want to introduce a concept I call the entrepreneur's curse—a common yet little-known malady I initially recognised in myself, before I realised it affects nearly every entrepreneur on the planet. When I am making a speech or presentation at a seminar or conference, I'm invariably introduced with the usual MC hype—'Our next speaker is a serial entrepreneur—Creel Price had eight businesses before he left school and at the age of 25 co-founded Blueprint Management Group with $5000, which had 10 businesses in 10 years and was eventually sold for $109 million. He is also a high-octane adventurer who captained Australia in the World Elephant Polo championships ... blah blah blah.' You get the picture. And while this overt promotion is necessary to build audience expectation and attention, it makes me extremely uncomfortable.

This discomfort and embarrassment occurs partly because I feel far more qualified to teach because of my failures rather than my successes, and partly because when I walk on stage there is a moment of silence when I'm convinced that at least half the audience is thinking, 'If this guy is so successful at business, why is it that I've never heard of him?' And if I'm right and that's what people are thinking, then it's a pretty fair point. For me the reason I'm thankfully not a household name is because I am an entrepreneur, not a businessperson. The type of people we know as business success stories are those individuals who are completely synonymous with their core business—think Bill Gates of Microsoft, Steve Jobs of Apple or Mark Zuckerberg of Facebook. They love their businesses so much that they often spend decades building their business and becoming embedded in the brand. An entrepreneur, on the other hand, is in love with the game of business, not necessarily any one business. They are a businesses person — plural. They spend their time building, growing and often exiting multiple businesses. It is this distinction that is the cause of the entrepreneur's curse and why I had so many businesses.

The entrepreneur's curse is our inability to focus on any one thing for very long. My 10 businesses in 10 years sounds impressive until you realise that we probably would have been a lot more successful a lot more quickly if we had focused on one business to make it successful before moving on to other opportunities. The entrepreneur's curse affects people in all walks of life, regardless of whether they are in business

> The entrepreneur's curse is [their] inability to focus on any one thing for very long.

for themselves or not. Those of us who have the curse are always coming up with brand new, incredibly important, life-changing projects that make everything else — including working on last month's 'incredibly important, life-changing project' — feel as inspiring as sorting through your sock drawer. Sound familiar? We are like the Border Collies of the business world — always falling in love with every opportunity, rounding everyone up around the new thing, giving it 100 per cent of our enthusiasm, only to lose interest just as quickly and move onto the next thing that takes our fancy.

On the positive side the entrepreneur's curse has our minds on the lookout for business opportunities. For instance, if I'm standing at a ferry terminal, instead of reading the paper or maybe doing some people-watching like everyone else, I will be thinking, 'Wow there's 40 people lined up here, and they've got to wait maybe half an hour or an hour to get into the city before they can get their coffee. If there was a coffee cart you could make an absolute fortune'. I would then do the mental arithmetic of how much revenue you could expect, despite having little intention of launching my entrepreneurial idea. In short, those of us who have the entrepreneur's curse have over-active minds, obsessed with creating business opportunities where others don't see them.

If you don't learn to curb this enthusiasm for entrepreneurial distraction you will never implement your decisions and realise the full potential of your ideas. You need great ideas, but you also need perseverance — even more so, you need to stick with the idea that you are already working on, despite its taking longer to be successful than you thought and despite your gradually fading enthusiasm. The best way to succeed at anything is to give it your undivided focus and attention.

The dangers of always looking elsewhere for the next big thing is demonstrated by a story I once heard about a greedy dog. Imagine a hungry dog foraging through the forest for food. After some time it finds a pretty decent-sized bone and, thinking all of its Christmases have come at once, with much anticipation it takes the bone down to the lake to eat it. Yet as the dog gets to the lake it notices in the mirrored surface what appears to be a bigger bone shining back at him. Mistaking the reflection for a better meal the greedy dog drops his bone and grabs at the reflection, only for both to disappear out of reach. The dog goes home hungry.

The same is true in business. If you don't appreciate what you have and focus on that until it's successful before getting distracted with other ideas in business, you're probably never going to achieve what you want and you too will go home hungry. Being conscious of the entrepreneur's curse and when it is having a detrimental effect on your business is often the key to ensuring your decisions are actioned. And actioning each decision is the key to building a great business that can eventually be sold. Then and only then do you start another business or pursue another opportunity, thus satisfying your entrepreneurial hunger.

The components of the decide step

The best way to overcome the entrepreneur's curse is through the last step in the decisionship process — decide. Once you have adequately defined an affirmative question that identifies two possible choices and you have assessed both of these choices using your foresight, insight and hindsight, it is time to decide. It's time to convert thinking into action. It's time to execute the decision.

Five components need to be in place to ensure successful execution:

- clarification — firming up the decision and communicating it
- commitment — fleshing out an implementation plan with time commitments

- reason — reminding yourself about why you made the decision
- objective — considering what success will look like
- next steps — identifying what to action immediately.

Seeking clarification

The first step is to firm up the decision. Proactively writing down a decision serves to remove it from the decision-to-make list that clutters your brain and can cause a lot of anxiety — essentially more bricks. It will also mean you aren't as likely to change your mind.

Start the clarification step by stating, 'I have decided to ...'. Being specific also serves to clarify the decision in your mind. So, for example, a decision to hire a salesperson might be framed as 'I have decided to hire a salesperson on $50 000 plus commission'.

Once you have made the decision you need to tell all the relevant people. Often a decision can be changed up until the point when you share it with someone — it is at this point that you have really decided. So whom do you tell? If you have been smart about the decision-making process you will have involved key people in that process from the start or delegated decisions to people who are best placed to make them, so the communication channels should already be open.

No-one likes having decisions made about them or decisions made that affect them without their input or involvement. This is just common sense and common courtesy. If you want people to buy into the decision and support it, then you need to include the people most affected in that choice. Even if the inclusion is somewhat superficial and you will ultimately have to make the choice regardless of their input, involving them in information gathering or making them aware of the challenge will not only smooth that process but it may also throw up some possible solutions that you never thought of.

Consider creating a communication plan so that everyone affected by the decision is informed. Obviously the nature of the decision will affect how you communicate it. If, for example, your decision involves changing someone's role then that deserves a face-to-face conversation so the person affected can ask questions and express their opinion about the move. If, on the other hand, you have decided to change your telephone provider, it may be appropriate to simply send out a company-wide email.

Finding the right way to communicate to the right people is a crucial part of success and buy-in. It is also wise to try to match the communication style with the person you are dealing with. Some people prefer hearing news in a team setting; others prefer email, face to face or a phone call. Your job is to communicate the decisions you have made in a way that will best be heard, and also matches the weight and gravity of the decision being made. It would be completely inappropriate, for instance, to fire someone by text.

Making commitments

Every decision needs to be actioned to make it come alive, and that actioning process needs an implementation plan that has clear timeframe commitments. Clearly not all decisions need an implementation plan as they can be easily actioned and resolved; for the rest, working out the how to is a crucial part of the process.

If, for example, you have decided to hire a receptionist then you need to decide how much that person will be paid, be clear about what that person will do and what their responsibilities will be, and decide how you are going to recruit that person. Do you plan to use a recruitment agency, for example, or are you going to advertise or put a call out to your network for the sort of person you are seeking. You need to interview the prospective candidates and you need to know specifically what skills and abilities you require, and which would be a bonus. You need to know what you will not compromise on, and you need to allocate a trial period and prepare an employment contract if necessary. And finally you need to think about what the key performance indicators for the role will be.

For every decision you make, you need to ask yourself how you are going to make this happen. What do you or someone else need to do in order to bring this decision to fruition.

Napoleon Hill, author of the famous book *Think and Grow Rich*, said that goals are just dreams with deadlines. It follows therefore that without the deadline, goals will evaporate into dreams. Daydreaming may be a nice way to spend a Saturday afternoon on the beach, but it won't get you any closer to your goals unless you make some time commitments.

Once you have made your decision and told the relevant people in the relevant way and worked out the nuts and bolts of what is required to action that decision, you have to commit to a timeline. When are you going to follow through on this decision? It is important to draw a line in the sand and commit to a date, otherwise the decision will just be put aside and never achieved.

Using reason

Decisions that have a strong 'why' involved are far easier to implement than those that do not. In fact the why should be easier, because essentially it will answer the affirmative question you developed in the define step. For instance if the affirmative question you came up with was 'Should we launch a new website for $10 000 or spend the money on a direct marketing campaign to increase sales and fix our cash-flow problems?' the why will no doubt be something like, 'Spending this money will bring in more sales which will improve our cash flow', but could include other personal elements, such as 'so I can sleep at night'; 'so I can pay myself an adequate wage'; or 'so I can have enough breathing space to have a holiday to Fiji'. The more personal you make the why, the more likely it is that you will follow through on the implementation plan in the timeframes you commit to.

You may have heard the theory of towards and away from motivations when goal setting. It is the proverbial carrot-and-stick approach to leadership and child-rearing techniques. Essentially, a towards (carrot) motivation is where you are motivated toward achieving something, such as 'If I lose weight and fit into this dress I will look great in the wedding photographs', or 'If you pass your exam I will buy you a bike'. Similarly, away (stick) motivation is where you are motivated away from something. For example, 'If I lose weight I won't die young due to heart disease'; or 'If you don't pass your exam you will be grounded for a week'. Both are very different motivators. Generally, individuals tend to be more compelled to action either by towards *or* away from motivation—if you aren't sure which you are try developing a reason that includes both toward and away from motivations.

If you are struggling to think of why you are doing a certain thing or making a certain choice then maybe it's not the right choice. If you don't have a big enough reason to follow through then you may just need to forget it. If it's a hard decision and you are just avoiding it then it's essential that you reconnect to why you need to make this choice and allow that motivation to drive you forward.

The clearer you are on why you are doing what you are doing—even when it's tough—the easier it will be to do what needs to be done. Focus on the benefits of the decision. Think about what it will cost you if you don't follow through on the decisions. What will you lose or miss out on? What negative consequence will occur? Just connect to the reason for your decision and get on with the job—no matter how hard.

American psychotherapist and psychologist Albert Ellis reminds us of something very important too:

> Some of us walk around all day long getting on our own cases: 'I've got to do this. I've got to do that. I should have said this to that person. I need to be more that. I ought to be more organised. I should be more attractive, intelligent, witty, popular and personable. I ought to be more assertive. I need to be less aggressive. I've got to speak up more. I really need to keep my mouth shut'... Some of us 'should on ourselves' all day long!

Ellis even refers to this type of unhelpful language as 'musterbation' and believes that it creates an internal prison for us. So forget about what you *should* do. Stop *shoulding* on yourself and either do it or don't do it. There is no middle ground.

Setting objectives

As entrepreneurs we spend so much time making decisions yet spend very little time considering what success looks like and keeping ourselves accountable to that objective. By documenting our success objectives for each decision we will not only achieve our goals more often but we will also become better decision makers in the future. Because of the way the brain works, we are far more likely to achieve documented objectives than fluffy ones floating around in our heads.

Giving our brains direct and measurable instructions will wire our conscious and unconscious minds to keep working on the objective, even when we are asleep. The other important benefit of getting a clear objective is that it helps with hindsight for future decisions. It's important to close the loop on your decision making by considering how you might know if you have made the right decision. Is it because of the impact on revenue or profit; is it the vibe or feeling you would rather have; is it hitting a key milestone; is it hitting break even for that particular purchase decision; or is it about making time so you can do something that's going to add a lot more value to your business.

Once you have documented what success might look like, you need to confirm a review date in the future so you can find out whether that success that you envisioned came about or not. Put the date in your calendar to remind yourself to review the decision.

Taking the next steps

As soon as you have made a decision maintain the momentum by defining what the first next step is. If possible do that first next step immediately or within the first 24 hours so the decision maintains momentum.

If your decision is to hire a receptionist, for example, the very first thing you can do is gather information online about what they should be paid. You could do that immediately. You could also start putting together a detailed description of what you need that person to do. Again, you could complete those tasks within the first 24 hours of making that decision, and breathe life and purpose into the choice. Once you have made those initial next steps, the next best step will become apparent and the task of appointing a receptionist will move forward.

If you decide to use a recruitment agency, for example, that choice will take you in a different but logical direction and illuminate what has to happen next. Your next steps will be to negotiate to find the three best recruitment agencies and then commit to getting a brief out to them by the end of next week. You will also need to put some time aside in your diary to interview the candidates, and communicate the plan to the rest of the team.

You must turn your decisions into actions, otherwise all the effort has been for nothing. Making good decisions requires a consistent process of define, assess and decide. Each is crucial to effective decision making and improves with practices, and each is made easier when you gain a heightened awareness of what you are trying to achieve, both personally and professionally. Although it may sound obvious, as an entrepreneur it's very easy to lose sight of why you started the business in the first place. Foresight, which we will explore in the next chapter, seeks to make your aspirations and motivations crystal clear so you can consciously align your decisions to your hopes and dreams.

Key points

» Entrepreneurs are notoriously good starters, who have loads of great ideas, and are excited and energised at the start of a project or venture. But they lose interest as the business idea flourishes past the interesting phase, so they are often great starters and lousy finishers.

» To counter this tendency, the third and final step of the decisionship process is decide, which includes all the vital components to ensure your decisions are implemented, and not ignored, delayed or forgotten.

» The decide step puts in place a protocol to ensure your decisions are effectively actioned.

» The entrepreneur's curse is the inability to focus on any one thing for very long. If you don't learn to curb your enthusiasm for entrepreneurial distraction you will never implement your decisions or realise the full potential of your ideas.

» Five components need to be in place to ensure successful execution— clarification, commitment, reason, objective, and next steps.

» You must turn your decisions into actions, otherwise all the effort has been for nothing. Making good decisions requires a consistent process of define, assess and decide.

Part III

How to use foresight to build a solid decision-making foundation

Business, more than any other occupation, is a continual dealing with the future; it is a continual calculation, an instinctive exercise in foresight.

Henry R. Luce, influential US publisher

Part III

How to use foresight to build a solid decision-making foundation

Chapter 8

The six lenses of clarity

As discussed in chapter 6 there are three skills or 'sights' that you can develop to allow you to make faster, better informed decisions without anxiety: foresight, insight and hindsight. Part III is concerned with foresight—the ability to predict what might happen, or what you want to happen, in the future. You can receive a massive return on investment from a small amount of time invested into generating foresight for future decisions.

I received an early lesson on the importance of pre-prepared clarity when I was in the market for my first house. Rather than thinking about any specific strategy for choosing my home, I figured I would know it when I saw it. Yet 50 house inspections later, in a wide range of suburbs and over the course of 18 months, I was fed up spending my weekends looking at houses. Somehow every one of the houses I had looked at didn't quite suit my needs—even though I really wasn't that conscious of what those needs were. Meanwhile, the booming Sydney property market had risen by 30 per cent since I had started looking, so my budget kept going up whereas the quality I could get for my money was going down.

I complained to a friend of my dilemma and she recommended that I get really clear on what I wanted. Not just clarity on how many bedrooms and in which suburb—she meant what potential streets, what aspect, the state of repair, number of garages, specific character traits, setting and what it felt like walking in. Taking her advice I sat down and within a couple of hours had a very specific list of what I wanted. Sure enough the very next weekend I was out looking and stumbled on a house that was minutes away from being auctioned. As the auction got under way I walked through and realised it ticked every one of my boxes except one! It was almost spooky! I made a fast decision and found myself the owner of the house 10 minutes later. And it was a decision I never regretted for a moment—I loved that home.

Similarly, to develop the art of foresight using your entrepreneurial eye you need to create a platform of reference points that will help you make decisions in the future. I was able to buy my new home quickly without the anxiety because I had a list of reference points about exactly what I wanted. So when the opportunity presented itself I was confident and ready.

Spending a day once a year to get clear about the six lenses, and then a couple of hours each quarter updating them, will save you countless hours. If I had had my list of requirements and house reference points earlier I wouldn't have wasted 18 months looking for a home. I would have been able to immediately discount the vast majority of the houses I viewed in that time simply on the basis of their location and the details available online.

When you have defined your lenses of clarity you will save thousands of hours a year because you will be able to say 'no' immediately when a new business avenue doesn't fit your business model. You will be able to give a quick 'yes' to expenditure decisions that are in line with your priorities. You will be able to make fast recruitment decisions when you become clear on what sort of company you want to be, and you will be able to provide fast, easy briefs to creative teams on your brand identity. You will also know which opportunities to pursue and when it is the right time to engage potential investors or purchasers.

Developing foresight

Pre-thinking who you want to be in business and what you want your business to be like allows you to create reference points that you can then compare all future decisions to. The six lenses of clarity make up your foresight decision-making platform (see figure 6.1 on p. 70) and they act like the lens combinations in the optometrist's eye-testing machine. They will allow you to increase the depth and detail of your entrepreneurial vision until finally you see the future ahead of you with 20/20 clarity.

> The six lenses of clarity make up your foresight decision-making platform and they act like the lens combinations in the optometrist's eye-testing machine.

Used individually, the lenses allow you to look at the future in an entirely different way, and when used together they create a whole new multi-faceted view of your entrepreneurial world. The six lenses are:

- *Passion lens*—focused on *your* motivations. It's important to know why you're in business and what *you* want to get out of it.
- *Philosophy lens*—focused on *your* beliefs. It's important that your business has a strong culture and brand that is aligned to *your* values.
- *Proficiency lens*—focused on *your* skills. It's important that you play to *your* strengths and understand how to overcome *your* weaknesses.
- *Progress lens*—focused on the *business stage*. It's important to know what stage a business is in so you can vary your approach accordingly.
- *Prototype lens*—focused on the *business model*. It's important to have a formula for the business that will help you produce and sell products and services that are financially viable and scalable.
- *Plan lens*—focused on the *business plan*. It's important that you follow a strategy and plan with a set of clearly defined priorities to keep the business on track.

You may remember that the lenses of clarity are split into those that relate to the entrepreneur and those that relate to the business (see table 8.1).

Table 8.1: entrepreneur-focused and business-focused lenses of clarity

Entrepreneur			Business		
1	**Passion lens**	Own motivations	4	**Progress lens**	Business stage
2	**Philosophy lens**	Own beliefs	5	**Prototype lens**	Business model
3	**Proficiency lens**	Own skills	6	**Plan lens**	Business plan

Business theory can often be dry and complex, and for the time-poor entrepreneur theory just isn't that practical. I have tried to use simple concepts that are easy to grasp and, perhaps more importantly, remember, and can be immediately applied to your business.

One of my favourite business writers is organisational theorist Charles Handy. In his ground-breaking book *Age of Unreason* he talks about teaching MBA students at the London Business School. Rather than bore them with stories or tell them theory in the classroom he chose instead to take them on excursions. Yet rather than visit the types of businesses they were trying to understand, he gave them a completely different perspective by taking the students on excursions that were far removed from business. He would have the group visit the emergency wards in hospitals, where they would study systemisation, or take them off to a basketball game, where they went to discover insights into leadership and branding. The concepts that were at the heart of the lesson were far easier to distinguish when presented in this way.

Likewise, entrepreneurs who come through my training programs often learn more from working with a fellow entrepreneur in an entirely different industry, company type or business size, than from working with a competitor in their own space that they can emulate. Internet businesses have learnt about colour coding logistics from recycling businesses; recruitment firms have learnt about inventory management from consumable companies; and large financial services businesses have learnt the power of hot-desking from a one-man-band consultant.

Like Handy's metaphoric training philosophy, I use metaphor and principles from non-related fields to help understanding, recall and usability of decisionship.

Each of the six lenses of clarity has its own mindset, personality trait and key outcome:

- *Mindset*—the stereotypical role taken from a number of well-known occupations. The mindset uses the metaphor of the profession to bring business learning outcomes alive. For example, the prototype lens is all about the business model, and we use the master chef mindset to demonstrate that a business model is similar to creating a successful recipe.

- *Personality trait*—the summary of how each of the different mindsets acts, or the key skills they bring to the table. The key trait helps the entrepreneur act in a certain way in a certain situation. Using the prototype lens as an example again—the experimenter key trait helps the entrepreneur recognise that the best chefs and entrepreneurs are ones that innovate and trial different ingredient combinations and methods in order to create their unique recipe or business model, knowing that some *will* fail.

- *Key outcome*—the one critical element to work on and be aware of above all others. The key outcome quantifies and qualifies something that the entrepreneur can focus on to achieve or live up to. For instance, in the prototype lens the key outcome is the magic metric which is all about discovering the one figure to measure and analyse that will ultimately have the biggest impact on the success of your business.

See table 8.2 for a full list of the lenses with their associated mindset, personality traits and key outcomes.

Table 8.2: the mindsets, personality traits and key outcomes of the six lenses

Lens	Mindset	Personality trait	Key outcome
Passion lens	Sailor	Inspirer	Endgame
Philosophy lens	Gardener	Caretaker	Values
Proficiency lens	Movie producer	Manager	Role
Progress lens	Mountaineer	Go-getter	Vision
Prototype lens	Master chef	Experimenter	Magic metric
Plan lens	Architect	Coordinator	Priorities

These six lenses effectively force you to clarify various aspects of your business that will, by default, facilitate better decision making. To bring all of the lenses alive I recently ran a business bootcamp on the decisionship methodology for 16 entrepreneurs from Richard Branson's Centre for Entrepreneurship in South Africa. To ensure that the theory translated to actual business lessons, given many hadn't had the good fortune of a solid education, I decided to experiment with teaching the six lenses of foresight through a series of fun outdoor competitions.

> These six lenses effectively force you to clarify various aspects of your business that will, by default, facilitate better decision making.

We headed to a game park about three hours north of Johannesburg and spent the most amazing five days there. Many of these inner-city entrepreneurs had never been to a game park or seen the wildlife of Africa. Add to this the adrenalin-fuelled competition and a willingness to learn, and it was always going to be a break-through experience. We had cooking challenges to demonstrate the master chef mindset; building competitions to demonstrate the architect mindset; treasure hunts for the passion lens; theatre productions for the movie producer mindset;

botanical painting challenges for the gardener mindset; orienteering challenges to demonstrate the sailor mindset; and climbed a mountain for the mountaineer mindset of the progress lens—although that didn't go according to plan, as I will explain in chapter 12. The next six chapters cover each of these lenses in detail, starting with the three lenses that apply to you as an entrepreneur—passion, philosophy and proficiency. These lenses will give you clarity on why you're in business, how you want to play the game of business and what role you are going to perform, based on your relative strengths and weaknesses. As the business grows, however, these perspectives expand to explore the motivations, skills and beliefs of other stakeholders in the business.

The chapters on the progress, prototype and plan lenses explore the business stages, business model and business plan respectively. And these lenses will give you clarity on what stage your business has currently reached, what you want to achieve, what you want your business to look like and how you are going to get there.

Key points

» Foresight is the ability to predict what might happen, or what you want to happen, in the future. You can receive a massive return on investment from a small amount of time invested in generating foresight for future decisions.

» Pre-thinking who you want to be in business and what you want your business to be like allows you to create reference points that you can then compare all future decisions with.

» The six lenses of clarity make up your foresight decision-making platform and they act like the lens combinations in the optometrist's eye-testing machine. They will allow you to increase the depth and detail of your entrepreneurial vision until finally you see the future ahead of you with 20/20 clarity.

» The six lenses are the passions lens (motivation), the philosophy lens (beliefs), the proficiency lens (skills), the progress lens (business stage), the prototype lens (business model) and the plan lens (business plan).

» The passion, philosophy and proficiency lenses are about you as an individual.

» The progress, prototype and plan lenses are focused on your business.

» Used individually, the lenses allow you to look at the future in an entirely different way, and when used together they create a whole new multi-faceted view of your entrepreneurial world.

» Each of the six lenses has its own mindset, personality trait and key outcome.

» The mindset uses the metaphor of well-known professions to bring business learning outcomes alive.

» The personality trait is the summary of how the different mindsets act, and the key skills they have.

» The key outcome is the critical element that the entrepreneur can focus on to achieve or live up to.

» These six lenses force you to clarify various aspects of your business that will, by default, facilitate better decision making.

Chapter 9

The passion lens

The first lens in training your entrepreneurial eye on foresight is the passion lens. As the name suggests, this lens is all about focusing your attention on what you are passionate about to ensure you remain motivated—either working in your passions or moving towards your passions in some way. The passion lens, therefore, is all about becoming clear on your *own motivations* for being in business in the first place.

Too many people start in business and they don't really know why. All too often the decision to get into business was driven not by a goal they wanted to achieve but a situation they wished to avoid or move away from. Going into business because you hated your boss or were sick of being told what to do by others or because you were made redundant and didn't have any other option are all valid reasons for going into business, but they will not drive you forward after the initial start up. You need something more.

> The passion lens is all about becoming clear on your *own motivations* for being in business in the first place.

Until you have a goal that is driving you toward an outcome then you are just treading water in your business. Whatever your motivations were for starting the business, you need to reassess those motivations and find a big enough reason to continue and move forward. You need to find your passion if your business is ever going to take off.

The problem is that most business owners don't know or have forgotten why they went into business in the first place. In addition, their vocation is outside of the business, or perhaps they realise that it's the game of business they love, not their own business! If you don't love what you do then the passion and excitement soon melts away and the business that was going to liberate you to a life of freedom and fulfilment slowly becomes your jailer.

It's unrealistic to think that everyone is going to love what they do. It's also unrealistic to think that you are always going to be passionate about the business you are in. That's just not possible, but when you know what inspires you, you can weather the tough times more easily and use that passion to direct your efforts. For example, if you went into business because you thought the company you worked for wasn't delivering value for customers and you could do better that's fine, because it got you to take the first important step. But it won't motivate you forward. You need to reassess your business and think about what you want to achieve now. If you don't particularly love the business you are in but you can see that it could be a cash cow that could provide you with enough time and money to learn to train horses, which *is* your passion, then suddenly the way you feel about your business can change.

I never woke up one day and said, 'I am passionate about direct marketing and I want to dedicate my life to creating the greatest marketing company in the world'. Truth is, I'm not actually that passionate about direct marketing at all. But I am passionate about business; I loved the challenges that we encountered. I loved the thrill of chasing a new client and landing them. I loved the challenge of dramatically reducing the cost of sales for our clients. I loved thinking up novel ways to inspire the team. I was passionate about the fact that too many businesses ignore their existing customers in favour of finding new ones. That idea seemed crazy to me and I was passionate about changing that. You don't need to be passionate about every aspect of your business — you just need to find aspects of it that really excite you so you can enjoy the journey.

Concentration camp survivor Victor Frankle said, 'Those who have a "why" to live, can bear with almost any "how"'. If you can uncover your passion and use it to drive you forward then you will do what needs to be done and not become despondent and discouraged in the normal course of any business.

Life's too short not to be doing what you love doing, when you want to be doing it, with the people you love doing it with. For me, business is one of the most powerful ways to achieve this — to finally have the freedom to work in areas that fulfil you.

Mindset: sailor

When looking through the passion lens you must take on the mindset of a sailor. I love sailing but I only came to it by accident when I took a trip with some friends around the Greek islands in my early twenties. One of the things that really struck me about sailors was their passion for what they do. They clearly love being out on the water. Particularly those salty old sea dogs that practically live on the sea. You can't wipe the smile off their face, whether they are faced with a beautiful clear blue day or a huge swell, gale-force wind and a dirty black cloud on the horizon. There is nowhere they would rather be.

SAILOR

The other aspect of the sailor mindset that parallels an important aspect of the passion lens is that while sailors love what they do, they usually also have a purpose. They will have decided on a destination that they are going to sail to or they are competing in an event and need to navigate a certain course—whatever the objective there is always a goal and that's the other important point to the passion lens. Yet business and sailing are not just solo pursuits, so it is important to consider not just your own passion but also your crew's. The best sailors inspire their crew with a sense of fun and purpose. Likewise, as the captain of your business, whether you have staff or not, you need to motivate your stakeholders. The sailor is the perfect embodiment of the passion lens because he or she loves what they are doing; they make this passion infectious; and they always have an endgame or goal that drives them forward. When my business achieved a certain level of success one of my first personal purchases was in relation to my lifestyle. I bought a 41-foot cruising yacht so I could experience that carefree feeling of sailing around without a care in the world. While things were a bit rocky to begin with, given this is how I taught myself to sail, I have developed a lifelong passion for yachting.

Personality trait: inspirer

The personality trait for the passion lens is the inspirer, which should remind you to be the captain in charge of bringing out the passion in everyone associated with your business.

In 2010 I took a navigation course for my offshore skipper's license and got a good reminder about how many things can conspire to throw you off course in business. The primary tool for navigation on a yacht is the compass. When navigating from point A to B you need to take numerous factors into consideration to ensure you get where you want to go, safely and in the timeframe required. Of course, the wind, tides and swell also need to be accounted for. You need to consider your yacht's hull speed and the various obstructions that you have to navigate around. And if this isn't enough, you also have to take into account the deviation between true north (what your map says) and magnetic north (what your compass shows).

Similarly, if you don't know what you are in business for and why you are in that business then it's very easy to be thrown off course. The model in figure 9.1 shows the various components you can use to help you navigate what you want out of business.

Figure 9.1: how to get what you want out of your business

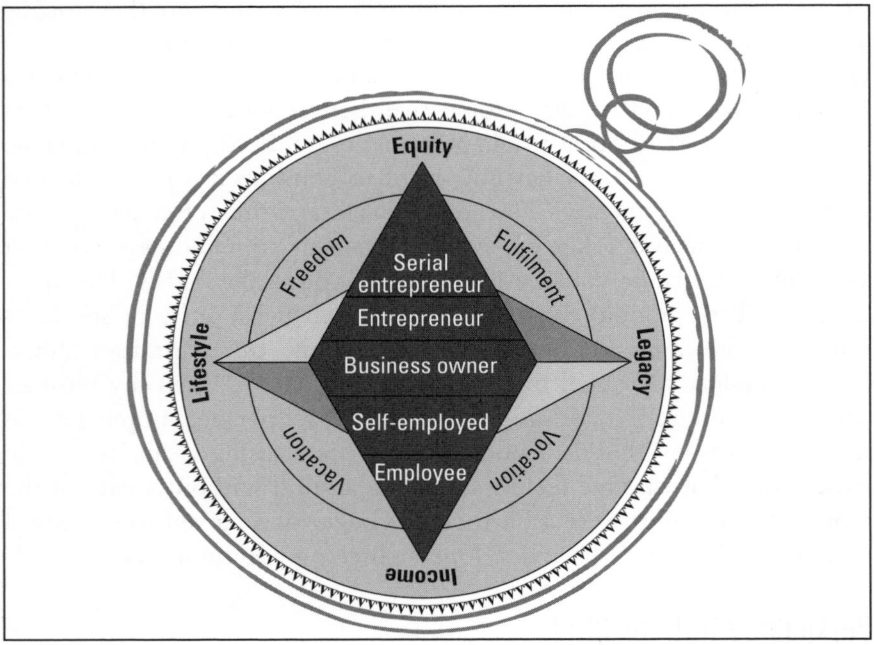

Why are you in business?

It is likely that you went into business to achieve some combination of freedom and fulfilment. You probably wanted to take control of your own life so that you could do what you love and perhaps create a legacy of some sort. You probably wanted more freedom to spend your time as you wanted, without needing permission from a higher power. You probably wanted to increase your income so you and your loved ones could enjoy a better, more relaxed lifestyle. And it's also likely that you wanted to create something that would provide for you into the future. Although the reality rarely lives up to expectation — especially in the early days — business does still offer an unprecedented opportunity for personal liberation.

I think it's fair to say that, for most people who venture out on their own, their primary focus is more freedom and more fulfilment. There are many different types of freedom and fulfilment and most people are driven by a combination of these motivators.

Freedom might include:

- financial freedom (I have financial options)
- time freedom (I do what I want, when I want)
- intellectual freedom (my views are my own)
- spiritual freedom (I am not owned).

Fulfilment might include:

- experiential fulfilment (what you love doing)
- creation fulfilment (what you are building)
- contribution fulfilment (who you are helping)
- relationship fulfilment (who you are doing it with).

Who do you want to be?

The first thing to consider is who you want to be in business. We can differentiate between five business-oriented roles: employee, self-employed, business owner, entrepreneur and serial entrepreneur. These roles differ according to the focus of the individual and can be compared to the various categories of sailor:

- *Employee* (crew). Someone who works for a business without an ownership interest; for example, a plumbing apprentice.
- *Self-employed* (catamaran skipper). Someone whose business is largely about selling their own time; for example, a plumber.

- *Business owner* (cruising yacht skipper). Someone who owns a business (often in a traditional industry) that employs staff whose efforts create value that can be sold to derive an income; for example, a plumbing supplies store.
- *Entrepreneur* (off-shore racing yacht skipper). Someone who owns a business (frequently offering an innovative product or service) with a goal to pay themselves a wage and to exit the business for an equity windfall; for example, an online plumbing supplies site.
- *Serial entrepreneur* (charter yacht CEO). Someone who loves playing the game of business and is always starting and exiting business for gain; for example, a group of online building sites.

The choice of role has an impact on the level of freedom and fulfilment that can be achieved. For instance, it can be much harder for an employee to achieve complete freedom if they have to work set hours, have defined holiday periods and answer to a boss or board. Whereas a successful serial entrepreneur rarely needs to answer to anyone and has the financial freedom to do exactly what they want. The freedom many employees and self-employed business people strive for is what you could best describe as a vacation. They work hard during the week so they can enjoy a stress-free weekend with their family, a well-earned holiday and long-service leave or a comfortable retirement.

Yet it is important to recognise that being an entrepreneur is not an easy or guaranteed route to freedom or fulfilment either. In fact there are just as many fulfilled and free employees as there are unfulfilled and trapped entrepreneurs. It all comes down to vocation — essentially your calling. You are working in your vocation when a day at work doesn't feel like a job and you are doing exactly what you would be doing even if you had all the choice and freedom in the world! For example, if you are obsessed with music then your vocation might be teaching kids piano. If you are completely happy when you are working with animals then your vocation could be in veterinary science. Or if you love working with computers and complex issues that stretch your brain then being a software programmer may just be your ideal vocation.

In his legendary book *The E-Myth*, Michael Gerber argues that the entrepreneurial myth is that people start a business to get freedom and fulfilment only for their business to take away all of their freedom. He tells a great story of a woman who makes incredible pies—something she is passionate about. Encouraged by her friends she quits her job and starts a pie-making business only to discover that due to its runaway success she ends up managing people to make pies rather than making pies herself. In other words she is doing HR, sales, marketing, finance and management, not her vocation of pie making. Essentially she has succumbed to the e-myth.

All of these issues are important because they will determine your endgame. A decision about whether you want equity or income, lifestyle or legacy will help to determine your endgame. The purpose of the passion lens is to gain clarity around what it is you are trying to achieve.

Key outcome: your endgame

Your endgame is what you want to get out of business. The purpose of the work you do and the value you add is to help you achieve your desired level of income and equity so that you can in turn enjoy your desired level of lifestyle and legacy.

First, consider what you would like your lifestyle to be like. What do you want to be doing every day? What time do you go to work on your vocation; how much time do you get to spend with your family; when, where and how often do you go on holidays; where do you live and what do you own? Write down a few things that you would really love to achieve as an ideal lifestyle now and into the future. This will change over time, but it will give you a target.

The next thing to consider is legacy. What is your purpose in life? What is it that you would like to create; whom do you want to influence; what would you like to see changed on the planet; and what will people remember you for? Write down some of the things that you will achieve through your business, in your spare time or after you sell your business.

You may want to step back from your business so you can pursue another dream, or you may want to float your company or leave a lasting legacy. You may want to continue in your business, and use the income to invest in real estate. You may want to franchise your business or leave it to charity. Your endgame is what you ultimately want to achieve from your business and what financial reward you are seeking for creating it in the first place. Consider the lifestyle it will afford you or the legacy that you intend to leave.

Alternatively, your legacy might be completely unrelated to business — it might all have to do with the amazing kids that you really want to raise and what sort of people they're going to be in the future and what sort of world you want to leave them.

Once you're clear on the lifestyle and legacy you want to achieve, the next thing to consider is what level of income you need in order to achieve that lifestyle. Consider how much you might need once all of your debts have been paid off and you are living your ideal life — how much would that cost? Once the level of income has been determined, you need to work out where you are going to get that income from. Is it going to be from doing a job; is it going to be working for yourself; or is it going to be from an investment that creates a residual income over a period of time?

Equity is about being able to receive something without actually having to do any ongoing work: it's the value of your business without valuing your labour. You could build equity from the value of assets that your business owns, the goodwill that builds up from the relationships your business maintains or from the value of your shares based on a multiple of the profits your business makes.

So putting these four things together is really what your in endgame is about. If you can be really clear on your lifestyle, legacy, income and equity goals, then your endgame is pretty much complete.

The endgame I set for myself in my business was to uncover the formula for why some businesses grow and thrive and others wilt and die, and then to float the company for over $100 million. This would allow me to retire by the time I was 35 so I could help incubate the next generation of entrepreneurs. Most of the elements of this endgame came true for me. I did come up with a business growth formula and retire by the age of 35. And while we sold the company rather than floated it, the result was uncannily close to my original goal of $100 million. This outcome has allowed me to work in my chosen vocation of training and developing entrepreneurs of all ages — which was the mission I first set myself all those years ago.

> If you can be really clear on your lifestyle, legacy, income and equity goals, then your endgame is pretty much complete.

Endgame by role

The internal compass that drives an employee is very different to the compass that motivates a serial entrepreneur. So how do we know what our endgame is?

Employees are often motivated by the income they receive so that they can live the lifestyle they want. For the fortunate few that role may be their vocation or the job that they love and, if it is, then they would be wise to continue being an employee. Your endgame could be moving up the corporate ladder or retiring with a certain amount of financial stability. And while it is possible for employees to gain equity through their superannuation benefits, pension fund or employee share plan, building wealth this way can be an agonisingly slow process. In fact it is the frustrating lack of freedom and fulfilment, not to mention any long-term financial security, that often provides the catalyst for the employee to take action by considering getting into business for themselves.

The next level of business occupation, self-employment, is where you are in business, yet your life and activities more closely parallel employment because you are selling your time for money. Generally you can make more income and have more freedom than being an employee because you are your own boss. Your endgame is usually to either achieve your desired level of income for the least amount of effort so that you can pursue your vocation outside of your work, whether that's surfing, fly fishing or working with disabled kids. Alternatively, if your vocation is the industry you are working in, then your endgame might be to make a name for yourself as the best in your field in order to have greater choice over which clients you work with.

If neither of these sounds like it would give you satisfaction, then you might consider being a business owner, entrepreneur or serial entrepreneur. How to differentiate between these occupations often comes down to the endgame. The endgame of a business owner might be to build the business to a stage where it is deriving an income for them to spend on their lifestyle, regardless of how much of their own time they invest. Alternatively, the endgame might also include becoming the best in an industry or creating a legacy that will benefit many generations after. Essentially business owners plan to have their business indefinitely.

The difference with an entrepreneurs' endgame is that it has a much more time-condensed purpose: essentially to start, grow and exit their business for an equity gain. Sure, they might enjoy an industry or love working in their company, but if they can't see themselves doing it until they retire then this is not their ultimate vocation. Their vocation is probably to sell their business so that they can either invest their time and money in a legacy outside their business — possibly a social entrepreneurial endeavour, doing something for the sheer fun of it or investing back into another business. It is the last that contributes to someone becoming a serial entrepreneur. They love the game of business so much that their vocation is not any one business, but business itself. A serial entrepreneur's endgame is usually to amass some combination of wealth, power and influence.

So take a moment to consider your endgame and the role best suited to that endgame. There are essentially three tests — the first around your vocation, the second around your exit and the third around your remuneration:

- *Vocation test.* Is the industry you are in your vocation? If it is then your endgame is most likely being the best employee, self-employed or business owner you can be. If the current role you perform is your vocation, then you are likely to be most fulfilled as an employee or self-employed. You shouldn't strive to manage people to do your role because, like the pie-making lady mentioned earlier, you will probably end up not doing the thing you are passionate about.

- *Exit test.* When do you plan to exit your business? If it is a long-term goal, say, when you retire, then you are self-employed or a business owner. If it is a short- to medium-term goal, then you are an entrepreneur or serial entrepreneur. Do you plan to go back into business when you exit? If you do, then you are a serial entrepreneur.

- *Remuneration test.* Is the reason you are in business predominantly to maximise your income? If it is then you would be best served as an employee, self-employed or business owner. If your primary reason to be in business is to make equity and an adequate income, then you are an entrepreneur or serial entrepreneur.

Personal mission statement

One of the things in relation to endgame that I have done throughout my business career, and I encourage others to do, is to create some kind of personal mission statement. While this can be a little bit corny, I have found that the repetition of being able to have something that brings your endgame to life is really helpful. A personal mission statement will serve as a continual reminder of what you want to achieve in your life. It's easy to forget why you are doing what you are doing in the day-to-day tasks of life. Having a mission statement and reviewing that regularly can help to keep you on track.

Your mission statement might include a verbal or visual affirmation about what sort of company you are going to create. It may be an emotively written future story of what your future business will achieve. Imagine you are on the cover of *Time* magazine — what is the paragraph of copy written underneath your picture that describes your business and your achievements? The other way of thinking about this statement is to consider it a type of obituary and what people will be saying about you after you're gone.

I developed an aspirational personal mission statement to act as a reinforcement of what I wanted to achieve and to help motivate myself through the hard times. And while it's embarrassing to share it here, it will give you a clearer idea of what I mean. My personal mission statement was, 'My name is Creel Price, one of the world's foremost entrepreneurs and inspirational leaders, widely respected for my innovation, humanitarian values and tireless sense of adventure. What my mind can achieve and my heart can believe, I can achieve. No mountain is too high.' Your mission doesn't have to be original or innovative: it just has to resonate with you on a very deep, personal level. My own mission was inspired by a quote from Jessie Jackson, which I adapted to make my own.

Repeating this mission statement over and over in my head until it became part of my DNA not only helped me achieve what I wanted out of business, it also helped me to become the type of entrepreneur I strived to be.

If neither of these verbal techniques motivates you then consider using some kind of visual or auditory affirmation. An auditory affirmation might be a particularly motivating song that captures what you're about and who you want to be. Every time it plays on the radio or you play it yourself it will serve as a reminder of your endgame. A visual affirmation might be a picture of a Spanish villa overlooking the Mediterranean if your endgame is to retire to Spain.

A visual affirmation I use to remind myself of my endgame and the goals I have set are small rocks! Every New Year's Day I climb a mountain and reassess my goals. I take a rock from the summit of each mountain I climb, and while I rarely find the time or inclination to refer to the goals I write down, the rock, which then sits in pride of place on my desk, acts as a constant reminder of my commitments.

I am a huge believer in the power of having a clear mission and a compelling endgame. If I told you the combination of the two create some sort of indescribable magic you would think I was nuts, but it's the truth nonetheless. In chapter 12 I will share a personal story of how making and setting goals not only came true for me but also came true nearly to the letter and nearly on the exact date I first set.

Passion in decision making

Getting really clear on your destination will give power to your decision making because you will be able to immediately assess if the decisions under discussion are taking you closer to your endgame or further away from it.

Having a key decision-making question for each of the six lenses brings foresight to bear in the assessment process much faster and more easily. The key question to consider when bringing passion to bear in your decision making is, 'Which option will accelerate my endgame and enable me to be working on my mission?' For example, if your endgame is to make $5 million from the business and your mission is to become a venture capitalist then you would need to consider carefully if you are thinking of selling a 50 per cent share of your business to a new partner. First, you will need to be very sure that having a partner will help you take the business to $10 million in less time than you could take the business to $5 million yourself. And second, you will need to ensure that having a partner will continue to give you the control of your reputation and exit timeframes you need to pursue your goal to become a venture capitalist.

During the boot camp for the Branson entrepreneurs in South Africa, to demonstrate the role of the passion lens and sailor mindset in decision making we created an orienteering challenge. Unfortunately any sizeable bodies of water at the game park tended to be full of lurking creatures, and many of the entrepreneurs couldn't swim, so we opted for a land-based treasure hunt. Given the passion lens is all about getting clear on your endgame and using your internal compass to get you there, the relevance to business was soon apparent. We organised a map of the park and gave the teams two hours to collect as many flags as possible. Flags were worth different points based on distance from the base and difficulty to find or reach — not dissimilar to the rewards gained from being in business.

> The key question to consider when bringing passion to bear in your decision making is, 'Which option will accelerate my endgame and enable me to be working on my mission?'

Hoping that the noise and daytime hours would keep many of the dangerous animals in the game park at bay, the starter's gun went off and the teams of four set off through the bush. Being able to go only as fast as the slowest person, given groups had to stick together, the different motivations of team members soon became apparent. Some wanted to stretch themselves and collect every possible flag regardless of the distance away even though they would risk getting disqualified if they didn't make it back in time. Others wanted to keep within their abilities and take a more ordered approach by ensuring they achieved all of the easiest points first. And others, who realised that this wasn't the activity for them, were comfortable having a leisurely stroll. The teams quickly realised that they needed to have a united goal or endgame before they could plan what they needed to do to achieve it. So point-targets were set that they could keep focusing their attention on to keep their energy levels up. Incorporated in the endgame would be how they wanted to participate as a team, or their mission. Some agreed that it was safety first; others put the slowest runner in charge so that they could dictate the pace; and other teams wanted to have fun, and so choose a more scenic route, which included a lookout.

The first group finished well inside the finish time with big smiles — they had achieved their modest target exactly; no-one was injured; and they had worked well together as a team. They were also chuffed to have made it up to the lookout — even taking some time to take a team picture. Their tally was unlikely to give them a win, but based on their fitness levels and motivations they knew that from the beginning. The next group came in puffing but exhilarated to know they made it just in the nick of time. Half way through the course they realised their target was too modest and decided to stretch themselves some more. This tactic worked well and their proud high-fives said the rest. As the time bell ominously chimed the last group were still out of sight. After 15 minutes they finally laboured into the lodge, tired and not on good terms. Their goal to get all of the markers had backfired and they hadn't taken into account that one of the team members had asthma. The lesson was that big goals are great but if they are beyond your capabilities you end up achieving nothing—and that is exactly how many points their team earned from the challenge.

The passion lens is crucial for developing your endgame, which will include your desired income, equity, lifestyle and legacy. To achieve this you need to decide on the role best suited to your objectives, from being an employee, self-employed, business owner, entrepreneur and serial entrepreneur, and bring your endgame alive through a personal mission statement. Understanding your passion drivers will bring you one step closer to ensuring that all future decisions will help you achieve your freedom and fulfilment goals.

Key points

» The passion lens is about becoming clear about your *own motivations* for being in business in the first place.

» You don't need to be passionate about every aspect of your business—you just need to find aspects of it that really excite you so you can enjoy the journey.

» When looking through the passion lens you must take on the mindset of a sailor.

» The personality trait for the passion lens is the inspirer, which should remind you to be the captain in charge of bringing out the passion in everyone associated with your business.

» The sailor is the embodiment of the passion lens because he or she loves what they are doing; they make this passion infectious; and they always have an endgame or goal that drives them forward.

» Your endgame is what you want to get out of business.

» Being clear about your destination will give power to your decision making because you will be able to immediately assess if the decisions under discussion are taking you closer to your endgame or further away from it.

» The essential question to consider when bringing passion to bear in your decision making is, 'Which option will accelerate my endgame and enable me to be working on my mission?'

» The passion lens is crucial for developing your endgame, which will include your desired income, equity, lifestyle and legacy.

» Understanding your passion drivers will bring you one step closer to ensuring that all future decisions will help you achieve your freedom and fulfilment goals.

Chapter 10

The philosophy lens

The philosophy lens is about reflecting on your *own beliefs*. That way your business stands for something meaningful to you, is congruent with you as an individual and will often help you stand out from the crowd as a result.

One of the misconceptions about entrepreneurial success is that you need to spend huge amounts of money to build a brand in order to mimic large corporate success stories. I see entrepreneurs waste thousands of dollars on advertising and superficial brand awareness campaigns, or think they have to pay top dollar to attract and keep great people. What these entrepreneurs don't realise is that there are many ways to build a business—and they don't all require buckets of cash. Attracting great staff, influential clients and resourceful investors and motivating them to do business with you without a big budget comes down to building a compelling philosophy or methodology.

All too often entrepreneurs go into business and become carbon copies of all the other businesses in their sector. And that is a mistake. There are millions of brands, products and services all competing for a limited amount of customer headspace. There was a time when a business could set up in a particular geographic location and those boundaries would limit their competition. That is no longer the case for the vast majority of businesses. With the exception of a few industries where the product or service has to be supplied locally, most businesses are competing with other suppliers who may be thousands of miles away from you.

> The philosophy lens is about reflecting on your *own beliefs.*

This explosion in competition means that now, more than ever, being conventional doesn't get you noticed; and if you can't get noticed then you won't succeed.

If you look at any major successful company, the business is usually a direct reflection of the person at the top. If you consider Sir Richard Branson, for example, his whole personality is hinged around having fun, breaking the rules, cutting new ground. He's a maverick and his businesses, even the ones that he is no longer involved in, still embody that philosophy.

Your core beliefs and values will be reflected in your business operation, whether you want them to be or not, and whether you are conscious of them or not. It is therefore far better to take conscious control of this process so that the philosophy that develops in your business is one that you want to develop. Say, for example, you are a poor timekeeper. It may be an attribute that really frustrates you and you wish you could change, but up to now you have never really got around to making an effort to change it. You go into business and that poor timekeeping will become embedded in your business. Managers and staff members will see you running late and assume it's okay for them to run late, too. You will tell your people how important it is to be early for client meetings, and so on, but they don't hear what you say, they see what you do and who you are. So who are you?

Mindset: gardener

When looking through the philosophy lens you must take on the mindset of a gardener. Good gardeners don't just throw everything together and hope things will grow: they decide on a theme. That theme may be Japanese garden, formal English garden or tropical garden, and the theme will determine what people will feel when they walk through the garden. A good gardener also understands that it takes time to grow a compelling garden that looks, feels and smells great.

GARDENER

In gardening a great deal of what happens above the ground is dictated by what happens below the ground. What grows depends on how good the soil is, for example, or how deep the roots are, and how much water and fertiliser gets to those roots. The same is true of business. The roots of the tree are like the values of your business and they determine how tall and how strong your business will grow. Like roots, the company's values ground the business, and while your philosophy and your company values may not be overt, they will manifest themselves in your business whether you like it or not.

One of my first businesses relied heavily on my skills as a gardener. At the ripe age of 11, I found myself as the aspiring strawberry baron of western New South Wales. Growing strawberries and selling them beside the highway taught me some valuable lessons. I was able to fully appreciate the dynamic and dependent relationship between above and below ground, and how what happens out of sight often determines the visible reality.

I got so hooked on gardening that I started a gardening business to put myself through university, and this early gardening experience was invaluable in teaching me about business.

Figure 10.1 shows a model that illustrates the key elements that make up the philosophy lens.

Figure 10.1: the elements of the philosophy lens

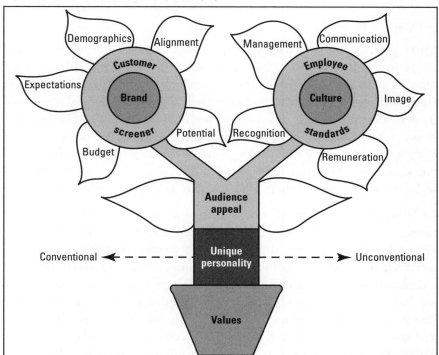

Personality trait: caretaker

The personality trait that brings the mindset of the gardener alive is that of the caretaker. The gardener is not only responsible for planning the garden, but also for constantly taking care of it, so that it continues to prosper in the future. They are constantly watering the garden and making sure that it has enough nutrients to flourish. They match the right plant to the right conditions to ensure it is successful and grows to its full potential.

You need to be the caretaker for your business, making sure everybody and everything aligns to your values and your methodology. You need to have the patience to create a unique company culture and a winning brand all based around your unique personality.

Key outcome: your values

The first element to consider in building your philosophy is your individual values. Like the roots of a plant they are often out of sight, but they will have a significant impact on the health and direction of your company philosophy.

Values go hand in hand with your unique personality, and when you can inject your business with those values you will be amazed at how much more motivated you and your stakeholders become, because it gives you a chance to share your authentic self. If you have a quirky, unusual or persistent personality, let those differences be expressed through the business. You need to stand out, otherwise you won't be noticed. Don't force quirky if you are not quirky — instead find something authentically different about you and your proposition. Drive that value home, and seek customers and suppliers who resonate with your difference.

At Blueprint, for example, we developed a list of five values with the team, and then constantly communicated and reinforced them with all employees in the company. They were written on the walls, and we recruited and managed staff with those values firmly in mind. I delivered a director's message focusing on one of those values every week. And we had off-site weekends and weekly firedowns that reinforced the importance of those values. Instead of having a meeting to fire-up the staff on a Monday morning we held a firedown on a Friday afternoon. These 30-minute sessions to finish the week on a high were delivered with some well-deserved drinks. A representative from each department would share their funny stories or events from the week, what they would change if they could and who the star performers were for the week. We also used this session to reinforce one of our company values and then recognise one or more individuals who had demonstrated that value in a big way. The firedowns usually finished with some kind of silly competition, such as karaoke, live crab races, belly slides, pie-eating contests and apple bobbing. They were fun and extremely significant in creating such a powerful culture in the business. We lived and breathed our values 24 hours a day.

Our five values were:

- fun and focus
- valued relationships
- our team
- mountainous success
- continuous innovation.

One of the different things about my personality is that I love climbing mountains, which is where our value mountainous success stems from. To reflect mountainous success into our company, rather than just paying lip service to it, our office was called base camp, and it had a fake open fire and a rock-climbing wall, and all the meeting rooms had mountain-related names. Our training program was called Ascend. People got carabiners when they won an award or went up a level in the training program, or for each year of service.

Each year we committed to some kind of adventure trip to reinforce this value, whether it was climbing a mountain or doing some other kind of adventure, so staff would know we were really serious about stretching ourselves and living the mountainous success value. Coming to work in this sort of environment, which was very much aligned to my values, helped to motivate me, and I guess inspired me to share this value with our staff, our clients, and suppliers. We wanted our clients to see how serious we were about creating mountainous success, not only in our own business but in their businesses too. Although I'm pretty sure everyone loved the philosophy, not everyone was thrilled about having to climb our two-and-a-half storey climbing wall in the atrium of our office.

Think about what you love and seek to drive this into your company philosophy. If you are unsure what you stand for, or what you want to stand for, take a moment to think about five companies that you respect. Think of businesses whose success you would like to emulate and for each company write down words and phrases that represent the aspects of those businesses that you aspire to. Then determine what it is about those companies that you admire so much. Are there any themes that emerge? Have you, for example, realised that the businesses that you most admire are courageous and innovative? Perhaps you realise that you most respect businesses that are doing something worthwhile for the planet. All of these things represent your values. All you need to do is articulate them to yourself and then to others.

Pictures can also be a great way to quickly determine your underlying values, provided you can choose something appropriate before you over-analyse it. So come up with an appropriate stack of random pictures unrelated to business, such as people shaking hands, a windy mountain road or someone playing a difficult golf hole—50 is a good number. Quickly flick through the 50 pictures like a stack of playing cards and work out the five to eight pictures that really jump out at you. And then work out why that particular picture caught your eye, what it means for you and your business in terms of values.

I recommend that you use two-word descriptions for your values rather than just one-word descriptions. For example, success could have been one of our values but mountainous success was more personal to us. Creating two-word values allows you to add extra meaning to the process so that you really own those phrases, and get excited and fired up about them. It also helps you to reflect your unique personality, which is what the philosophy lens is all about.

But remember philosophy is not a one-time gig. It's not a matter of coming up with your corporate values and then filing them away never to see the light of day again. Rather, values are to be cultivated (hence the mindset of the gardener). Instilling a corporate philosophy takes time and effort.

You can't fake your values and beliefs, but you can strengthen them by documenting them and communicating them to others as the business grows and develops. If an entrepreneur is really clear on what drives them and creates their unique personality, then they can convert that unique personality and direct it towards a particular audience. So if it's a client audience, you need to bring your brand alive, and if it's a staff audience, you need to bring your staff culture alive.

Building a unique brand

One of the major benefits of having a really strong business philosophy is that it will drive everything you do, including the personification of your brand. Certain brands attract certain types of people and if your brand is a true reflection of who you are, what you stand for and what sort of business you want to create, then it stands to reason that only customers who want to work with such a company will approach you. And clients who love what you stand for are more likely to be loyal to your business over the long term. They are also much more likely to tell others about your business and allow you to tap into the power of referral marketing.

> One of the major benefits of having a really strong business philosophy is that it will drive everything you do, including the personification of your brand.

The customer screener

One of the tools we used to protect and enhance our brand was a customer screener. A customer screener is just a list of key attributes that you want your potential customers to have. Having this ideal client profile allows you to make better informed decisions about whether to do business with a particular customer or not. Screening customers prevents you from wasting time seeking out, selling to or doing proposals for customers who are not in your target market, aren't profitable or don't build long-term value into your business and brand.

Elements to consider when formulating your customer screener include the following:

- *Demographics.* These include the type of business, business size, location or age. For example, you may decide you only want to deal with businesses in your geographic area or businesses that employ more than 100 people.
- *Alignment.* You may want customers who fit with your brand and values; otherwise you may find it hard to work with them. For example, you may choose not to work with a cigarette company or arms production company.
- *Potential.* You may want customers that you can keep and grow. For example, you may choose to select customers who are willing to sign a contract with you.

- *Budget.* You may want customers who can afford to pay along the way. For example, you may be seeking customers who are happy to pay an application fee.

- *Expectations.* You may chose to select only customers who have realistic expectations about what can be delivered. For example, unrealistic timeframes will almost always result in future grief and conflict.

As you get clear on your customer screener, it's going to help with your business niche, which is essentially the segment of your target market you choose to do business with in order to dominate it. There are two ways to use a customer screener—where you ask the questions and where you get the customer to ask the questions. For example, one of the entrepreneurs that came through my training program had a publishing business for those who wanted to self-publish their books. Initially the business attracted lots of customers but they were tyre kickers, who actually didn't have the money to publish their own book. So one of the customer screeners she implemented was to immediately tell prospective customers of the minimum cost and range upfront. Those who were serious proceeded with the discussions, and those who were not quietly disappeared. This allowed her to screen her customers and saved her wasting time with customers who were never going to use her service anyway.

Another entrepreneur I worked with has an online business called Taste of Ireland, which supplies food and beverages to Irish people living in Australia, or to people in Ireland who want to send someone in Australia a unique Irish gift. His niche was focused on the Irish and was therefore self-screening. On visiting the website, anyone not Irish or looking for Irish goods or wanting to send goods to someone from Ireland would immediately realise the site was not for them. This allowed the customer to screen themselves.

Building a unique culture

Having a strong philosophy is also important when it comes to creating the right company culture, and often that comes down to employing the right people. If your philosophy is strong, then only people who resonate with your values will want to work with you. Having a team whose values are aligned is a powerful motivator towards success because everyone is singing off the same hymn sheet and everyone is inspired by what you and your business are trying to achieve.

The best way to ensure you develop the right culture and employ the right people is to have employee standards. Employee standards are documented or implied policies and expectations for your team that ensure a consistency of operation and hiring. Having employee standards is not about building unpopular, inflexible or time-consuming procedures that don't make life easier for you or your employees, but rather consciously building the company the way you want it to be built. If there is standard policy, then you don't have to keep re-inventing the wheel and answering the same questions over and over again.

You have employee standards to ensure that you can more easily defer and delegate decisions while maintaining a consistent outcome. Think about the things that you are constantly asked and the answer always seems to be the same. For example, having a standard around which staff get a business card and what it says and how many to order will save you time organising business cards and responding to business card requests. Having employee standards means that everyone knows what is expected of them and what sort of working environment they are entering into.

Areas to consider when developing your employee standards include the following:

- *Management.* This may include how the employees will be managed, by whom and how their performance will be reviewed. It may also include the types of decisions they can make and the leeway they have in making those decisions. For example, you may have an employee standard that states that every employee can spend up to $500 to fix a customer issue or problem without prior approval.

- *Communication.* This may include expectations about how your employees deal with you, your customers and each other. For example, you may chose to update your employees each quarter with the company's strategy and priorities so as to keep everyone informed and motivated.

- *Image.* This may include standards around how employees dress, how information is presented to customers and each other, how correspondence is quality controlled and how common areas are kept presentable. Don't assume others will see the importance of certain things just because you do. If it matters, make it part of the employee standards.

- *Remuneration*. It's important to maintain consistency around remuneration and salary levels, incentives and bonuses. A remuneration standard might also deal with how requests for salary increases are dealt with. For example, your company might have a standard that pay reviews are dealt with at the end of the financial year.
- *Recognition*. This may include the standards around how you recognise new staff and leaving staff. It might include how employees are promoted and motivated, and how incentives and awards are given, to keep within your company's personality. For example, you might always announce annual award winners at your Christmas party.

Some of the basic yet powerful employee standards we had at Blueprint included policies on simple things like when and how employees are reimbursed for parking, mobile phone calls and travel expenses. One of the communication standards we had was that the phone at reception had to be answered within the first three rings. We also set a standard of inviting all staff to a formal communication from the executive team on the first Wednesday in each quarter.

Remuneration standards we implemented included a review process for everyone's salary, each December. So if someone wanted a pay raise in March, we didn't say you're not getting a pay rise, we said they would find out when we reviewed everyone's pay in December. Also, we kept a methodology around why different people were paid different amounts. So when someone invariably found out what someone else was on, having a standard enabled them to make sure that they understood that it was a standard and not a whim of their manager. We also had standards around how bonuses were distributed.

Another great thing about standards is they are a great way to empower your employees, which gives them a lot more decision-making ability.

Philosophy in decision making

Becoming really clear on all of the elements that make up your philosophy will give you decision-making power, because you will be able to immediately assess if the decisions under discussion are in alignment with your core values and beliefs. The key question to consider when bringing philosophy to bear in your decision making is, 'Which option will cultivate our company values and reinforce our brand and culture?'

If, for example, one of your values is to emulate the quality of Rolex, and you are approached by a would-be supplier who says they can offer you components that you need for a fraction of what your current supplier is delivering those same components for, but they are not of the same quality, then the answer is clear. If you are keen for your business to have a social conscience and do no harm, then the same offer may be turned down because of the working conditions of employees in that business.

The philosophy lens was put to the test at the South African boot camp's next challenge, which was to reflect the gardener mindset in a collage of canvases. Each team was given four blank canvases, paints, two hours and the instruction to create a masterpiece that joined the canvases together in a united garden theme. Points would be awarded based on the strength of the brand they created, the expression of their unique personality and how aligned the paintings were to the whole, despite each canvas having to be painted by a different entrepreneur.

Team culture was again put to the test, given that some participants were great artists and a great painting next to someone else's average painting would look out of place. They all took the key element of the gardener mindset to heart by coming up with a theme for their combined masterpiece. One of the teams of entrepreneurs painted a canvass for each of four vegetables that together made up their favourite soup. Another conjured up a vine that interlinked all of the canvases together, changing colours as it went. The other team declared they were all about international relations, painting a flower from four countries: the English rose, Singapore orchid, African violet and Australian wattle.

> The key question to consider when bringing philosophy to bear in your decision making is, 'Which option will cultivate our company values and reinforce our brand and culture?'

All of the groups of canvases were strong and vibrant, and very different in image and meaning. The best designs were strong, with a consistent use of few colours but with simple geometric shapes that were easy enough to paint—not unlike the characteristics of a good logo. The groups were chuffed with their achievements, given some of them had never painted on a canvas and had considered themselves to be without any artistic talent. Getting clear on their culture, brand and unique personality served to unify the teams even more — a clear reinforcement of the learnings from the philosophy lens. They could see how these lessons could translate into their business decisions by ensuring future decisions aligned a consistent image and culture that reflected their values and unique personality.

Key points

» The philosophy lens is about reflecting on your *own beliefs*.

» Attracting great staff, influential clients and resourceful investors, and motivating them to do business with you without a big budget, comes down to building a compelling philosophy.

» Your core beliefs and values will be reflected in your business operation, whether you want them to be or not, and whether you are conscious of them or not.

» When looking through the philosophy lens you must take on the mindset of a gardener.

» The personality trait that brings the mindset of the gardener alive is that of the caretaker. The gardener is not only responsible for planning the garden, but also for taking care of it, so that it prospers into the future.

» The first element to consider in building your philosophy is your individual values. Like the roots of a plant they are often out of sight, but they have a significant impact on the health and direction of your company philosophy.

» A strong business philosophy will create a unique brand through the customer screener and a unique culture through employee standards.

» Being clear on all of the elements that make up your philosophy will help you immediately assess whether decisions align with your core values and beliefs.

» The key question to consider when bringing philosophy to bear in your decision making is, 'Which option will cultivate our company values and reinforce our brand and culture?'

» The philosophy lens ensures future decisions align to a consistent image and culture that reflects your values and unique personality.

Chapter 11

The proficiency lens

Proficiency is the last of the three lenses that are about you as an individual, and it focuses your attention on your *own skills*. You must gain clarity around your personal strengths and weaknesses so that you can manage them appropriately in your business.

The widely held belief is that entrepreneurship can't be taught: you are either born with that business flair or you are not. As I said earlier, I don't necessarily agree with this idea. I do accept that some people are naturally more entrepreneurial in their approach to life, but I also believe that entrepreneurialism has a skill set that can be taught.

If you asked someone to describe an entrepreneur, you might hear about attributes such as resilience, courage, inquisitiveness, humour, optimism, a never-say-die attitude, charisma, drive, determination, sense of adventure, stamina, perseverance or confidence. There can be no doubt that many of these attributes occur naturally, but many can also be taught or developed over time. You can, for example, act bravely once and develop courage over time. You can commit to perseverance and diligently refuse to give up over time.

What is perhaps more important, which too many business owners forget, is that there are business skills and competencies that can be developed and they are every bit as important as any attribute you may or may not have been born with. Everyone can improve their skills and abilities through practise and finetuning their entrepreneurial intelligence.

The only thing standing in your way is an inferiority or superiority complex. Those who have an inferiority complex assume that nothing will work and they will never be able to be a brilliant entrepreneur. They think they don't have enough skills and are constantly comparing themselves with others and finding personal fault. Or they have a superiority complex and don't believe there is anything new and useful they could possibly learn about business. This is something that I see time and time again from people who have successfully climbed the corporate ladder and then decided to go into business for themselves. They automatically assume that their competence and success in working in someone else's business will easily and naturally migrate to their own business. It doesn't.

Everyone is different. We all have certain skills and abilities that are slightly different from everyone else's. It is the combination of those skills that creates our unique proficiency and it is that proficiency that lends itself to particular roles and tasks.

I'm a great believer in continuous learning and personal development, but a great deal of the personal development industry has done us a disservice by convincing too many people that they can do anything they want if they just want it badly enough. Nothing could be further from the truth. If we could all do what we wanted to do, and if drive and determination was all that was required, then surely everyone would be rock guitarists, round-the-world yacht captains, catwalk models, celebrity chefs or silver screen actors.

The proficiency lens is about becoming really clear about what your strengths and weaknesses actually are. You can't be anything you want to be, regardless of how much effort you put in — you can only be really great at the things that you are actually already pretty good at. So instead of beating yourself up about the things you can't do or are not very good at, focus on finding out what your unique talents and abilities are and use them.

> The proficiency lens is about becoming really clear about what your strengths and weaknesses actually are.

The really successful entrepreneurs have the foresight to know their proficiencies and limitations and how to build a successful team that allows them to reinforce their strengths and counter their weaknesses.

Mindset: movie producer

When looking through the proficiency lens you must take on the mindset of a movie producer. The movie producer is the talent manager on a film set. They know who they need to put in each role. They manage to pull all the relevant people together, from directors to casting managers, props and design managers to technicians, special effects teams, camera crew, actors, scriptwriters and make-up artists. They know that everyone has a specialist role to play in the creation of the finished product.

MOVIE PRODUCER

A great movie producer knows that nothing brilliant can be created by one person alone, and that their job is as much about matching people to roles as it is about having a clear vision of what the end result will look like.

Personality trait: manager

The personality trait most appropriate for the movie producer is the manager—someone who is great at hiring, firing and motivating a team of people to achieve great things.

In business it's just the same. As an entrepreneur it's your job to manage all the talent in your business in the same way that a movie producer manages the talent on a movie set. You're always on the lookout for the best talent and making sure that the best talent is doing the tasks they are most suitable for—including you. Your business will not grow until you cast other people in key roles in your business and manage them to fulfil their potential.

Incidentally, this is a lesson I have to constantly remind myself of. In an effort to leverage my Winning at the Game of Business training program, I decided to generate more than 50 three-to-five minute videos and upload them to my website. Not listening to my own teachings about having the movie producer mindset in business, I found myself doing everything—scripting, directing, filming, acting, editing and uploading each clip myself. Not only was this a tremendously laborious exercise, it was also very expensive when I compared my hourly rate to what I could have paid a specialist to do it for me. Sure enough, half way through the exercise I began to outsource each element. Not only was the result much better, but I could also get back to focusing my time and energy on what I was good at!

Key outcome: your role

One of the things you'll notice about being in business for yourself is you need to start to have a much broader range of skills and you need to be conscious of the role you play in your business. In some ways you need to be a Jack of all trades. Yet some skills are just not worth focusing your time and attention on. While you may be born with attributes that underpin the inherent qualities and proficiencies of the entrepreneur, you can unpack those proficiencies or skills to see what makes up entrepreneurial intelligence. That way you can quickly identify which you are good at, which can be improved and which you suck at!

The proficiency model (see figure 11.1) highlights the various components that make up the proficiency lens.

Figure 11.1: the components of the proficiency lens

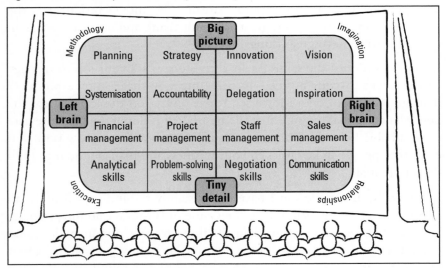

Entrepreneurial intelligence

Every entrepreneur or business owner needs to oscillate between the big picture and the tiny detail—the vertical scale on the proficiency model. In the corporate world, roles are more defined and range from the entry-level employees doing the tiny details up to the executives who focus on the big picture. When you are running your own enterprise, however, you need to be proficient in both, and yet generally you will have a tendency to like or be good at one over the other. There are those that love the big picture, future thinking and strategising, but hate the nuts and bolts of making it happen. There are those who couldn't care less what's going to be happening in five years time but want to focus on making today successful.

The horizontal scale on the proficiency model tracks an entrepreneur's tendency towards either left-brain or right-brain thinking. The left-brain focused among us are more logical than the right-brain focused; they thrive on objective, rational assessment and are interested in analysis of the parts, not necessarily the whole. Those who are more right-brained are more intuitive, subjective and interested in people rather than things. The right-brained people are interested in the whole, not the parts. The tricky part is that to be successful you have to be focused on both big picture and tiny detail, and you have to use the right and left sides of your brain.

These four, often conflicting, forces revolve around four key skill areas: methodology, imagination, execution and relationships. Generally, an entrepreneur will fit into one of these quadrants; for instance, you might be a left-brain big-picture thinker.

Think of the process of making a movie. Directors are often all about the methodology. They have a process to follow to make a great movie and bring their big picture, often left-brain, thinking to bear. Whereas scriptwriters are all about imagination—the right-brained big-picture quadrant. They need to consider the whole, in order to bring everything together in a natural but entertaining sequence.

The actors in a movie are probably more like right-brain, tiny-detail thinkers; they're all about relationships and people. They need to be able to express themselves so that their character comes to life as you watch the movie. And then finally there's the computer-generated imagery (CGI) team, who are likely to be left-brain, tiny-detail thinkers. They have specialist technical skills and they're very good at analysing and executing a system that works.

Clearly these roles don't rely only on the quadrant they most identify with. Directors also need to bring creative right-brain thinking to their roles as much as actors need to understand the big picture that they are part of. Yet what makes a movie work is that there are specialists who really are performing their own role.

However, things can go horribly wrong when someone doesn't understand the limits of their role. For instance, an actor who thinks they can also direct. I read an article recently about a famous actor who wanted more and more creative control over the directing process the more famous he got. And yet, in the movies he is best known for and has won an Oscar for, he let the director do his job and focused all his attention on his acting.

> The last thing your business needs is another you. Instead you should be finding someone complementary who's good at the things that you aren't good at.

Likewise, one of the biggest mistakes an entrepreneur can make is employing someone who is the same as or similar to themselves. The last thing your business needs is another you. Instead you should be finding someone complementary who's good at the things that you aren't good at.

So considering you don't possess all the appropriate skills required for your business, what are you to do? Simple — you recognise the proficiencies you do have and focus on them; you work on ones you could improve on; and you outsource or delegate the ones you are not good at. And you make sure your business model doesn't require the things that you are weak in.

To help you identify what those proficiencies are, figure 11.1 (see p. 130) shows the 16 separate proficiencies that make up entrepreneurial intelligence. They can be split into the following four quadrants.

Quadrant 1: left brain and big picture

There are four proficiencies in this quadrant of the left brain.

- *Planning.* The ability to develop and stick to a well-considered and achievable business plan and set of milestones.
- *Strategy.* The ability to effectively conceive, flesh out and prioritise potential avenues for improvement.
- *Systemisation.* The ability to organise systems, processes and prototypes, both small and large, for each aspect of your business.
- *Accountability.* The ability to keep yourself and others accountable for following through on actions, responsibilities and commitments.

Quadrant 2: right brain and big picture

There are four proficiencies in this quadrant of the right brain.

- *Innovation.* The ability to create untried and unproven ways of solving problems and capitalising on opportunities.
- *Vision.* The ability to have clarity on a future goal or outcome, and use foresight to recognise what will be required to get you there.
- *Delegation.* The ability to delegate tasks to employees by giving them clear objectives and empowering them to become successful, with latitude to learn from failure.
- *Inspiration.* The ability to motivate others, to create elegance in your brand and message, and inspire new ideas from your team and partners.

Quadrant 3: left brain and tiny detail

There are four proficiencies in this quadrant of the left brain.

- *Financial management.* The ability to understand financial statements, to manage the set-up and delivery of the accounting function, and to budget effectively.
- *Project management.* The ability to lead yourself or a team to execute a project from inception to completion using appropriate trade-offs between cost, time and quality.
- *Analytical skills.* The ability to analyse figures, analyse the relative merit of opposing strategies and decisions, and identify strengths and weaknesses in people.
- *Problem-solving skills.* The ability to quickly develop solutions to problems without overreacting or unnecessarily delaying.

Quadrant 4: right brain and tiny detail

There are four proficiencies in this quadrant of the right brain.

- *Staff management.* The ability to hire, fire and motivate staff to achieve results, conduct performance appraisals, establish incentives, and understand human resources laws.
- *Sales management.* The ability to promote your business through marketing, lead generation, database management, pitching, closing sales, and upselling existing clients.

- *Negotiation skills.* The ability to buy better and sell more through your skill in negotiating terms that suit your business's cost, price and timings.
- *Communication skills.* The ability to communicate your message in a compelling and clear way, using both verbal and written media, including questioning and listening.

From the list of 16 proficiencies above, highlight which four proficiencies are your strengths and which four are your weaknesses.

A major mistake entrepreneurs often make is trying to fix their weaknesses. As American humorist Jack Handey once said, 'If you think a weakness can be turned into a strength, I hate to have to tell you this, but that's another weakness'. Don't waste your time and energy trying to be good at something you have no aptitude for or hate doing. So for the four proficiencies that you have identified as your greatest weaknesses, find someone either inside or outside the company who is good in those areas or loves the tasks you hate. For instance, if you hate or are not good at systemisation, employ a second in charge who is.

From the four proficiencies you identified that you were good at, you should design a role for yourself that capitalises on those talents and abilities. Armed with the insights about your personal strengths, consider how you will lead. The fact is that more often than not the things we are good at tend also to be the things we most enjoy doing, so designing a role for yourself based on these attributes creates a situation where you are not only adding the most value possible to your business but you are enjoying the process too. If, for instance, you love sales management, make sure that you aren't hidden behind the scenes in your business and that you can devote as much time to sales as possible. A true win–win.

Finally, of the eight proficiencies that are neither strengths nor weaknesses: it is worth investing some time to improve those areas. Make a commitment to focus on one improvement area each month or quarter. You will need to implement a plan to ensure this happens. Think about the habits you're going to start to change, the people that you're going to ask for advice, the training programs you need to do, the books you need to read, or the people who you need to model. Also share your plans with your team, so they know that you are focusing on that proficiency. Being overt about your efforts will serve to remind you of the commitments you are making and hopefully will allow others to gauge and positively reinforce your improvements.

So, for instance, if my objective was to improve my financial management, I might commit to preparing my own financial statements each month and analysing them to determine which expenses are going up unnecessarily or are larger than they should be. Or if I was going to try to improve my analytical skills, I might commit to doing a lot more spreadsheet modelling in order to compare two options when trying to make a decision. Or if I wanted to get better at negotiation, I might have a little competition with myself or my team on working out ways to get better prices and terms from my suppliers. If you wanted to improve your communication skills, you might commit to doing a monthly director's message that you can send out to staff.

Your dream role

Looking back at my own business, the idea of focusing our time on our respective strengths was pivotal to Blueprint's success. My business partner, Trevor, and I were very different. He was a real people and relationship person and was great with clients and staff, whereas I was much more systems oriented and analytical. We were, however, both big-picture thinkers, so we were very mindful of recruiting people who could bring that tiny detail focus to the business operations. Also, both of us being quite prone to the entrepreneur's curse — the inability to focus on the same thing for very long — we constantly sought ways to get more variety in our job roles. To achieve this we often alternated job roles, or mixed and matched responsibilities as the business needs changed. This gave us not only more job satisfaction but also allowed us to work on areas or skills we wanted to improve.

Entrepreneurs can also often find themselves torn between the demands of each of the three business areas that make up their business model: sales, operations and support (we will cover these in more detail in the discussion of the prototype lens in chapter 13). Often a focus on sales (bringing new customers) will create more operational demand, so attention shifts to operations (delivering for clients); only for you to realise that sales have slumped. Or, because your businesses back end was not organised before a flood of sales, you spend too much time looking after support (non–income generating activities), which is taking your eye off sales and operations.

Your business role needs to change as your business evolves, so it is worthwhile to determine how much of your time you currently spend in each of the sales, operations and support areas of your business. Then consider the time you actually should be spending in each of these areas—there is often a big difference.

For instance, if you estimated that you spend only 10 per cent of your time in sales, 50 per cent in operations and the rest in support, then it's hardly surprising if the business isn't growing that quickly. You might instead commit to focusing 50 per cent of your time in sales and split the rest of your time between operations and support. The only way to achieve this is by rationalising, outsourcing or delegating some of the tasks in operations and support, so consider how to do this and commit to the change.

One of the entrepreneurs who came through my program found herself spending way too many hours completing support functions at the expense of sales and operations. She did these tasks because she wanted to save money, but it turned out to be counterproductive. To overcome her unwillingness to delegate and outsource, we hatched a plan where she started to charge herself out to her own business at $1000 an hour. When she realised her theoretical cost to the business was over $2 million a year and most of this wasn't bringing in sales or delivering operationally, she changed her mindset. She made some decisions to outsource and delegate tasks, starting with those she wasn't good at, followed by those that she realised could be achieved faster and cheaper by someone else. The exercise worked wonders as she was able to focus on her strengths and grow her business. The proficiency lens is about identifying where you should be spending your time and energy so you can work smarter, not harder, and, perhaps more importantly, enjoy the process.

Proficiency in decision making

Becoming really clear on your proficiencies will give you decision-making power because you will be able to assess immediately if the decisions under consideration are going to play to your strengths or help to enhance the combined strengths you have as a business by matching people with roles. The key question to consider when bringing proficiency to bear in your decision making is, 'Which option will let me perform my role and play to my strengths or strengthen my improvement areas?'

Consider, for example, that you are approached by a client who wants you to diversify into a new area of business and give them support in a new way. It may seem like a no-brainer decision, because you want to keep your client happy, but if they are asking you to do something you have no experience or proficiency in, then the answer should probably be no. Otherwise you risk diluting your focus and area of expertise, and you also risk damaging your existing relationship should things not go according to plan.

> The key question to consider when bringing proficiency to bear in your decision making is, 'Which option will let me perform my role and play to my strengths ...?'

Another example might be a decision around outsourcing all of your finances, not just the bookkeeping but also the management reporting. Yet if one of your improvement areas, for instance, is all about financial management, you might want to keep it in-house until you have a really good handle on that, so you then have confidence when you finally want to outsource.

In the boot camp for the South African entrepreneurs, we used a theatre challenge to help reinforce the lessons of proficiency and the movie producer mindset. We gave them two hours to produce a show with whatever they could find to use as props and inspiration. Teams drew straws for a production that was all about singing, dancing or acting. Their performances would be on successive nights to entertain and engage the entire conference.

Each night we were entertained in a unique way—the entrepreneurs again amazed themselves with talents they didn't realise they had. We watched as each team put on a show in that lovely African way of presenting performing arts that is so different from what we get in the West. Of course song and music were well represented, but so too were parody and satire. All performances were vastly different, but also endearing, so it was very hard to choose a winner.

What this exercise did as much as anything was help us discover people's unique talents, which of course is what the proficiency lens is all about. The participants also learnt who should be leading, who should be front of house and who should be controlling the lighting and back of house. To create a production takes people who have different kinds of skills. The worst thing you can do is match a task to someone who is not proficient in that area or does not like doing that task or have any interest in learning it. All of the lessons were easily translatable into business decisions—getting yourself and others to play to their strengths and what they love doing.

Become the movie producer for your business: be the talent manager who not only brings in the right people in the right roles but also works on what their ideal job role should be.

The proficiency lens is the last of the three lenses that focus on you as an individual. Gaining clarity around your motivation and endgame, your beliefs and values, and your skills and ideal role can massively simplify the decision-making process. If you are clear about what you as an individual are trying to achieve, what you stand for and what's important to you, as well as what you are good at and what you are not good at, then those parameters will guide your choices. Becoming consciously aware of them is the first step.

The next three lenses, progress, prototype and plan, focus on your business and they will be discussed in detail in the following three chapters. Together the six lenses provide a complete decision-making perspective that helps you align decisions to your personal and business objectives.

Key points

» Proficiency is the last of the three lenses concerned with you as an individual, and it focuses your attention on your *own skills*.

» The proficiency lens is about being clear about what your strengths and weaknesses actually are.

» When looking through the proficiency lens you must take on the mindset of a movie producer.

» The personality trait most appropriate for the movie producer is the manager—someone who is great at hiring, firing and motivating a team of people to achieve great things.

» When you are in business for yourself you will need a much broader range of skills than you had as an employee, and you need to be conscious of your role in your business.

» Your business doesn't need another you. Find someone complementary who is good at the things that you aren't good at.

» Don't waste your time and energy trying to be good at something you have no aptitude for or hate doing.

» The proficiency lens helps you identify where you should be spending your time and energy so you can work smarter, not harder, and, perhaps more importantly, enjoy the process.

» Being clear on your proficiencies means being able to assess immediately if the decisions under consideration will play to your strengths or enhance the combined strengths you have as a business by matching people with roles.

» The key question to consider when bringing proficiency to bear in your decision making is, 'Which option will let me perform my role and play to my strengths or strengthen my improvement areas?'

» Gaining clarity around your motivation and end game, your beliefs and values and your skills and ideal role can massively simplify the decision-making process.

Chapter 12

The progress lens

The progress lens is the first of the lenses that is concerned with your business rather than you as an individual, and it helps you to explore your *business stage.*

It is really important to appreciate the various stages of business from start-up to exit, because success at each stage requires a different focus, and the progress lens helps you to consciously recognise where you are in your business evolution so you can apply that focus appropriately. The reason so many business owners are frustrated with their progress is because they don't realise what business stage they are in and that

> The progress lens is the first of the lenses that is concerned with your business rather than you as an individual, and it helps you to explore your *business stage.*

they will need a different approach to move successfully through the various stages. Some may reach a point where they are generating a good income, but can't get out of the habit of working long hours. Others may plateau at a particular stage when their profit is brilliant but the business is completely reliant on their own reputation, work and leadership. And there are those entrepreneurs who plateau because they can't see an appropriate exit.

Understanding the business stages is also a useful antidote for guarding against the entrepreneur's curse of the short attention span. Whether you want to start, grow and exit the business, or simply start and grow the business you need a plan. If you don't have a plan that guides you through the various stages then you could fall prey to the curse where you either turn your business into a messy conglomerate of half-finished ideas, like I did for a while, or else boredom sets in, closely followed by lack of motivation, which results in a downward spiral.

And before you know it your business has become a prison — far from the freedom you envisioned when you started it in the first place.

If your goal is to exit the business, you will also need to be careful that you keep an eye on whether you're likely to outgrow your business or your business is likely to outgrow you. Very few entrepreneurs start a business and think about how they want to exit. By the time they realise business exit is important, it can be too late, because they have built the business around their own personal brand, own skills or their own passion, which all make the business very hard to exit successfully. One of the problems I see with the people who attend my training programs is that they started the business to gain more freedom and fulfilment so that they could perhaps pursue other goals, but sooner or later they realise they have become trapped by their own creation and have in fact created a situation where they have less freedom and fulfilment than ever before. And that's frustrating. It's caused by their not fully understanding the business stages, so they don't know where they are and where to direct their focus.

At one end of the spectrum you have those entrepreneurs who are so focused on value that they barely have enough money to survive personally. This was the mistake we made. We were so focused on our long-term aim of floating the company that we didn't care enough about how much money we were drawing from the business. But this meant that we were broke, and that's not a productive mindset. Success breeds success, and you have to feel as though you are making progress, so starting with a goal to earn a good wage is the best place to focus your initial attention. At the opposite end of the spectrum are those who only focus on earning a good income. That too is a mistake, because these entrepreneurs often just want to look the part rather than actually take the business to its full potential. In addition, income is directly affected by effort, so if you are overly focused on income you can be working like a dog and never actually growing the business, which can be disheartening.

Knowing the stages of business evolution and where you are in your journey will ensure that none of this happens to you. We will discuss each stage and some success strategies to fast track your journey.

Mindset: mountaineer

When looking through the progress lens you must take on the mindset of a mountaineer. The goal of the inexperienced mountaineer is to reach the top. They get summit fever and don't leave enough energy in the tank or light in the day to make it down the mountain alive. The goal of the experienced mountaineer is to reach the summit and to descend successfully too. They will always have planned their exit strategy, even if it means having to call off their summit attempt.

MOUNTAINEER

It is thought, for example, that George Mallory may have been the first person to reach the summit of Mount Everest in 1924, but because he never made it back down the mountain alive that accolade went to Sir Edmund Hillary and Sherpa Tensing Norgay 30 years later. Mountaineers are great at being clear on their goal and then having dogged determination to get there. They plan their journey and are flexible enough to deal with unexpected obstacles as they crop up.

Personality trait: go-getter

The personality trait of the mountaineer mindset is that of the go-getter — someone who leads from the front and get things done regardless of how tough or how frightening things first appear.

When I was 25 years old I decided to climb Mount Kilimanjaro. Kili is the highest freestanding mountain in the world, rising from sea level to nearly 6000 metres. It takes five days to climb and, although it's not a technical climb, the huge increase in altitude makes it extremely dangerous. In fact it is thought that more people have died climbing Kili than climbing Mount Everest! The reason is acute mountain sickness (AMS), a debilitating condition that makes it very hard to breathe — your heart feels like it might explode and every step requires herculean effort! According to the Kilimanjaro National Park, only 30 per cent of those who attempt Kili successfully summit the mountain.

When I climbed Kili I got the early stages of AMS and felt pretty bad. I was thinking of turning back, when one of my climbing buddies handed me Richard Branson's book *Losing My Virginity* and it really inspired me. Apart from taking my mind off how horrible I felt, I was fired up about this daring guy who had dyslexia and left school at 15, but had created a business empire. I decided that if I got to the top of Mount Kilimanjaro, I was going to go back to Australia, start a business and become a millionaire by the time I was 30.

That was my mission. The only way to climb Kili successfully is very, very slowly. The porters would constantly tell us, *pole, pole,* which is Swahili for 'slowly, slowly'. And every ten steps I would repeat my mantra, 'I'm going to be a millionaire before I'm 30'. 'I'm going to be a millionaire before I'm 30'. A statement I kept repeating in my mind. I just kept putting one foot in front of the other and repeating my goal, and eventually I saw this beautiful, weather-beaten sign declaring I had made it to the summit. I put my arms around it, clinging to it for support really, and then proceeded to vomit profusely all over it. That's all I remember from the summit, because being sick is a very bad sign and the porters turned me straight back around and took me down the mountain as quickly as possible.

I think the lesson I drew from my somewhat harrowing experience is that business and mountain climbing are very similar. You need to have a goal and constantly overcome both physical and mental obstacles to make it to the top and back down safely. In fact mountaineering and being an entrepreneur, or what you might call entrepreneering, for me have forever since been intertwined. So much so that when I achieved my goal of becoming a millionaire before I was 30, Trevor and I took 10 of our staff to climb Mount Kilimanjaro.

Entrepreneurship is an adventure. There will be ups and downs; you will probably have feelings of nausea at times; and there will be false summits and numerous paths to the top, but if it wasn't tough at times everyone would be doing it and there would be few opportunities left. Mountaineers wouldn't climb a mountain if there was an elevator to the summit. And the same thing is true in business. It's not always easy, but that's what makes it rewarding and that's what creates the opportunity.

Key outcome: the vision

Running a business, like climbing a mountain, requires a focus on two often conflicting elements. You need to keep your eye on where you are heading—the vision—while also keeping an eye on the success factors that will get you to the next level.

Having a big-picture vision is great and it can be a really powerful motivator, but treated as some distant dream it can become counterproductive to success, or simply forgotten about. This lens is often the one that causes the most confusion because ascertaining the vision can sound similar to working out your endgame from the passion lens. The endgame, however, is all about what you as an individual want to get out of the business or how you want to benefit from the experience. The vision of the progress lens is all about the vision for the business. Sooner or later, preferably sooner, every entrepreneur must separate themselves from the business they create. There will probably be crossover between your endgame and your vision, but the vision is focused on what the business will become beyond the individual's involvement in it. Creating a business is a little like having children: you may create your children but you don't own them and you can't control them forever. You have to raise them as best you can and let them go out into the world and make their own way. Think of endgame as your hopes and aspirations, and vision as the hopes and aspirations of your children.

> You need to keep your eye on where you are heading—the vision—while also keeping an eye on the success factors that will get you to the next level.

Part of the vision–creation process is to create a vision statement, which will also help you use the progress lens in your decision making. First of all, create what's commonly referred to as a BHAG—a big hairy audacious goal. Next, convert your BHAG into something that can be easily communicated and understood. Vision statements usually consist of a sentence or two that use emotive and descriptive words, which may include mention of your stakeholders, your position within your marketplace, and what people might say about you or know about your company.

Examples of vision statements include the following:

- 'To be the best company in the world in the eyes of our customers, shareholders, communities and people. We expect and demand the best we have to offer by keeping always Alcoa's values top of mind.' (Aloca)

- 'To become the World's leading consumer company for automobile products and services.' (Ford)
- 'To be the World's premier food company offering nutritious, superior tasting foods to people everywhere.' (Heinz)

That gives you an idea about how these large companies see themselves and how they fit into the larger world stage.

What level are you at now?

There are always going to be a series of key stages that you will encounter and have to successfully navigate in your business adventure, just as there are in climbing a mountain. Broadly speaking, your focus will shift from income to profit and then finally to value as you progress through the eight stages outlined in figure 12.1.

Figure 12.1: the stages of the business venture—the progress lens

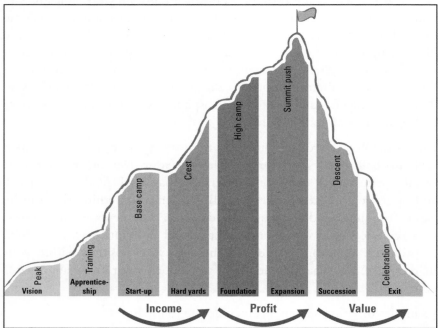

A few years ago I undertook a nonstop 100-kilometre walking challenge to raise money for Oxfam. At first look, the challenge appeared beyond

me, but rather than thinking of the whole 100 kilometres, I started to break the trip down into eight bite-sized pieces. Planning each leg in 10–15 kilometre stretches, and organising a support team to meet us at the end of each leg helped get my mind around how we could succeed and keep motivated. During our training we undertook each of the different legs—noting the differences between the rugged bush tracks, road stretches or big hill climbs and descents. When the big day came we focused on completing each particular leg and focused only on that immediate stretch of terrain. We never thought about the next leg or the leg after that—instead our only goal was to complete each individual leg—a strategy that allowed our entire team of four to complete the challenge in 30 hours.

Similarly, to be successful in business you can't allow yourself to become overwhelmed by how you are going to go from a start-up to a multimillion dollar exit in one attempt. Instead you need to divide your journey into achievable, bite-sized pieces. This makes the journey feel much more realistic and manageable, and you can more easily establish the success factors you are aiming for at each given stage.

Before we discuss the eight stages that make up your business journey, let's consider the three broad phases of focus—income, profit and value.

- *Income.* In this phase of the business you are focused on making enough money to survive, and beyond that to afford the lifestyle you want.
  Income = your own salary before tax (dividends are bonuses down the track).
- *Profit.* In the profit phase you are focusing on building your profit so that the business can scale and stand on its own.
  Profit = earnings before interest and tax (EBIT) and after paying yourself a wage (not dividends).
- *Value.* In the value phase you are focusing on creating a business that is saleable and independent of you.
  Value = the valuation amount you can sell the business for (usually expressed as a multiple of EBIT, such as six times).

The focus on income, profit and value vary according to the stage of business you are currently in.

The eight stages of business

The eight distinct stages you will go through in business are:

- vision — dream it
- apprenticeship — trial it
- start-up — commence it
- hard-yards — keep at it
- foundation — crack it
- expansion — milk it
- succession — delegate it
- exit — leave it.

Vision and apprenticeship are both pre-start-up stages in business evolution.

Vision

The first of the pre-start-up phases is vision, where you decide what mountain it is you want to climb. Vision is all about deciding what the goal of the business is, what product or service you want to supply and what legacy you wish to leave as a result of your business. The vision is all about where you want to be in the future. And, unlike an endgame, which is mostly about you as an individual, the vision can even outgrow your involvement in the business, because it is about where the business will be in the future.

It's important that this vision be compelling, inspiring and audacious. It has to ignite your passions and propel you forward, and you need to share it with others so it can inspire them too. Your vision has to be powerful enough to keep you going through the inevitable tough times and ideally motivate others to do the same.

In Blueprint, our vision was to revolutionise the marketing industry through a concept we called marriage marketing where we focused our attention on existing customers, not on acquiring new ones. It sounds a pretty basic concept today, but this was in an era before customer relationship management (CRM) was a commonly accepted practice. In fact, most large organisations spent most of their marketing budget attracting and giving the best offers to new customers, often at the expense of existing customers, who started to leave them in droves. The customer divorce rate was massive and extremely costly, and so we set out to change the marketing landscape. We worked with companies to create a happy marriage with their customers—to build trusting communication with them that would not only help them stay married to the company, but also allow our clients to upsell and cross-sell more products. We decided that we would know we had achieved this vision when we were working for a large number of corporations and attracting a significant percentage of our clients' marketing budgets.

In order to successfully complete the vision stage you have to *dream it*, and be clear on what you want to achieve in your business.

Apprenticeship

The second pre-start-up stage is the apprenticeship stage, which can take many years. Everything you do before starting a business is in some way an apprenticeship for that endeavour. In your apprenticeship you are building your knowledge and expertise in readiness for starting your own business. Sometimes that apprenticeship might have been a previous business, which served as an apprenticeship for the main game, and it may be that you need to close down one business to start up and focus on the business that is going to become your legacy.

Another form of apprenticeship that people often ignore is working for others. Instead of being resentful of your job, as though it is in some way holding you back from your true purpose, view it as your apprenticeship and use it to your benefit. How, for example, could you use the knowledge, contacts and insights that you have gained in your role as an employee to further your entrepreneurial goals? Perhaps you need to start your business without leaving your employment, so you reduce the need for income from your new enterprise. This is especially important if you have a family to support and have responsibilities and commitments outside your own drive for success. It may be sexy to pack it all in and fly by the seat of your pants, but that approach is not for everyone and can add an enormous amount of unnecessary pressure.

It is also important to appreciate that vision and apprenticeship are often interchangeable. Some people may start with vision and seek out an appropriate apprenticeship, while others may find themselves in the apprenticeship stage and only then become excited about a possible vision. For me, my apprenticeship before Blueprint was forged in three parts.

First, as a kidpreneur I had eight businesses before I left school and two at university, including my strawberry and gardening businesses. Second, I worked in various sales and management roles for a major American financial organisation that understood the power, and profit, that comes from focusing on existing customers. And finally my apprenticeship started when I worked for a few months doing menial sales jobs for four different marketing companies that would be the closest thing we had to competitors.

In order to successfully complete the apprenticeship stage you have to *trial it*—to get the skills and connections you need to start your business in earnest.

Start-up

Once you have gained the experience and confidence to go out on your own it's time to start your own business. The first goal in these early days is income and income alone, knowing your revenue is likely to be half what you project and your expenses will be double what you expect. Start-up is an exciting and terrifying time. It is always fuelled by unrealistic expectations and overly optimistic projections.

Our start-up in Blueprint was an equal mix of excitement and naivety. I can still remember the feelings of awe and pride I felt sitting in my office. I was in a pokey little office with second-hand, beaten-up furniture without any staff except myself, but it felt amazing. The possibilities felt endless. Yet, because we started with such a small amount of start-up capital—Trevor and I had thrown in $5000 each—we really struggled to make ends meet in those early days. We focused too much on the value without considering income, and consequently often found ourselves without even enough money to buy a train ticket! I had to jump the turnstiles at the station a few times, which I'm very embarrassed to admit now and it didn't feel great then. It's hardly the way to generate self-respect when you're trying to create a world-beating business.

In order to successfully complete the start-up stage you have to *commence it*—to decide to get started even though you don't have all of your bases covered or your plan thought through.

You have completed the start-up stage when you are paying yourself enough income for you to survive financially without going backwards. You may require some short-term modifications to your business model to focus on cash flow, which is what enables your business to maximise your income, not profit.

Hard yards

After the initial flurry of excitement has passed and you begin to settle into business life it's time for you to put in the hard yards. Hard yards is when the rose-coloured glasses are taken off and you realise that perhaps not everyone on the planet actually does want what you are selling. It's when you realise that closing a sale takes three months, not three hours. It's when you realise that you are working harder, for longer and less money than you ever did in the comfort of your corporate office. It's also when you start to second-guess your decision to go into business in the first place.

But giving up is not an option—you have to keep the faith. The biggest challenge of the hard yards stage is working out how to grow the business while growing your income to a sufficient level, beyond survival.

At Blueprint the hard yards were not only our hardest and darkest times, they were also the most memorable. Success achieved through adversity is what makes the best stories, and our business was no different. Trying to drum up clients when we didn't have a reputation or showcase office was never going to be easy. To land a major Australian bank we had to resort to what we later came to call our Hollywood set. We hired new furniture, staff, computer monitors and set them up in the vacant office next door just so we looked bigger than we actually were. We knew we could do a great job for them, but sometimes first impressions count and they did—this client went on to be a multimillion dollar a year account for us.

In order to successfully complete the hard yards stage you have to *keep at it*! You need to keep motivating yourself and surviving as a business despite the various obstacles thrown at you.

You have completed the hard yards stage when you are paying yourself a level of income that is equivalent to what you could dictate as an employee on the job market. And while nearly every accountant will encourage you to split dividends with salary for the tax advantages, I encourage you not to listen. Pay the little extra in tax, because before you can be paid for your equity investment (dividends) you first need to be paid as an employee (salary). This keeps the honesty in the system and ensures you aren't overcomplicating the different reasons why you are in business—to first earn a wage, then to build a dividend stream and finally to create an equity windfall. So with income achieved, there is no longer an opportunity cost of being in business and you can move on to the profit phase.

Foundation

In the profit phases your focus shifts to building a profitable business. You are no longer primarily concerned with how much salary you can draw from the business; instead, you are looking for ways to maximise business earnings, before interest and tax but after paying yourself a wage.

With your income needs met, your focus must move to creating a profitable business model (more of that in chapter 13). This stage can take a while to get right as you experiment with different ways of working to find the ideal combination. You need to develop a product or service that customers are willing to pay for without increasing your overheads too much so you can turn a profit. Too many entrepreneurs prematurely scale up their business without first having a solid foundation—essentially a business model that works.

We knew that we hadn't cracked our business model at Blueprint until we had ticked three crucial boxes. First, we had to be in a market where people were buying what we had to offer. Second, we had to be the purchase of choice in this market based on our differentiation. And third, we had to be able to deliver our product profitably every time. This took us much longer than we would have liked, particularly waiting for the market to catch on to the different proposition we were offering, but when it finally happened we knew we were onto a winner.

In order to successfully complete the foundation stage you have to *crack it*! When you have a proven formula and are able to clearly articulate your business model, then you are ready for expansion.

You have completed the foundation when you no longer need to experiment or try new business avenues. This can be challenging for an entrepreneur who is constantly thinking about new ideas but it's absolutely essential. When our chairman asked us which two of our four businesses we were going to move forward into expansion we were shocked because all four were doing okay, but it was a brilliant question that transformed our business success. Sooner or later you need to stop experimenting and throw all your effort behind one avenue. The foundation stage is complete when you can see proof of the enormous opportunity the product you have is attracting in the market you have chosen. Weak business models fall apart when you expand full tilt: crack the business model first and then put your foot on the accelerator—not the other way around.

Expansion

Expansion is the second part of the focus on profit. When you appropriately invest in a solid foundation or business model the expansion phase is your time to reap the rewards. This is the time to grow the business as fast as possible without growing so fast that your income or profit is jeopardised.

Blueprint appeared in the *Business Review Weekly* Fast 100 for two consecutive years, first as the sixth fastest growing and then the third fastest growing company in Australia. After that we dropped out of eligibility for the awards because we employed more than 250 people, but that didn't stop us growing just as quickly. Our revenue doubled every two years and we finished with more than 1000 employees.

In order to successfully complete the expansion stage you have to *milk it*—make hay while the proverbial sun shines: essentially, simultaneously maximise your revenue and profit.

You have completed the expansion stage when you outgrow the business or it outgrows you. When you outgrow the business you can no longer see yourself leading the growth of the business because you don't enjoy the industry or the size of the business, or it no longer challenges you. The business outgrows you when you find that your skills are not suited to the size of company you have created or the new challenges created by your business reaching the size it has grown to.

Succession

Once you have a winning business model and you have maximised the revenue to within your ability or interest, you need to get your succession plan right. This stage is all about creating value in the business. And this must be done without negatively impacting either income or profit.

A business is always more valuable if the people who started the business are no longer in the business. This is something we learned from our advisers and which ultimately made us double the personal return in the final sale. The reason is simple. If a business has a strong succession plan and the people who started the business are no longer running it and it is still a successful and profitable business, then that reduces the risk for the potential buyer. One of the biggest concerns when buying an existing business is that the success of that business is somehow down to a magic formula that only the owner knows, or that the success is attributable to a key figurehead, and without that figurehead the business will crumble. If you can prove that this is not the case, then your business will be much more valuable because you have shown the buyer that the business functions and thrives with or without you.

At Blueprint, like at many entrepreneurial-led businesses, our succession was not easy. In fact we made four failed attempts before we finally got it right. In our first attempt we tried to promote an existing employee who was young and particularly promising because we thought that this would be the best way to replicate our unique culture. This attempt failed not because of capability but because we had underestimated how big a shadow the founders of a business cast. In fact, getting staff and clients used to someone new taking control instead of dealing direct with the owners can be a real struggle. We then experimented with bringing in an executive from a competitor, without success. Then we had an unfortunate episode where we thought it would be a good idea for the management team to democratically elect a successor. This failed experiment in human psychology caused a lot of harm to the business that took years for it to recover from. Finally, we took a more traditional solution and used an executive recruitment agency to appoint a proven CEO. This appointment was also assisted and given greater authority when I threw a retirement party—finally signalling to our staff that this was the last succession attempt and it was time to embrace the change and move forward with a new leader.

In order to successfully complete the succession stage you have to *delegate it*—hand the reigns over to a management team of one or more employees and empower them to make decisions around the running and direction of the business.

You have completed the succession when you appoint a CEO and become the chairman with less day-to-day responsibility for the business. Or you take on a non-essential or less central role, such as starting a new business initiative within the company or working in sales, or taking an easily replaceable position that has no direct management reports or responsibility.

Exit

With your succession plan identified and implemented, your team become responsible for continuing to build value in the business with the aim of achieving a financial or physical exit. Not everyone wants to sell out and start again. It very much depends on your character and your passions. If your passion is what your business does and you love it, then why sell? It may be that you simply want to be able to come and go a little more or that you want to work for six months and take the rest of the year off. If this is the case, you won't need to execute a financial exit.

If it is the thrill of business that you love and you are not particularly passionate about what the business actually does, then you may want to sell up and start the adventure all over again or do something completely different. None of these outcomes is better than any other, but you have to know what that outcome is from the outset instead of meandering along.

In Blueprint our financial exit happened in two parts. First, we sold 20 per cent of the business to give us enough security to allow us to fully empower our successors. This stage also coincided with the introduction of an attractive options scheme for the management team and board. The second part was 18 months later when we sold the business in a private equity–funded buyout.

In order to successfully complete the exit stage you have to *leave it*—to finally say goodbye to the company that you love and the people that make it what it is. Like a teenager leaving home, business exit is a rite of passage that allows your company to grow up and grow out from under you as the founder.

You have completed the exit when you are no longer physically working in or for the business other than as a board member, director or chairperson, or when you have sold the business in any one of the many possible options, including a public float, a trade sale, a management buy-out or buy-in, or a leveraged private equity buy-out.

Creating compelling milestones

Business is not just about the destination—it's meant to be challenging and rewarding too and it can only be those things if you enjoy the journey. To me business success is about keeping your eye on the prize *and* enjoying the adventure toward that prize through the creation of compelling milestones. To simplify this approach, you need to concentrate on creating empowering milestones for each of the three main business stages—income, profit and value.

If you are in the income stage, identify the income you need and then identify the best opportunities that will generate cash-positive revenue without substantial investment. Think about tapping into existing markets, using existing expertise, leveraging existing relationships or networks, or even moonlighting between your business and paid employment.

If you are in the profit stage of your business, seek to identify sales, support and operations activities that could have the greatest impact on profitability. Think about your assets and expenses, the opportunity for residual income, pre-paid income, outsourcing to save operational costs and minimise staff requirements, increasing your price or defering expenses.

If you are in the value stage of your business, conduct industry research into what similar businesses have sold for and the multiple of earnings they achieved. Identify what you need to do to ensure your business is valued at the highest possible value so you can achieve the best possible price and embed those features into the business. Think about your succession plan—a company is always worth more if the person who started it is no longer running it—and ensure that the revenue is steady or increasing. Think about your positioning in the industry and how you are different. Consider how you can protect and secure your position moving forward through contracts, assets or patents.

Progress in decision making

Becoming really clear on your progress will give power to your decision making, because you will be able to immediately assess if the decisions under consideration are going to help or hinder you in climbing to the next business stage and eventually exiting the business successfully. The key question to consider when bringing progress to bear in your decision making is, 'Which option will help us reach our business vision and climb to the next business stage?'

While you need to view your decisions in the context of your overall vision, you also need to focus on the very next step to keep grounded in the present. If, for example, your vision is to make a net profit of $1 million in one year and you currently make $15 000, that's so far from the current situation that the goal can be too daunting.

If, instead, you focus on the incremental steps between where you are and where you want to be then the plan is much more motivational and exciting. You could, for example, initially focus on taking $50 000 out of the business as earned income. Once that milestone has been achieved, you could shift your focus to making $100 000 profit, and so on. The achievement of these goals is in line with your big vision, but each is also taking you to the next level.

> The key question to consider when bringing progress to bear in your decision making is, 'Which option will help us reach our business vision and climb to the next business stage?'

Given my passion for mountaineering I decided to take the Branson Centre boot camp entrepreneurs to climb a nearby mountain—well, hill, by Himalayan standards. Rather than run through the eight stages of the progress lens in the classroom I aimed to unpack each as we completed each stage of the climb. With much anticipation we set off through the African bush, winding through some rugged terrain, then stone hopped over a sizeable river, and then fought our way through some head-high undergrowth to the base of this sizeable *kopje*, or small mountain.

Looking at the sheer slope and assessing the inexperienced climbers, I started to regret my bravado in thinking we could just pick a mountain in the middle of nowhere and get to the summit without a track and without injuring someone. So giving the participants instructions to await my return, I set off at a fast scramble to see if the most likely route up was safe. Within 30 minutes I was at the top and while the route was hard, I figured at least some of the stronger members of the group would make it without having to turn back. Rushing back down to join them I suddenly found myself flying through the air, tumbling head over heels to finish 25 metres down the slope with a jarring crack against one of the red granite boulders. My ankle had shattered and I lay whimpering in the dirt wondering what had happened.

It turns out I had unwittingly come across a baboon slide. As these aggressive primates slide down a slope they release an oil from the glands in their pink behinds, creating a slip-and-slide surface. My mind wasn't on this technicality; I was more focused on the pain and how I was going to get off the mountain and continue the boot camp. Fortunately the shock soon kicked in and the pain was somehow masked. I yelled for the team to meet me up on the rock, and put on a brave face to meet them. Pretending everything was okay, I put in charge a new leader and instructed them to head up and down at a snail's pace while I organised the next activity — essentially, to buy me time to think about my predicament.

I managed to limp down to the river and rest my ankle in its cool waters; waves of stars appeared before my eyes as I faded in and out of consciousness. A few hours later when the entrepreneurs returned jubilant at their success, I told them the news — their leader was incapacitated. I was living proof that the most dangerous part of a mountain climb is the descent and, similarly, in business, one of the hardest things they would ever do is a succession. So the next activity I announced was for them to get me safely off the mountain. Without prompting from me, the teams volunteered themselves into one of three stages for my rescue. I was impressed that they had learnt that it is advisable to split your bigger mission into manageable stages — a key lesson from the progress lens and mountaineer mindset.

The first group had to carry me through the undergrowth, and the next group was charged with getting me over the river safely. And finally the last group were given the responsibility of building a stretcher and getting me the 3.5 kilometres back to the truck. It took a few hours and some hair-raising moments where I thought I would go from bad to worse, but they took the succession seriously and I arrived back at the lodge in one piece. I now have a steel plate and six pins in my ankle to remind me of the dangers of the descent, and the entrepreneurs have had a lesson about the progress lens that they are unlikely to forget.

When making decisions, remember to take on the mountaineer mindset to ensure each decision gets you closer to your next business stage and long-term business objective. Gaining clarity through the progress lens means that you are constantly aware of the business stages. When you understand what stage your business is in you can manage your decisions accordingly so that you move more easily from start to grow to exit. Assuming, of course, you have a solid business model, which is the subject of the next lens — prototype.

Key points

» The progress lens is the first of the three lenses concerned with your business rather than you as an individual, and it helps explore your *business stage.*

» Appreciate the various stages of business from start-up to exit, because success at each stage requires a different focus. The progress lens helps you recognise where you are in your business evolution so you can apply that focus appropriately.

» When looking through the progress lens you must take on the mindset of a mountaineer.

» The personality trait of the mountaineer mindset is that of the go-getter—someone who leads from the front and get things done regardless of how tough or how frightening they first appear.

» As you navigate a series of key stages in your business adventure your focus will shift from income to profit and finally to value.

» The eight distinct stages of business are vision, apprenticeship, start-up, hard yards, foundation, expansion, succession and exit.

» Being clear on your progress means you will be able to immediately assess if the decisions under consideration will help or hinder you in climbing to the next business stage and eventually exiting the business successfully.

» The key question to consider when bringing progress to bear in your decision making is, 'Which option will help us reach our business vision and climb to the next business stage?'

» Take on the mountaineer mindset when you are making decisions to ensure each decision gets you closer to your long-term business objective.

» Gaining clarity through the progress lens means that you are constantly aware of the business stages. When you understand what stage your business is in you can manage your decisions accordingly so that you move more easily from start to grow to exit.

Chapter 13

The prototype lens

The prototype lens is all about creating a compelling *business model*. Every successful business has a unique formula or way of operating, even if you don't call it a business model. There are far too many entrepreneurs or business owners who have really poor business models. They find it too hard to sell the product or service, too expensive and difficult to deliver, or the business model causes too many headaches, or they are trying to do too many things, which confuses their stakeholders. It's also much harder to make enough money to pay yourself and generate enough cash flow to fund your expansion if you aren't clear about your business model. Your business model is a strategic rationale for how your business will create and deliver value. It includes core business issues, such as purpose, product or services offerings, delivery and pricing, and explains how you will make money in the business.

> The prototype lens is all about creating a compelling *business model.*

One of the mistakes entrepreneurs make around their business model is that they don't specialise their offering to a specific market and they don't systemise the way they do business. The result is a watered-down brand, or a chaotic company culture. Most people go into business with a set idea of what will make them successful, but things don't always go to plan. In fact, in the early stages you have to have the flexibility to see when something isn't working, and the courage to try new approaches until you find a model that works for you.

One of the benefits of a well thought-out and executed business model is that it helps you with two of the most enduring clichés in business: namely, how do you work smarter, not harder; and how do you work *on* your business, and not *in* it. I'm sure you've heard those things many times before. By figuring out a winning business formula, you can start to focus on working less for bigger results. Your business model will also help you evolve so that your business is less reliant on your skills and personality and you can start to delegate and outsource activity, which allows you to become more strategic rather than being dragged into the day-to-day operations of your business all of the time.

Mindset: master chef

When looking through the prototype lens you must take on the mindset of a master chef. Master chefs are great at creating innovative dishes that their customers love, creating a unique blend of taste and presentation. They know the ingredients to use, the exact blend of spices, when to include what, and the cooking times for an optimal result. Once perfected, they then get their junior chefs to replicate the dish over and over and over again, so they leverage their input without having to do all of the work.

MASTER CHEF

The master chef mindset encourages you to think about the ingredients you need for a successful product or service, and how you will combine those ingredients to wow your customers. This doesn't have to be complicated; often the simplest recipes are the best.

Personality trait: the experimenter

The personality trait of the master chef is that of the experimenter. In your own kitchen there are two ways you might choose to cook. You can either follow your grandmother's recipe that's been handed down from generation to generation. If you follow that recipe to the letter, you will end up with the desired result. This is like buying a franchise: a great way to start your business, but not a great way to create an entrepreneurial business where there is a high risk and a high take-out return.

The other way to cook, which I think is more fun, is to experiment like a master chef. Open up the fridge, see what you have and throw some random ingredients together to see what works. Sometimes you end up with an inedible mess and you have to order in pizza. And occasionally the experimenting results in a really unique and tasty dish. When it comes to business, it's your job to experiment in every part of your business, so you can find the very best recipe for your business success, which essentially is your business model. Endless planning and researching won't produce a great business model. It will either produce a copy of someone else's model, or it will crumble under pressure because your assumptions were based on guesswork, not facts. Experimenting will eventually get you to a unique business model that's hopefully going to make you a lot of money.

When I lived in a share house in Melbourne I used to cook a really great red wine stir-fry. This one time when I went to make it I discovered half way through that I was missing two vital ingredients—red wine and teriyaki sauce. So I improvised and put red cordial and vegemite in the stir-fry instead. My flatmates came home and I didn't tell them what was in it and they thought it was the best meal I'd ever cooked. Had I not been game enough to experiment I would never have discovered my now infamous red cordial and vegemite stir-fry!

Essential business model considerations

So what elements need to be considered for a compelling business model? Unfortunately the bulk of business theory about how to develop the right business model is far too complicated. These theories are often developed by academics with little or no firsthand experience of business, or they come from corporate success stories which bear little resemblance to smaller entrepreneurial businesses.

In truth there should be nothing complicated about a business model—I have outlined my simplified business model in figure 13.1 (overleaf).

The first thing to consider is that there are three core stakeholders in any business—customers, investors and employees. An entrepreneur is actually both an investor and an employee, especially in the early stages. If your business model isn't helping you build relationships and success with these stakeholder groups, then it is unlikely it will be successful. Starting with your stakeholders is a crucial step in building a business model that will be relevant and not based all around you.

Next we need to consider the three capabilities that you'll have to develop to serve your stakeholders—sales, operations and a support capability:

- *Sales.* This encompasses your efforts to increase your revenue through new or existing customers, and includes marketing, PR, advertising, prospect management and sales.

- *Operations.* This is your focus on delivering on the products and services that have been sold, or building products and services that you can sell in the future. It includes fulfilment, warehousing, production and customer service.

- *Support.* These are all of the functions keeping your company in business, but these are also elements that don't directly make money, like accounting, legal, IT, and HR capabilities within your business.

Figure 13.1: simplified business model

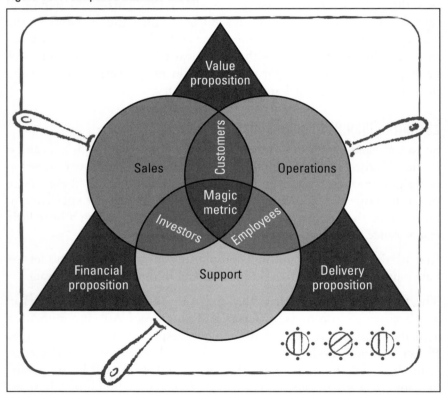

The next element in the prototype model is your propositions, which includes your value proposition, your delivery proposition and your financial proposition. By combining these three propositions with your sales and operations and support capability, you will start to serve your stakeholders better, and you'll find that your business model will start to become really clear. And if you use the magic metric, which I will explain, to track the critical measure you will be better able to stay focused on what really matters in order to achieve business success.

Value proposition

The value proposition is concerned with sales and operations, and is customer focused. It is what you are offering to your customers to entice them to buy. It includes the features and benefits that your frontline sales team present to the customers.

The value proposition is concerned with sales and operations, and is customer focused. It is what you are offering to your customers to entice them to buy.

By developing your powerful value proposition and factoring it into your marketing and sales effort, you will begin to sell more products and services to more customers. You will also keep those customers for longer and hopefully you will also be able to charge more for your products and services. There are five steps in a process for building your value proposition:

- *Decide on a niche target market.* Consider who is going to buy what you're selling. If the market is too broad, start to narrow it down into niche groups, understanding your competitive positioning. Compared with other products or service provisions that are out there, how does your offer rate, or what could you do to make a better offer than is already on the market? Find a niche that you can really own. It's better to be a big fish in a small pond than a small fish in a big pond.

- *Map the customer buying process.* Consider the stages that a customer goes through in buying your particular product or service. It might include initial awareness, research, testimonials from friends, getting quotes and then finally making the purchase. You then need to ensure that you match your sales process to the buying stage of your customers. Doing a hard sell when a customer doesn't even think they need your product is simply not going to work. Or if customers are used to buying this type of product or service you offer online, or over the phone, they may not appreciate a door-to-door sales approach, for example.

- *Identify rational and emotional needs.* To achieve a new customer or upsell to an existing one will require a value proposition that talks to both the rational and emotional needs of your prospective customer. You need to think about what will motivate a customer to buy from you, what problems will your product or service solve, and how will you make that person feel. Consider rational needs, which include how to make something easier, faster, cheaper, superior, greater or scarcer; and emotional needs, such as fear, greed and pride — which might include the fear of missing out on a special offer, the greed of getting a good deal, or the pride of having something that not everyone else has.

- *Formulate features and benefits.* Consider the service, product and price features and benefits that you can own in your customer's mind. Staying top of mind will ensure your company is more likely to be chosen when a customer is making a purchasing decision. Customers will not necessarily make the mental leap between a feature of your product or service and a benefit. Features are what the product or service has and benefits are how these features are perceived by the customer and how they will help the customer. For instance, a feature of modern vehicles is an airbag. A benefit is that it keeps your family safe. So spell out the benefits of your products and services in all of your marketing and sales efforts.

- *Evolve through testing.* Try to test your product or service through selling rather than research. You don't necessarily have to completely build a product in order to be able to see if it's going to sell. Use the information developed from feedback to refine the offer and evolve your value proposition.

In summary, the value proposition is all about the customer. You need to develop a compelling value proposition if you want to make more sales for your business.

Delivery proposition

The delivery proposition is concerned with operations and support and is employee focused. It is about how you produce or deliver the product or service you have sold, or will sell. It is where the bulk of your non–sales oriented employees will spend their time.

One of the keys to creating a compelling delivery proposition that can be replicated as you scale up the business is to create systems. Systems will create scalability for your business because you don't have to start from scratch every time. It will help you create more innovation. If systems ensure consistent delivery then no-one needs to keep reinventing the wheel, which leaves time for innovation. It also promotes delegation, because you are sure that the work will be done to an existing system. Your people will therefore be more accountable if you include measurement of key outcomes as part of the system. And finally, systems are going to help you with succession, because they're going to be easier to hand over to a new staff member or owner.

There are hundreds of theories on introducing systems into your business, so rather than discussing these I will demonstrate a system with an example. One of the elements that most companies require is some kind of lead-tracking process. They need to know where their leads are coming from so they can determine where to put their marketing budget. The first step in creating a lead-tracking system would be to list all the possible sources where leads could come from and update them monthly, based on the marketing campaigns that you are conducting. For example, you might look at referrals or the Yellow Pages or seminars or Google ad words, affiliates or advertising. The next step might be to list where the leads could come into contact with your business. For instance, do leads come from inbound phone calls; outbound phone calls that you have made; web search; through emails or social media; or from walk-ins off the street, or SMS or even mail.

The next step is to create some kind of system to find out the lead source. You could ask the customer by phone, or have them select from a list before they can make their inquiry, or have sales people ask the source before pitching something; or have an automatic way of tracking, so for instance, you could have a separate toll-free number for each campaign, or a separate landing page on your website, or domain name, or maybe even a special offer code that the customer types in.

You also need to ensure that every database entry has a lead code, the date the lead was first entered into the system and who has since taken responsibility for it. This quality control will make sure that your system is being followed.

The last step is to have someone periodically match the sales to the date they were first entered, and to which channel they're being derived, so you can work out where you need to spend your marketing dollars in the future. Because it's not all about leads: it's about leads that turn into sales.

As you can see from this example, even a relatively small area of your company can be systemised. It is the combination of these systems that make up your delivery proposition. It is all about producing a quality, reputable product and service at the lowest cost possible with the fewest faults or issues. The way to develop a compelling delivery proposition is to focus on systemisation in every single part of your business.

Financial proposition

The financial proposition is concerned with support and sales and is investor focused. It is the economics of how you sell a good or service, deliver on it and then support it for profit.

It's amazing how many businesses—some that are household names—actually aren't nearly as successful as they sound. Just because you are the biggest in the category or you have lots of revenue or lots of staff doesn't mean you are successful. Focusing on the financial proposition will help you be the right kind of successful. So how do we create a winning financial model? For me there are two parts—price right and keep your costs down.

One of the hardest elements to get right for your financial proposition (and one that has the most profound influence on your profit) is setting your price. A useful exercise is to break down your price into the key components:

- cost of sales
- labour costs
- production costs
- variable costs
- overheads
- profit
- tax.

So many entrepreneurs just pluck a figure out of the air or they look at what the competition is charging and price in a similar manner. I remember doing this exercise in one of my training programs when one entrepreneur volunteered to go through the pricing exercise in front of a group of peers. By the end she was almost in tears because the figure she had been charging, which she thought was more than fair and would make her a decent profit, actually meant she made a loss on every job she had done.

This process can be a real eye-opener for the entrepreneur and business owner, and it can also be used to educate your staff and clients on how you price and why. Those connected to a business both inside and out rarely realise how expensive things are to deliver and how small a percentage of the revenue or turnover you actually make as profit. If you are selling a big-ticket item, for example, it's an easy mistake for staff to assume you're rich or the business is rich and not perhaps be as frugal in their purchasing as they could be. If, however, they understand how much of the price is actually profit, they are likely to behave differently. In addition, selling becomes easier because you can articulate how you arrive at your price rather than it being an arbitrary number.

Clearly this approach works best if your margins are small and the cost of the product or service seems high to staff and customers. If your margin is high then transparent pricing could backfire!

The second part of the financial proposition is to be really clear on what makes up the costs of your business. There are four types of costs you need to consider:

- *Cost price*—how much you pay for your goods. Essentially the cash register price and you should remember that this can usually be negotiated.
- *Real cost*—how much your goods really cost. For instance, while the cost price of a new person might be their wage, you also have to factor in benefits, recruitment fee and training, bonuses, phone calls, workstation and chair, management time and training. Things usually cost a lot more than they at first appear and sometimes the cheapest sounding goods have the highest real cost.
- *Opportunity cost*—this is the cost that one purchase decision rules out in making some other purchase. For instance choosing Mac computers instead of PCs determines your future software and hardware choices.
- *Financial cost*—this is where you factor in the cash flow, balance sheet and profit and loss impact of your business approach. For instance, if you can defer the terms of a purchase or if you can depreciate a cost, it is better for your business.

Communicating your business model

Once you have developed your business model, you have to communicate it to your stakeholders. So many business models or success formulas are floating around in the entrepreneur's head, which means it's hard to make your business scalable, or else they're so complex and loaded with jargon that they aren't easy to communicate. To overcome this, I'm going to share with you five powerful ways to communicate your business model:

- *Diagram.* Often a flowchart or other visual model that outlines the key components of your business and their relationship to each other.

- *Financial model.* Often a summary spreadsheet that calculates the relative success of your business based on a variable set of assumptions that you can alter to help predict outcomes.

- *Metaphor.* Painting a picture in someone's mind, or telling a compelling story from a completely different field. Use a hook that already exists in someone's mind; for instance, in our business we used marriage marketing as a metaphor to demonstrate the types of committed relationships we helped our clients achieve.

- *Paradox.* Choosing between two diametrically opposing strategies. For instance, some businesses are really powerful when they promote themselves locally in one suburb, while other businesses are really powerful when they promote themselves globally, but doing both or being somewhere in the middle is not as successful. The paradox is choosing between local or global, both potential winning strategies.

- *Comparison.* Creating a hybrid model using a mixture of signature traits from other companies. An example might be wanting to be to housing what McDonald's is to hamburgers. This lets people know what you are trying to achieve very simply because you are borrowing from existing knowledge.

The best way to work out what communication method or methods are going to work for you is to trial pitching them to your stakeholders.

Key outcome: the magic metric

Considering all the essential factors of a successful business model, it is easy to see why entrepreneurs can become so swamped in numbers they forget to analyse them or stop to challenge their relevance. As such they can either drown in information or ignore it, and neither is a useful outcome. Instead you need to come up with a magic metric.

The idea behind the magic metric is that you shouldn't count everything—only count what counts. At the heart of your business model will be one or two tell-tale metrics that you can easily access to establish the health and vitality of your business. Your magic metric therefore is the variable that has the biggest influence and impact on driving business success.

Every business or industry has a different metric. In the hotel and airline industries, for example, it is percentage occupancy. In car manufacturing the magic metric is percentage market share. In real estate it's number of listings (which explains how enthusiasm for your property always wanes after an agent gets your listing!). Lawyers and accountants are interested only in billable hours, and fund managers, for example, measure performance by amount of funds under management.

Coming up with, sharing and keeping a magic metric foremost in your team's mind will help drive behaviour and strategies, and how you judge and celebrate success. Note that profit is an outcome and not a cause in itself, so it doesn't make a good magic metric. If your magic metric is not immediately obvious don't worry—they rarely are. In most cases it takes a few attempts to arrive at the magic metric that is right for your business.

To help you come up with some options for your magic metric consider whether your business success is driven largely by sales, operations or support.

If the success of your business is mostly driven by sales, consider sales-oriented metrics, such as number of new clients, number of premium clients, number of leads, cost per sale, length of time a customer stays with your business or churns, the percentage of sales to leads, or the number of new customer referrals per month.

If the success of your business is mostly driven by operations and capacity utilisation, consider metrics such as average billable hours, gross profit per hour, average unit cost, percentage returns or complaints, or average cost per product.

And if the success of your business is mostly driven by how you execute on your support areas, consider metrics such as percentage of overheads to revenue, percentage of debt to equity or number of debtor days.

Now take the three or four most appropriate variables and assess their suitability as your magic metric against the following parameters:

- *Measureability.* Which metric is best able to be measured in the following ways:
  - *Quantifiability.* Is it easy to quantify and collect accurate data? Note, for instance, that staff surveys are often quite subjective.
  - *Regularity.* Can the data be collected regularly? Note, for instance, that a quarterly staff survey doesn't allow for the frequent assessment of improvement.
- *Motivationability.* The best metric used to motivate your staff to action, for example, if you find a positive metric that your team can focus on, then morale can be boosted as progressive goals are kicked.
- *Profitability.* While profit is not a good magic metric in itself, a magic metric does need to have a high resulting positive impact on profit. Assess each potential metric on its ability to directly link to profitability.
- *Influenceability.* How easy is it to influence the variable? As an example, if you are a business liquidation expert, although your business may increase in an economic downturn, you don't have the ability to influence the variable of the economy.

Further road test your proposed magic metrics by considering these additional questions:

- Which metric enables you to experiment with different strategies and assess their impact?
- Which variable helps you compare your company with your competitors?
- Which variable is the key to helping you make it to the next growth stage?

Once you have your magic metric you can then use it to improve your success by developing a business model that helps you maximise your magic metric: setting goals for your staff and your company; recognising when key landmarks are reached; evolving your strategy to ensure the magic metric improves; and finally, spending funds or making expense decisions only when they will maximise your magic metric.

Don't worry if you start with a magic metric and you realise after a couple of months there is something more suitable. This experimentation will get you closer to and clearer on what will be the most appropriate metric for your business.

Prototyping in decision making

Becoming clear on your prototype lens will give you power in decision making because you will be able to immediately assess if the decisions under consideration are going to help or hinder you in refining your recipe for business success. The key question to consider when bringing prototyping to bear in your decision making is, 'Which option will improve our magic metric and enhance our business model?'

Considering the impact of your magic metric can help you arrive at the best decision. For instance, trying to decide between buying a new computer or spending those funds on a new marketing brochure when your magic metric is new customers per month would be quite simple. A computer is unlikely to bring in new customers, whereas a brochure might.

In terms of enhancing your business model you might also consider which decision allows you to experiment. Say, for example, you're confronted by a decision on whether to trial a marketing avenue but have only a small budget. You could either spend $10000 on a print ad, or $10000 on a direct marketing campaign. You might find that the latter gives you much more latitude to experiment. The print ad, once produced and run, won't allow you to trial various approaches. So you might realise way too late that it didn't work because you chose the wrong magazine or the wrong copy, or you didn't have the process in place to cope with and convert enquiries.

> The key question to consider when bringing prototyping to bear in your decision making is, 'Which option will improve our magic metric and enhance our business model?'

The direct marketing campaign, on the other hand, may allow for more experimentation or latitude because you can constantly evolve who you contact, what offer you approach them with, how you sell, and the mix between email, telephone and mail. This experimenting will have more chance of ending in a successful formula before your budget has expired.

Back at the game park in South Africa the challenge to bring out the master chef mindset was one of the most rewarding. In the tradition of Gordon Ramsay and *Masterchef* we completed our own version — safari style. The exercise was split into two stages. In the first stage participants had to follow a recipe and in the second they could conjure up their own creations — points to be awarded based on presentation, taste and innovation. They were given a budget to cover both activities.

For the first course we started with three groups of ingredients and recipes that the teams needed to bid on — recognising that they would need further funds for the second challenge. Limited funds would be a crucial lesson of the financial proposition. Cooking over a simple open fire with monkeys stalking from the branches above gave an extra element of challenge. A real lesson in the importance of the delivery proposition for one team, who didn't think to get their fire going before preparing the food, resulted in them having to rush to finish in the timeframe. Dishes were cooked and presented with the entrepreneurs promoting the value propositions of each — pointing out their unique selling points. Interestingly the team that spent the most didn't achieve the best outcome. Following a recipe at least ensured that everyone had a meal that was edible.

The second cooking challenge consisted of having the entrepreneurs bid on the remaining ingredients in order to cook another meal — but this time to experiment with their own recipe. In this society, which can be quite segregated in terms of male and female roles — having men argue with the women for a particular recipe was quite an experience. While there were clearly some disasters, particularly when they overcomplicated things, all of them agreed that they enjoyed the experimentation more than merely following someone else's recipe — a key learning for the prototype lens's application to business.

Adopt the master chef mindset and experiment to create a compelling recipe or business model for your business. Gaining clarity through the prototype lens means that you are focused on finding the perfect recipe for business through your ideal business model. When you know your business model and why it works, decision making is greatly simplified. The final decision-making lens, the plan lens, is discussed in the next chapter.

Key points

» The prototype lens helps you create a compelling *business model*. Every successful business has a unique formula or way of operating, even if you don't call it a business model.

» Your business model also helps you evolve so that your business is less reliant on your skills and personality.

» When looking through the prototype lens you must take on the mindset of a master chef and the personality trait of the experimenter.

» The three core stakeholders in any business are the customers, investors and employees.

» You will have to develop three capabilities to serve your stakeholders—sales, operations and a support capability.

» The next element in the prototype model is your propositions, which include your value proposition, your delivery proposition and your financial proposition.

» Entrepreneurs can become so swamped in numbers they can either drown in information or ignore it, and neither is useful.

» Instead of many numbers, entrepreneurs need a magic metric, which means they shouldn't count everything—they should only count what counts.

» Being clear on your prototype lens will help you immediately assess whether the decisions under consideration will help or hinder you in refining your recipe for success.

» The key question to consider when bringing prototyping to bear in your decision making is, 'Which option will improve our magic metric and enhance our business model?'

» Adopt the master chef mindset and experiment to create a compelling recipe or business model for your business.

» Gaining clarity through the prototype lens means that you are focused on finding the perfect recipe for business through your ideal business model. When you know your business model and why it works, decision making is greatly simplified.

Chapter 14

The plan lens

The plan lens is the last of the business-focused lenses. It is all about being clear on what you need to achieve and how you are going to achieve it with your current resources. Essentially, it is about creating a well thought out and achievable *business plan*.

Entrepreneurs usually approach planning in one of two ways. Some plan everything to death, creating a tomb of paperwork where every detail and financial figure is mapped out—then they never look at it again. Having a plan like this won't necessarily build a great business and it certainly won't build a business if you don't follow it.

> Essentially, [the plan lens] is about creating a well thought out and achievable *business plan.*

The other type of planner keeps the plan to themselves. Whether detailed or vague, the plan remains in the mind of the entrepreneur. And while this approach gives them flexibility, it is not useful in building a business. It is also far too easy to quietly change direction on a whim, be pulled off purpose and never finish or follow through on anything.

A good plan is a happy medium between a huge plan and none at all, and it should run for about one or two pages at the most. It takes more time and effort to create a concise and compelling plan than it does to make a long one. As Mark Twain famously said, 'I didn't have time to write a short letter, so I wrote a long one instead'. The same applies to your planning process. Once you develop this concise plan you need to work out how you will stick to it.

Mindset: architect

When looking through the plan lens you must take on the mindset of an architect. What separates a good architect from the rest is their ability to deliver the vision while staying mindful of the budget. It's easy to create a design masterpiece if you maintain the vision and disregard the budget and it's easy to create a bland living space on budget if you disregard vision. What makes a good architect great is their ability to maintain both vision and budget. These rare architects are able to

ARCHITECT

hold both the big picture and the tiny details in mind and at the same time project manage the creation of that structure. They will make it happen by keeping people accountable, and finish on time, on budget and on brief.

When you're assessing decisions from this mindset, therefore, it may be useful to imagine yourself as a skilled architect pulling the plan together to achieve success.

Personality trait: coordinator

The personality trait of the architect is that of the coordinator. Keeping projects moving forward and coordinating various resources is critical to success. Good architects realise that unexpected things will crop up from time to time that they will have to deal with. They also realise that there will always be trade-offs between three elements — time, cost and quality. For example, if they get too many rainy days on their work site, they might need to either extend the time frame or bring in more workers, which will cost more, or get their existing contractors to work faster, which could jeopardise quality.

In business you will also have to make trade-off decisions that affect time, cost and quality. I remember in our early years we couldn't afford to keep excess capacity, so that when we secured a new client we would have to find and fit out additional office space, often over the space of a weekend. Once we promised our client a new piece of technology that enabled us to track the average length a customer had to wait in our call centre's phone queue. Unfortunately, we found out a few days before the campaign commenced that the promised technology would be delayed by a few months. The options initially appeared straightforward—we could either defer the campaign, which would probably mean we lost the client, or we could have gone to the huge expense of having a new phone system installed, something we couldn't afford.

Instead we used the architect mindset and coordinator personality trait to implement an innovative solution. Our five-minute man turned out to be the best of both worlds. We employed someone to call the number every five minutes and join the queue. Using a stopwatch he would then record how long it took to answer a call and the result was tracked in a spreadsheet. Although it appeared clunky it was a surprisingly workable solution. Not only did it come in at the right cost, it could also be actioned within the right time frames, and the quality was no worse than that promised by the software. Although it caused a raised eyebrow or two with our client, it was a great solution that delivered the required data on time, on cost and on quality.

Start building your business using the architect mindset so you coordinate the vision effectively while staying within the budget.

Building blocks of business success

Developing a business plan to help with foresight in your decision making incorporates financial projections, strategies and priorities as outlined in figure 14.1

Figure 14.1: model of a business plan using foresight

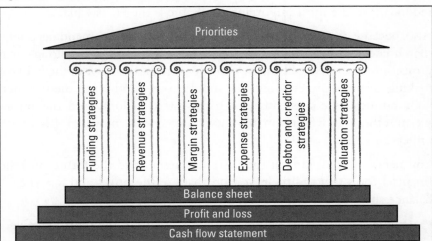

Financial projections

As an entrepreneur you should never absolve yourself of responsibility for your accounts. It's advisable to employ experienced bookkeepers or accountants to manage this area and prepare your financial statements, but it's still up to you to manage these people and interpret the results.

Don't just prepare financials for your tax or statutory requirements. Prepare them as a health check for your business, or what's called management accounts. The financial statements are the foundation of your business plan. But historical tracking is not enough. It is also important to have a clear financial plan of what you want your business to achieve in the future. This keeps you on track and heading towards a target, but it also allows you to keep track of how you are travelling against your financial objectives.

Financial goals are really useful because they are easy to measure and quantify. Money is a universally recognised yardstick of success, so knowing what you are projecting financially and being able to measure that against what actually happens is an essential part of the business planning process.

I'm a huge fan of having quarterly projections and then making myself and my team accountable for hitting this budget. Sure, in small to medium-sized enterprises it's worthwhile looking ahead two, three and five years as well as the next 90 days. Yet the landscape changes so quickly that you can't adapt quickly enough if you only look at 12-month projections or more. If you have a couple of bad months, the projections become redundant so the most important timeframe is the 90-day plan.

Also, because as entrepreneurs we don't usually have demanding public shareholders to keep happy or freak out if we change our long-term projections, focus on getting the short term right first. Get in the habit of making accurate projections three months out, and hitting them. When your business is consistently doing this, start to look into the future six months, and when you hit those projections, move to 12-month projections and beyond.

You need to be looking at the past, the present and the future, and the financial tools that will help you do that are the profit and loss (P&L), balance sheet and cash flow statement.

- *Profit and loss* (past). The P&L is the statement of the return received over a defined period of time, calculated as sales minus costs.

- *Balance sheet* (now). This is the statement of net assets at a particular date, namely the assets (goodies) minus liabilities (baddies).
- *Cash flow* (future). This is the statement of funds required going forward (based on expected cash inflows and outflows).

Of course you can still project into the future with a profit and loss statement, and balance sheet. Once you consider these three statements, the building blocks or foundation of your business plan will start to emerge and you can start to put it into place in reality. It is also important to counter this obsession with profit and financial success with other metrics that create a more balanced approach. In his book *Screw Business as Usual*, Sir Richard Branson calls for business to switch from a profit focus to caring for people, communities and the planet.

Strategies

The strategies are the methods and tactics by which you can plan to achieve your long-term objectives and win at the game of business. Often, though, entrepreneurs focus on growing small, by never investing in their business, or they focus on growing too big, with only sales and marketing strategies, completely disregarding how important other parts of the financial equation are.

Strategies can be broken down into the following:

- *Funding strategies.* How can I bring more cash into my business?
- *Revenue strategies.* How can I increase sales?
- *Margin strategies.* How can I make more from each sale?
- *Expense strategies.* How can I keep my overheads and costs down?
- *Debtor and creditor strategies.* How can I improve payment terms?
- *Valuation strategies.* How can I increase the business valuation by focusing on elements that increase the multiple of earnings?

The combination of strategies that you choose to focus on will depend on the stage of your business. When you're in the income to profit stage, for example, you can dramatically increase your ability to pay yourself a wage by focusing your plan on improving revenue, debtors and creditor collection, and then reducing your overheads. You could, for example, double your take-home pay by negotiating with debtors or creditors for better payment terms. You can make an even bigger difference if you also improve your revenue without increasing overheads.

And in the profit to value stage of your business evolution, you can dramatically increase your valuation by focusing on your plan and improving four key areas — increasing your revenue, improving your margin, minimising your overheads, and having a succession plan. For example, obtaining a long-term contract from your biggest client will improve the predictability of your revenue and result in potential investors paying a higher multiple of earnings when they value your company.

Key outcome: the priorities

Your priorities are key focus areas to keep you on track and ensure you execute your strategies and hit your projections. In business your priorities will change over time, and you need to revise and reset your priorities every quarter. These priorities should include four to eight key focus areas, and you should stick to them over the quarter unless there is a genuine need to change them. If you jump around and shift your focus continually, then you will dilute their impact.

If you want to add priorities, get into the habit of removing one of the priorities you already have. Having a list of 20 things to focus on merely turns your priorities into a to-do list, which doesn't help you achieve the plan you are striving for.

Say that one of your goals is to double your take-home pay this quarter. Your priorities might therefore include things like improving cash flow by prioritising fast invoicing, and keeping on top of debtor collection. You could also maximise revenue by prioritising existing client revenue that doesn't take as long in the sales cycle from upselling into high-value products, and avoid chasing clients you don't think you have a high chance of success with. And finally you might prioritise keeping your overheads at the current level so that any increase in cash flow can go straight into your pocket.

The next thing is to road test your priorities against these four questions:

- Will this priority help me achieve my projections?
- Do I really think I'm going to adhere to this priority?
- If it is a priority, what would it give my business?
- If I didn't have it as a priority what would happen to my business?

If you find that you don't often achieve your priorities, you need to stop and reflect on what stopped you and how you can prevent that happening in the future. You may need to reduce your priorities or reward yourself when a priority is met, or you may benefit if you communicate your priority to someone who will keep you accountable. Unfortunately, entrepreneurs are a bit like kids when they get their new books at the start of the school year, saying, 'Wow I'm going to be really neat this year', but after a week or two, they're as messy as ever. To overcome this habit, try to match up with someone who will keep you accountable. Consider putting an advisory board in place, having a team management meeting where priorities are pledged and reviewed, finding a peer entrepreneur who could be your accountability buddy, or hiring a business or executive coach.

Priorities are the key outcome you need to think about when you consider the architect mindset and the plan lens.

Planning in decision making

Being really clear on your plan lens will give you power in decision making because you will be able to immediately assess if the decisions under consideration are going to help or hinder you from reinforcing your priorities. The key question to consider when bringing planning to bear in your decision making is, 'Which option will help us adhere to our priorities and help us meet our projections?'

For instance, say you set your projections as achieving $200 000 in profit this quarter and one of your priorities is to keep your overheads contained. If an opportunity comes up to hire a personal assistant recommended by a friend, the decision is easier to make because hiring a PA will increase overheads and, although the appointment may make you more efficient, it's unlikely to increase profit. At this stage of business evolution, based on projections and priorities, it would be better to stick to the plan and defer the decision about hiring a PA until later.

> The key question to consider when bringing planning to bear in your decision making is, 'Which option will help us adhere to our priorities and help us meet our projections?'

The last challenge I set the Branson Centre entrepreneurs in the boot camp was an old favourite designed to bring out their architect mindset — to participate in the infamous marshmallow challenge, a worldwide team competition I found on the TED, Ideas Worth Spreading website <www.TED.com>. In this challenge, each team received 18 pieces of spaghetti, a metre of string, a metre of masking tape and a marshmallow. They had 18 minutes to build the tallest free-standing structure with the marshmallow on top. The challenge is used all around the world, and generally architects, engineers and kids perform the best, and MBA students perform the worst, so I was keen to find out how this group of eager, developing-world entrepreneurs would do.

Typical of many of these groups, teams spent too much time on planning to death and not enough time on doing—leaving 10 seconds to place the marshmallow on top only to see it topple over. Each of the Branson Centre groups managed to make a structure, although, as usual, two had fallen over a few minutes before judging, leaving as the winner the group that was a little less ambitious and who finished with time to spare. Regardless of whether they were successful, the teams had already learned the importance of having a short and simple plan and then executing it—essentially what we were encouraging them to do in business. They could apply the activity lessons around planning and project management to their business, recognising the need to trade-off time, cost and quality boundaries.

The plan lens is all about viewing the business from an architect mindset so that you can become the coordinator for your business—to formulate financial projections, strategies and key priorities that work together to help you achieve your business goals.

Once you have spent time on each of the six lenses of clarity, you will have a far greater and deeper appreciation of what is important to you as an individual, as well as what you are seeking to achieve in business and why. Each of the six lenses gives you the foresight of a unique perspective that provides more relevant information to the decision-making process. In essence, the lenses encourage you to stay mindful of six key questions:

- Which option will accelerate my endgame and enable me to work on my mission?
- Which option will cultivate our company values and reinforce our brand and culture?
- Which option will let me perform my role and play to my strengths or strengthen my improvement areas?
- Which option will help us reach our business vision and climb to the next business stage?

- Which option will improve our magic metric and enhance our business model?
- Which option will help us adhere to our priorities and help us meet our projections?

The resulting clarity speeds up your decision making while also giving you greater confidence in the final decision. We will discuss what happens when the decisions are assessed using insight in part IV.

Key points

» The plan lens is the last of the business-focused lenses. It is about being clear on what you need to achieve and how you are going to achieve it with your current resources. Essentially, it is about creating a well thought out and achievable *business plan*.

» Develop your business plan and work out how to stick to it.

» When looking through the plan lens you must take on the mindset of an architect and the personality trait of the coordinator.

» Developing a business plan to help with foresight in your decision making incorporates financial projections, strategies and priorities.

» Financial goals are easy to measure and quantify.

» The strategies are the methods you can use to achieve your long-term objectives and win at the game of business.

» Your priorities are key focus areas to keep you on track and ensure you execute your strategies and hit your projections.

» Being clear on your plan lens will allow you to immediately assess whether the decisions under consideration are going to help or hinder you from reinforcing your priorities.

» The key question to consider when bringing planning to bear in your decision making is, 'Which option will help us adhere to our priorities and help us meet our projections?'

» The plan lens is about viewing the business from an architect mindset so that you can become the coordinator for your business.

» Each of the six lenses gives you the foresight of a unique perspective that provides more relevant information to the decision making process, which speeds up your decisions while also giving you greater confidence in the final decision.

Part IV

How to use insight by focusing on the information you have at hand to make decisions in the present

Nothing is more terrible than activity without insight.

Thomas Carlyle,
Scottish satirical writer, teacher and historian

Chapter 15

Introducing the perpetual growth principles

Entrepreneurs need a way to bring insight into their decision making to help them make faster, better-informed decisions without the angst. The right insight helps you make faster decisions, because you don't have to second-guess your outcomes. Insight helps you be more informed, as you take into consideration all of the crucial data. And finally, insight helps reduce your angst, or anxiety, because you have a proven decision-making methodology to follow.

Methods for gaining insight

Some of the typical methods of gaining insight in business decision making are:

- developing a business case
- seeking an external opinion or advice
- conducting a scenario analysis
- conducting some research or testing
- using a decision-making methodology.

One of the common methods used to bring insight into business decisions is the creation of a business case to justify and illustrate the reasoning behind the decision under review. The business case seeks to provide evidence that the options for consideration will meet a specific business need, such as return on investment, and are not just the result of a managerial whim. The problem with business cases is that they are not always used as an analysis tool but as a way of getting support for a desired course of action. It's too easy to manipulate the business case to deliver the result that is required. Just like in debating competitions, you can find compelling evidence for either side of an argument if you look hard enough. As a result the business case is of little genuine help to a small or medium-sized enterprise, where you're both the person preparing the case and the ultimate decision maker.

The next method you might choose is to get insight from various sources of external advice. I am a huge fan of this approach and at Blueprint we constantly sought external advice in our business, but there are some limitations to this method of gaining insight. First, your external advisers are not always available and if you get their advice on too many things too often, their cost and the time it takes can really mount up. And second, no-one knows your business like you do, particularly the interrelated aspects of the business to be considered in each individual decision. To brief someone on all of these would take too long, so while you may get advice, it may not adequately account for all the relevant facts.

Completing a scenario analysis is another insight methodology that can have useful application to business decisions. Essentially this involves documenting the important factors for consideration between opposing decisions, in order to tally up the best course of action. This can be worthwhile in some circumstances, but it is best suited to the analytical aspects of a decision. Also, this method can be quite arbitrary, as you will almost always have a natural bias towards one of the scenarios, which can effectively defeat the purpose of doing an analysis in the first place.

Another useful tool is to complete research and testing. This background work will certainly work for some decisions, such as choosing the right marketing offer, but it simply isn't applicable to most decisions. That's particularly the case when you don't have the luxury of testing before a decision is implemented or when research bamboozles you with many choices.

While each of these methods has its place the most powerful method is to use a decision assessment methodology — essentially an agreed process or theory for quickly deciding between various courses of action. The perpetual growth principles (PGP) form one such methodology, which had enormous impact on making our business one of the fastest growing in Australia.

Developing the perpetual growth principles

The PGP consist of four universal business principles (see figure 6.2 on p. 73), which actively focus your entrepreneurial intuition to provide powerful insight into your decision making in real time. And because they have been proven over nearly a decade in my business and by many of the entrepreneurs I have trained, you can have the confidence that they work.

I love this comment by American writer Ralph Waldo Emerson:

> The man who knows will always have a job. The man who also knows why will always be his boss. As to method there may be a million and then some, but principles are few. The man who grasps principles can successfully select his own methods. The man who tries methods, ignoring principles, is sure to have trouble.

I think Emerson's comment highlights the importance of scaling up your thinking around assessing options and making it first about principles. You can then be empowered to use that methodology in any decision. The PGP transcends industries and size, and the particular quirks of individual companies. Yet to fully embrace the PGP, you will need to take a leap of faith. They will probably represent a different approach from anything else you would have come across in business theory, and yet understanding the PGP was the single biggest thing that helped underpin the fast growth we achieved at Blueprint.

In fact, this theory was the first piece of intellectual property that I developed, and I still hold it as the most original and the most powerful method I have created. So how did the principles come about? It all started with my first attempt at a succession. We announced that we were handing over to a general manager. Trent, the new GM, soon found me hanging around the office lending my wasabi to various problems and issues. My presence undermined his ability to exert his own management style in the company. And so, insightfully, he encouraged me to work at home in order to develop the theory of what had made our company so successful.

What he said next, though, set my thinking on a course of action from which there was no return. 'There's a real science behind how you guys operate business compared with any of the other companies I've worked for—you need to get that science out of your head and into a form we can teach the management team.'

The next day when I got a blank sheet of paper at my desk at home—banished from my own company—I thought wow, what's the science behind how we do what we do? And second, how can we make this replicable so other people in the company can use the theory to help the business grow to the next level?

The first thing I thought about was that we tended to look out for our stakeholders, but it was more than that. We went to great lengths to make it easier for our staff and clients to get ahead—to create a frictionless path to our goals and theirs. And then thinking of that word, friction, I had a vivid memory of a year nine science lesson that involved some link between friction and Newton's laws of motion.

So I started to do a little research and was amazed at just how applicable Newton's laws are to business: we could apply their insights to make our business grow faster. What I realised is that the laws that dictate what happens in the physical universe are equally relevant to what happens in the business universe. Newton's principles have stood the test of time for more than 300 years, and while his laws have been challenged by quantum mechanics, they remain the best explanation of physical objects in motion. Using Newton's laws of motion I derived four business principles that enable entrepreneurs to gain immediate insight into how a decision between alternatives will affect the acceleration, or growth, of their business.

> Using Newton's laws of motion I derived four business principles that enable entrepreneurs to gain immediate insight into how a decision between alternatives will affect the acceleration, or growth, of their business.

Newton's laws of motion and PGP

Newton's first law of motion states that every object in a state of uniform motion remains in that state of motion unless acted upon by an external force. Essentially, for an object to move faster it needs a push or a reduction in the frictions slowing it down. From this law, I derived two principles, namely the need to reduce frictions and to foster actuators, the two opposing forces that need to be considered if you don't want your business to plateau or experience inertia.

Principle one is the need to reduce frictions. It is about maximising force by reducing the negative forces, or frictions, that can so easily derail a business. Principle two is the need to foster actuators. It is also about maximising force, but through fostering the positive forces or actuators that can fast track a business's growth. Actuators are simply positive forces that help move an objective or business forward.

Newton's second law of motion gave rise to the third PGP. Newton's law states that the relationship between an object's mass, acceleration and applied force is mass $\times$ acceleration: you might remember the formula $f = ma$ from your school days. In other words, if you want to maximise acceleration you must reduce mass. Principle three is therefore minimise mass. If you want to grow quickly and minimise the impact of inertia you must be lean and mean.

And lastly, Newton's third law of motion, which states that for every action there is an equal and opposite reaction, gave rise to the last of the principles. Principle four is the need to maximise balance. Whatever we do in business affects someone else—the idea of this law is that we seek balance and win–win outcomes for all stakeholders. There is nothing to be gained in the long term if a decision benefits you but disadvantages all the other stakeholders, or vice versa.

The four principles in brief

We will discuss the four principles in more depth over the next four chapters, but for now the PGP, briefly stated, are as follows.

Principle one: reduce frictions

Arising from a shortage of time, knowledge, money and momentum, the eight business frictions are negative influences on your business. So if the decision you are about to make will reduce one or more of the eight business frictions that are holding you back, then you will grow faster and more profitably.

Principle two: foster actuators

If you enhance the positive forces in your business then you will naturally accelerate your business. So if the decision you are about to make fosters one of the eight actuators then you will gain more forward momentum, which will speed up the growth and, in turn, increase the profitability of your business.

Principle three: minimise mass

If you minimise the mass that can slow down a business (or prevent it growing) then you will naturally accelerate your business. So if the decision you are about to make reduces one of four areas of corporate mass then you will move forward faster without unnecessary cost and clutter weighing you down.

Principle four: maximise balance

If you actively seek win–win sustainable outcomes then you will naturally accelerate your business. So if the decision you are about to make will result in mutual benefits to some or all of your stakeholder groups then it is a good decision, paving the way for increased growth and profitability of your business.

> If you can reduce the frictions in your business, foster actuators, minimise mass and maximise balance then your business will prosper.

The PGP offers a framework that, with time, you will instinctively run through, helping you to quickly and accurately assess your decisions from all angles. If you can reduce the frictions in your business, foster actuators, minimise mass and maximise balance then your business will prosper.

Key points

» Entrepreneurs need a way to bring insight into their decision making to help them make faster, better-informed decisions without the angst.

» Insight helps you make faster decisions because you don't have to second-guess your outcomes. Insight helps you be more informed, as you take into consideration all of the crucial data and it helps reduce your angst, because you have a proven decision-making methodology to follow.

» Some of the typical methods of gaining insight in business decision making are developing a business case, seeking an external opinion or advice, conducting a scenario analysis, conducting some research and testing, and using a decision-making methodology.

» While each of these methods has its place, the most powerful method is to use a decision-assessment methodology. The perpetual growth principles (PGP) form one of the most effective methodologies for assessing decisions.

» The PGP consists of four universal business principles that actively focus your entrepreneurial intuition to provide powerful insights into your decision making in real time.

» I derived four business principles from Isaac Newton's laws of motion that enable entrepreneurs to gain immediate insight into how a decision between alternatives will affect the acceleration, or growth, of their business. The four principles are reduce frictions, foster actuators, minimise mass and maximise balance.

» The PGP offers a framework that, with time, you will instinctively run through, helping you to quickly and accurately assess your decisions from all angles. Activating them will help your business to prosper.

Chapter 16

Principle I—reduce frictions

Let's cut to the chase. Business is not easy. It can be fun, inspiring and extremely rewarding, but it's rarely easy. As a business owner or entrepreneur you will invariably come up against a huge number of obstacles and roadblocks in the course of your business journey. These challenges can range from the small day-to-day decisions of business life to life-altering choices that could make or break your business. Often the sheer volume of choices, challenges and decisions can result in a feeling of being overwhelmed and out of control.

Reducing frictions is, therefore, at the centre of insight in the entrepreneurial eye because it is the most important part of business evolution, growth and success. In the end it doesn't matter how proactive you are in your business operations or how smart you are in your strategic thinking; if you don't actively seek ways to reduce the frictions in your business then you are going to limit your success and slow your growth and development. Frictions are the negative forces, events or situations that act as speed bumps on your business journey.

It's impossible to create a completely frictionless working environment, but if you train your entrepreneurial eye to actively eliminate those frictions then you will exponentially accelerate the growth and success of your business. If you clear out the obstacles as fast as possible, then it follows that you will travel far faster and much further. There are four things that every entrepreneur or business owner needs in various quantities at various stages of the business journey:

- time
- knowledge
- money
- momentum.

An entrepreneur needs time to focus their energy on growing the business. It is a shortage of time, or at least time well spent, that often causes their business to stagnate. Entrepreneurs also need enough knowledge not just about their own industry but also about how to operate a business. So many entrepreneurs start business without enough experience or training and this shortage of knowledge causes their business to be held back, or worse. The shortage of money is one of the biggest frictions for entrepreneurs. That might include inadequate funds to pay the entrepreneur an adequate wage or insufficient growth capital for the business. Yet with all of the time, money and knowledge available, your business will still not accelerate. You also need momentum, which includes things like sales, opportunities and systems. It is the shortage of momentum that results in the business not going forward fast enough.

The eight frictions

A shortage of time, knowledge, money and momentum creates eight core frictions that can easily derail your business growth and success. Those eight frictions are:

- lack of funding (shortage of money)
- lack of scale (shortage of money and momentum)
- lack of growth (shortage of momentum)
- lack of control (shortage of momentum and control)
- lack of support (shortage of time)
- lack of focus (shortage of time and knowledge)
- lack of guidance (shortage of knowledge)
- lack of direction (shortage of knowledge and money).

The reason why reducing frictions is at the centre of insight in the entrepreneurial eye model (see figure 16.1) is that focusing on reducing frictions can have a profound effect on the success of your business. If you can identify the biggest frictions within your business and make decisions that will actively reduce them, your business will grow faster. The eight business frictions incorporate every conceivable friction or obstacle that holds an entrepreneur back.

In order for you to work out which frictions are affecting you in your business, complete the diagnostic on my Accelerate Global website at

<www.accelerateglobal.com/frictionsdiagnostic>. Being aware of the frictions affecting you and your business will help you make better-informed decisions.

Figure 16.1: reducing frictions is at the heart of the entrepreneurial eye

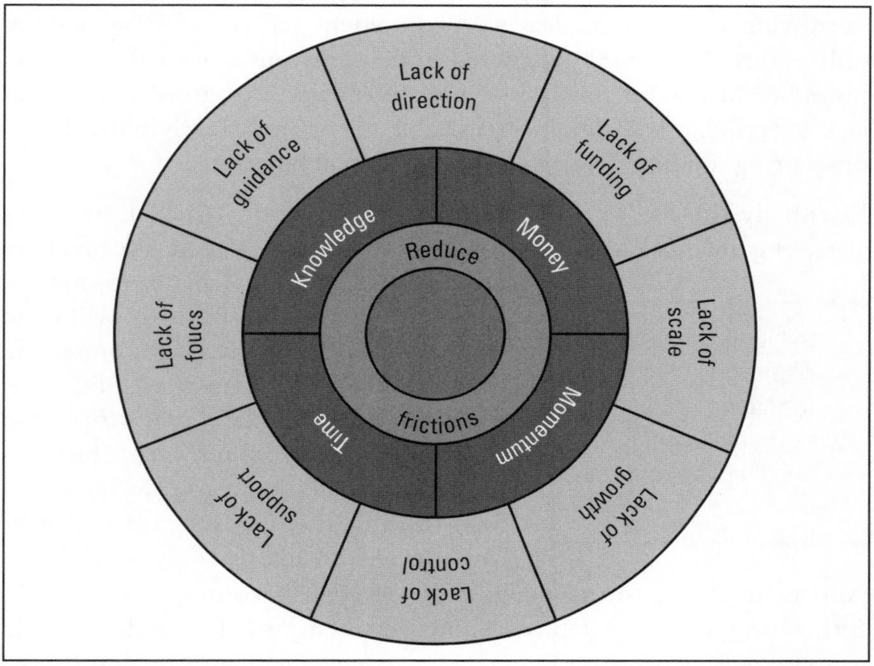

Lack of funding

The two types of funding friction are:

- inadequate personal funding; that is, I'm not getting enough money to support my lifestyle
- inadequate business funding; that is, I'm not getting enough money to support the growth of my business.

Too many business people think that their biggest friction is a lack of funding, but if you scratch the surface a little it's almost always something else. In other words, it doesn't matter what the real friction is, most people will instinctively come back to money as both the problem and solution. And yet the truth is that money is rarely the real issue and it's almost never the best solution.

When we started Blueprint we each invested $5000. As you can imagine, this shortage of money caused not only a shortage of capital in the business, it also meant that it took nearly two years before we were paid an adequate wage. During that time we also found it nearly impossible to borrow money or raise equity. In fact, right up until I retired the only borrowing was for some leases on equipment and an overdraft, and the only equity was $25 000 we raised from a previous work colleague and his father-in-law. Yet this lack of investment into our growth wasn't for lack of trying: it was simply attributable to the notoriously difficult task of securing funding if you are running a small business.

Essentially there is a frustrating catch-22 situation when it comes to attracting investment or borrowing in business. If you already have money and don't need more money, banks and financial institutions will bend over backwards to give you more and that is as relevant today, post–GFC, as it was before. If, on the other hand, you don't have money, but need it for business expansion then the banks will make a loan so difficult to secure you will have lost the will to live, or they will charge you so much for the privilege that the loan becomes unserviceable. Either way, securing debt or equity financing in the modern world is extremely hard work for the average small and medium-sized business owner.

> Securing debt or equity financing in the modern world is extremely hard work for the average small and medium-sized business owner.

To increase your business funding without borrowing and selling shares, it's worth considering:

- focusing on cash-flow positive (upfront) sales
- negotiating terms to bring forward your debtors
- negotiating terms to stretch out your creditors
- leasing rather than buying your assets
- reducing your non-core expenses.

Whatever it is that you are trying to achieve or resolve, you need to decide if your choices will reduce your funding frictions or increase them. Addressing your lack of funding will help pave the way for faster business growth.

Lack of scale

Lack of scale is about clout. If you are experiencing a lack of scale you have a shortage of money and momentum. Two components make up lack of scale:

- inadequate track record — you don't have the reputation to attract new business
- inadequate resources — you don't have the operational capacity to grow.

Another business conundrum is that you need a reputation to get experience, but you need experience to get a reputation. Building a track record is all about getting a name and developing your personal and business brand. A brand, reduced to its simplest explanation, is nothing more than a consistently delivered promise. Building a good track record starts the moment you open the doors for business. It involves demonstrating your ability and credentials to do what you say you can do. It involves going the extra mile, making it easy for your clients to do business with you, and helping your customers and staff get what they want. It's about underpromising and overdelivering time and time again. It also involves looking the part and playing the game of business.

No matter where you are in your business journey, you need to instil confidence: people buy track record and they need to trust that you will deliver what they need when you said you would. You need to project professionalism in everything you do and, if you can do that, then you will develop a loyal following and a solid and reputable track record, which will provide you with some momentum toward success.

When you are starting out you may not have hundreds of clients and millions of dollars but you can build a track record. You have a code of ethics and a set of values that will and should drive your business. It is those things that make up your reputation and it is those things that other people buy.

The best ways to develop your track record is to do what you do and do it better than anyone else, because excellence influences people. Forget six-figure brand-building campaigns, the likes of which the Coca Colas and Microsofts of this world can afford — focus on projecting the right image and doing the right things. This means building your individual profile as an entrepreneur.

There are many ways to build your track record, including:

- surrounding yourself with credible companies
- having a smart business address
- creating a professional website or brochure
- gathering case studies and testimonials (even if conducted for free)
- building your personal brand through published articles or public speaking assignments, or writing a book.

Lack of scale is also caused by a lack of resources—everything from infrastructure to staff to equipment. It could be that you don't have the equipment you need to grow your business as fast as you would like. It might be that your office space is too small or not in the right location or not impressive enough. Or it might be that you haven't got access to the people resources you need to fulfil promises for your clients.

There are many ways to address your resources challenges, which might include:

- doing non-cash contra deals
- establishing partnerships or alliances
- conducting your business on your client's site
- outsourcing or offshoring
- utilising someone else's excess capacity.

Whatever it is that you are trying to achieve or resolve, you need to decide if your choices will reduce your scale frictions or increase them. Addressing your lack of scale will accelerate your business growth.

Lack of growth

Lack of growth is traditionally about sales. But it's also about creating products and services that people want to buy, and about creating new business avenues. Most businesses are heavily dependent on sales. Yet despite this it is amazing how little time entrepreneurs spend selling.

Igor Ansoff, a pioneer of strategic management, in an article called 'Strategies for diversification', published in 1957 in the *Harvard Business Review*, identified the following four ways to increase revenue:

- sell more of the same product or service to your existing market
- sell the same product or service to a new market

- sell something new to your existing market
- sell a new product to a new market.

Selling more of the same product or service to your existing market is known as upselling. If your company is in the business of selling photocopiers, you might be able to upsell your customers so that they buy more than one photocopier. This is a quick win strategy, particularly if you give your customers an incentive to buy more than one of your products.

Selling the same product or service to a new market is a common expansion method used by businesses as they start to grow. They might consider a new geographical market, such as the next suburb or state, or they might consider a new niche market. If the photocopier company sold mainly to office firms, they might consider expanding to include companies in the mining sector.

Selling something new to your existing market is known as cross-selling. Once you have a relationship with a customer and know their needs, it becomes much easier to sell them other relevant products. For instance, the photocopier company might consider cross-selling a range of printers to their photocopier customers.

And lastly, selling a new product to a new market is one of the hardest things to do. Selling can be tough without experience with the product or a relationship with the market. New market in this context is new to you, not creating a totally new market, though there are a few companies who have pulled off this even harder combination. One of the best recent examples is when Apple launched its iTunes store. A hardware provider offering its own platform to download songs and applications completely changed the game. Other hardware vendors have taken years to catch up. Educating someone about a product is hard enough, but educating them about their need for that product when you have no or limited track record is almost impossible if they don't already use a similar product.

Whatever it is that you are trying to achieve or resolve, you need to decide if your choices will reduce your growth frictions or increase them. Addressing your lack of growth will accelerate your business faster than almost anything else.

Lack of control

Lack of control can be one of the hardest frictions to describe and pin down. Essentially, you are doing things to gather momentum and circumvent your scarcity of time, but those activities could result in lack of control.

Two of the biggest ways to lose control are:

- complicating business shareholding; that is, selling equity
- exposing yourself to disputes; for instance being taken to court or taking someone else to court.

So, for example, you may need money so you decide to sell 50 per cent of the business to a client. This immediately solves your funding friction, as you bring in a major investor and the business gathers serious momentum. However, it isn't long before you realise that the new business partner wants much more say in the running of the business than you had imagined, which results in a lack of control.

Alternatively, you take someone into partnership without adequate documentation and your partner steals your intellectual property (IP). You may end up in court and be unable to use the IP until the matter is resolved.

Lack of control friction often comes about as a result of the law of unintended consequences, which is an adage that warns us against the naive belief that we can fully control anything. The law of unintended consequences suggests that when we intervene in complex situations or make decisions without enough forethought, we can create unanticipated and often undesirable outcomes.

There are many ways to overcome lack of control, but some of the things I would recommend include:

- documenting agreements and keeping a paper trail or electronic record of events
- adding back-out or unwind clauses to agreements
- registering ownership around IP, trademarks and domain names
- creating systems that can be tracked and followed
- limiting the ownership of your company.

Whatever it is that you are trying to achieve or resolve, you need to decide if your choices will reduce your control frictions or increase them. If you address your lack of control you will ensure you don't end up with a business headache in the future or an unnecessary distraction in the present.

Lack of support

Lack of support occurs when the entrepreneur or business owner doesn't have enough time to get things done. This is a common friction and one that affects everyone in business sooner or later. The dilemma is that there are only 24 hours in any day, so a business owner might end up spending too much time on sales, operations or support. If they spend too much time in sales and bring in a lot of extra work that their operations are not equipped to handle, then the business will fall over. If they spend too much time in operations and support, then there will be no sales to fulfil and the business will also fall over. Getting support in each of these areas will ensure they all consistently improve.

Very few successful businesses are created alone. If you want to achieve stellar success then you had better work out how to reduce this friction and solve your support challenges. The question you need to ask is, how do you get enough support so that you can get a more balanced life?

There are many ways to deal with lack of support, but some common strategies include:

- delegation
- outsourcing
- business partners.

Delegating sometimes feels unnatural to an entrepreneur who started their business doing every job possible. Yet without getting others who are less expensive than you to do some of the non-crucial tasks, and specialists to do the important tasks, you will not have enough time to focus on what you are good at and what the business needs. The trick to delegation is not completely absolving yourself of responsibility, but rather supporting the person you are delegating to until they are comfortable and have proven they are capable.

Outsourcing has been one of the biggest buzz words of the last two decades, as companies realise they need to focus on what they are good at and outsource the rest to a company or individual who can do it better or more cheaply, or with less management time required. You can outsource in nearly any field you can think of, including accounting, sales and marketing, recruitment and HR, software development, IT, call centre and recruitment.

Starting business with a partner or bringing a business partner on board part way through can dramatically reduce lack of support. Having someone with complementary skills to rely on without having to give them management support can be a real blessing for any entrepreneur. Sure, you are going to have a smaller share of the pie, but it really should be a bigger pie if you work together successfully.

Whatever it is that you are trying to achieve or resolve, you need to decide if your choices will reduce your support frictions or increase them. Addressing your lack of support will give you more time and create forward momentum in your business.

Lack of focus

Lack of focus is the friction that occurs when entrepreneurs spend most of their time on the things they have the least knowledge of.

People who suffer from lack of focus usually find themselves in this situation for a number of reasons. First, it can be a byproduct of the previous friction, in which the business owner doesn't have enough support and finds themselves trying to be all things to all people. If you don't have the support to be able to effectively delegate tasks and move through the workload, then you can end up jumping around between tasks. This approach is scattered and the lack of focused attention means you never actually get much done.

This is accentuated by the fact that you are spending more time trying to do tasks that you have no knowledge of. So, for example, you may decide to do your own accounts and it might take you a week of stress to complete them. Because you're not a trained accountant, you don't actually know if you have done them correctly and you have hated every last minute of it. And there is a huge opportunity cost involved in this strategy. Say you are a marketing consultant and that's your area of expertise, and you billed yourself out to clients at $300 an hour. Even if you look at the number conservatively and allow for only five billable hours a day, you have just wasted $7500 preparing those accounts. You could have engaged a professional accountant to prepare your accounts and it would have cost you a fraction of that figure, and you would have been able to focus your energy on doing what you do best and making money.

The other situation that causes lack of focus has nothing to do with support and is a result of the entrepreneurial curse — your natural inclination to get bored and want to come up with and implement brand-new ideas. If not kept in check, your tendency towards the entrepreneur's curse will cause a great lack of focus.

There are many ways to deal with lack of focus, but the best are:

- narrowing your focus into what you are good at and enjoy
- preventing the entrepreneur's curse by having a business plan
- getting an executive or business coach or mentor who keeps you accountable
- having a daily to-do list of things to achieve
- splitting your day into sections with allocated time slots for important, but less exciting functions.

Whatever it is that you are trying to achieve or resolve, you need to decide if your choices will reduce your focus frictions or increase them. Addressing your lack of focus will save you time and help you get more done.

Lack of guidance

Lack of guidance is a friction that comes down purely to a scarcity of knowledge. There are two types of knowledge that are relevant to business:

- business knowledge, or how to set up, operate and grow a business
- industry knowledge, or how you become a specialist at what your company does.

The first is knowledge about how to be good at the process of business. It involves knowledge of all the separate aspects of successful business: sales, marketing, hiring and firing, management, leadership, operations, administration, customer service and finance.

The second type of knowledge is how to be good at the thing you do in business. This will depend upon what your business specialises in. For instance, if you are in the legal profession then your knowledge will need to encompass the type of law you are practising, such as commercial contracts.

By the very nature of these different types of knowledge, any business owner or entrepreneur is much more likely to already have the second type of knowledge than the first. Just think about it for a moment. Most people go into business in an area of interest or expertise. Often they have been made redundant and decide to pursue their dreams of self-employment, or they just decide they don't want a boss any more. Whatever the catalyst, most business owners set out in business doing the thing they were trained to do or used to do for an employer. You might be a plumber in a large contracting firm and decide one day to strike out on your own. In that very moment you go from having to be a good plumber to having to be a good plumber *and* a good salesperson, marketer, recruitment expert, leader, administrator, accountant and manager.

Some people go to university to study just one of those disciplines and dedicate their entire life to that specialisation, and yet now you have set up Plumbers R Us and you have to be a specialist in all of them, as well as what it was you wanted to do in the first place, which was fix clients' plumbing problems.

The bottom line is that you need both types of knowledge to be successful. There are many ways to address lack of guidance, but some areas to consider include:

- reading books, journals, articles, blogs and newspapers
- talking to peers and other specialists
- surrounding yourself with mentors and advisers
- attending training courses
- teaching someone else (one of the best ways to become an expert).

Yet the reason why entrepreneurs often don't get adequate guidance is not because they don't know where to get it, rather they don't allocate enough time to knowledge building. If you are one of those people, consider some strategies to get yourself in a continuous-learning frame of mind. Maybe pay for a course or program upfront that will commit you to learning about a topic; allocate an hour first thing in the morning or last thing at night to learn something you didn't already know; or consider sharing your knowledge with someone else — often one of the best ways to learn is to teach. So commit to writing a book, an article, a blog, or to public speaking at a conference or event that you organise.

Whatever it is that you are trying to achieve or resolve, you need to decide if your choices will reduce your guidance frictions or increase them. Addressing your lack of guidance is a way to get your business moving forward.

Lack of direction

Lack of direction is where you don't have enough knowledge or a clear enough idea of your financial goals to get you to the next stage. You constantly change direction, and never seem to get anywhere significant.

Those who lack direction suffer from either not having a clear strategy for where the company is heading, or they aren't clear about their reason for being in business in the first place.

Business direction and strategy go hand in hand. If you decide where you want the company to be in 12 months, two years, five years and so on, you can then start to work on the strategies that will help you get there. When US President John F. Kennedy stated his goal of putting a man on the moon before the end of the 1960s, he was met with a lot of scepticism, given this was a big hairy audacious goal of galactic proportions. Yet having set the direction, he ensured the various stakeholders were moved to action, and his audacious goal was achieved a little over eight years later, just six months before the end of the decade. Similarly, companies that set a very clear direction that is inspiring for their employees will go on to achieve more than those who are merely in business.

Because of the nature of small and medium-sized enterprises, it is imperative that the company direction and the entrepreneur's own direction are aligned. Often one of the reasons entrepreneurs experience a lack of direction is because they haven't devoted the time to become really clear on what they want to get out of the business. Is it to build the business up to be sold; is it to make some kind of difference in their industry or with their stakeholders; or is it to create a family company that will last hundreds of years?

There are many solutions to lack of direction, but my tips are:

- set personal goals and share them with anyone who will listen
- hold an annual company strategy session, even if it's only with yourself
- have a peer or adviser challenge your stated direction.

Whatever it is that you are trying to achieve or resolve, you need to decide if your choices will reduce your direction frictions or increase them. Addressing your lack of direction is one of the best ways to get you and your team motivated towards achieving something significant.

Using frictions

There are essentially two ways to use the frictions — proactively and reactively. First, you can develop strategies or business models that seek to reduce as many frictions as possible. Or you can use the frictions when making a decision between two options — the one that reduces the most frictions in the business is the better course of action.

Removing the frictions in your business is common sense, but until you are consciously aware of those frictions it's almost impossible to remove them. Understanding all the possible frictions and the interplay between them can massively speed up decision making. If, for example, the two biggest frictions in your business were lack of focus and lack of support, and you were presented with an opportunity to diversify the business into a new area, the decision is considerably easier. The diversification may lead to growth, but if the business already suffers from lack of focus and lack of support, diversification is only going to amplify those frictions. In addition, the diversification is almost guaranteed to fail if you don't fix your focus and support issues first. When you are aware of the frictions facing you and your company, you can make more informed decisions that will either fix them or at least not make them any worse.

In reality you may continually meet the same frictions and never experience others, but knowing the full range of frictions that can and will slow you down gives you a greater chance of staying on track. The entrepreneurial eye acts as a visual reminder to reduce frictions both from an individual decision-making perspective and in the way you design business processes, so you seek to reduce frictions at all times and all levels of the business. If you can do this then your business will flourish.

On the opposite side of the maximising force spectrum, if you can also foster the business actuators then you will do even better. These actuators are the subject of the next chapter.

Key points

» Entrepreneurs come up against a huge number of obstacles and roadblocks on their business journey, requiring everything from the small day-to-day decisions of business life, to life-altering choices that could make or break your business.

» Frictions are the negative forces, events or situations that act as speed bumps on your business journey.

» The four things every entrepreneur or business owner needs in various quantities at various stages of the business journey are time, knowledge, money and momentum.

» The eight frictions are lack of funding (shortage of money), lack of scale (shortage of money and momentum), lack of growth (shortage of momentum), lack of control (shortage of momentum and control), lack of support (shortage of time), lack of focus (shortage of time and knowledge), lack of guidance (shortage of knowledge), and lack of direction (shortage of knowledge and money).

» The two ways of using the frictions are proactively and reactively. First, you can develop strategies or business models that seek to reduce as many frictions as possible. Or you can use the frictions when making a decision between two options — the one that reduces the most frictions in the business is the better course of action.

» The entrepreneurial eye is a visual reminder to reduce frictions both from an individual decision-making perspective and in the way you design business processes.

Chapter 17

Principle 2—foster actuators

While the frictions are the negative forces that slow the growth of your business, eat away at your profit and derail your success, the second of the perpetual growth principles (PGP), actuators, are the positive forces that can speed up growth, fulfilment and prosperity.

The eight actuators

Like the frictions, there are eight actuators, and if you make decisions that foster these actuators then your decision making will automatically improve and you will reach your business objectives faster with less stress and anxiety. The eight actuators are:

- empowerment
- innovation
- inspiration
- flexibility
- replication
- leverage
- simplicity
- reputation.

Empowerment

Empowerment is where a staff member or supplier is delegated responsibility for a task or project within a set of clearly defined guidelines. Whether you are looking at empowerment in relation to a particular decision, or whether you are seeking ways to incorporate the philosophy into your business model and culture, empowerment is a major actuator toward success.

If you expect the best from your people and give them the support and encouragement they need in the early stages of learning, then they will invariably thrive.

It's not rocket science. If people are excited about working for you and they feel challenged and trusted to do a good job, then their confidence and productivity increases. Countless studies in psychology prove beyond question that individuals will rise or fall to meet expectations. If you expect the best from your people and give them the support and encouragement they need in the early stages of learning, then they will invariably thrive.

This idea that people will rise and fall to meet expectation is often called the Pygmalion Effect, after George Bernard Shaw's play *Pygmalion*, in which a professor makes a bet that he can teach a poor flower girl to behave like a lady.

But the effect is not fiction. In a study named 'Pygmalion in the classroom', Harvard social psychologist Dr Robert Rosenthal gave a non-verbal intelligence test to 18 classrooms of elementary school students in a Californian public school district at the start of the school year. Twenty per cent of the students were then selected randomly and identified as being 'intellectual bloomers' and their teachers were told they could expect to see remarkable intellectual gains in the coming year.

Remember these kids were selected randomly and *not* according to their test scores, so the only difference between these students and the other 80 per cent was the expectations created in the teachers' minds. When both groups of students were retested eight months later the 'bloomers' had gained in IQ points over the other group. Expectation of outcome can clearly result in changes in behaviour that can dramatically influence outcome — both good and bad.

If you demonstrate that you trust your people and have confidence in their ability then you will be astonished at the value they bring to your organisation.

There are many ways to foster empowerment, including:

- effective delegation techniques, such as agreeing outcomes up front
- a focus on building the résumés of your employees
- giving employees the latitude to fail.

Whatever it is that you are trying to achieve or resolve, you need to decide if your choices will empower others. If the answer is yes, then your choice will foster this actuator and become a positive force for your business.

Innovation

Innovation uses creativity and lateral thinking to develop solutions that haven't been developed before. The reason innovation is such a powerful actuator is because of the nature and pace of modern business. Twenty years ago you could be great at something and repeat the process and stay great for another 20 years. That simply isn't true any more. A great quote from the American humorist Will Rogers says it all: 'Even if you are on the right track, you will get run over if you just sit there'.

No business can rest on its laurels—regardless of its previous strength. Just think of corporate legend Microsoft. It made every right move and transformed the personal computing market. But it overestimated the importance of the physical machine. With the advent of the internet and, more recently, cloud computing, the market is shifting. Hardware and software are not so important if people put their lives on the internet and can access that information from any machine anywhere in the world. As a result, one of the most successful companies of all time is behind the eight ball. And quite frankly, if that can happen to Microsoft then it can happen to every business on the planet.

It's ironic really because Gates always said he was not worried about his competitors, he was worried about some guy in a garage somewhere who was coming up with the next technology. And that's exactly what happened—though I'm sure this is not the end of Microsoft as we know it.

There are many ways to foster innovation, though I find it helpful to first consider the things that destroy innovation, or what I have come to call the Seven Deadly Sins of Innovation:

- Lust for innovation for innovation's sake is dangerous. Don't appoint a chief innovation officer or start an innovation division for a select few—make innovation core to everyone's role.
- Gluttony is having too much red tape and hierarchy, which both stifle innovation. You need to be lean and mean if you want to innovate.

- Sloth is having a culture where it's okay for people to do the absolute minimum to survive. If you want to avoid this, then get your staff competing and striving for big goals and have a culture of doing more in less time.

- Envy occurs where companies always look beyond their employees for the genius who can help their company innovate. You need to look beyond someone's sexy résumé and start ensuring your existing employees innovate.

- Pride appears where companies think they have arrived, and forget to constantly innovate to stay ahead.

- Greed is where companies focus only on short-term profit. Innovation won't happen if you aren't prepared to invest and have some patience as to the outcome.

- Wrath is the last of the seven deadly sins — the anger that often surrounds initiatives that have failed. Celebrate failure and learn from it rather than point fingers if you really want to foster a culture of innovation in your business.

If you can avoid these seven deadly sins then innovation will work for you. Whatever it is that you are trying to achieve or resolve you need to decide if your choices will foster innovation. If the answer is yes and the innovation will be useful and profitable then it fosters this actuator and is a positive force for your business.

Inspiration

Inspiration means leaders motivate their stakeholders by communicating a compelling vision or leading by example. Inspiration is fairly obvious: if people are inspired they are going to put a lot more into their jobs. When your clients are inspired to be working with you, then they are much more likely to accept your advice and develop a great working relationship. When your suppliers are inspired by what you are doing, then they are much more likely to want to work with you and will therefore be more open to negotiating terms and giving good prices and service.

Inspiration is rarely about money. Sure, money can offer a short-term boost to productivity, but being inspired is something much more than money — it's about how someone feels about being part of your organisation. Most of us want to feel valued and as though our contribution matters in some way. We want to feel proud of our work and that we are making a difference. That can't happen if your people aren't inspired or, worse, they aren't proud to work for you.

There are many ways to foster inspiration, including the following:

- launch products that revolutionise markets
- embrace creativity, design and individual expression
- incentivise and recognise your employees
- get your people to look up to you by leading by example
- communicate the good and bad about what's going on.

We experimented with countless incentive programs at Blueprint and the results were often a revelation. In one initiative we launched an incentive plan for our front-line staff to raise money for charity. The agreement was that for every sale a team made the company would donate a set amount to charity and that money would be pooled across all the teams. The more sales that were made, regardless of what team made them, the more the charity fund would increase. And at the end of the day the team that made the most sales would get to select which charity would receive the charity fund for that day. The opportunity to make a contribution and possibly present a cheque to a charity of their choice turned out to be one of the most successful incentive programs we ever ran—a result that categorically refutes the idea that salespeople are only interested in individual or financial incentives.

Whatever it is that you are trying to achieve or resolve, you need to decide if your choices will inspire others or not. Will your employees be inspired? Will your clients and suppliers be inspired? If the answer is yes then the decision fosters this actuator and is a positive force for your business.

Flexibility

Flexibility occurs where a business has the ability to adapt to change or unforeseen circumstances. It is an actuator because of the changing nature of business. The strongest businesses have a degree of flexibility built in so that they can move and adapt to whatever comes up. It is this versatility and ninja-like quality that often allows smaller businesses to respond far faster to changing market conditions than a large company ever could.

The many areas where you can foster flexibility include:

- contractual agreements
- infrastructure and equipment
- job descriptions
- product features.

Entrepreneurs from a corporate background often fall over when it comes to flexibility because they try to implement the familiar rigid job descriptions of their corporate life into their small enterprise. Smaller businesses need to be more flexible because business changes so quickly and people within the business need to be able to adapt, without getting shirty and complaining, 'but that's not in my job description'. Incentives based around a job description are unlikely to be motivating if the job requirements and expectations keep changing. You need to work out a way to have flexibility but still give employees direction and responsibility.

To overcome the shortfall of traditional job descriptions at Blueprint, we implemented a unique type of job description that we called a project and prototype list. Everyone's role was made up of a group of projects, essentially tasks that have a beginning and end, such as building a website or recruiting a new sales manager. In addition, their role included one or more prototypes for which they were responsible — tasks that were ongoing in nature, such as accounts receivable or answering phones at reception. Dividing employees' roles into groups of projects and prototypes enabled us to effectively promote and demote staff continually. But because the roles were split in this way there was no animosity or expectation around those changing roles and responsibilities. If someone turned out to be unsuitable to a particularly task they were just moved off that task to something else — there was no fuss or fanfare. This gave us enormous flexibility to change the company as our business model evolved.

We motivated staff to excel at their groups of projects and prototypes by tracking their results and giving new projects and responsibilities for bigger and better prototypes to the individuals who performed. This job satisfaction and recognition was enough to motivate staff, and we changed from individual to team-based incentives, where employees shared in the company's profits.

Whatever it is that you are trying to achieve or resolve, you need to decide if your choices will bring more flexibility to your business or more rigidity. If your decision brings more flexibility then the decision fosters this actuator and is a positive force for your business.

Replication

Replication allows a process, product or service to be delivered consistently and easily through repetition. Success is a result of doing something well, finding a market and repeating the process. Replication is an actuator because it encourages entrepreneurs and business owners to focus on duplication. It is replication that has allowed companies like McDonalds to become global phenomena. McDonalds has perfected a system that allows for low-cost, consistent replication of products and services, regardless of country or store, and it is this consistency of delivery that keeps customers coming back for more.

If you have developed a good idea and are making good money in the income stage of your business you will *never* move into profit and value unless you master replication. You may understand what you do, yet in the process of building your business you may have forgotten some of the nuances of how that success was achieved. You hire people but fail to tell them how to repeat your success, so results fall away and you wonder what happened.

What happened is that you did not adequately pass on the formula to the person you expected to do a certain job. Replication is about coming up with a formula and being able to pass that formula on to others so that they too can replicate and deliver consistent results, regardless of who is doing the tasks involved.

Often businesses baulk at the idea of replication because they think it will take too long, but the alternative is a false economy. If everyone in the business is clear about how certain things are done and they don't have to second guess themselves all the time, then they are freed up to focus on other things that really matter, like customer relationships, innovation and creativity. If your people are wasting their creativity trying to work out the best way to do things that already have an optimum process but no-one has bothered to tell them, then it's a waste of resources.

There are many areas where you can foster replication, including:

- implementing job descriptions that encourage continuous improvement for your staff

- tracking and sharing results to reduce time and cost inputs
- implementing replicable systems and processes into every part of your business.

Whatever it is that you are trying to achieve or resolve, you need to decide if your choices will bring more opportunities to replicate or less. If your decision is going to allow for more replication of the things that really matter to the bottom line, then it fosters this actuator and is a positive force for your business.

Leverage

Leverage involves an entrepreneur using fewer resources to gain greater impact from relationships or capacity. Leverage is essentially about trying to get the biggest bang for your buck and how you can spend the least amount of time, money and effort for the biggest gain.

> Leverage is essentially about trying to get the biggest bang for your buck and how you can spend the least amount of time, money and effort for the biggest gain.

Ancient Greek mathematician and inventor Archimedes said, 'Give me a lever long enough, and a prop strong enough, I can single-handedly move the world'. This is what leverage is all about—using what you have, or gaining access to what others have, to massively impact your business.

There are many areas where you can foster leverage, including:

- client, supplier and peer partnerships
- reputation and relationships
- excess capacity within your or someone else's business.

One of the fastest growing sectors on the internet is group buying. This relies on reselling the excess capacity of companies such as hotels, restaurants and service companies. If you have latent assets, selling your services at a discount through a group-buying company like Groupon is an example of leverage at work. And the group-buying company is also using leverage smartly by using other companies' capacity to make a market and build a customer following for themselves. They can then leverage the sheer numbers of customers on their database to get increasingly better offers for their customers. Regardless of the long-term future of these type of businesses, given customers are driven to shop only on price, it is a business model that is a great example of leverage at work.

Whatever it is that you are trying to achieve or resolve, you need to decide if your choices will bring more opportunities for leverage or less. If your decision is going to allow for more leverage, then it fosters this actuator and is a positive force for your business.

Simplicity

Simplicity simply means that your business is easy to do business with and its functions and products are easy to understand. There is a strange paradox in business that seems to encourage the notion that complicated is better. We have a language that is often needlessly complex to anyone outside that industry, and business memos and communication are often deliberately bamboozling so that the writer can feel intellectually superior. What's the point?

Warren Buffett, the richest and most successful investor of all time, believes in simplicity and is known for never investing in things he doesn't understand. He says, 'There seems to be some perverse human characteristic that likes to make easy things difficult'.

He's right of course and, frankly, if simplicity is a touchstone for one of the most successful investors in history it should be good enough for you and me.

There are many areas where you can foster simplicity, including:

- having systems that aren't over-complicated to follow
- making it easy to understand what your business does
- making it easy to buy from you.

In his book *Simplicity* Edward de Bono calls for companies to realise that consumers sometimes want less, not more. Citing video players as an example he states that only a tiny percentage of people use more than the basic features on their video recorders. This study, other than showing its age, given that recorders have been replaced by DVD players and are themselves being rapidly replaced by downloadable files, is a great example of why consumers want less not more. In fact, the concept of simplicity was really embraced at Apple when they launched their first iPod. For the first time, an electronic device could be functioned with one button. This revolution changed the game completely — and it was all about embracing the concept of simplicity in design and function.

It amazes me how some companies overcomplicate doing business with them. Pick from this long list of options, fill out this form, get it signed by an authorised person, send it off, come into the branch, and so on. The companies that understand how to make it simple for their customers to access their products become the market leaders. Just look at the success of Google as an example — Google search engine is a clean, white screen with a search box. That's it. There is nothing much else on that page, no clutter, no wordy explanations — just a simple little box and some nice white space.

Whatever it is that you are trying to achieve or resolve, you need to decide if your choices will bring more simplicity to your business or less. If your decision is going to allow for more simplicity, then it fosters this actuator and is a positive force for your business.

Reputation

Reputation is where an entrepreneur looks after their image and standing in their business and the wider community. A lot of entrepreneurs think success is all about branding and getting their brand out into the marketplace, but in the early stages of business evolution you need to brand yourself, and that means developing your own entrepreneurial track record and reputation. Only as the business progresses into the profit stage would you shift your attention from personal reputation to building the reputation and brand of the team. Finally, when you are in the value stage of business then you can focus on the reputation and brand of the business.

When you are in the income stage of your business it's too expensive to build the business brand. Spending money on branding isn't going to bring in sales. Instead, focus your attention on developing the right reputation with your staff, suppliers and customers. Remember a happy customer will tell a few people if you are lucky, an angry one will scream if from the rooftops. Don't tell people what you can do — get out there and do it so others can tell potential customers. And now, with the advent of online feedback, happy and unhappy clients can reach millions of other potential customers.

As I said earlier, there is a catch-22 around reputation. If you haven't got a reputation it's difficult to get business, and without the experience you get from winning that business you can't build a reputation. That's why reputation is such as powerful actuator. If you can work out a way to use reputation to get ahead you will go further and faster.

There are many areas where you can foster reputation, including:

- not taking on business that you can't deliver successfully
- exceeding expectations, practising humility and not burning bridges
- aligning yourself with companies that will give you implied reputation.

When we purchased technology for our call centre, wherever possible we bought the best-known and respected brand. Sure, this sometimes cost us more but the implied reputation we earned for being reliable made the difference between winning large corporate contracts and not. We were also prepared to go to greater lengths to win business with well-respected companies because we knew if they were our clients other companies would follow.

Whatever it is that you are trying to achieve or resolve, you need to decide if your choices will enhance your reputation or tarnish it. Would you be proud if this decision was splashed across the front pages of the newspaper? If your decision is going to build your reputation, then it fosters this actuator and is a positive force for your business.

Using actuators

There are essentially two ways to use actuators: either reactively or proactively. First, you could proactively develop strategies or business models that serve to harness the power of as many of these actuators as possible. Second, you can reactively use the actuators when making a decision between two opposing courses of action.

For instance, one of the social enterprises I helped bring to Australia is One Water—at the time, a unique business model that funded water projects in Africa from the sale of bottled water. If you unpack the business model, you will find many of the actuators we just covered. The model is firstly innovative because the water projects we fund are called Play Pumps—as kids play on the merry-go-round water gets pumped out of the ground into a holding tank so they can go to school rather than spend hours a day collecting water. The play pump is empowering because the kids are doing something to help their village by doing what they enjoy most — playing. And this is simplicity in action, because the motion of the kids playing doesn't require an engine that could break down or fuel that might run out. The model is leveraged because we don't need to install the Play Pumps, because installation is handled by a specialist company in Africa. And lastly, we use inspiration because people like to see smiling kids on a merry-go-round doing good for their village. Five out of the eight actuators are well factored into this particular business model and I think that is why it's been so successful raising, globally, nearly $5 million in funds for Africa since inception.

It is easy to use the actuators in your decision making, because you can quickly assess which options harness the most or most important actuators. For example, if you were considering launching an incentive scheme for staff and you were trying to decide between an equity scheme and a team bonus, you could analyse the benefits based on the embedded actuators. The equity scheme may provide more inspiration and leverage, given you don't pay cash until the company sells, but the team bonus would be simpler, easier to replicate and give you more flexibility as you bring on new staff and the business changes. So in making that choice you would need to work out which of these actuators is probably going to be harnessed more than the other, and for me it would probably depend on what stage your business is in.

Actuators are the positive forces that you can call on to help accelerate your business. The more of these you can harness, the faster your business will grow.

Key points

» PGP actuators are the positive forces that can speed up growth, fulfilment and prosperity.

» The eight actuators are empowerment, innovation, inspiration, flexibility, replication, leverage, simplicity and reputation.

» Whatever you are trying to achieve or resolve, you need to decide if your choices will empower others.

» Decide if your choices will foster innovation. If the answer is yes and the innovation will be useful and profitable then it fosters this actuator.

» Decide if your choices will inspire others or not. Will your employees, clients and suppliers be inspired?

» If your decision brings more flexibility then the decision fosters this actuator and is a positive force for your business.

» Whatever it is that you are trying to achieve or resolve, you need to decide if your choices will bring more opportunities to replicate or less.

» Decide if your choices will bring more or less opportunities for leverage. If your decision is going to allow for more leverage, then it is a positive force for your business.

» If your decision allows more simplicity, then it fosters this actuator and is a positive force for your business.

» Decide if your choices will enhance your reputation or tarnish it. Would you be proud if this decision was splashed across the front pages of the newspaper?

» The two ways to use actuators is reactively and proactively. You can proactively develop strategies or business models that harness the power of as many actuators as possible. Or you can reactively use the actuators when deciding between two opposing courses of action.

» The more actuators you can harness, the faster your business will grow.

Chapter 18

Principle 3—minimise mass

Mass is anything that slows down business. A business that has excessive mass is like an ocean liner, and a business that is lean and mean is more like a speedboat. The speedboat is nimble and can change direction quickly, depending on the obstacles and conditions it encounters. It can get in and out of tight spots quickly and go places a larger vessel can't. An ocean liner, on the other hand, often takes kilometres just to slow down, let alone turn around.

The idea of mass is a little contradictory because you do need some mass to get momentum. But too much will slow you down. The trick is finding a happy medium. In my view it's always better to have a little less than you think you need. That way all your resources are utilised to their maximum potential. Having a little less than you need makes people better planners, smarter innovators and more creative individuals. Greek philosopher Plato's statement, 'Necessity is the mother of invention', pretty much says it all. If everything you need is always to hand, you don't need to plan or strategise about how to solve your resource issues. A perfect world may have all you need in terms of money and resources, but that creates its own inertia.

Since my retirement from business I have been very fortunate to have the opportunity to work with many entrepreneurs in the developing world and I have loved every minute of it. I have worked with subsistence farmers in the mountains of Papua New Guinea, helping them establish micro-businesses to sell products and services to Western trekkers. I have worked with young entrepreneurs from townships in South Africa in collaboration with the Branson Centre for Entrepreneurship, and with young people in Zimbabwe who are trying to create a better life for themselves through business. I'm also involved in a project to foster micro-business along the Kokoda Track in Papua New Guinea. What is so inspiring is that all these entrepreneurs have developed an uncanny ability to get things done without easy access to all the resources they need. All of these individuals struggle with adversity every day, but they rise above it using their resourcefulness. If their businesses survive, it's because of innovation and determination, not because they have everything they need at their fingertips. One of the entrepreneurs at the Branson Centre even made a business out of the shortage of resources in one of the townships in South Africa. He realised that no-one had bathrooms, but everyone still had to look presentable for jobs in the city. So he established portable showers at bus shelters and his business took off.

The four areas of business mass

Businesses founded with too much mass often focus on the wrong things. They create sloppy business models that are supported by initial funding, not business smarts, and the business spends way too much money on purchases and processes before a single cent has been made. There were countless examples of this excess during the dot-com era, when companies were able to raise huge amounts of cash despite ridiculous business models, and they then spent most of that investment creating unnecessary mass. To be genuinely successful, you need to minimise mass in order to go faster and further.

Mass can be inadvertently taken on board by too many:

- people
- products
- purchases
- processes.

People mass

Having too many people to deal with is a type of mass. The people involved in your business include staff, customers, suppliers and investors. One of the traps entrepreneurs often fall into is that they think the more people involved in their business the better—but nothing could be further from the truth.

The burden of too many people was driven home to me when a friend of mine told me about his experience during a 28-day trek through Pakistan. For any trek of this type the travelling party will always have porters who will carry supplies, travel ahead and set up camp, make the food and often put up tents, and so on. When my friend told me how many porters accompanied him and his four trekking mates I was astounded. They needed 88 porters. The trek followed a route where there were no villages, so it was necessary to carry all of their water and food. Those on the trek needed porters, and the porters needed porters, and the porters' porters needed porters. The mass created for that expedition was huge and that's what it can be like with people in your business if you aren't careful.

Staff mass

As soon as you hire a staff member you need to manage that person until you grow to a stage where there are too many for you to manage, and then you need a manager to manage the staff. And then you grow further and you need managers in different areas including sales, operations, accounts, IT and HR. The problem is that managers are essentially overheads that don't directly make your business money, so it can be counterproductive to have too many people working in your business.

Possible ways to minimise staff mass include the following:

- Hire casual staff unless they are crucial for the long term.
- Consider outsourcing all but the vital core elements of your business.
- Minimise management layers by employing staff who don't need to be micro-managed.

Customer mass

The next type of people mass that businesses often collect is customer mass. And while customers are the lifeblood of any business, your focus needs to be on quality not quantity. The Pareto principle, or 80/20 rule, applies to most businesses, which means that you will make 80 per cent of your profit from 20 per cent of your customers. In fact, when you add up all of your overheads and management time you might find that at least some of the remaining 80 per cent of your customers are actually losing you money. The banking industry, for example, worked out that their top 20 per cent of customers made the vast majority of their profit—hence the difference in service. The top tier gets personalised private bankers, whereas the bottom 20 per cent are given poor service because the bank doesn't care if they leave.

Possible ways to minimise customer mass include the following:

- Track which customers are profitable and which are not.
- Have a customer screener (as outlined in chapter 10).
- Treat different customers differently.

Supplier mass

Supplier relationships are another area where businesses create unnecessary people mass. Every business relies on a variety of component or service suppliers in order to be successful in what they do. Finding the right suppliers who provide goods or services of the right quality and at the right price is a crucial part of business success.

Getting three quotes and choosing the cheapest may make the shareholders happy in large companies, but it doesn't build solid partnerships. Having fewer reliable suppliers that offer good value without having to brief them and micro-manage them makes more business sense and is worth paying that little bit extra for. Good, loyal relationships with a few suppliers will almost always save you money in the long run.

Possible ways to minimise supplier mass include:

- Don't chop and change based on price alone.
- Invest the time to train your suppliers on how you want to work.
- Get your suppliers to coordinate other subcontractors.

Investor mass

Lastly, investor mass is another area where entrepreneurs find themselves overwhelmed by having to deal with the different personalities and needs of more and more people. In their eagerness to grow, many entrepreneurs try to attract investors into their business. While this can be a powerful strategy to get ahead, it can also create a huge management headache for the entrepreneur if the investors are high maintenance.

Possible ways to minimise investor mass include:

- looking for the investors who can invest both now and in the future
- getting a smaller number of investors who each make larger investments
- finding investors who will add more value than just money.

Whatever it is that you are trying to achieve or resolve, you need to decide if your choices will reduce people mass or increase it. Unless there is a very good reason and you can financially justify having to deal with more people, reducing people mass is a positive force for your business.

Product mass

Every business must sell either products or services. Yet offering too many products or services can create unnecessary mass. There is an adage that says that too much of anything is a bad thing, and products and services are no exception. Product mass becomes a problem when you have to market multiple brands, and the choice confuses your consumers and causes operational and delivery challenges.

> Every business must sell either products or services. Yet offering too many products or services can create unnecessary mass.

Too many brands

Strong brands are unambivalent: they are what they say they are; they do what they say they will do; and they do so consistently. There is no confusion about what that brand is about and what the company is trying to achieve. If you have too many different or competing brands, then you water down the impact of each. And I know this because we made this mistake time and time again in our business. We would launch a new business and create a totally separate brand for each. This required a logo, a website, a unique phone number, a brochure and different business cards for people working in that business. It also meant that people working across businesses needed to carry multiple business cards. We inadvertently created brand mass for ourselves that was not only costly and time-consuming to manage, it also confused our clients about who we were and what we did. Don't make the same mistake.

Too many products or services

The second type of product mass is trying to sell too many products or services. It used to be that restaurants would have 30 to 40 dishes on the menu, but the best restaurants quickly worked out that if you give people a smaller number of things to choose from it makes it easier for them to choose and implies better quality.

In the book *Yes! 50 Secrets from the Science of Persuasion*, authors Noah J. Goldstein, Steve J. Martin and Robert B. Cialdini write about how behavioural scientist Sheena Iyengar and social scientist Mark Lepper ran an experiment that demonstrated how too much choice can actively depress buying behaviour. They created a jam display in a supermarket. They wanted to see how many passers-by would taste and buy jam depending on how many varieties they offered. Although the display of a large choice of 24 varieties of jam attracted more people to the tasting table, only 3 per cent bought jam. When only six flavours were displayed on the stand, 30 per cent of those attracted to the tasting table bought jam—a great lesson in why less can achieve more.

Minimising product mass

Product mass also hinders your ability to deliver a good quality product, in the least time at the lowest cost. In the restaurant example, think how much easier it is for the chef and his team to prepare just 10 dishes instead of a possible 40. The ingredients can be fresher, and much more care can be taken so the dish is of a consistently high quality every time. Your business is exactly the same—the fewer products or services you offer, the more of a specialist you will become and the more opportunity you will have to finetune the delivery for maximum efficiency and consistency. And specialists get to charge more for their goods and services.

Possible ways to minimise product or service mass include:

- Don't have too many brands, and ensure your brand says what you do.
- Don't give customers too many options.
- Deliver fewer products or services so you can have an efficient operation.

Whatever it is that you are trying to achieve or resolve, you need to decide if your choices will minimise product and service mass. If your choice helps to reduce product mass, then it is a positive force for your business.

Purchase mass

Earlier we explored the idea of cost price, real cost, financial cost and opportunity cost. Mass is often created when we don't adequately consider the real cost of any purchase. The real cost is how much your goods really cost once you factor in all of the other up-front and ongoing costs that often come with making a purchase.

By considering your purchases carefully, you will help to prevent unnecessary mass. For example, the decision to have a new office in another city is not just about the cost of rent; there are other costs to consider too, such as cleaning and fit-out. You may also need a reception area and receptionist, and there are all the travel costs associated with visiting that office, and staff from that office visiting you. You will need more management, and before you know it your company has taken on a lot more cost and mass than you originally bargained for. Creating new offices in different locations takes time and money. In today's world where technology plays a crucial everyday role in sales and communication, it may no longer be necessary to create physical offices, which will allow you to minimise your mass.

Other purchases that can increase mass include inflexible contracts for technology or communications. While $100 per month might sound reasonable for access to equipment, by the time you add up the real cost over the term of the contract and compare that to how long you actually need the equipment for, you might realise it's not so reasonable after all. Be very wary about long-term contacts that lock you into a decision, as they can add mass and remove flexibility from your business model.

Possible ways to minimise purchase mass include:

- Always consider the real cost of a purchase, which includes all of the additional up-front and ongoing costs.
- Negotiate not just on price but also on the terms, including additional services, payment terms and contract length.
- Do without; use someone else's spare capacity; or hire as you need to.

Whatever it is that you are trying to achieve or resolve, you need to decide if your choices will minimise purchase mass or increase it. If your choice helps to reduce purchase mass, then it is a positive force for your business.

Process mass

Mass can also be inadvertently taken on board through the processes you develop. We have already discussed the importance of systemisation;

however, the drive for systems can go overboard and create unnecessary mass. You need to find a balance between structure and processes, and the flexibility needed to just get on with the job. Excessive red tape, too many layers of management and unnecessary or overly complex systems will slow the business down by adding mass. You just need to look inside a typical government department to see how excessive process and red tape can stifle growth and progress.

Reducing process mass is about seeking ways to make your operation faster, leaner and more productive with the same resources. Remember the South African bus shelter shower entrepreneur I mentioned earlier? His business was thriving but he noticed a process problem developing, which was a classic bottleneck. Each person paid the same to use the shower facilities, but the men took about 10 minutes to shower and change and the women took about 20 minutes. Although the women were paying the same as men they were taking twice as long, and he was effectively losing one sale every time a woman went for a shower. To solve this problem the entrepreneur set-up a separate cubicle for the women, so they would have their shower in the same time as the men and then transfer to the separate cubicle to do their hair and make-up. Although this increased mass slightly due to the need for the separate cubicle, it increased revenue substantially and kept his customers happy.

Possible ways to minimise process mass include:

- Work with your team to come up with simple systems that are efficient but not overly laborious.
- Have a flat management structure without too many levels.
- Use technology to enable your systems by taking out the boring processes.

Whatever it is that you are trying to achieve or resolve, you need to decide if your choices will minimise process mass or increase it. In all cases minimising unnecessary process and red tape is a positive force for your business.

Using mass

Once you have a clear idea of the types of things that can increase mass in your business, you can use the understanding in two ways. You can look around your organisation and seek ways to reduce the current mass.

Are there too many people? Is there a client you want to sack, or a staff member or supplier that has passed their use-by date or an investor who consumes too much of your time? Are there too many products, especially products that rarely sell or confuse the customers? Have you made purchases or created processes that are unnecessarily slowing you down? The reduction of any type of mass will pave the way to greater and faster business success.

The other way to look at mass is to seek to minimise mass in all your decision making. The next time you are making a decision to hire people, launch new products, make purchases or develop processes, consider the mass implications. If you are going to increase mass you had better make sure that it is going to deliver a tangible benefit to the business. When you consciously seek to reduce frictions, foster actuators *and* minimise mass you will *always* improve your decision making. When you also seek to maximise balance, which is the subject of the next chapter, your decision making will become even stronger.

Key points

» It's always better to have a little less than you think you need, so all your resources are utilised to their maximum potential.

» Working with the minimum makes people better planners, smarter innovators and more creative individuals.

» You need to minimise mass to go faster and further—reducing mass is a positive force for your business.

» Mass can be a result of too many people, products, purchases or processes.

» Decide if your choices will reduce mass or increase it.

» Once you understand the types of things that can increase mass in your business, you can use the understanding in two ways. You can minimise current mass, and you can minimise mass in all of your decision making, choosing the option that results in the least mass.

Chapter 19

Principle 4—maximise balance

The last perpetual growth principle (PGP)—maximise balance—is all about the drive to create win–win outcomes. Consider a motor vehicle that has one wheel out of balance—not only do the wheels wear out much quicker, fuel economy and car safety are both compromised. The same is true in business—it is important to see competition as a healthy and necessary part of business success, but it's not mortal combat. Other people—be that your family, your clients, your suppliers or your staff—don't have to lose out in order for you as the owner or entrepreneur to win. Far from it! Success is far more likely and will arrive much more quickly if you ensure that other people win also. I can still hear the Texan drawl of US author

> Maximising balance is about walking the proverbial mile in someone else's shoes and having an awareness of how your choices and decisions impact on the people around you.

and speaker Zig Ziglar who said, 'You can get everything in life you want if you will just help enough other people get what they want'.

Maximising balance is about walking the proverbial mile in someone else's shoes and having an awareness of how your choices and decisions impact on the people around you. If you take a moment to view your choices from the perspectives of your stakeholders, then you become more aware of other people's perspectives, and you are then more likely to see and secure win–win outcomes. This is not always possible, but we should always try.

Many business mistakes that end up hurting or damaging others are done so inadvertently. They are the product of ignorance rather than malice, and happen because the person making the choice didn't adequately consider the other stakeholders. If you do consider others, you will maximise balance in your decision making. Just taking a moment to consider alternatives, and review how your action will impact on others, will give you insight to ensure that you can benefit more people most of the time—and that will always be beneficial for your business.

Stakeholders in your business

There are, of course, many stakeholders connected to a successful business. Of those there are three direct stakeholders and five indirect stakeholders. Your role in maximising balance is to ensure that as many of those stakeholders as possible also benefit from your choices as much as possible. The stakeholders are:

- direct stakeholders
  - employees
  - clients
  - investors.
- indirect stakeholders
  - family and friends
  - suppliers
  - partners and alliances
  - competitors
  - community.

Direct stakeholders

Direct stakeholders include the employees, clients and investors involved in the business.

Employee stakeholders

In Blueprint we were often accused of being too staff-centric but we found that focusing on win–win outcomes for our staff created a bunch of benefits we didn't initially anticipate. Staff turnover was lower and it took less time and effort to manage staff because empowered employees just get on with the job without have to be hassled or cajoled. As a result we achieved greater results because employees were motivated to achieve our vision. The idea is simple: if your people are happy then they are much more likely to deliver good service and attract more customers; if customers are happy, they will buy more products more often, which will in turn make the shareholders happy.

The conventional business philosophy is that the shareholders are the most important, followed by customers, and then staff, but you only need to look at the disastrous morale in modern banking to see just how flawed that approach is.

Whenever we made a decision or were reviewing options and choices, we worked out how it was going to affect our people. If the impact was negative, even if there was additional profit to be made, we wouldn't proceed. Instead we would try to think of alternatives that would allow us to find a solution to tap into the positive and mitigate the negative so that the decisions would yield reward without having a detrimental impact on staff. It wasn't always possible, but at least we exhausted potential avenues before implementing something negative.

Our employees were always very clear about how highly we valued them. When we were employing for a key role we would get the staff that would eventually report to this person involved in the recruitment process, so people felt ownership in hiring their own boss.

Possible ways to maximise employee balance include:

- determining what your employees' career goals are and helping them get there
- recognising output rather than the time people spend at work
- giving employees flexibility to attend to personal matters.

Whatever it is that you are trying to achieve or resolve, you need to decide if your choices will positively or negatively impact your people. If the decision will negatively affect the people who work for you then there needs to be a *very* good reason for proceeding. If the decision will positively rather than negatively affect your people then chances are the decision is a good one.

Client stakeholders

In the traditional win–lose business environment, it's assumed that we should all negotiate hard with clients so we can get the best deal for the business. You should always know where your breakeven is, and you should seek to receive a fair margin for the effort and service you deliver, but if you are too expensive you risk pricing yourself out the market. If you are too difficult to work with, clients will go elsewhere for a stress-free existence. At the end of the day your business exists to provide solutions to your clients' problems. If you do well at this, profit will follow.

Business is a two-way street—if you look out for your clients as well as your own business then you become partners, not combatants. If you are always looking for ways to give your clients better service then you develop the relationships and build loyalty.

Remember, without your clients you're in real trouble, so you need each other. It's not a competition to see who wins. Seek ways that you can offer greater benefit to your clients for choosing you over your competition. Exceed expectations at every opportunity and give unexpected value.

I remember one instance where we were working with one of Australia's largest banks, and they were taking forever to pay us. We were under serious cash-flow pressure as a result. Normally smaller business just accepts this reality as the nature of doing business with large companies. I approached the bank with our dilemma and they shared their own dilemma, which was they were getting pressure from their procurement team to achieve a volume discount. So together we worked out a solution that allowed us to receive our funds within 48 hours and for our client to get a 1 per cent discount. Everyone agreed. It worked for the bank because that percentage discount equated to a considerable amount of money and it worked for us because it solved our cash-flow problems and allowed us to focus on doing our job.

In our case it worked because there was a financial incentive for the bank to agree to the fast payment. If you are not in that position, however, there are many other ways that you can introduce an additional benefit if the client pays quickly. For example, you could offer to give them some form of preferential treatment or value if they pay faster.

If you can get what you want while also making it advantageous for your client then everyone wins. Not only does that help both parties, but it also strengthens the relationship and makes it less likely for them to shop around.

Possible ways to maximise client balance include:

- finding out the goals of your client so you can help your client achieve them

- giving more value when you increase your price
- having an open and transparent relationship with your clients.

Whatever it is that you are trying to achieve or resolve, you need to decide if your choices will positively or negatively impact your clients. You need your clients as much as they need you, so work with them and ensure you consider your clients in the decision-making process.

Investor stakeholders

If you have investors in your business, it is important that they are considered when you make decisions. Don't forget that, as an entrepreneur, you are both an employee and an investor, and you should expect to be paid as such. If the company is making money, as an investor you can expect to be paid a dividend. If it makes more sense to re-invest these dividends in future growth so that the equity windfall is larger, it's fair to expect your investors to want a say in this type of decision.

In traditional business, investors are the people who are looked after the most. Senior management traditionally spends more time worrying about keeping their shareholders happy than anything else. Personally, I think that if you focus your attention on keeping your staff happy and making sure they have what they need to do a good job then your customers will be happy, and if your customers are happy then your shareholders will benefit.

If you focus on your shareholders first, then it's very easy to create win–lose scenarios that negatively affect the other stakeholders in your business. If all you care about is returning a profit for your shareholders then you could just sack half your workforce. Cutting costs so dramatically can look very good on a balance sheet, but will be short-sighted for long-term success. In fact, when we sold our business that is exactly what transpired soon after the deal was signed. One of the first things to go was our unique culture—deemed an unnecessary expense by the incoming investors. Little did they realise that not cultivating our values would ultimately end in the company's downfall.

> If you focus on your shareholders first, then it's very easy to create win–lose scenarios that negatively affect the other stakeholders in your business.

The goal for all business people should be to build a long-term profitable business that will benefit investors in the long term.

Possible ways to maximise investor balance include:

- finding the right mix between risk and return that investors are seeking
- aligning the exit horizons between you and your external investors
- giving regular reports and updates and involving investors in the big decisions
- giving current investors first right of refusal over future share offers.

Whatever it is that you are trying to achieve or resolve, you need to decide if your choices will positively or negatively impact your investors. It's always smart to try and keep your investors happy, but never at the expense of the other direct stakeholders.

Indirect stakeholders

Indirect stakeholders include friends and family, suppliers, alliances and partners, the competition and the community.

Friends and family as stakeholders

In my view, the most important of the indirect stakeholders are your friends and family. It will be these people who will support you through the tough times of business and bring you down to earth during the good times. If you are working 20-hour days and can't remember the last time you saw your own children then it's unsustainable — for your health and your relationships with the people you care about.

Most people go into business because they want more control over their own lives. Invariably the entrepreneurs and business people I meet were ultimately driven to create more freedom. No longer content with pouring their heart and soul into some nine-to-five rut they yearned to break out so they can do something they love, and spend more time with friends and family. They wanted to feel the sense of achievement that comes from building something that was uniquely their own. There are always times of growth that demand a huge commitment of your time and energy, but these stages should be temporary phases, not a constant state of play.

If the decisions you make negatively affect the quality of your life and your ability to unwind and enjoy time with the people you love, then you have to ask yourself whether it is really worth it. Whatever it is that you are trying to achieve or resolve, you need to decide if your choices will positively or negatively impact your friends and family.

Supplier stakeholders

Suppliers are another of the indirect stakeholders that can make a massive contribution to your business. Sure, the idea in business is often to negotiate hard with your suppliers so you can minimise your costs. But if you grind your suppliers down to the bone and reduce their margin to the point that it's barely worth working with you, then they will not have the leeway to ensure you get the very best service. When things go wrong—which they often do—your suppliers won't have the time or inclination to bend over backwards to help you.

Your suppliers are critical to your success. They need to deliver what they do in order for you to deliver what you do, so you need to get used to seeing your suppliers as your partners. You need to find ways to make your relationships with your suppliers critical to their business too. Add value and add benefits that make them want to help you—not just because they like working with your company, but also because they make money from your relationship. If your suppliers win, you win too.

Whatever it is that you are trying to achieve or resolve, you need to decide if your choices will positively or negatively impact your suppliers — especially your important suppliers.

Partner and alliance stakeholders

Partners and alliances are another type of indirect stakeholder that you should consider before making decisions. Partners might include advisers or consultants. Alliances might include companies that you have established a common purpose with. An alliance might be forged to help each other achieve more clients, keep costs down or help a stakeholder group.

Whatever it is that you are trying to achieve or resolve, you need to decide if your choices will positively or negatively impact your partners and alliances.

Competitor stakeholders

Including the need to achieve balance with your competitors might appear unusual, but some healthy competition is important and usually inevitable, so whether it is this competitor or a new one that emerges to replace them, it's only a matter of time before you have competition, even if you don't already. As such it is important to foster good relationships with competitors. Don't belittle them in your customers' eyes if you can help it. You might even find that by referring or recommending them business that isn't suitable for your business can be a win–win. Both companies will get a reputation for the niche that you fill. Also, many industries have associations that bring together competitors to make sure they are investing in best practice and that they have a united voice in working with regulatory bodies on new legislation. Something that is clearly win–win if you get it right.

Whatever it is that you are trying to achieve or resolve, you need to be aware of how your choice will impact your competitors. Although this indirect stakeholder is not as crucial as the other stakeholders, and often your decisions will adversely affect them, it's always wise to consider how your decision will affect everyone so you get a rounded picture.

Community stakeholders

And lastly, an element of business that is often forgotten is your impact on the community that you live and work in. It's important that your presence in that community doesn't negatively impact others. For instance, those companies who have harmful emissions or don't treat their employees well are not conducive to a thriving community.

Whatever it is that you are trying to achieve or resolve, you need to decide if your choices will positively or negatively impact your community stakeholders. This is the community you work in, and your staff will often live in that community so wherever possible you want to honour that relationship.

Using balance

When assessing decisions, it is best to pursue options that will create win–win outcomes for you *and* your stakeholders. While it is unrealistic for all stakeholders to win on all occasions, it is amazing how you can develop options that can be better for everyone with a little lateral thinking.

Say, for example, you are considering closing an underperforming division within your business. This may be considered a good decision for your company and its investors, but a bad one for staff and customers. If you thought a little differently and explained the situation to staff and customers they might find a better, more balanced solution. If the customers really want you to deliver that service they might offer to pay more for it, or accept a service less costly to deliver. And staff might decide to take over the division and run it as their own business, or agree to lower pay and higher incentives until the business is back on its feet.

There are always a lot more solutions to any problem than you may first realise. Getting your stakeholders involved earlier rather than later will help maximise balance for everyone.

The PGP provide insight into any decision so that you can appreciate the choice ahead from a number of significant perspectives. When you actively seek to reduce frictions and foster actuators you create a double boost to your business by removing the negative *and* fostering the positive. When you also minimise mass and maximise balance to create more win-win decisions then growth is almost inevitable. But don't take my word for it: read the next chapter to appreciate how the PGP works in practice.

Key points

» Other people — your family, your clients, your suppliers and your staff — don't have to lose out in order for you as the owner or entrepreneur to win.

» Maximise balance by walking the proverbial mile in someone else's shoes and being aware of how your choices and decisions impact on the people around you.

» There are three direct stakeholders and five indirect stakeholders in any business. They are employees, clients, and investors (direct); and family and friends, suppliers, partners and alliances, competitors and community (indirect).

» Decide if your choices will positively or negatively impact your people. If the decision will negatively affect the people who work for you then you need a *very* good reason for proceeding.

» Decide if your choices will positively or negatively impact your clients. You need your clients as much as they need you, so work with them and ensure you consider your clients in the decision-making process.

» Decide if your choices will positively or negatively impact your investors. It's smart to try to keep your investors happy, but never at the expense of the other direct stakeholders.

» Decide if your choices will positively or negatively impact all your indirect stakeholders, especially friends and family. If the decisions you make negatively affect the quality of your life and your ability to unwind and enjoy time with the people you love, then ask yourself whether it is really worth it.

» When assessing decisions, pursue the options that will create win–win outcomes for you *and* your stakeholders.

» The PGP provide insight into any decision so that you can appreciate the choice ahead from a number of significant perspectives.

Chapter 20

Perpetual growth principles in practice

One of my passions is training entrepreneurship, but I hate stuffy seminar rooms. So once we have covered the perpetual growth principles (PGP), the entrepreneurs split off into pairs and we all set off on a walkshop — a training session on the move. As we wander along discussing the frictions or actuators that each entrepreneur is currently experiencing, I manoeuvre the group to a flat grassy section where I get the opportunity to physically demonstrate the power of putting the four principles into action — an exercise that helps embed the principles much better than explaining the theory in a classroom can ever hope to achieve.

First, using a croquet ball and mallet, each pair has a minute to hit the heavy ball around a course approximately 30 metres long — while hopping! They must hold the mallet low down the handle over the rough grass and we track how well each pair did. Then we begin to change the variables. First, pairs are allowed to run rather than hop, which usually doubles the number of laps they complete. They have maximised their balance by being able to use both of their legs and are now not accidentally missing the ball or falling over.

Next the teams are encouraged to use the full length of the croquet mallet, which demonstrates what happens when you increase an actuator (positive force). The ball of course now goes much faster and travels further, and the laps are often doubled again. The next variable we change is the size of the ball, swapping the larger and heavier croquet ball for a smaller and lighter golf ball. Again the laps are doubled. Even with the same effort, minimising the mass of the ball results in the ball going further and faster. And finally, just as the teams are becoming exhausted, we make the last change, which is to allow them to hit the ball on a smooth concrete surface rather than the rough grass. This reduction in friction (negative force) has one of the most profound effects of all as they can hit the ball the full length of the course without running, dramatically increasing the number of laps they can complete in the time.

Not only does this get everyone outside for some fun, but it also dramatically illustrates the potency of the four principles in practice. Participants go from barely achieving one lap to making it to 12 to 15 laps, just by making a few changes that harness the PGP—principles that work in the business universe as much as they do in the physical universe.

> I have seen the PGP create vast improvement in everything from sales to staff productivity, and from efficient resource utilisation to profit optimisation.

Imagine what can be achieved when the laps are monthly sales? Is it possible to use these four principles to get a 1000 per cent increase—to go from say $100 000 in sales to $1 000 000 in sales per month? The short answer is yes. I have seen the PGP create vast improvement in everything from sales to staff productivity, and from efficient resource utilisation to profit optimisation.

Case study: Joe's story

One example that sticks out in my mind is Joe, who achieved a similarly massive increase in sales by tweaking just a few things in his business. Joe's business was in direct mail DVD sales, and over a couple of years he had built a solid foundation with monthly sales that averaged a little over $40 000.

When Joe completed the frictions diagnostic (available online at my website <www.accelerateglobal.com/frictionsdiagnostic>) he discovered his biggest frictions were a lack of scale, lack of funding and lack of support. Joe's funding and scale issues were interrelated: his small office was his warehouse, mailing room, retail shop and call centre, and it was starting to hinder his growth. Managing staff to complete these somewhat labour intensive tasks was also taking a lot of his time. The other issue was that as the business grew his cash-flow issues seemed to get worse and worse, given he had to stock DVDs for an average of three months before someone bought them. This didn't leave any extra funds to invest in a larger, more efficient space, nor did it allow Joe to draw a very significant wage from his business.

The decision to reduce the frictions also took into consideration how he was going to foster actuators, minimise mass and maximise balance. The first change Joe made was primarily around cash flow. He realised that if he changed his business model from buying DVDs and reselling them to only paying for DVDs once an order was made, his cash flow tripled immediately. This also minimised mass because there were fewer DVDs to store and cut out the time-consuming step of storing the DVDs alphabetically.

The next change Joe made was to outsource the call centre function that handled the phone ordering. Realising this was an area that wasn't core and that occupied three of his five staff, getting a specialist call centre bureau to handle the calls would be more efficient, free up his time and create more space in the office. It also minimised his costs per DVD shipped. The bonus was that he negotiated to pay the bureau on a 30-day basis, which was much more efficient than paying his own staff weekly, and this made a positive difference to cash flow. The decision to outsource the orders reduced Joe's funding, scale and support frictions in one strategy. He reduced mass by converting the call centre overhead to a variable cost; he was also able to save management time and harness the actuators of replication and empowerment. Whether he received 100 orders or 10 000 orders, the call centre was empowered to look after each call in exactly the same way through a systemised process that Joe helped them develop and stick to.

Finally, with Joe's time freed up, improved cash flow and a business model change that allowed him to scale up, it was time for Joe to invest in a sales and marketing push. He evolved his business model away from list purchase and mailing catalogues to a much more cost-effective and successful referral program with his existing customers. He tapped into his growing reputation with his existing clients and leveraged those relationships in a win–win scenario. His existing clients referred new clients in return for a free DVD. He also set up a win–win alliance with some direct mail houses that specialised in book distribution and agreed to promote their products to his database if they promoted Joe's DVDs to theirs. This was a great leverage of assets and reputation that worked much better than a cold approach to a purchase list. Not only did the percentage of sales per database double, it cost half as much to promote.

Essentially these three changes—selling DVDs on consignment, outsourcing the call centre and leveraging affinity groups—tripled Joe's sales in a few months, which turned into a profit increase of five times and an even better cash-flow benefit. Simultaneously focusing on reducing frictions, fostering actuators, minimising mass and maximising balance proved to Joe the power of these universal business principles.

The PGP gave Joe greater insight into his business, what was going wrong and how to fix it so he could quickly and easily road-test decisions against the four principles. We used to train our staff on this simple yet effective decision-making methodology and it meant that they made better decisions more often.

Identifying no-brainer decisions using PGP

A no-brainer decision can be one that is either a categorical No or a categorical Yes. These types of clear-cut decisions probably make up about a quarter of the decisions you're likely to make and so they can be signed off without too much delay or worry. So long as you know how to identify them.

Where all elements of the PGP are optimised, then the decision is in the sweet spot. This can be demonstrated using a three-axis graph (see figure 20.1.)

The first axis, mass versus force, is optimised where the mass is the lowest and the force is the highest (that is, the difference between the positive forces, or actuators, and the negative forces or frictions).

The second axis is between balance and force, and this is optimised when both balance and force are at the highest.

The third axis, between balance and mass, is optimised when balance is at its highest and mass is at its lowest.

Each axis is optimised where these lines intersect; this is what you could call the sweet spot, and points to a no-brainer decision.

In other words, any decision that simultaneously reduces frictions, fosters actuators and minimises mass while maximising balance is going to be a good decision. So if you find a no-brainer decision that is in the sweet spot then proceed and move on to the next decision.

Figure 20.1: location of the sweet spot for a no-brainer decision

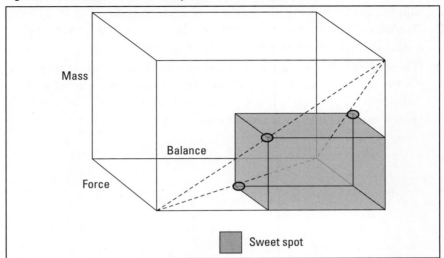

The opposite is also true. Any decision that simultaneously increases frictions, reduces actuators and maximises mass while minimising balance is a bad decision, and you should not proceed, as it's almost guaranteed to be bad for your business.

The decisionship accelerator, which you will learn about in chapter 24, is a powerful tool that allows you to easily bring your newfound foresight and insight to bear. It is a one-page reminder of the key foresight and insight distinctions that will guide your decision making; when added to the final sight of hindsight, which is the subject of part V, then your ability to accurately assess decisions will greatly improve.

> Any decision that simultaneously reduces frictions, fosters actuators and minimises mass while maximising balance is going to be a good decision.

Key points

» The PGP can create vast improvement in everything from sales to staff productivity, and from efficient resource utilisation to profit optimisation.

» Where all elements of the PGP are optimised, then the decision is in the sweet spot.

» Any decision that simultaneously reduces frictions, fosters actuators and minimises mass while maximising balance is going to be a good decision. If you find a no-brainer decision that is in the sweet spot then proceed and move on to the next decision.

» The opposite is also true. Any decision that simultaneously increases frictions, reduces actuators and maximises mass while minimising balance is a bad decision, and you should not proceed as it's almost guaranteed to be bad for your business.

Part V

How to use hindsight to develop perspective to reflect on your own results

Hindsight provides new eyes.

Wayne W. Dyer,
US author and personal development speaker

Chapter 21

Developing hindsight

The decisionship process of define, assess and decide is dominated by the assess process. In the assess stage you must view the decisions you face with the three sights: foresight, insight and finally hindsight. Where foresight is focused on the six lenses of clarity and insight is provided by the perpetual growth principles (PGP), hindsight is made possible through the creation and application of the decision bank (see figure 6.3 on p. 75). Your decision bank is simply a record of all the decisions you make, so you can look back on those decisions and learn from them so you can take that learning into your new decisions. Hindsight is all about gaining perspective into your decision-making skills by anticipating, evaluating and relating to the decisions you have made in the past. Hindsight is located in the centre of the entrepreneurial eye model.

Even if you read this book or attend a seminar or take a decisionship training program, it doesn't mean you will miraculously activate your entrepreneurial eye. Your entrepreneurial eye needs to be trained if you are to reach a point where the decisionship process becomes instinctive and consistently accurate. That is only possible once you have followed the steps of foresight, insight and hindsight, and applied the entrepreneurial eye to your business decisions. In doing so you will build up a database of all the decisions you have made and the results of those decisions—this data is your decision bank.

> Hindsight is all about gaining perspective into your decision-making skills by anticipating, evaluating and relating to the decisions you have made in the past.

Only when you close the loop in the learning process does new information become knowledge and eventually wisdom. Learning about the entrepreneurial eye is not the end of your journey: it is the start of it. Understanding this methodology intellectually is not the goal: applying it in practice and gaining feedback from the process is what will exponentially improve your decision-making skills.

You will close the knowledge loop when you turn theory into practice and reflect on the outcomes of your decisions. When you apply the learning, reflect on the results, finetune your approach and re-apply the learning, you have a real opportunity to transform information into practical wisdom.

This is why hindsight is such an important part of the decision-making process. If you spend all this time looking to the future and following a process to make effective decisions when you need to, but don't ever look back to see how accurate you were, then you are never going to truly learn from your decisions. You need to know whether your decisions worked out or not. You need to know if your foresight was accurate or not. You need to know if you could have made better decisions had you taken more time, gathered more information or been less anxious.

And if you think you will remember these things, you're wrong.

Hindsight is often the part of the decisionship model that meets with the most resistance. More often than not, when I initially explain hindsight, entrepreneurs want to skip past it as soon as possible. By their very nature entrepreneurs are usually forward thinkers — they are instinctively drawn to the future. To them the past is the past and they need to move on, regroup and get into action. In an effort to demonstrate the importance of hindsight I often conduct a secret experiment.

In our program we encourage entrepreneurs to come up with their own magic metric. You may remember this concept from chapter 13. Basically, the idea is that if a business owner can focus on the one metric that makes the most difference to the business's success and focus their energy on improving that metric then they will transform their business as a result. I wanted to see just how reliable the memory was for the decisions we make and commit to, so in one session the entrepreneurs were asked to pledge how much their magic metric would increase in the coming quarter. Just one month later we all got together again and I asked each of the participants how they were travelling towards that outcome. What they didn't know is that we had made a record of each entrepreneur's magic metric and what they had pledged to deliver in the quarter. What we found was that almost everyone in the group thought they were achieving against their magic metric, but when we examined the details almost everyone thought they had pledged to something lower than what they had actually pledged to. In short, they had mentally shifted the goal posts. Whether this was a deliberate tampering with the truth to look good or whether they genuinely thought they were on track doesn't really matter. What this exercise did for the entrepreneurs was highlight just how fickle the memory can be. Unless you write down what you decide, you will never have the opportunity to harness the power of hindsight to improve your decision-making process moving forward. One of the outcomes of this exercise was for the entrepreneurs to learn with hindsight that they had nearly all set goals that were unachievable. So if they were to then implement their hindsight learnings into future decisions I would hope that they would remember to be more realistic when they set goals in the future.

Hindsight is therefore about looking back at the decisions you have made and assessing them — subjectively and objectively. And you can't do that unless you document them and are accountable for them. And that is achieved through the creation of your decision bank.

Before we talk about the decision bank, though, let's first look at the process you need to consider to close the loop on your decisions, so you can make faster, better-informed decisions without the angst.

Hindsight process

Creating the systematic habit of looking back at the decisions you have made in the past will help you to develop hindsight and bring a new level of perspective into future decisions. And this will always improve your results. Hindsight requires the creation of a feedback loop, which is embodied in the three-step hindsight process outlined in figure 21.1 (overleaf).

This process ensures that you use hindsight to learn from past decisions in order to make faster, better-informed decisions without the angst. The three steps are:

- *Anticipate.* At the time you make the decision you need to outline what you expect the outcome to be and what success will look like. You also need to commit to a date in the future for review, so you can work out if the decision was a good one or not.
- *Evaluate.* At the review date, you need to evaluate the outcome to see if it was what you expected or not, and whether the decision was a good one or not. Take the time to consider what you did well and what you would have done differently.
- *Relate.* Turn the learning from the evaluate step into knowledge that you can use to change poor decision-making habits and make more effective decisions in the future.

Figure 21.1: the three-step hindsight process

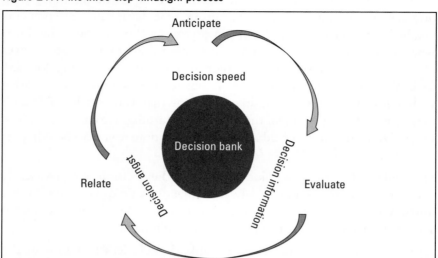

Anticipate

Anticipate is in effect a postscript to the insight stage of decision making. When you are using your entrepreneurial eye to help you make faster, better-informed decisions without the angst, you will travel through a process of define, assess and decide. As you become increasingly familiar with the entrepreneurial eye model and how to use it to train *your* entrepreneurial eye, the process will eventually bed down into instinct.

Every time you make a decision and choose an option to action, you need to document that decision in your decision bank and take a moment to anticipate what the outcome will be. You need to ask yourself what you think will happen as a result of this decision. What has to happen for you to consider this decision to be successful? How will you know if you made the right decision? How will you know if it turns out to be the wrong decision? What will failure look like? You need to anticipate the future and make a note of how you think things will work out. That way you will have a benchmark for your hindsight.

As part of anticipating the outcome you also need to know when you expect the decision to bear fruit. This could be a date in the future or a significant outcome. You might, for example, only get to know if the decision was a good one based on an event, when you're operating at full capacity, a client renews a contract or when you take your annual holidays. Alternatively you may know by a key date in the future, such as the end of the month, end of the financial year or by Christmas.

The two things you need to anticipate are:

- How will you know if the decision was a good one?
- When will you know if the decision was a good one?

Make a note of the information you had at hand when you made the decision, how quickly or slowly you made the decision, and how anxious you were about making the decision. Making a note of this information will allow you to finetune your decisionship profile and embed decision-making excellence into your company.

Also document what process you followed. For example, did you anticipate that the decision would foster at least three actuators and reduce five frictions? Were you confident that the decision would maximise balance with your stakeholders? On what basis did you make the decision?

You don't have to write an in-depth report, simply a snapshot of what you did and why you did it, and what you expected the outcome would be, together with a reminder in the calendar to evaluate if you were correct. And don't assume you will remember why you made a particular choice or what your logic was: write it down. You won't remember or you will fudge your prediction and if you can't look back on the facts then you will not be in a position to genuinely learn and improve.

And don't panic about how much information you need to record. You are already very familiar with the decision and why you chose certain options, so it will take you two minutes to make a record in your decision bank and allocate a review date.

Evaluate

This is what we do when we get that reminder in the calendar. If you make a decision in June and you anticipate that you will know if the decision worked or not by Christmas, then when Christmas roles around you need to evaluate whether your decision was right or wrong.

You need to apply the often harsh critic of hindsight to your outcomes to see how effective you are. This is not always easy or comfortable, but it is critical for learning and improving as a decision maker. Only by articulating your decisions and anticipating the future will you be able to arrive in that future and work out if you were right or not. Knowing what you know now, how would you have made the decision differently? Could you have simply asked better questions earlier to establish that information? If the answer is yes, then you have an opportunity to fine-tune your approach and improve your future decision making.

What did hindsight teach you that you could incorporate into your foresight and insight? Remember that just because the decision didn't result in the success you were looking for doesn't mean that you made the wrong decision or followed a flawed decision-making process. You might have made the best decision with the information you had at the time. It may be that something emerged from left field that no-one could have predicted.

You can evaluate outcomes from a qualitative output, that is, what effect did your decision have on stakeholders? Did you think staff would be enthusiastic and motivated, and they were not, for example? Did you think your decision would improve client relationships, but it didn't? Did you think you would want to spend more time in the office than you do? These are all subjective indicators and as such don't have hard and fast answers, but they are nonetheless important to business success. Remember what physicist Albert Einstein said: 'Everything that can be counted does not necessarily count; everything that counts can not necessarily be counted'.

It is also essential that you evaluate quantitatively to bring in a more objective measure of the outcome. In this case you need to consider the metrics — did profit increase or decrease? If you anticipated that you would get 10 new clients as a result of the decision, did you get those 10 new clients? Or did you only get six new clients?

You have an opportunity to glean some incredible insight into your decision making if you just have the courage to look back on the results and learn from them. By looking objectively and subjectively at the results we can gain understanding, expertise and knowledge from past decisions to improve future decisions. Without this retrospective assessment we are destined to repeat the same mistakes over and over again, and that's the official definition of insanity.

As an entrepreneur you have an opportunity to create the business you want. You are the master of your own fate and you have the power to be a very positive force for good. There is increasing talk of such concepts as the triple bottom line, whereby companies are called to measure their success not just in terms of profit. The triple bottom line relates to:

- *People*. How are our stakeholders affected, including staff, community and customers?
- *Profit*. How do the numbers stack up, and are the investors happy?
- *Planet*. How do our choices impact the planet and the wider community?

There are plenty of critics of the philosophy of the triple bottom line. The argument is that because of shareholders, when push comes to shove profit will always win out over people and planet. In truth, triple bottom line is a tricky business for large, publicly listed companies who have shareholders baying for dividends, but you and I don't have that problem so we can create businesses that do take into consideration people, profit and the planet.

So I encourage you to evaluate your decisions both objectively and subjectively so that you can really see the impact of your choices in action, and use that information to refine your approach and make faster, better-informed decisions without the angst, and that also let you sleep at night!

Relate

When you are evaluating your decisions between what you thought would happen and what actually happened, you have an opportunity to improve.

That improvement becomes a reality when you can relate the learning from the past to your future decision making. If, for example, you become consciously aware of your propensity to make fast decisions and those fast decisions don't work out, then you have the opportunity to do something about that. If you never look back you will never see the correlation between speed and poor decisions and will continue to think you are effective when, in fact, you are not. These understandings can finetune your decisionship profile and make you a better decision maker.

Hindsight allows you to see what you need to put in place to make sure you don't repeat the same mistakes, and also improve your decision making in real time. Say you discover through the hindsight process that you frequently hire the wrong people because you are making decisions too quickly. Or perhaps you recognise that your judgement of character is not what you thought it was. Maybe you believe everything people tell you in an interview and don't have an objective enough viewpoint. If you have come to that realisation because you had the courage to look at your recruitment decisions, then you could have someone else conduct the first interviews and reference check, so you are only involved in the second interview. In this instance, you have taken the learning that perhaps you rush to a conclusion too quickly and that you are not always a great judge of character, and put a process in place that allows you to stay involved in the process while mitigating your shortcomings. In this way you avoid the error in the future and recruit the best people possible for your business.

Success and failure leave clues—hindsight is all about finding those clues so you are more successful more of the time. Consistently applying hindsight to your decision-making processes is like having your own board of directors without having to pay them. You make yourself accountable for your decisions; you bring them to your own attention long after the decision was made so you can effectively assess

> Success and failure leave clues—hindsight is all about finding those clues so you are more successful more of the time.

if your decisions were good choices or not. That hindsight offers up invaluable learning that can then be used to improve your future decision making and ultimately your business. Not to mention your peers and colleagues will often ask your opinion and advice and having a databank will help you easily access the information you need to help them.

You need to ensure that for every significant decision you make you anticipate how you will know if it was a good decision, and when you will know. Remember to put a reminder of that date in your calendar, so you can then evaluate the success of the decision or understand what you need to learn. Finally, you need to continue to relate your learnings back to how you will change these types of decisions in the future. Now you understand the purpose of hindsight and the importance of developing a database of your decisions, in the next chapter we will explore how to effectively create that decision bank so you can add the final touches to the assess process.

Key points

» The decisionship process of define, assess and decide is dominated by the assess process.

» In the assess stage you must view decisions with foresight, insight and finally hindsight.

» Where foresight is focused on the six lenses of clarity and insight is provided by the PGP, hindsight is made possible through the creation and application of the decision bank.

» Your decision bank is a database of all the decisions you make, so you can look back and learn from them so you can take that learning into your new decisions.

» Hindsight is located in the centre of the entrepreneurial eye model.

» Creating the habit of looking back at past decisions helps you develop hindsight and bring a new level of perspective into future decisions.

» Hindsight requires the creation of a feedback loop, which is embodied in the three-step hindsight process. The three steps are anticipate, evaluate and relate.

» Anticipate means outlining, at the time of making the decision, what you expect the result of your decision to be and what success will look like. You must commit to a future date for review, so you can work out if the decision was a good one or not.

» Evaluate means that at the review date, you evaluate the outcome to see if it was what you expected, and whether the decision was a good one or not. Consider what you did well and what you would have done differently.

» Relate means turning the learning from the evaluate step into knowledge that you can use to change bad decision-making habits and make more effective decisions in the future.

» Success and failure leave clues—hindsight is all about finding those clues so you are more successful more of the time.

Chapter 22

Building a decision bank

The only way to bring hindsight to bear on your decision-making process is to actively seek and apply it. And that can't be done effectively or accurately if you rely on your memory or assume that you will remember to think about past decisions. Even if you make a serious error and the pain is so bad that you think you will remember that lesson forever, unless you create a process to make you remember the learning, then chances are you won't.

Your decision bank, which is effectively a database or written record of all the decisions you've made and their respective outcomes, will allow you to mine that valuable knowledge and make better decisions in the future. This chapter is about how you create that decision bank and it's not as daunting as you might at first imagine.

The decision bank is at the centre of the entrepreneurial eye model (see figure 6.3 on p. 75) and is the tool that facilitates hindsight because it is the decision bank that allows you to effectively close the knowledge loop and work out what works and what doesn't work for you individually.

Decisionship is the ability to make faster, better-informed decisions without the stress and anxiety that often prevents entrepreneurs sleeping at night. At the moment you have a decision-making profile based on your innate character and what you have learnt as you go along. But do you know if your decision-making style works? The fact is that most of us have no idea whether our decision making is flawed or not because we don't spend enough time looking back at the results of those decisions. It is hindsight that will set your decision-making skills on fire.

Your decision bank allows you to monitor your individual decision speed, decision information and decision angst, as well as the overall outcome of the choices you make. If your decision-making profile indicates that you make decisions quickly, can you validate that approach from the results your decisions achieved? You need to ask yourself, 'Did I make the decision too fast?' or 'Should I have made the decisions sooner?' Hindsight will help you to finetune your decisionship profile. If, for example, you look back on your decisions and you repeatedly see that you are making decisions too quickly, then you can address this in future by making the decision and always agreeing with yourself that you will sleep on it. You could implement a protocol that short-circuits your capacity for rash choices, which will improve your strike rate over time.

The same is true of information. Say you are the sort of person who makes a point of gathering all the possible information. It may be that, once you start to retrospectively assess your choices, you see a pattern where you get an initial gut response, but you don't trust yourself enough so you delay the process by gathering more information. If you can gather retrospective validation for your initial gut response, then you will increase your self-confidence in making decisions based on your instincts in the future. Alternatively you may be the sort of person who skirts over the details and jumps into action without all the facts. If you can look back at the results of those decisions and appreciate that if you had just asked your customers or your staff a little more about the situation you could have made a better decision, the hindsight gained can allow you to improve your decision making in the future.

> Hindsight will help you to finetune your decisionship profile.

And finally, how stressed do you get about making decisions? The stress and anxiety you feel about decision making comes down to confidence. I believe that every entrepreneur needs to develop confidence that only time can provide. They need experience of making good decisions, making bad decisions and altering the process to make better ones. This is only possible when hindsight brings your decisions and their outcomes into conscious awareness.

Only when you assess the amount of anxiety you felt at the time of making the decision can you work out if the stress was worthwhile. If it turns out that you are super-anxious and are quietly giving yourself an ulcer, but things often work out, then maybe you need to trust yourself a little more, maintain the process you run but give yourself permission, based on past performance, to reduce your stress levels and chill out a bit. If, on the other hand, you don't feel anxious at all and the decisions you make turn out to be terrible, then perhaps you need to pay more attention, be less cavalier and take your responsibilities as an entrepreneur more seriously.

The decision bank will provide accurate hindsight to improve your decisionship profile and also your decision-making process. Normally when entrepreneurs use what *they* consider to be hindsight, it's when they happen to remember something important from the past. But without accurate facts and data about that situation and what *actually* happened, the hindsight can be flawed and can perpetuate poor decision making. Even in our test where we asked a group of entrepreneurs to report how they were travelling against a magic metric they committed to a month before they didn't accurately remember what they had committed to, so how do you seriously expect to remember the facts around a decision you made 12 months ago? Developing a decision bank to record all the decisions, especially all the really important decisions, means that you have an accurate, robust and useful record of past decisions and outcomes that you can then use to guide future decision making.

By way of demonstration, following are a few examples of the hard-won hindsights I learned in business, which address four common decisions.

Should I hire this person?

As you grow your business you will invariably need to make more staff-hiring decisions. The first crucial lesson I learned through hindsight is that just because someone knocks on the door or sends in a résumé doesn't mean you have to hire them. There is rarely anything to be gained from being overly accommodating to a friend's long-lost relative.

First rule — there needs to be a position that you need to fill before you consider hiring someone or waste your time interviewing them. And although it sounds obvious, I doubt there is an entrepreneur alive who hasn't been cajoled into hiring someone to help someone else out. Make sure there is a real position that needs to be filled and that the person under scrutiny is a good match for that role — regardless of who it is.

One of the other mistakes we made — and that I see a lot of entrepreneurs make — is that our reasoning for hiring a new employee was flawed. It ran something like this: 'If we pay them $50 000 we only need $50 000 more in sales and they will pay for themselves.' Given that the real cost of having an employee is usually at least 50 per cent more than their salary, once you take into consideration bonuses, infrastructure, management time, extra expenses, and other statutory fees, not to mention that sales revenue also incurs cost, then the new employee needs to bring in at least three times their wage in additional revenue for the position to be viable.

> Hindsight taught me to always employ based on someone's personality, cultural fit and motivation rather than just their experience.

If there is a genuine position available based on affordability, then you should still write down what you are looking for. Consider experience, cultural fit, growth potential and personality type. Hindsight taught me to always employ based on someone's personality, cultural fit and motivation rather than just their experience.

Interviewing people can be a time-consuming process, so we would often conduct group interviews for multiple positions to save time and narrow down those who suited our culture and wanted the role. It also meant we only needed to give an overview once rather than to each individual. For higher-level positions I would ask the candidates to make a presentation and I would invite their potential direct reports and peers to help assess their suitability.

Once you have found someone suitable, you need to consider their terms of engagement so that you can build in as much flexibility as possible. Our hindsight taught us that hiring people as casuals to start with and converting them into a permanent position only *after* they had proven themselves in the role was always the best approach. For higher-level positions this wasn't always possible, especially if they were leaving a permanent job to join the business. But even then you need to ensure that there are some performance assessment criteria woven into the position so that you have an exit should the person turn out to be a poor fit. It doesn't matter how good your interviewing skills are, there is no better way to test someone's suitability than to test them in your environment.

And finally, setting expectations before a new staff member starts work is crucial. Don't promise the world. Be honest and tell them up front what they can expect from the role — both the good and bad. We learnt that it paid to always have someone else in the business sell a potential employee *off* the role as much as on. That way the person starts with their eyes open to the good and not so good about the business and is less likely to change their mind and quit when they encounter challenges. People really just want to be told the truth so they can make an informed choice, so don't over-blow your trumpet or slide past the challenges they will face — they will work it out soon enough anyway, so be honest.

What office should I rent?

Having had to keep upgrading our office as our business grew we developed some hindsight around how best to choose and negotiate the right space at the right time. Due to our fast growth we probably had about five or six offices over a decade, but even within those offices we were always trying to improve the office, or acquire more space. The first lesson we learned was that location is crucial if you want to attract and retain the best employees. And with people being more and more critical to any business, you can't underestimate the importance of getting this right.

We could have located our office in the suburbs and saved 25 per cent on our rent bill, but locating in the city had a number of positive implications. First, we got a better reputation by being in the heart of the city — people felt better about the company and their role if the company they were working for was based in the most happening part of town. This flowed over into looking more professional for potential clients. Second, this central location meant there were transport options from any part of the region, which increased the potential pool of employees. And finally, the central business district had the highest density of office space, which gave us more options to consider.

Flexibility was also critical to making good location decisions. In the early years, before our business model was proven and we had consistent business, we aimed, where possible, to limit our lease length to month by month, but have the first option on additional space. The trick was to get space with some room for growth but not be paying for what we weren't likely to use. And finally, we became experts at office layout so we could maximise capacity utilisation. This included limiting the amount of space used for meetings. We always went for the minimum number of meeting rooms. If there was a meeting room clash, then one party had to undertake what became known as a walking meeting. Rather than having your meetings in a room or coffee shop, the meeting would go outside for a walk. I had a 30-minute walking circuit, and one that took an hour. It was amazing how much more got achieved in these settings, as everyone felt more exhilarated being outside in the fresh air. Also, it has been scientifically proven that motion helps activate both sides of your brain more than sitting down—another reason to reduce the meeting rooms you need and encourage staff to get outside.

When should I give up on a potential client?

Looking back, we made some pretty bad sales decisions. One decision in particular stands out. We probably went for about six months trying everything we could think of to bring this particular client on board and they just weren't interested. So, wanting to focus on other opportunities, we decided to give up. Only to find out six months later that one of our competitors had picked up this huge piece of business and, if we had just persevered, we would probably have won it. Missing the opportunity for this business, worth more than $5 million, taught me the importance of perseverance and that sales can sometimes take 12 months or more to get over the line. You only lose the business when you walk away.

We also learnt to be more conservative in projecting the length of time it took for a new client to come on board. So many entrepreneurs build their projections based on an overly optimistic potential client-conversion rate. We learnt the hard way that clients almost always take longer to bring on board than you think and rarely make you as much money as you imagine. So while you should never give up chasing key clients, don't count your chickens before they hatch and always downplay the number of golden eggs they will eventually lay. This also means that you need to have a much larger prospect list than you think in order to bring in a certain amount of business. We slipped into the same trap I see so many other entrepreneurs trip up on, in that we expected to achieve a 10 per cent market share. Just because you have a great product and have sky-high enthusiasm doesn't mean that everyone you speak to will be equally enthusiastic.

The trick is to be very targeted, and then to have some good excuses to keep in contact, such as relevant research for them, updates on your products, newsletters and other industry expertise. Then mix up your communication among phone calls, person to person meetings, social media, emails and traditional mail. Think of the rule of seven contacts, which states that a potential customer will need to be exposed to your product or service seven times before they are willing to buy, and this is probably higher for big-ticket items. Trust builds up over time, so don't go for the sale unless a client has a genuine need; just keep making contact over the long term and build up their trust.

How should I work with a business partner?

I learnt some great lessons through the relationship I had with Trevor, my business partner of 12 years. Creating a partnership can be one of the most rewarding things you do in business, but if you get it wrong it can also be one of the most destructive.

For a business partnership to be successful and productive you should always go into business with someone who has different skills from you — there is no point duplicating yourself. You also need to make sure you define your roles very clearly, not only for yourselves, but also to communicate to the other staff members and your clients, so they don't become confused about who does what, and when they should be speaking to you or your business partner. Often these lines are drawn between one partner who focuses on sales and the other on operations. We also learnt through hindsight that you need to leave egos behind and appoint one partner the CEO. Staff and clients are used to this structure and having two people to escalate decisions to is untenable and can so easily become political. It doesn't mean that the partner who is the appointed CEO doesn't work closely with the other partner on major decisions, it just means you aren't confusing reporting lines and duplicating effort.

Trevor and I also learnt the importance of being aligned in our values and endgame. Individually, we would work closely with our executive coach on what we ultimately wanted out of the business and the things we would need to enjoy our roles. Each quarter we got together with our coach and shared what each of us could do to be more accommodating to the other's role. By creating this regular review in a safe environment, where the point was to benefit the business and not just our own points of view, we made sure any problems were nipped in the bud before they became an issue.

Getting started on your decision bank

A decision bank in its most basic form is a list of business lessons with their outcomes. Often entrepreneurs believe they already have a decision bank stored in their brain, but as I mentioned before this isn't nearly as powerful as something written down and therefore more rigorous. I would recommend creating your own database or simply keeping a journal to record your decisions, why you made them and what you expected them to deliver. Then all you need to do is diarise the review date, and when that date rolls around simply go back to the database or journal to record what happened. But you will have to impose some personal discipline in order to take the time to record the decisions as they happen, otherwise you won't have accurate real-time data to look back on.

To make life easier for you and to ensure that you build hindsight into your future decision making, I have developed a Smartphone application that allows you to record in real time when you make a decision. It is called Decisionship and it can be downloaded from your app store. The great part of this system is that it will remind you at the review date.

The other tool I have developed to help you to use the entrepreneurial eye effectively is the decision accelerator. The decision accelerator is a simple one-page reminder of the key foresight and insight distinctions that you need to bring to bear on each decision. I will explain more on the decision accelerator in chapter 24 and how to use it as a simple way to collect and store your decisions. Using the decision accelerator is another very simple and convenient method of recording decisions, because each one-page sheet documents the decision as you made it and why. All you need to do is set a review date and record the learning in the hindsight section of the accelerator, and you have your decision bank.

It is hindsight that pulls all the three sights together and closes the knowledge loop so you can assess the decisions you need to make from the perspective of where you want to be, where you are now and what's happened in the past. Part VI will explain decisionship in practice and give you a greater understanding of how everything fits together in the real world.

Key points

» The only way to bring hindsight to bear on your decision-making process is to actively seek and apply it.

» Don't rely on your memory or assume that you will remember to consider past decisions.

» The decision bank facilitates hindsight because it allows you to effectively close the knowledge loop and work out what works and what doesn't work for you individually.

» The decision bank provides accurate hindsight to improve your decisionship profile and also your decision-making process.

» Developing a decision bank to record all of your decisions means that you have an accurate, robust and useful record of past decisions and outcomes that you can then use to guide future decision making.

» Create your own database or keep a journal to record your decisions, why you made them and what you expected them to deliver. Put the review date in your diary and when that date rolls around simply go back to the database or journal to record what happened.

» The decision accelerator—a one-page reminder of the key foresight and insight distinctions that you need to bring to bear on each decision—will also help you develop your entrepreneurial eye.

» Hindsight pulls all the three sights together and helps you assess your decisions from the perspective of where you want to be, where you are now and what's happened in the past.

Part VI

Decisionship in practice

In any moment of decision, the best thing you can do is the right thing, the next best thing is the wrong thing, and the worst thing you can do is nothing.

**Theodore Roosevelt,
26th President of the United States**

Chapter 23
Practising the art of decisionship

Decisionship is the One Thing that separates successful entrepreneurs from the rest—the ability to make fast, better-informed decisions without the angst. And while decision making is the One Thing, learning how to make better decisions involves many different processes and relies on the development of three crucial sights: foresight, insight and hindsight. So far the book has unpacked the process and those sights for greater understanding. Now it's time to put them all together again so you can hone your entrepreneurial eye and begin to practise the art of decisionship.

There are many practical ways to use the entrepreneurial eye and the decisionship theory.

By making the distinction that your role as an entrepreneur is to primarily focus on one thing and one thing only—making decisions—you can dramatically improve your business success. Having an appreciation of the profound importance of decision making and the accompanying sense of relief that you don't have to be brilliant at everything, just good at one thing, can make a huge difference to individual productivity and stress levels. And knowing that there is a framework to systematically help you to make faster, better decisions without the angst can also remove a great deal of internal pressure. There is a light at the end of the tunnel after all, and it's not an oncoming train!

How far you go in learning this methodology and applying it will depend on your situation and your personality. For some people, awareness of the need to focus on decisions is enough to guide them. For others, the further distinction around the importance of defining the challenge properly, assessing the potential options with due diligence and finally closing the loop by taking genuine real-world action will be enough to massively improve their decision-making success rate.

Others will be inspired to take the process one step further to where the real juice can be found, and they will seek to use foresight, insight and hindsight in their decision-making process. Developing foresight takes time, but it is absolutely worth the effort. And once it's done it's done: all you need to do is tweak it all from time to time. By looking at your business through the six lenses you effectively gain a conscious 360-degree appreciation of what you are trying to achieve, as well as all the critical details of your product or service and what success genuinely looks like for you. These are things that all too often remain vague and unexpressed for the entrepreneur. The real power of foresight is that it encourages the entrepreneur to bring all those things that are swimming aimlessly around in their head into conscious awareness by putting them down on paper in order to guide the direction of the business. If you don't write things down, then everything remains too vague, and it is this vagueness that is often the root cause of poor decision making. After all, if you don't fully appreciate the fundamentals of what you are trying to achieve and what your business is all about, it's very easy to be pulled off track. If you are inspired by the power of foresight, insight and hindsight, but you are feeling a little daunted, just remember you don't have to use the formula that I follow to bring these sights into play to make great decisions. You may choose to use your own method or use foresight, insight and hindsight simply as a reminder to always look forward to the future and back at the past, and assess what's really going on in the present in order to make better, faster decisions without the stress.

> By looking at your business through the six lenses you effectively gain a conscious 360-degree appreciation of what you are trying to achieve.

Still others might be most inspired by the importance of role-playing in the decision-making process. When you understand that you must assess the problems and opportunities that arise in your business from the mindset of a sailor, gardener, movie producer, mountaineer, master chef and architect, you will always become a better entrepreneur.

For some entrepreneurs the information in this book that has resonated most may be the perpetual growth principles (PGP) that underpin business success. You may be motivated by the knowledge that you can simply assess your decisions to ensure that they are reducing business frictions, fostering actuators, minimising mass and, wherever possible, creating win–win outcomes for as many stakeholders as possible. Do that and your business success is much more likely.

And finally, I hope there are entrepreneurs who can see the benefits of following the proven process I have mapped out in this book in its entirety. If you are one, then I hope you use the six lenses to build foresight. I hope you use the PGP to build insight, and use the decision bank to develop valuable hindsight. Like any new skill, this methodology can feel uncomfortable and laborious at first, but as you gain confidence and begin to see the results, the process will become familiar and it will become a powerful habit. Finally, you will have the tools, skills and knowledge to create the business of your wildest dreams.

Like anything in business and life, the trick is to work out what works for you and follow it.

Using the entrepreneurial eye for powerful decision making

The process of defining what question you are trying to answer, assessing the various options and then deciding on your preferred course of action is a pretty straightforward process. In fact, whether you are aware of it or not, your brain automatically follows a very similar process. Just being aware of the three stages of define, assess and decide will improve your ability to make decisions.

Remember to invest the time in defining the question you are trying to answer before ploughing straight to the solution. By doing this you will be much more likely to make the right decisions. To ensure that you become good at this, start turning meeting agendas into a list of questions and using the meeting to reach a decision. This exercise will encourage you to view the problems and opportunities as questions, which will facilitate the answering process.

Once you have defined the issue you need to assess the options with your new-found skills in foresight, insight and hindsight. It is the combination of these three sights that I believe are the key to assessing the right things at the right time. You might not always have the time to use the six lenses, but start to think of the impact of your decision in six months, 12 months or five years down the track. You might forget what makes up some of the four PGP, but just remember to consider the things that will make your business accelerate or grow faster. And if you forget the feedback loop required to develop hindsight, then just think about past decisions you have made and heed the lessons from them.

And finally, take the time to complete the powerful process using the decide step. A decision hasn't been completed until you write it down, along with your commitments, a note of why you made the decision, and how and when you will know if it was the right decision.

Using the six lenses

We might like to believe that business is an unemotional entity—it is not. Human beings create businesses and work in businesses, and so trying to ignore their inherent subjective bias is foolish. Instead, we have to put on our subjective, personalised hat and view the situation from those important points of view and then systematically move around the six lenses to gather a 360-degree subjective and objective awareness of the situation. Then and only then are you in a position to make strong, effective decisions.

We are all slightly different people at different times, depending on the situation or the people we are with. This adaptability and flexibility is one of our greatest strengths as a human being. Viewing each situation from the different mindsets is just a formalisation of that skill. And once you are familiar with it, it will take moments to switch from one mindset to the next in quick succession, and this ability will become one of the easiest to use and yet most powerful tools in your business.

Each of the six lenses needs to be viewed in isolation so you understand what each lens is focused on and how understanding each lens will give you clarity in different but crucial areas of your business. Each lens has one simple question that you must apply to each decision under assessment to establish if the decision is in line with your personal and business focus or not.

As a simple reminder, the six questions are repeated here. You may want to write them out and put them on your wall, or turn them into a screen saver.

- *Passion.* Which option will accelerate my endgame and enable me to be working on my mission?
- *Philosophy.* Which option will cultivate our company values and reinforce our brand and culture?
- *Proficiency.* Which option will let me perform my role and play to my strengths or strengthen my improvement areas?
- *Progress.* Which option will help us reach our business vision and climb to the next business stage?

- *Prototype.* Which option will improve our magic metric and enhance our business model?
- *Plan.* Which option will adhere to our priorities and help us meet our projections?

The lenses ask you to explore yourself and your business in greater depth, to really get behind what you are doing and why you are doing what you are doing. They force you to unpack the detail and become really clear about your values, goals and objectives, as well as how you are going to achieve them. This clarity is then brought to the decision-making table so you can properly weigh up the pros and cons of each decision in accordance with your predetermined objectives.

The lenses are therefore not just a decision-making tool: they are a tool for gaining clarity in your business. Like the optometrist making adjustments in an eye test, these lenses allow you to see your objectives clearly and use that foresight in a positive way moving forward.

Your endgame, your values, your role, your vision, your magic metric and your priorities are not one-time, 1 January ideas. These key outcomes have to live and breathe in your business if they stand a chance of materialisation. If, therefore, those concepts are built into your decision-making process, it's much easier for you to stay on track.

Using the perpetual growth principles

Using the PGP outlined in part IV of the book will undoubtedly give you the framework to make better, faster decisions without the angst. After all, if the decision on the table will reduce frictions, foster actuators, minimise mass and maximise balance, then it's a no-brainer, Yes decision. If, on the other hand, the course of action you are considering will increase frictions, inhibit actuators, increase mass and create an imbalance with stakeholders then it is a no-brainer No decision. Granted, there may be few such easy choices to make, and more likely your choices will cause some positives and some negatives, but it's your role to weigh up the relative value of each.

Start to envisage an organisation that is frictionless, lean and mean, super-powered yet balanced. This could be your business — where nothing slows growth and there are no insurmountable challenges or obstacles: a business that looks forward and sees a smooth, straight highway, not a bumpy road with curves, potholes and countless dead-ends. Imagine your company as small yet powerful, an organisation that has minimal mass but plenty of clout, nimble and free to adapt to changing business conditions. How would you feel if you were the head of a business that could harness all of the powers available to it to get ahead and stay ahead—a dynamic, exciting company energised by continuous forward momentum and focus on actuators? And finally, how satisfying would it be to win alongside your stakeholders among whom you have fostered loyal, sustainable relationships through the good times and the bad, within a community of people all striving for a similar vision, and sharing in the fun and rewards along the way. All this is possible when you embrace decisionship and use the entrepreneurial eye for faster, better decisions without the angst.

Using the decision bank

Whether you use the tools we provide or you develop your own method of learning from the past to build your own hindsight, the decision bank will be a central repository—a way to acknowledge that business is a game. A game where the decisions you make determine your success and you must live or die by the choices you make. Having a central place to store those decisions and reflect on them will always improve your decision making in the future. If you learn to develop your hindsight, what you learn gives you greater foresight into the future and insight into the present. You will create a powerful cycle where each sight develops and adds to the next, in an endless loop of decision-making expertise.

> If you learn to develop your hindsight, what you learn gives you greater foresight into the future and insight into the present.

Then, with your decision bank building, you need to start to heed the lessons learned and share these lessons with your team and other entrepreneurs. This will help you learn even more. And don't forget that other entrepreneurs and advisers are also a good source of hindsight. Use these resources to make better decisions more often.

Ensure that you review the merit of the decision at the follow-up date and embed these learnings for future hindsight, making particular note of your decision's speed, decision information and decision angst, or anxiety.

Applying hindsight is both an active decision-making tool to improve your decision-making skill in the here and now, and a retrospective assessment tool to improve your decision making into the future. Both perspectives allow you to constantly improve your results and consistently achieve your desired outcomes.

The decision bank is a great way to categorise your knowledge. As an active decision-making tool, for example, I immediately identify what type of decision it is that needs to be made. This definition of the challenge is a crucial step in the insight phase; remembering to use hindsight at that point is just about recognising that you may already have experience of a similar decision in your decision bank, and you would be crazy as an innovative entrepreneur not to tap into that hindsight to offer insight into the decision at hand. And by defining the decisions, you know where to go in the decision bank to get the information, and all you need to do it is to refer to and apply that knowledge in the future to improve your decision in the present.

Making it happen

Decisionship is clearly all about how to make better, faster decisions without the angst, but nothing happens until you action those decisions, so you need to do more than just make decisions—you need to do something about them. Too many entrepreneurs make decisions but then don't follow through. Don't make that mistake. Hold yourself accountable for committing to actions and putting dates around these actions, and be sure to connect to why the decision is important so you maintain momentum to see it through.

When you make a decision, write the details of the decision down and lock in a date for review. In the next chapter I'll explain more about the decisionship accelerator I mentioned in chapter 22—a powerful tool to make and record your decisions.

Key points

» Decisionship is the One Thing that separates successful entrepreneurs from the rest—the ability to make fast, better-informed decisions without the angst.

» Your role as an entrepreneur is to focus on one thing and one thing only—making decisions. Do that, and you can dramatically improve your business success.

» Being aware of the three stages of define, assess and decide will improve your ability to make decisions.

» Once you have defined the issue you need to assess the options with your newfound skills in foresight, insight and hindsight.

» View each of the six lenses in isolation so you can understand what each lens focuses on. Understanding each lens will give you clarity in different but crucial areas of your business.

» If the decision to be made will reduce frictions, foster actuators, minimise mass and maximise balance, then it's a no-brainer, Yes decision.

» If the decision will increase frictions, inhibit actuators, increase mass and create an imbalance with stakeholders then it's a no-brainer, No decision.

» Hindsight gives you greater foresight into the future and insight into the present. Each sight develops and adds to the next, in an endless loop of decision-making expertise.

» Be accountable for committing to actions and putting dates around these actions, and be sure to connect to why the decision is important so you maintain momentum to see it through.

Chapter 24

The decisionship accelerator

To help with the application of the decisionship methodology I have created what I call the decisionship accelerator—a reference guide that will allow you to quickly make decisions. The decisionship accelerator is a one-page double-sided form that will help you define, assess and decide using foresight, insight and hindsight. You can download the decisionship accelerator from my website at <www.accelerateglobal.com/accelerator>. A complete copy of the decisionship accelerator is also included in the appendix. Each part of the accelerator is explained here.

The decisionship accelerator is a simple ready-reckoner that speeds up the decision-making process because it:

- reminds you to be concise about your key outcome so you can stay focused on the big picture
- reminds you to separate the facts from the feelings
- reminds you to consider the problems and opportunities through the different lenses and mindsets and ensures you ask the *big* question from each lens
- reminds you to draw on your decision bank and tap into your hard-won hindsight
- reminds you to consider how the options will affect frictions, actuators, mass and balance
- reminds you to take action, commit to a decision and more forward.

The decisionship accelerator has been developed to provide a summary of everything you need to consider when making a decision so you can develop the habit of making faster, better-informed decisions without the angst.

The decisionship accelerator helps you make faster decisions because once you have invested the time necessary to gain clarity on your six lenses, you don't need to keep reinventing the wheel. Instead you immediately bring that clarity to bear on all future decisions, and that can save a huge amount of time. You can complete an accelerator in less than five minutes once you get used to the format, and that's considerably faster than fumbling your way through a decision in your mind. Also, having faith in using a formalised process will allow you to make faster decisions. You will start to allow your natural decision-making instinct to emerge in order to assess the various options faster than your conscious or rational brain can.

The decisionship accelerator helps you make better-informed decisions because it reminds you to bring foresight, insight and hindsight to bear on each decision, which massively improves the information you use in the decision-making process. You will consider areas you might normally forget about or dismiss too readily, and it will ensure that the data you are considering covers a range of areas that are important to include in your decision making.

The decisionship accelerator will also reduce your anxiety. When you know you have a tried-and-tested process that you can follow, a great deal of the stress is removed. Much of the angst of decision making is actually the result of not having a proven process, rather than just the decision itself. We stress about whether we have got the decision right, whether we have forgotten something or whether the decision will impact something in the future. If you have a proven process to work through all those grey areas, you will be able to relax — especially once you start to see the results. This process won't always yield a correct decision, but it will dramatically reduce the errors and thus the angst.

Using the decisionship accelerator

The decisionship accelerator is split into three parts:

- define
- assess
- decide.

Define the challenge

The define section of the decisionship accelerator covers the five elements we discussed in chapter 5 — view, illumination, transparency, screen and focal point. See figure 24.1.

Figure 24.1: the define section of the decisionship accelerator

DEFINE	Problem/opportunity		
	Facts		**Feelings**
	Size: Minor ☐ Major ☐ Mega ☐		**Screen:** Defer ☐ Delegate ☐ Decide ☐
	Should I/we	**Option 1**	**or** **Option 2**

Write down your problem or opportunity in the top section of the decision accelerator. Then outline the facts you know and the feelings you have about this problem or opportunity. Next, decide whether the decision is a minor, major or mega decision, which should help you determine how much time to put into it, and the level of anxiousness you should feel—in other words, don't get too anxious if it is only a minor decision. Screen the decision to consider whether you should defer, delegate or decide.

This pre-work will help you move on or develop an affirmative question based around two options worthy of consideration. Take the time to ensure you are asking the right question, as this will massively influence the outcome. If you ask the wrong question the answer is irrelevant. Write your two options into the accelerator.

> If you ask the wrong question the answer is irrelevant.

Assess the challenge

The assess section of the decisionship accelerator is split into three parts, as you would expect: foresight, looking into the future; hindsight, looking into the past; and finally insight, assessing in the present. While each of these is important, you might find your decisions tend to lean on one of these sights more than the other, particularly for minor decisions. And while you will arrive at a score for each, your decision should not be based merely on adding these three scores together. Instead, you should engage with the score and make an informed decision, using your instinct once this comprehensive process has been completed. You might find that you decide to heed foresight more than insight for a particular decision. Or because the hindsight and foresight scores are quite similar for both options, you might rely on the big disparity in the insight scores to choose an option.

Before making any decisions, you should ensure that the outcomes for each of the six lenses have been updated at least within the last quarter. I find it beneficial to carry around a folded, double-sided A4 booklet that outlines the key concepts and outcomes as they stand in the business. Included in this pre-work document should be your two biggest frictions and the hindsight learnings from past decisions. The decisionship accelerator form includes the key outcomes of endgame, values, role, vision, magic metric and priorities for each of the lenses.

> Before making any decisions, you should ensure that the outcomes for each of the six lenses have been updated at least within the last quarter.

With this form, or a version of it, at your fingertips you are ready to assess using your three sights.

Using foresight

Starting with foresight you will ask yourself the six key questions that embody the mindset and key outcome as outlined in figure 24.2.

Figure 24.2: the assess—foresight section in the decisionship accelerator

	To what level will each option... on a scale of 1 (low) to 10 (high)		Option 1	Option 2
ASSESS — FORESIGHT	**Passion (Sailor)**	... accelerate my ENDGAME and enable me to be working on my MISSION?		
	Philosophy (Gardener)	... cultivate our company VALUES and reinforce our BRAND and CULTURE?		
	Proficiency (Movie producer)	... let me perform my ROLE and play to my STRENGTHS?		
	Progress (Mountaineer)	... help us reach our business VISION and climb to the next business STAGE?		
	Prototype (Master chef)	... improve our MAGIC METRIC and enhance our BUSINESS MODEL?		
	Plan (Architect)	... adhere to our PRIORITIES and help us meet our PROJECTIONS?		
		TOTAL:		

For instance, starting with the passion lens, you will rate each option on a scale of 1 to 10, 1 being the lowest and 10 the highest, by asking yourself to what extent each option will help you to accelerate your endgame and allow you to be working on your mission. Repeat for both options against each key question in each lens.

In scoring the answers for each option, try to avoid hesitating for too long—simply put down the first thing that comes into your mind. The power of asking yourself each of these affirmative questions and logging a score immediately is that the first thing to come to your mind is usually right. Second-guessing your answer will usually only lead to overcomplicating the issue and taking into consideration other variables that will be covered later in the accelerator.

Using hindsight

List the relevant learnings from similar past decisions, and the learnings you have acquired from other entrepreneurs and advisers that may be relevant to this decision. See figure 24.3.

Figure 24.3: the assess—hindsight section of the decisonship accelerator

ASSESS — HINDSIGHT	Learnings from similar past decisions I have made	Learnings/advice from other entrepreneurs or advisers		
	To what degree will each option...on a scale of 1 (low) to 10 (high)		Option 1	Option 2
	...take into consideration my learnings?			
	...follow the learnings/advice from other entrepreneurs or advisers?			
		TOTAL:		

Bring hindsight to bear by asking yourself, on a scale of 1 to 10, to what degree will each option:

- take your learnings into consideration
- follow the learnings or advice from other entrepreneurs and advisers.

It's important to differentiate between the things that you have learned, and the things that other people have learned, because over time this could be one of the aspects that you need to take on board and change.

For instance, you might find that the advice from other entrepreneurs isn't nearly as valuable as your own experience, or vice versa.

Using insight

In order to bring insight to bear, you need to ask the questions that help you consider frictions, mass, actuators and balance in the perpetual growth principles (PGP). See figure 24.4.

Figure 24.4: the assess — insight section of the accelerator

		To what level will each option ... 0 (none) 1 (insignificantly) 2 (somewhat) 3 (significantly)	Option 1	Option 2
ASSESS—INSIGHT	**Frictions**	... reduce my biggest friction [lack of_____]		
		... reduce my next biggest friction [lack of_____]		
	Mass	... minimise the need for too many stakeholders?		
		... minimise unnecessary products and brands?		
		... minimise the real cost of purchases?		
		... minimise onerous structure and processes?		
	Actuators	... foster empowerment and replication?		
		... foster innovation and inspiration?		
		... foster flexibility and simplicity?		
		... foster leverage and reputation?		
	Balance	... maximise employee satisfaction?		
		... maximise customer satisfaction?		
		... maximise investor satisfaction?		
		... maximise indirect stakeholder satisfaction? (suppliers, family, community, and so on)		
		TOTAL:		

You need to know what your top two frictions are to successfully complete this section. To help with this process I've created a friction diagnostic which you can complete on my Accelerate Global website at <www.accelerateglobal.com/frictionsdiagnostic>. The option that reduces your biggest or second-biggest friction will most certainly be a better decision, because it will remove or reduce one of your major obstacles to success. Complete the remaining questions in the decisionship accelerator and score each option under consideration against mass, actuators and balance.

It will only take you two to three minutes to consider the 16 insight questions, and yet the additional information you will glean will massively improve the outcome. Using the PGP brings much-needed objectivity to the decision-making process and helps to propel your business forward.

Decide on the outcome

You need to record what you have decided based on your assessment. See figure 24.5.

Figure 24.5: the decide section of the decisionship accelerator

I have decided to:	
Commitments: what actions will you take to follow through, by when?	
Calibration: scale of where you are now from 1 (low, not started) to 10 (high, complete)	
Why is this decision important to you? List what it means personally	
How will I know if this is the right decision? Include measurable outcomes	
When will you likely know if this is the right decision? Specific date in the future	

Be as specific as possible: for example, if the decision is to hire a general manager then you would complete the box, 'I have decided to …' with the words 'hire a general manager by the end of July for a package of $100 000'.

To ensure that the decision gains immediate momentum, you also need to record your commitment, so that you know what actions you will take to follow though and by when.

The calibration process underneath the commitment section has two purposes. First, it's to let you know if you're confirming an existing path, or starting a brand new path; and second, if you're working with an accountability coach, which I highly encourage you to do, then this will help the coach calibrate where you're up to in your decision.

It's also important to outline why the decision is important to you personally, so that you connect to your inner motivation to follow through. And finally, you write in the essential steps necessary to create your decision bank and improve your hindsight. Specify how you will know if this was the right decision, and when you might know it, so that you have a specific date for review. Try to include any measurable outcomes applicable. For example, if you decide to employ a new salesperson, you might specify that you want a 20 per cent increase in sales by Christmas, or that they are bringing you $50 000 of sales per month within six months.

Practice makes perfect

Like most things in life, practice makes perfect, so I strongly encourage you to make as many decisions using the accelerator as possible over the next 90 days to ensure this new skill of decisionship becomes instinctive. And then you can do away with the form for all but the most difficult and important decisions.

The time invested in populating the accelerator will save you huge amounts of time and make for much-improved decision making. You will also be able to develop your foresight as your business needs change rather than having to start from scratch every time you want to work on your business. You will be able to easily remember the elements that make up the principles of insight and you will be able to remember to include the feedback loop to ensure you continue to develop your hindsight and build your decision bank.

This powerful tool will dramatically increase your understanding of decisionship while making the entrepreneurial eye model practical so you and your business can benefit from your new-found knowledge. So don't forget to download a copy of the decisionship accelerator from my Accelerate Global website <www.accelerateglobal.com/accelerator>. The final chapter will showcase some case studies so you can see how decisionship works in the real world.

Key points

» The decisionship accelerator is split into three parts: define, assess and decide.

» The define section of decisionship accelerator considers view, illumination, transparency, screen and focal point.

» If you ask the wrong question the answer is irrelevant. Write your two options into the accelerator.

» The assess section of the decisionship accelerator is split into three parts: foresight, looking into the future; hindsight, looking into the past; and insight, assessing in the present.

» Starting with foresight, ask yourself the six key questions that embody the mindset and key outcome.

» List the relevant learnings from similar past decisions and the learnings you have acquired from other entrepreneurs and advisers that may be relevant to this decision.

» To bring insight to bear, ask the questions that help you consider frictions, actuators, mass, and balance in the PGP.

» To ensure that the decision gains immediate momentum, record your commitment so that you know what actions you will take to follow though and by when.

» Practice makes perfect in decisionship, as in other parts of life. Make as many decisions using the accelerator as possible over the next 90 days to ensure this new skill of decisionship becomes instinctive.

Chapter 25

Decisionship in the real world

In order to give you a greater appreciation of how to use the decisionship accelerator and how decisionship works in the real world, I have included case studies showing how two decisions were made by entrepreneurs who have taken our 12-month mentoring program. These are real examples from real entrepreneurs who have given me permission to include their completed decision sheets in the book. The advantage of looking at these case studies is that they give decisionship context and show you how someone else has used the entrepreneurial eye model and decisionship accelerator to improve their decision making.

I have chosen two decisions that many entrepreneurs come up against, namely:

- when to bring on a general manager for succession
- which marketing option to pursue.

Case study 1: succession plan

When Bevan first joined our training program—*Winning at the game of business*—I could tell he was distracted. Although he recognised the need to spend time on his business, it was done so almost begrudgingly. Bevan had grown a successful IT infrastructure business to 17 staff and $6.5 million in turnover, but he knew that something had to give: the company had grown out of his skills and he had grown out of the company. He no longer felt motivated to manage the day-to-day running of the business, lead the team or work with clients. Yet there was one problem—all his clients wanted to deal with him, and Bevan was the only person responsible for winning new business.

Like so many time-poor entrepreneurs, Bevan jumped straight to solution mode and announced that he was considering employing a general manager who would eventually succeed him in the CEO role. But the first thing Bevan had to do was define the problem or opportunity that had prompted his arrival at that solution, which meant he needed to backtrack a little. Bevan was excited about the day when he could collect a residual income without effort or sell the business and focus on his passion for rally-car racing. Figure 25.1 shows what Bevan wrote in the define section of his decisionship accelerator.

Figure 25.1: defining the problem or opportunity

DEFINE		
Problem/opportunity *Business growth same as last year: problem is reliance on me at a time when I am not motivated.*		
Facts *June 15th* *2009 revenue: = $6.1M* *2010 revenue: = $6.05M* *All nine clients and prospects in pipeline are due to me.*	**Feelings** *I'm tired.* *I want to do something else.* *I'm nervous handing over the reins.* *Current managers not suitable for GM position.*	
Size: Minor ☐ Major ☐ Mega ☑	**Screen:** Defer ☐ Delegate ☐ Decide ☑	
Should I/we	**Option 1** *Employ a GM on $120K next quarter.*	**or**	**Option 2** *Employ a sales manager on $80K + bonus and get Frank to look after operations as well as finance.*

As you can see, Bevan identified the problem as business growth. Bevan wanted to increase growth, but it had levelled off, due in no small part to the fact that he was solely responsible for new business and he was no longer motivated to win new business. He summarised the facts and his feelings, and decided that the scale of the decision was mega and that he really needed to decide now.

Bevan identified several potential options, including doing nothing, spending the money on marketing, bringing in a business partner or merging with a competitor. He identified the two options he preferred and converted them into these affirmative statements:

» Employ a general manager on $120 000 per year next quarter.

» Employ a sales manager for $80 000 + bonus and get Frank to look after operations as well as finance.

Bevan's next task was to assess these options using foresight and the six lenses of clarity (see figure 25.2).

Figure 25.2: assessing two options using the six lenses of foresight

	To what level will each option ... on a scale of 1 (low) to 10 (high)		Option 1	Option 2
ASSESS — FORESIGHT	Passion (Sailor)	... accelerate my ENDGAME and enable me to be working on my MISSION?	8	6
	Philosophy (Gardener)	... cultivate our company VALUES and reinforce our BRAND and CULTURE?	5	8
	Proficiency (Movie producer)	... let me perform my ROLE and play to my STRENGTHS?	8	8
	Progress (Mountaineer)	... help us reach our business VISION and climb to the next business STAGE?	7	6
	Prototype (Master chef)	... improve our MAGIC METRIC and enhance our BUSINESS MODEL?	6	9
	Plan (Architect)	... adhere to our PRIORITIES and help us meet our PROJECTIONS?	3	9
		TOTAL:	37	46

Bevan's endgame was to build the business up and sell it by the year 2014 for $10 million, and he had a personal mission to buy a share in a rally car and be accepted on the amateur circuit. Therefore, looking through the passion lens option 1 rated higher than option 2 because this strategy seemed more in line with getting him to his endgame more quickly.

In terms of the philosophy lens, Bevan had already completed an exercise to identify his personal and company values, which combined into Go Fast, Be Good and Have Fun. The personality of his company was a reflection of his love of speed, which was reflected in his company's brand and culture. He expected his employees to foster their reputation for responsiveness, which was the company's key differentiator. In line with this culture he preferred to reward his employees with career opportunities rather than bring someone in from the outside. But in making this decision he realised there was no-one currently on staff who was cut out for the GM role. So he scored option 2, employing a sales manager and continuing to foster opportunities internally, as the better of the options.

Next Bevan considered his options from the perspective of the proficiency lens. This was a little hard to rate, because he was the best salesperson in the company; he also knew how to deliver for customers and he had shown himself to be a strong and capable leader. Yet his desired role was to be more strategic and not have to deal with sales and operations. Both of the options seemed to achieve this, so he gave them an equal high rating.

When considering the business-focused lenses, Bevan had already identified that his business had completed the expansion phase and it was now time to move into succession. This didn't mean that he didn't still want the company to grow to meet its ultimate vision: it just meant it was time to acknowledge succession if he really wanted to exit or step back from his business. Weighing up the two options Bevan thought that hiring a GM would help the company through the succession stage the fastest so gave this a slightly higher score.

Bevan's magic metric was the number of contracted maintenance clients paying more than $2000 per month, and he thought that having a dedicated sales manager would contribute most to achieving the metric. The GM might be better at finetuning the business model, but he was pretty happy with that, so option 2 was better from a prototype perspective.

As for the plan lens, Bevan thought option 2 would be better, because hiring a sales manager in a specific function and promoting an existing employee to a function he was already adept in would reduce the down time as the team came to grips with the changes. Hiring a GM would probably mean a short-term dip in productivity, which would not help him achieve one of his key priorities — acquire eight new contracted clients by the end of the financial year. As a result option 2 was perceived to be better by a large margin.

As you can see by the overall scores, employing a sales manager and promoting the financial controller to the head of operations came out on top by a fair margin. The best result of the exercise, though, was that each of the options resulted in quite a high score, which should have given Bevan confidence that both options, according to foresight, were likely to result in success.

With foresight completed, Bevan filled in the hindsight section of the decisionship accelerator (see figure 25.3).

Figure 25.3: using hindsight in the decisionship accelerator

	Learnings from similar past decisions I have made	Learnings/advice from other entrepreneurs or advisers		
ASSESS — HINDSIGHT	• New staff time in training wheels. • Sales is last priority for generalists. • Finding one person to do all my tasks will be hard.	• Work on biz not in it (AP). • Successor = danger. • Don't give over complete control on day 1.		
	To what degree will each option… on a scale of 1 (low) to 10 (high)		**Option 1**	**Option 2**
	…take into consideration my learnings?		5	8
	…follow the learnings/advice from other entrepreneurs or advisers?		4	7
	TOTAL:		9	15

Using hindsight skills, Bevan identified three personal learnings that he thought were relevant to the decision — that new employees always take longer to get up to speed than you expect; that sales are the last priority for generalists, so staff often use any excuse not to put effort into sales; and finally, finding one person who can do many varied tasks is hard. Considering these issues, Bevan thought that option 2 posed less risk for the business, based on his existing hindsight.

The second part of hindsight considered the learnings and advice of others. Bevan had a mentor who counselled him that he should be strategic — working *on* the business not *in* it. He had also read lots of business biographies where the difficulties created by appointing the wrong successor often derailed a business for years. This was reinforced by his friend Tom's experience: he had appointed a CEO who quickly turned the staff against him and left to set up his own business in competition with Tom's. Summing up the hindsight from these people Bevan was quick to conclude that option 2 would be the safer strategy.

The last of the assess elements in Bevan's decisionship accelerator were the 16 questions around the perpetual growth principles (PGP) of insight (see figure 25.4).

Figure 25.4: answering the 16 questions associated with the perpetual growth principles

		To what level will each option... 0 (none) 1 (insignificantly) 2 (somewhat) 3 (significantly)	Option 1	Option 2
ASSESS — INSIGHT	Frictions	...reduce my biggest friction [lack of___*growth*___]	5	8
		...reduce my next biggest friction [lack of___*support*___]	8	4
	Mass	...minimise the need for too many stakeholders?	4	4
		...minimise unnecessary products and brands?	—	—
		...minimise the real cost of purchases?	3	7
		...minimise onerous structure and processes?	4	8
	Actuators	...foster empowerment and replication?	7	5
		...foster innovation and inspiration?	7	6
		...foster flexibility and simplicity?	4	8
		...foster leverage and reputation?	5	7
	Balance	...maximise employee satisfaction?	5	7
		...maximise customer satisfaction?	3	8
		...maximise investor satisfaction?	6	7
		...maximise indirect stakeholder satisfaction? (suppliers, family, community, and so on)	7	5
		TOTAL:	68	84

The two biggest frictions that Bevan was experiencing were lack of growth and lack of support. Bevan thought that a sales manager would help bring in more revenue than a GM, and scored accordingly. From a support point of view, Bevan thought that hiring a GM would give him someone to rely on—particularly for taking responsibility for the issues that needed resolution and cropped up every day.

In terms of people mass, both options were essentially the same, as they required the recruitment of an additional member of staff and neither had an impact on products and brands. When figuring out the real cost of each option, Bevan figured that a GM would not only be more costly, given their larger salary, they also might not be as frugal on expenses as Bevan had been, so he deemed option 2 the better from a purchases point of view. Option 2 was also better from a structure perspective, because it wouldn't create another level across the entire company.

The actuators came out pretty much even, with option 1 better for empowerment, replication, innovation and inspiration, and option 2 faring better for flexibility, simplicity, leverage and reputation.

And finally, Bevan rated the impact of the two strategies in terms of balance. He decided that his employees would be most satisfied if he promoted Frank, who was popular and competent, rather than bring in someone unfamiliar from outside. He felt sure his customers would also prefer option 2, because they had already expressed a desire to maintain connection to Bevan. While he didn't have any external investors and was the sole equity holder, Bevan knew that the company would be worth more if it wasn't so reliant on him. Both strategies potentially increased the value of the business, but there was slightly more risk in employing an external GM who might negatively impact the business. The main indirect stakeholder who was affected by Bevan's decision was his fiancée, and employing the GM would potentially be a better solution, because he would be less stressed, more motivated and would spend less time in the office if he appointed a GM. The overall score for the PGP also came out in favour of option 2, although there were pros and cons for both, depending on the principle.

With foresight, hindsight and insight now completed, it was Bevan's job to use these scores to make a decision. Sometimes going through the process confirms that neither strategy is worth considering, but in this case both came out as good options. Yet with a winning score for each of the three areas, option 2 seemed like the winning strategy, so Bevan felt comfortable moving forward, especially as he had done the assessment using a thorough and systematic process. This outcome was a bit of a surprise, however, as he had set his heart on employing a general manager. Using decisionship allowed him to pull back from his initial response, and he realised that hiring a GM would have been too much of a succession jump.

Finally, Bevan documented his decision on the accelerator. You can see that Bevan's decision (see figure 25.5) is documented not only in an affirmative form — 'I have decided to' — but also with some elements that make it more concrete, such as timeframes, salary and recruitment method. His commitments included the immediate next steps of developing a job description for the sales manager and appointing a recruitment agency. He also committed to work with his financial controller on the promotion and how he was going to communicate the changes to his staff. Bevan was in the early stages of his decision, which was reflected in his low calibration score, unsurprising considering given this particular strategy option wasn't even something he had considered the week before.

Figure 25.5: Bevan's decision after using the decisionship accelerator

I have decided to: *commence my succession plan by handing over operations to Frank and employing a sales manager on $80 k by the end of June using an agency.*	
Commitments: what actions will you take to follow through, by when? 1. *Type up job description.* 2. *Appoint recruitment agency (estimate 15% salary).* 3. *Appoint Frank and work with him on role responsibilities.* 4. *Staff announcement during May staff retreat.*	
Calibration: scale of where you are now from 1 (low, not started) to 10 (high, complete)	*1*
Why is this decision important to you? List what it means personally · *Reach endgame faster and less risk than GM now.* · *Work on business.* · *Motivation.*	
How will I know if this is the right decision? Include measurable outcomes *Met projections and business grows 15% per annum.* *I spend less time managing staff and clients.*	
When will you likely know if this is the right decision? Specific date in the future	*1: 1/7/10* *2: 1/7/11*

(left margin label: **DECIDE**)

Bevan nominated that the decision was important for him because it would get him to his endgame faster, without risking everything. It would allow him to be more strategic, but still oversee the business and staff. The changes would also give him a fresh lease on life in his role, as it felt like the company was growing up. He also nominated that the decision would be the right one if they met their projections this year, the company had grown by an additional 15 per cent within 12 months, and that he was doing less staff and client management. He planned to review the decision in two stages at the end of the quarter and at the end of the next financial year.

What were the results?

So how did Bevan's decision pan out? On reflection he thought that he had made the right decision at the right time with the information that he had. The recruitment agency took longer than expected, which meant that the salesperson started only a few weeks before the end of the quarter. As a result, the appointment couldn't affect the sales results and they were below those projected. Also, the sales manager had brought in some business, but not nearly the number of clients that Bevan had expected in the new financial year. The shortfall was, however, brought in by Bevan, given that he had more time because he no longer had to look after operations. Yet despite the sales mostly coming from Bevan, the sales manager had helped build the pipeline and they had together designed a new sales process, which would enable the sales manager to sell without too much involvement from Bevan. The appointment of Frank, the financial controller, to head of operations also worked out well. Staff responded well to his management style and the business was becoming much more systemised as a result. Clients took longer to adjust and respect the changes, but were now dealing more and more with Frank.

So what did Bevan learn from this decision and its outcome that he could add to his decision bank and hindsight? First, he needed to factor in a longer recruitment process, and while using a recruitment agency saves some time, he still needed to invest the time with them for the process to be successful. Bevan acknowledges that the stepped approach to succession was the right choice. He feels that if they had appointed a general manager straight away, the clients and staff would have rebelled. Also, he learnt that the owner of a business finds it easier than an employee to sell the company's products. This comes from their knowledge, passion and position of authority. But all in all, Bevan was happy with the decision given that the company has grown in revenue and maturity, and he is feeling much more motivated by his role. He plans to be ready for the next part of the succession, to appoint a GM or CEO, within 12 months.

Case study 2: choosing a marketing strategy

In this example we follow a relatively minor decision made by Rebecca, who was considering whether or not to spend $5000 on a stand at an industry trade show.

Rebecca operated a boutique consultancy that specialised in brand development. Complaining to a friend who was organising a trade show about her lack of new clients, Rebecca was given the opportunity of taking a stand at half price at an IT expo. Rebecca had not exhibited at a trade show before, so she needed to make the decision on whether to take up her friend's offer.

Like many reactive decisions, which are prompted by an external person, event or situation, defining the decision becomes imperative. Rebecca defined her situation as shown in figure 25.6.

Figure 25.6: defining the decision

DEFINE	**Problem/opportunity** *Have stall @ the Auspac IT summit to help bring in new clients.*		
	Facts *June 15th* *Stall cost = $5,000* *Labour = $1,800 inc F/U* *Signage = $1,000* *Brochures = $600* *Promo items = $1,200 = $9,600*	**Feelings** • *I need more clients.* • *Four weeks before expo is tight.* • *Nervous that will be a lot of effort and no clients.*	
	Size: Minor ☑ Major ☐ Mega ☐	**Screen:** Defer ☐ Delegate ☐ Decide ☑	
	Should I/we	**Option 1** *Pay $10,000 to attend trade show on 15 June.*	**or**	**Option 2** *Pay $10,000 to conduct a direct marketing campaign over eight weeks commencing 15 June.*

The opportunity was whether Rebecca should attend the trade show in order to fix her problem of needing more clients. She recorded the facts and her feelings, detailing the costs involved as well as her nervousness about whether it would work and the timelines involved. The decision size was considered minor, but her friend needed an answer by the end of the week so it was something that couldn't be deferred or delegated.

Rebecca could have put down her options as to do the trade show or not to do the trade show, but comparison would have been difficult. Also, when one strategy is positive (being proactive) and one is negative (not doing something) your entrepreneurial brain will lean toward your own personal bias—getting into action or sitting on the fence. With my encouragement, Rebecca first had to work out the real cost of attending the expo. Given she would need to pay the fee, organise signage, prepare new promotional documents, employ an assistant, and then follow up all of the leads that she received, she realised that the real cost of the opportunity was just over $10 000, which was double what she had originally bargained on. Next Rebecca was challenged to find an alternative marketing strategy that would cost $10000 in real cost so the two strategies could be compared.

The second option Rebecca came up with was to undertake a direct mail and telemarketing follow-up campaign to businesses in her local area. So the two options then became:

» Pay $10000 to attend the trade show.

» Pay $10000 for a direct marketing campaign.

Filling out the foresight section of the decisionship accelerator was made easier because Rebecca had already invested the time to document the key outcomes that made up each of the lenses as follows:

» Endgame = build passive income stream of $25000 per month by 2015.

» Values = astound our clients, invest in our partnerships, inspire our industry, amaze ourselves.

» Role = thought leader, key consultant, chief rainmaker, head strategist.

» Vision = to be recognised as the leader in brand strategy for companies that had fewer than 100 employees in Australia.

» Magic Metric = average weekly billings per consultant.

» Priorities = contracted clients, off-the-shelf products to sell, financials out by the tenth of each month, 10 sales presentations each week.

An excerpt from Rebecca's accelerator outlines her findings for the six lenses of foresight (see figure 25.7).

Figure 25.7: assessing two options using the six lenses of foresight

	To what level will each option … on a scale of 1 (low) to 10 (high)		Option 1	Option 2
ASSESS—FORESIGHT	Passion (Sailor)	… accelerate my ENDGAME and enable me to be working on my MISSION?	4	6
	Philosophy (Gardener)	… cultivate our company VALUES and reinforce our BRAND and CULTURE?	7	5
	Proficiency (Movie producer)	… let me perform my ROLE and play to my STRENGTHS?	6	6
	Progress (Mountaineer)	… help us reach our business VISION and climb to the next business STAGE?	8	6
	Prototype (Master chef)	… improve our MAGIC METRIC and enhance our BUSINESS MODEL?	5	8
	Plan (Architect)	… adhere to our PRIORITIES and help us meet our PROJECTIONS?	6	7
		TOTAL:	36	38

She discovered from ranking the various lenses that a direct marketing campaign accelerated her endgame more than the expo. The expo was a one-time deal, whereas if she could find a formula that worked for the direct marketing campaign, then it could be scaled up to increase client numbers in the future, thus helping to meet her passive-income endgame. She felt that the expo was more aligned to her values, given it was less 'salesy' than a direct marketing campaign, and it would help inspire and amaze if they could pull it off.

When it came to playing to her ideal role, Rebecca was in two minds. On one hand the expo would enable her to be a thought leader and rainmaker, but it would take a lot more of her time than the direct marketing campaign. She decided to rate them equally. The option that best moved her towards the vision of being recognised as an industry leader leant towards the expo strategy. The expo would get their name out there while bringing in clients — both essential to achieve her vision.

The direct marketing campaign had more of a chance to provide a continual flow of clients rather than the rush of clients that the expo might produce. Hence the magic metric of average weekly billings per consultant would be more likely to be achieved by the direct marketing strategy. And, finally, Rebecca felt that her priorities would best be adhered to and achieved through the direct marketing program.

With total scores of 36 and 38 respectively there was really no difference between option 1 and option 2 using the six-lens analysis. Also, while the scores were not extremely high, they were above average, so either option looked as though it would help her business.

Next Rebecca considered the learnings she could apply to this decision — both her own and others (see figure 25.8).

Figure 25.8: using hindsight in the decisionship accelerator

	Learnings from similar past decisions I have made	Learnings/advice from other entrepreneurs or advisers		
HINDSIGHT	· *Direct marketing needs telemarketing.* · *Consulting must be sold not bought.*	· *Tyre kickers @ expos.* · *Need a honey pot to attract customers.* · *Direct marketing = sales.*		
ASSESS	**To what degree will each option** … on a scale of 1 (low) to 10 (high)		**Option 1**	**Option 2**
	… take into consideration my learnings?		*6*	*8*
	… follow the learnings/advice from other entrepreneurs or advisers?		*4*	*5*
	TOTAL:		*10*	*13*

Looking at her own experiences first, Rebecca realised that she didn't have experience with expos, but she had conducted a direct mail campaign. This previous campaign didn't work very well, however, and the learning from that was that in order for direct mail to work you must follow up by phone. In hindsight, she realised that the first time you try something it is unlikely to be as successful as you hoped. Her business was one that needed to be 'sold' rather than one that clients 'bought'. Considering this learning Rebecca opted to score the more known and proactive direct marketing campaign higher than the unknown expo.

In terms of advice from peers and advisers, Rebecca consulted a few friends who had exhibited before at expos and the advice was somewhat conflicting. Her first friend said it was an expensive waste of time, full of tyre kickers. The second friend said if you put in the effort you can come out with lots of leads — but you need to have some way to attract them to your exhibit. In terms of advice about direct marketing for consultants, an online learning program she had downloaded from the internet was a huge fan of direct mail and telemarketing follow-up, which had given her the idea in the first place. Weighing up this advice she decided to rate option 2, the direct marketing campaign, slightly higher than option 1, the expo. The upshot of hindsight was slightly in favour of the direct marketing campaign, though only by a slim margin.

Moving on to the insight section of the decisionship accelerator, Rebecca next rated how each of the options harnessed the four PGP (see figure 25.9).

Having conducted the frictions diagnostic, Rebecca identified that she was experiencing lack of scale and lack of guidance. The expo, she figured, would give her business some increase in scale, particularly around reputation, but it would be 12 months before the same expo rolled around, so this marketing solution wasn't that scalable. The direct marketing campaign, if successful, would give her scale. She could outsource both the mail-out and the telemarketing, which meant she and her team could concentrate on converting leads and delivering on new business. So the direct marketing campaign came out ahead. The campaign that would help her get the most guidance, particularly around sales, would also be the direct marketing campaign — a friend, Gregor, did direct marketing for a living, so she could lean on him.

Neither option increased stakeholders, though the expo would require a short-term additional resource. Both campaigns would require new product development, but Rebecca deemed this healthy as the team were fed up with selling something tailored every time. The real cost of the campaigns was identical, though Rebecca felt an additional cost to include was her time, and the expo would take more of this so she rated this option worse than option 2. There was no real impact on process.

Figure 25.9: answering the 16 questions associated with the perpetual growth principles

<table>
<tr><td colspan="3" rowspan="2"></td><td colspan="4">To what level will each option ...
0 (none)   1 (insignificantly)   2 (somewhat)   3 (significantly)</td><td>Option 1</td><td>Option 2</td></tr>
<tr></tr>
<tr><td rowspan="16">ASSESS — INSIGHT</td><td rowspan="2">Frictions</td><td colspan="4">... reduce my biggest friction [lack of____scale____]</td><td>6</td><td>8</td></tr>
<tr><td colspan="4">... reduce my next biggest friction [lack of__guidance__]</td><td>4</td><td>7</td></tr>
<tr><td rowspan="4">Mass</td><td colspan="4">... minimise the need for too many stakeholders?</td><td>5</td><td>6</td></tr>
<tr><td colspan="4">... minimise unnecessary products and brands?</td><td>4</td><td>4</td></tr>
<tr><td colspan="4">... minimise the real cost of purchases?</td><td>6</td><td>8</td></tr>
<tr><td colspan="4">... minimise onerous structure and processes?</td><td>—</td><td>—</td></tr>
<tr><td rowspan="4">Actuators</td><td colspan="4">... foster empowerment and replication?</td><td>5</td><td>7</td></tr>
<tr><td colspan="4">... foster innovation and inspiration?</td><td>8</td><td>3</td></tr>
<tr><td colspan="4">... foster flexibility and simplicity?</td><td>3</td><td>9</td></tr>
<tr><td colspan="4">... foster leverage and reputation?</td><td>6</td><td>6</td></tr>
<tr><td rowspan="4">Balance</td><td colspan="4">... maximise employee satisfaction?</td><td>4</td><td>6</td></tr>
<tr><td colspan="4">... maximise customer satisfaction?</td><td>6</td><td>4</td></tr>
<tr><td colspan="4">... maximise investor satisfaction?</td><td>4</td><td>5</td></tr>
<tr><td colspan="4">... maximise indirect stakeholder satisfaction? (suppliers, family, community, and so on)</td><td>—</td><td>—</td></tr>
<tr><td colspan="6" style="text-align:right">TOTAL:</td><td>61</td><td>73</td></tr>
</table>

Five out of the eight actuators favoured the direct marketing campaign. It would be more empowering, replicable, flexible, simple and leveraged. The expo, on the other hand, would be more innovative, inspiring and enhance their reputation. Where two of the actuators resulted in opposite outcomes, she rated them equal.

And finally, assessing which of the options would minimise balance, Rebecca put herself in the position of employee and investor. She felt win–win was more likely in the direct marketing campaign, whereas the less proactive sales approach of the expo would be better suited to customers. There was no real impact on the balance of indirect stakeholders.

Overall the PGP, indicated that option 2, the direct marketing campaign with a score of 73, would harness the principles more than option 1, the expo, with a score of 61. This difference continued the trend from the analysis conducted under foresight and hindsight. As a result, Rebecca decided to choose option 2, the direct marketing campaign. She was particularly happy because not only would that mean she wouldn't have to spend the next three weeks organising for an expo, there would also be scope to evolve the campaign if things did not working initially.

Completing the decide section of the decision accelerator was easy, since Rebecca had decided to roll out a direct mail with telemarketing follow-up commencing 15 June for eight weeks using an outsourced provider (see figure 25.10).

Figure 25.10: Rebecca's decision after using the decisionship accelerator

I have decided to: *Spend $10,000 on launching a direct marketing campaign (mail + telemarketing) over eight weeks starting on 15 June.*	
Commitments: what actions will you take to follow through, by when? 1. *Turn down Auspac IT expo (attend as delegate).* 2. *Engage outsourcer (contract has flexibility to evolve).* 3. *Meet with Gregor.*	
Calibration: scale of where you are now from 1 (low, not started) to 10 (high, complete)	*2*
Why is this decision important to you? List what it means personally *Evolve business model = replicable + sustainable Endgame more likely + build skills in marketing + business growth*	
How will I know if this is the right decision? Include measurable outcomes *At least five new clients (BE), ideally 10+ by Xmas. Roll out direct marketing in future.*	
When will you likely know if this is the right decision? Specific date in the future	*Xmas 2010*

(The left edge of the table is labelled vertically: **DECIDE**)

Rebecca's commitments were to respectfully turn down her friend's offer at the expo, but to attend it as a delegate to get a better understanding of the opportunity. Next she committed to outsourcing the direct marketing campaign, ensuring the appointment allowed for flexibility. She planned to meet with Gregor to get his advice on whom to engage as an outsourced provider.

Rebecca's calibration of the decision was at 2, given there was already quite a bit of work done for the direct marketing campaign they had conducted in the past. Rebecca deemed the decision important to her because it would help her evolve a business model that was replicable and sustainable. If successful, it would help her endgame and build skills in marketing that she wanted to gain. New clients would also mean a growing business.

Rebecca would know if it was a good decision by Christmas if she had brought in a minimum of five new clients, and ideally more than 10. More importantly, if the trial gave her confidence to roll out something more regularly this would mean the decision was the right one. So with the decision made, Rebecca threw her energy behind her chosen marketing strategy.

What were the results?

So how did Rebecca do? First of all she did bring in some new clients. Over the eight weeks of the direct marketing campaign they met with and converted four clients. Also, a further six clients were deemed likely to buy within the next three to six months. Assuming that a third of these came through, then the direct marketing campaign worked out at a cost of $1666 per new client. Rebecca's learnings included how best to target the most relevant prospects, and booking appointments in blocks to maximise time, but on the whole it was a successful trial. Rebecca had come up with a new marketing formula, which she decided to run out every month.

Yet probably Rebecca's biggest learning for her decision bank was to ensure that expense-related decisions shouldn't be just Yes or No decisions: they should be based on the question 'For the same amount of money or time investment, what else could I do to achieve a better outcome?' Stretching your mind to come up with alternative options this way can be a great way to make decisions.

Key points

- » The decision accelerator provides a short, simple reminder of the three-step decisionship process of define, assess and decide.
- » The accelerator is a visual reminder to help you properly define the problem or opportunity requiring a decision.
- » It prompts you to differentiate between the facts and the feelings of the situation and encourages you to gain perspective on the size of the decision so you can choose whether this decision is one you can defer or delegate, or one that you genuinely need to make now.
- » The accelerator will prompt you to bring the decision down to two options that you must then assess.
- » Using the accelerator allows you to quickly assess the decision at hand from the perspectives of foresight, hindsight and insight.

» Consider each option through the six lenses of clarity, scoring each lens as you see fit.

» Think of past decisions plus learnings and advice for similar situations so you can bring that hindsight to bear in this current situation and score each option.

» The decision accelerator will also prompt you to bring insight to the decision by considering each option from the perspective of the PGP so you can score each option appropriately.

» Finally, the accelerator reminds you to review the assessment constructively and logically so you can arrive at the best course of action. Being asked to decide and document your commitments helps move the decision forward while also providing valuable information to add to your decision bank.

» The accelerator helps to simplify the decisionship process and fast track your learning and mastery of the method.

» Decisionship is the One Thing that can transform your success: it will ensure that you make faster, better-informed decisions without the anxiety.

Conclusion

As an entrepreneur, the best way to achieve your aspirations is to master the art of decision making through the decisionship process of define, assess, decide. You need to train your entrepreneurial eye to apply foresight, insight and hindsight to your decision assessment so you can win at the game of business.

Thousands of moving parts make up any successful business. What should you sell? How much should you sell it for? Who do you hire? Who do you fire? Where do you locate yourself? What about contracts? Who should you chose as a supplier? Will they let you down? What happens when the wheels fall off? The list is endless.

If you asked 20 experts, you would get 20 different opinions about what it is that makes a successful company. It's also quite likely that all 20 would be correct. This ambiguity is difficult for most business owners and entrepreneurs to cope with. Most people in life are searching for some form of certainty, and yet there is very little certainty about business.

In addition, there is a vast amount of information available about how to make a business successful, and this is growing all the time, especially when you consider online resources. Some of it is good and some of it completely useless, but most of it is irrelevant because either it's written by trainers or experts who have never been in business before, or the good stuff is so hard to find amongst the rubbish that the time-poor entrepreneur never finds it.

As well as being time poor, entrepreneurs are also an impatient lot, and we are always in search of the quickest solution. For the most part, we don't have the time to pore over business books or theory that might point us in one direction, only to read something else that points us in another direction entirely.

Surely there has to be some sort of formula for success. Surely success leaves clues. Well, it does. It is my belief that there really is One Thing that can help you cut through the clutter of theory and rhetoric and allow you to forge your own path with confidence. The common denominator to all the thousands of moving parts in a business is that they all require a decision to move forward. Even if that decision is to delay the decision, someone has to decide a course of action and follow through.

And that's why decisionship is the One Thing.

If you can forget everything else and just focus on improving your decision-making skills so that you get to the point where you can internally run through the aspects of the entrepreneurial eye in a flash, then you will be making better, faster decisions without the anxiety. Mastering decisionship gives you the control, freedom and confidence you have been searching for and will allow you to reach your goals faster than you ever dreamed possible.

> Decisionship is the One Thing.

Given this book is about training your entrepreneurial eye to be effective at decisionship, it is ironic that half way through writing it, I found myself suddenly unable to see out of my right eye, even with glasses on. So off I went to the optometrist to once again experience that sensation I explained in chapter 3 of resting your chin on that wild-looking contraption. The optometrist asked a series of questions about which is clearer, the first lens or the next. Strangely, even when I had my glasses on I couldn't see a thing. Some further investigation and a trip to an optical surgeon later, I was diagnosed with what's called a trauma cataract: a blurred film over your lens is often caused after a significant fall—obviously caused by the 25-metre fall that I had while climbing in South Africa a few months before.

The upshot was that it needed to be replaced by a synthetic lens—something that I became immediately squeamish about. However, after this relatively simple operation and some laser corrective surgery on my left eye, I now find myself with a new set of eyes. For the first time in 20 years I have 20/20 vision without glasses. The changes to my life have been miraculous, particularly for the water and adventure sports I enjoy.

This experience has only reinforced for me the importance of being able to see with absolute clarity—especially in business. It is my hope that the decisonship methodology will also help you to see with 20/20 vision all of the possibilities that lie in front of you and your business—to use your newfound skills in foresight, insight and hindsight to grow your business to levels you never expected. And to have more fun in business as you realise that your role is as simple as making good decisions.

And decisionship is not just a tool that is useful only in business. All of us are called on to make personal and professional decisions every day. The quality of those decisions directly affects the quality of our lives. In his book *Predictable Irrationality*, professor of psychology and behavioural economics and founder of the Center for Advanced Hindsight Dan Arierly writes:

> One of my colleagues at Duke University, Ralph Kenney, recently noted that America's top killer isn't cancer or heart disease, nor is it smoking or obesity. It's our own inability to make smart choices and overcome our own self destructive behaviours. Ralph estimates that over half of us will make a lifestyle decision that will ultimately lead us to an early grave. And as if this were not enough, it seems that the rate at which we make decisions is increasing at an alarming pace. I suspect that over the next decade, real improvements in life expectancy and quality are less likely to be driven by medical technology than by improved decision making.

And if that's true—and I believe it is—then mastering decisionship will not only bring your entrepreneurial dreams alive, but it might even just save your life!

Appendix: the decisionship accelerator

<table>
<tr>
<td rowspan="4">DEFINE</td>
<td colspan="2">Problem/opportunity</td>
</tr>
<tr>
<td>Facts</td>
<td>Feelings</td>
</tr>
<tr>
<td>Size: Minor ☐   Major ☐   Mega ☐</td>
<td>Screen: Defer ☐   Delegate ☐   Decide ☐</td>
</tr>
<tr>
<td>Should
I/we   Option 1</td>
<td>or   Option 2</td>
</tr>
</table>

	To what level will each option … on a scale of 1 (low) to 10 (high)	Option 1	Option 2
ASSESS — FORESIGHT	**Passion** (Sailor) … accelerate my ENDGAME and enable me to be working on my MISSION?		
	Philosophy (Gardener) … cultivate our company VALUES and reinforce our BRAND and CULTURE?		
	Proficiency (Movie producer) … let me perform my ROLE and play to my STRENGTHS?		
	Progress (Mountaineer) … help us reach our business VISION and climb to the next business STAGE?		
	Prototype (Master chef) … improve our MAGIC METRIC and enhance our BUSINESS MODEL?		
	Plan (Architect) … adhere to our PRIORITIES and help us meet our PROJECTIONS?		
	TOTAL:		

ASSESS — HINDSIGHT	Learnings from similar past decisions I have made	Learnings/advice from other entrepreneurs or advisers		
	To what degree will each option … on a scale of 1 (low) to 10 (high)		**Option 1**	**Option 2**
	… take into consideration my learnings?			
	… follow the learnings/advice from other entrepreneurs or advisers?			
		TOTAL:		

ASSESS — INSIGHT		**To what level will each option …** 0 (none) 1 (insignificantly) 2 (somewhat) 3 (significantly)	**Option 1**	**Option 2**
	Frictions	… reduce my biggest friction [lack of_____]		
		… reduce my next biggest friction [lack of_____]		
	Mass	… minimise the need for too many stakeholders?		
		… minimise unnecessary products and brands?		
		… minimise the real cost of purchases?		
		… minimise onerous structure and processes?		
	Actuators	… foster empowerment and replication?		
		… foster innovation and inspiration?		
		… foster flexibility and simplicity?		
		… foster leverage and reputation?		
	Balance	… maximise employee satisfaction?		
		… maximise customer satisfaction?		
		… maximise investor satisfaction?		
		… maximise indirect stakeholder satisfaction? (suppliers, family, community, and so on)		
		TOTAL:		

DECIDE	
I have decided to:	
Commitments: what actions will you take to follow through, by when?	
Calibration: scale of where you are now from 1 (low, not started) to 10 (high, complete)	
Why is this decision important to you? List what it means personally	
How will I know if this is the right decision? Include measurable outcomes	
When will you likely know if this is the right decision? Specific date in the future	

Index